INTO FOCUS

INTO FOCUS:
UNDERSTANDING AND
CREATING MIDDLE
SCHOOL READERS

Editors:

Kylene Beers

Barbara G. Samuels

Christopher-Gordon Publishers, Inc.
Norwood, Massachusetts

Credits

Every effort has been made to contact copyright holders for permission to reproduce borrowed material where necessary. We apologize for any oversights and would be happy to rectify them in future printings.

All student work and comments are used with permission.

Chapter Seven:

"Poem" from *The Dream Keeper and Other Poems*, by Langston Hughes, copyright © 1932 by Alfred A. Knopf Inc. and renewed 1960 by Langston Hughes. Reprinted with permission of the publisher.

Cover photo of *Presidents: A Library of Congress Book* © 1995 by Martin Sandler used by permission of HarperCollins Publishers.

Excerpts from "Dialogue With a Text," copyright © 1988 by The National Council of Teachers of English. Reprinted with permission.

Excerpt from "Twenty (better) Questions," by Kris Myers, copyright © 1988 by the National Council of Teachers of English. Reprinted with permission.

Chapter Sixteen:

Excerpt from *Dear Author: Students Write About the Books that Changed Their Lives,* copyright © 1995 by Weekly Reader Corporation. Used with permission of Conari Press.

Cover of *The Los Angeles Riots: America's Cities in Crisis,* by John Salak, copyright © 1993 Black Birch Graphics; photo copyright © Jean-Marc Gibroux, and reprinted with permission of The Millbrook Press, Inc.

Material photographed courtesy of the Library of Congress.

Excerpt from *Here Is The Southwestern Desert,* text copyright © 1995 by Madeleine Dunphy. Reprinted with permission from Hyperion Books for Children.

Illustration from *Stephen Biesty's Cross-Sections Castle,* by Stephen Biesty published by Dorling Kindersley Publishing, Inc.

Illustration from *So Many Dynamos* by Jon Agee, copyright © 1994 by Jon Agee. Reprinted with permission of Farrar, Straus & Giroux, Inc.

Chapter Twenty:

All Web-sites used with permission

Christopher-Gordon Publishers, Inc.
1502 Providence Highway, Suite 12
Norwood, MA 02062
1-800-934-8322

Printed in the United States of America

10 9 8 7 6 5 4 3 2   03 02 01 00 99 98

ISBN: 0-926842-64-1

TABLE OF CONTENTS

Linda Robinson

Robinson sets the stage for the book by describing the interesting, exciting, and challenging nature of middle school students. Chapter 1 describes the physical, emotional, cognitive, and social development as well as the stages of reading development of teens in the context of a middle school classroom.

Hollis Lowery-Moore

Reading instruction begins with the particular needs and interests of the students. Lowery-Moore records the voices of middle school students as they discuss their literacy in reading autobiographies. Readers tell why, when, and what they read.

Kylene Beers

Do you find it difficult to connect students to texts? Beers explores the various reasons some teens choose not to read. Listening to the students themselves, she categorizes their responses and then develops activities that help aliterate teens make the connection with reading.

Barbara Baskin

Gifted students present different challenges for reading teachers, although few programs seem to acknowledge it. This chapter suggests strategies and materials to meet the unique needs of gifted adolescents in both heterogeneous and homogeneous classrooms.

Margaret Hill

Do you have students who have made it to middle school without being able to read above a third-grade level? Chapter 5 describes strategies including independent practice, guided reading and shared reading, vocabulary instruction, retellings and think-alouds that provide a framework to help teachers enable emerging readers to develop literacy.

Yolanda Padrón

ELLs, or English Language Learners, constitute a growing portion of our school populations. By the year 2020 it is projected that 25.3 percent of our student population will be Latino. Padron suggests ways to create an environment conducive to effective reading instruction in culturally diverse classrooms.

SECTION II: A FOCUS ON RESPONSE

Robert Probst

How do we make meaning in our minds when we read? Probst outlines the process we use to build response to a text. His chapter makes clear the nature of aesthetic response to literature and suggests ways classrooms can be structured to encourage transactions with text.

Mary Santerre's classroom is a reading community centered around a reader's workshop based on a series of
thematic units. Her chapter outlines a step-by-step
process for organizing units, presents some sample reading units, and demonstrates how her students move from
response letters to critical analyses and literary writing.

At the heart of effective reading instruction is a stimulating, student-centered discussion. In this chapter Poe
provides an overview of practices that promote book
discussions, including how to prepare for a discussion
and how to assess students' participation.

Scott and Wells assert the benefits of using literature
circles as a way to facilitate critical response to literature, furnish the comments one group of middle school
students made during a literature circle meeting, and
offer suggestions/strategies for implementing this structure in middle school classrooms.

In this chapter Robertson demonstrates how she uses
dialectical journals with her middle schoolers to encourage them to form questions about what they are reading,
make note of confusing pieces of text, recognize parts
that strike them as significant, and move from initial
response to critical analysis. A look at one student's
journal provides insight into this process that moves students from response to analysis.

Judy Wallis

Teachers with students who have difficulty comprehending texts will find this chapter valuable. Wallis not only explains the difference between reading skills and reading strategies, but she offers examples of many reading strategies as she explains when, how, and why students should use them.

Teri S. Lesesne

Lesesne reviews the benefits of reading aloud to middle school students and discusses the advantages of reading aloud short stories, of sharing picture story books with older readers, of offering a read and tease with specific parts of high interest novels, and of encouraging students to perform reader's theater. Lists of books and stories to read aloud help teachers plan their read aloud program.

Karen M. Feathers

Many students have failed to develop strategies for reading informational texts. Feathers discusses the structural differences between narrative and informational texts and suggests strategies for engaging prior knowledge, note taking during reading, and organizing information after reading. Her "trouble slips" offer ways to build vocabulary.

Devon Brenner and P. David Pearson

A strong authentic assessment program is built upon a teacher's goals for teaching and learning. Students' accomplishments are demonstrated by artifacts which document performance. Brenner and Pearson describe the process of establishing curricular goals, deciding what counts as evidence, and what the evidence means. Case studies provide specific examples.

SECTION IV: A FOCUS ON MATERIALS—FROM BOOKS TO COMPUTERS

Betty Carter and Richard F. Abrahamson

Nonfiction reading is often a forgotten favorite of today's teenagers; it's also the type of reading found on standardized tests. Carter and Abrahamson provide an overview of the structure and patterns of nonfiction books and suggests materials that both teens and teachers will find outstanding.

Donald R. Gallo

Don Gallo surveys the world of short stories for middle school students. He suggests classroom contexts and teaching tips as well as categorized lists of short stories aimed at specific interests of young teens.

Barbara G. Samuels

Young adult novels can unlock the door to a lifetime of reading. Samuels argues that these novels engage teens in reading about coming-of-age issues that are central to the lives of middle school students. She also suggests that well-written young adult novels serve as models for learning about the structure of the novel and therefore are a bridge to adult fiction and the classics.

Ted Hipple and Elizabeth Goza

Although print has always dominated the school curriculum, technology offers new media for the classroom. Hipple and Goza suggest ways of using audiobooks, comic books and graphic novels, and CD-ROMs in the classroom. Their lists of each of these materials make it easy to incorporate a new kind of language in the curriculum.

Elizabeth Stephens

A genie in one teacher's computer shows her how middle school scholars can access and produce multimedia programs for information, reading materials, and communication with the world. She learns how the Internet can provide an audience for her students' writings as well as sources of information on her entire curriculum.

SECTION V: A FOCUS ON TEACHERS

PREFACE

Into Focus: Understanding and Creating Middle School Readers is about middle school readers: who they are; why they read; why they don't; what they read; how to encourage reading; what to do when they can't read; and how to make reading meaningful in the content areas. This comprehensive handbook addresses the needs of English Language Learners, remedial readers, avid readers, gifted readers, dormant readers, reluctant readers, and readers in content areas. It connects teachers to books for middle schoolers by offering multiple lists of trade books that different types of middle school readers enjoy.

The handbook describes computer programs for middle schoolers, tells how the Internet can motivate some to read, offers methods for assessment, explains response theory, discusses short stories, explains the importance of reading aloud, walks us through CD-ROMs, audio books, reference books, fiction and nonfiction trade books, and outlines what successful staff development ought to entail. It describes classroom practices that show how to:

- use thematic units within a workshop setting,

- establish literature circles,

- encourage literature discussions,

- teach remedial readers how to decode, and

- teach vocabulary.

In short, this is a handbook with one goal: to help middle school teachers connect their middle school students to reading.

Background

We started this book in 1964. More accurately, part of the we started this book in 1964, when Bobbi (Barbara Samuels) began her career as a high school English teacher. She almost immediately saw that much of the traditional literature she had expected to use with her secondary students didn't meet their needs. What troubled her the most was that these students didn't read the assignments and seemed to care little about Hester, Pip, or Julius Caesar. Bobbi didn't realize at that time, but her first years of questioning what she was teaching, why she was teaching with that material, and how she taught those classics are the beginning of *Into Focus*.

As with most projects, this book had a lull. Bobbi's focus shifted from high school to elementary school and then to middle school as her own children progressed through the grades. During those years, she discovered that she wanted to know more about how to teach students to read. So, in 1978, she went to the University of Houston to earn a doctorate that focused on reading and young adult literature.

Kylene began her teaching career in 1979. With a secondary teacher's certificate to teach English and no courses in reading, she began teaching seventh-grade language arts. After a very short time (about a week!), Kylene recognized that knowing how to find the symbols in great works of literature and plot the meter in a sonnet were not very helpful. Furthermore, she discovered that standing at the front of the room with teacher's guide in hand asking the questions prescribed there was at best boring for herself and at worst frustrating, brain-numbing, and unmotivating for her students. To find a different way to teach, she began work on a master's and then a doctorate at the University of Houston.

Soon, we were enrolled in some of the same classes and began sharing concerns with one another. Our questions seemed endless: "What kinds of readers are in schools?" "What kinds of materials work with secondary students, in particular middle school students?" "Why do some kids like to read while others don't?" "How can we encourage all kids to connect to what they read?" "What do we do when kids get to middle school and can't read?" Finding answers seemed impossible.

As each of us continued to pursue these questions, we focused on different aspects. Bobbi's interests focused on teachers' attitudes toward teaching literature, while Kylene concentrated on middle school readers' attitudes toward reading.

Eventually we knew enough to know we would never know enough. Luckily, in the process of this discovery we had met many people—students, teachers, librarians, administrators, supervisors, publishers, authors, and scholars—who knew answers to specific questions. As we watched them work with students, as we read their articles and books, we saw that each individual was an invaluable resource to our understanding of what creates and sustains middle school readers.

We invited these experts to join us in the creation of a handbook that would help middle school teachers everywhere connect their students to reading. Like a chorus of industrious red hens, when asked "Who will help us make this book?" all answered "I will." We were thrilled, for we understood that no one person could address all the issues we wanted discussed with authority. But we suspected that if we could bring the finest minds in reading, literature, and middle school education together, if we let them write about the topic which they knew best, then we surmised the result would be a handbook that spoke to the questions that most teachers have concerning middle schoolers and reading.

Contributors

While we may have been the birth parents of this book, the contributors became, like adoptive parents, the real parents. Their thoughts, ideas, practices, and knowledge formed the book. These authors, 24 in total, represent the fields of reading theory and practice, juvenile literature, response theory, library science, and middle school philosophy. They include a middle school principal, a librarian, middle school teachers, a language arts supervisor, and scholars, many of whom have published their own books on the topics they write about in *Into Focus*. Though they each bring something different to this book, they all share the same goal: a real desire to sustain or create the love of reading. They all know that middle school is challenging enough for teachers without facing the problems of not knowing what to do. Finally, they share a similar philosophy toward teaching reading and literature.

Philosophy

We agree that if anyone had asked what our philosophy toward teaching reading at the middle school level was when we first started teaching, we would have stammered through something that in reality said nothing. We did not base our teaching on a philosophy. We based it on textbooks our districts gave us. If an excerpt from *The Diary of Anne Frank* followed the short story "Paul's Case," then we taught it. If students were to write answers to questions found at the end of the stories, then they wrote them. If the teacher's guide suggested that more able readers might enjoy reading all of *The Diary of Anne Frank* orally, then we did that. Since there were never any suggestions for what to do with those students who couldn't read, we often took the highly ineffective path of having these students reread the same story again, or we just gave them the failing grades we were sure they had earned.

However, the longer we attended classes, taught classes, watched students, watched outstanding teachers, read books and articles, attended conventions, and talked and talked and talked with colleagues, the more we realized that good teaching first means knowing what you believe about learning and learners. From there, we developed our philosophy of teaching, in particular teaching reading and literature to middle schoolers. Our philosophy is nothing new. In fact, we stole blatantly from people such as Louise Rosenblatt, Nancie Atwell, Robert Probst, and Frank Smith. We believe that reading is more than decoding, for without comprehension reading is only word-calling. We contend that reading and literature education must be driven by students' needs. Consequently, in terms of what we want to see students doing, we believe they must have some ownership in what they read, must be given time during the day to read, and must be allowed the opportunity to respond to texts.

Throughout this book, you will see how that philosophy plays itself out in the classroom. The examples you'll find here are from real middle school classrooms with teachers who want their students to read aesthetically and who have structured reading events that allow that to happen.

Organization of the Book

A quick look at the Table of Contents provides an overview of the organization of the book. The chapters in this book are divided into five sections.

Section I of *Into Focus* provides the setting by discussing the characteristics of middle school students. Robinson sets the stage by describing the students who sit in our middle school classes. Lowery-Moore follows Robinson's description of middle school students with a discussion of what these students say about reading. Then some approaches for meeting the needs of different types of readers are discussed: Beers writes about aliterates, Baskin describes gifted readers, Hill explains remedial readers, and Padron tells about readers who are English Language Learners. Just as our philosophy for teaching is based on understanding learners, this book is grounded on understanding the students who fill the classrooms of middle schools.

Section II moves into understanding response. Here we begin to see the importance of a transactionalistic philosophy toward literature. Probst explains this philosophy and how it plays itself out in a response-centered classroom. Then Santerre, Poe, Scott, Wells, and Robertson provide specific scenarios that show how they have turned response into a verb in their classrooms.

While Section II describes how to involve students in literature, Section III explains how to improve middle school students' reading. Wallis begins this section by explaining the difference between strategies and skills. Lesesne builds on this by showing how reading aloud helps students construct meaning. Feathers takes this view into the content areas. Brenner and Pearson show how assessment can complement the type of instruction discussed throughout the book.

Section IV pulls the first three sections together. After teachers understand their students, after they understand how a philosophy turns into action in a classroom, then they must know what materials support this type of learning. No more qualified people could have written this section. All gurus in their fields, each one gives us specific information about certain topics: Carter and Abrahamson tell us about nonfiction, Gallo writes about short stories, and Samuels discusses the novels middle schoolers enjoy. Then, recognizing that increasing numbers of middle schoolers think more in terms of home pages than book pages, we invited Hipple, Goza, and Stephens to take us beyond books into the world of technology.

Section V takes us back to how this book began with questions that teachers have about their own learning. In this section, Pope and Kutiper explain what needs to happen in staff development to implement some of the changes described in the previous sections. Wilson concludes the handbook by showing us all where to go when there is more we need to know.

As these contributors worked on their individual pieces, our task was to create connections among and between chapters. You will notice references from one chapter to another that link related topics in the book. Also, at the back of the book there is a bibliography of all the trade books mentioned throughout the text and several indexes that will guide you to particular books, authors, and topics.

Many authors listed books for you to consider using in your classrooms within figures and appendices. Complete bibliographic information for these titles may be found in the list of trade books that begins on page 435.

Important Thanks

We are proud to be the editors of this volume. For the two of us, working on this project has been a collaborative effort involving our publishers at Christopher-Gordon, the contributors, each other, and our families. Our publishers Hiram Howard and Sue Canavan believed in this project from the start. Laurie Robinson and Jake Schulz helped us stay focused on details. Their understanding of when to push, when to advise, and when to disappear was superb. The contributors left us little to do as editors. Their talents and expertise brought them to this project; their commitment to excellence, to reading, and most importantly to students of all ages kept them involved. This book exists because of these contributing authors.

The collaboration continued from publisher to author to us, the editors. The "co" in co-editor is the operative word, for we relied heavily upon one another during the final two-plus years of this book's birth. Along with the book came a respect and friendship for one another that perhaps only writing partners know. Our names on the front are listed alphabetically, not hierarchically.

Finally, our husbands, Brad and Vic, and each of our children were an important facet of this collaborative effort as they listened, talked, didn't talk, left us alone, and kept us company. In all that we do, our families light the way.

FOREWORD

Linda Rief

When I was ten, my dad set a playhouse in the backyard for me. It was a small log cabin, a "prefab" from Grossmans. It was almost too small for me right from the start, and I had to bend down to get through the precut doorway. I set up two small chrome chairs side by side and covered them with an afghan as a couch. I put an Allied Van Lines moving box in the opposite corner, spread the box with a royal blue cloth, set a jelly jar filled with lilacs in the middle, lit the candle I had taken from the house, stretched my legs across the "couch," and opened a Nancy Drew mystery. I don't remember a single story—what the mystery was, or how she solved it—but I do remember the smell of lilacs and the rain splashing down on the log roof, while I remained dry inside my space. I was alone—and smart—because smart people read books, and there were no books in my house. The only literature in my house was the *Reader's Digest*, on top of the wicker hamper alongside of Dad's ashtray and his Camel cigarettes, near the organdy curtains that always smelled of smoke.

But in my log cabin I was smart, as smart as Debbie and Pam and Charlie, who were all in the Robins reading group. Here in my log cabin no one laughed when I stumbled over words. Here I was alone with Nancy Drew, and she had the problems to solve, not me. Here in my log cabin I knew books were important. Just piling them in my lap made me feel important, smart. But I didn't know how to make the words in these books meaningful to me.

Growing up, no one read books to me. No one asked me to read books to them. I never saw my father, or my mother, read. I had very few teachers who made me love books, let alone introduced me to the possibilities of all that reading offered.

Despite my austere history as a reader, something in my life told me reading was important, even if no one around me did much of it. I read well enough to take notes and take tests and, sadly to say, that's the only kind of reading I needed in order to do well in school.

There weren't enough models in my life to show me how to become a reader, someone who took meaning to, and from, a text. Someone who read for comfort. Someone who read to understand the lives of others. Someone who read with a desire to learn. Who read to write. Who read to laugh, or cry, or think. Who read for the pure pleasure of a good story. Someone who read to know she was not alone. Someone who read to make order out of chaos. Someone who gave all those ways to read to me. No one showed me *how* to read, or *what* to read, for any of these reasons. For the past 20 years I've been trying to catch up.

So when Karen, an eighth grader in my language arts class, asked, "Have you seen *The Crucible*, Mrs. Rief? What did you think of it compared to the play?" I had to be forthright and say, "I don't know, Karen, I haven't seen or read it."

"You have *never* read *The Crucible*? . . . Who hired you? I mean, how can you be a language arts teacher if you never read *The Crucible*?"

Other students tried to cover for me.

"Don't you remember, she told us at the beginning of the year she only read Cliff notes to take the tests?"

"The *Crucible*'s not the only book in the world. . . ."

"Play. . . ." said Karen. "Play."

I had to say again, "Remember, you're the lucky ones. I'm still catching up."

The writers in this book and the students they talk about are the lucky ones, too. These teachers are readers who know that it takes understanding middle school students in order to create readers. They know, too, that it takes knowing books of all kinds, nonfiction as well as fiction. They know that it takes not only surrounding students with good reading, but opening these texts to them—by reading aloud, encouraging personal responses, and balancing choices with requirements.

"Catching up" doesn't mean I'm behind. I'm running alongside. Like the writers featured in this collection, I am still trying to know adolescents by centering myself in their midst. Linda Robinson, in the first chapter, knows them well when she writes: "Adult in many ways, yet children at heart; independent, yet seeking guidance, support, and love; full of confidence, bravado, and spunk, yet shy and tentative inside, middle school students are a walking set of opposites."

Because reading and writing are the most important things our students need to be able to do well in life, and for life, we have to know adolescents if we want to teach them. Beers and Samuels know that. They have literally made that the first section of this collection, as contributors write about everything from understanding adolescents to working with remedial, gifted, second language, or reluctant readers. We have to know kids so well that the books we surround them with are the ones they really want to read. Betty

Carter and Richard Abrahamson show us the value of nonfiction. Don Gallo reminds us of the value of short stories, and Barbara Samuels knows the kinds of novels adolescents want to read. Each provide extremely helpful, comprehensive lists of reading possibilities. Elizabeth Stephens, Ted Hipple, and Elizabeth Goza show us how to extend our thinking about what constitutes reading as they discuss everything from the Internet to audiobooks.

But just surrounding adolescents with reading isn't enough. We have to open those books to them—to invite them in. We read to them—the way Teri Lesesne suggests in her chapter—passages, short pieces, whole works. We work hard at knowing these young men and women, so we will know what words, what kinds of books, will grab them. Consider the following range of interests.

In my eighth-grade classroom, what Sally writes about *The Giver* makes me believe I finally found a meaningful book for her: "This book made me cry. I finished reading it and I went to my window and peered out at the crusted snow. I was so glad there was snow. I was so glad I was crying. I put my hands and my cheek against the window and I was so glad it was cold. I am grateful that I have love, compassion, grief, anger, and even hate. My life would not be worth living without feeling, color, sound, music, differences. Yes, most of all differences. I am different from everyone else and I take pride in being different."

When Damian, Rob, and Mike gather around mountain biking magazines, taking turns reading to each other on Fridays, I can't rip these from their hands because they're magazines, not novels. Instead, I must respect their choices.

When Kaitlin responds to the case study of Torey Hayden's *One Child* with "I finished this book standing in the bathroom, and cried. My mom, who had been passing by, asked if I was okay and spoiled the moment," or Ayshe writes me a thank you note that says "I just want to thank you for the book *I Live in Music* . . . I love the book. It is so beautiful. The words, the art, and my feeling of relationship. But mostly it made me feel really good that you knew me well enough to know I would love it," then I know, as their teacher, I'm beginning to catch up.

Robert Probst, Elizabeth Poe, Mary Santerre, Judy Scott, and Jan Wells, who value reader response in aesthetic as well as efferent ways, honor these students' voices by showing us ways their students bring meaning to texts. Judy Wallis, Sandy Robertson, and Karen Feathers show us more explicit ways of promoting meaningful reading.

This collection is about knowing adolescents, knowing books and materials, and knowing ways to bring them together so the readers can bring meaning to, and take meaning from, all their reading. The educators writing here surround adolescents with all kinds of reading materials: fiction, nonfiction, poetry, essays, newspapers, magazines, audiobooks, comic books, and CD-ROMs. It is reading of the highest quality that makes adolescents think, feel, learn, and enjoy. The writers here know the value in finding so many ways into reading individually, in small groups, and in whole class. And as Devon Brenner and David Pearson show us, there are many authentic, sensible, and extensive ways to validate all that our students know and can do as readers without "testing" them.

The contributors in this volume know that adolescents need to be given choices about what they read, how they respond to that reading, and how they're evaluated on what they accomplish. These educators make conscious decisions about what their students are given and/or invited to read, and how they ask them to read, based on all they know about adolescents, schools, communities, and curricula demands. All of the contributors encourage and solicit a variety of interpretations and possibilities, yet still know how to value the integrity of the written word. These authors know it is crucial to allow students to read about ideas and issues that matter to adolescents. These teachers read. Because of that, Beers and Samuels were able to create a collection that helps us understand how to get, and keep, those students in the middle reading. To help teachers keep reading and growing, they end the collection with chapters that discuss selection aids and explain how to implement ongoing effective staff development.

Through *Into Focus*, Beers and Samuels invite us into more than a handbook for teachers; they invite us into the what, how and why of reading, *for* and *with* our students, and *for ourselves* as teachers and learners. What these writers have done is give us as teachers ways of working with adolescents so that reading becomes theirs for life. When it works we see students asking for books the way Oliver Twist asked for gruel: "Please, sir, I want some more." All of the writers in this collection have put understanding and creating middle school reading into much clearer focus, so our students *will* ask for more.

References

Dickens, C. (1996). *Oliver Twist*. New York: HarperCollins.
Hayden, T. (1980). *One child*. New York: Avon.
Lowery, L. (1993). *The giver*. Boston, MA: Houghton Mifflin.
Miller, A. (1995). *The crucible*. New York: Viking Penguin.
Shange, N. (1994). *I live in music*. New York: Stewart, Tabori & Chang.
White, E. B. (1945). *Stuart Little*. New York: Harper & Row.

Linda Rief is a full-time classroom teacher in Durham, NH, the author of *Seeking Diversity: Language Arts with Adolescents* (Heinemann, 1992), and co-editor with Maureen Barbieri of *All That Matters: What Is It We Value in the Classroom and Beyond?* (Heinemann, 1995), and *Voices from the Middle* (a quarterly journal from NCTE).

A Focus on Middle School Students

Chapter 1

UNDERSTANDING MIDDLE SCHOOL STUDENTS

Linda Robinson

The title of this chapter is a misnomer. No one really understands middle school students—not teachers or administrators, not parents or psychologists; actually, not even middle schoolers themselves. Perhaps, then, a truer title is "Toward an Understanding of Middle School Students."

Yes. That's better. I can discuss how we move toward an understanding of middle schoolers; in fact, as a middle school principal, I discuss this topic often. However, when I begin talking with people about middle schoolers by telling them that I am a middle school principal, I am often interrupted with less than supportive comments. The comments often lean toward bewilderment or condolences: "Oh, really? Why?" or "I am *so* sorry!" or "How can you stand it—all those hormones!" Sometimes I cringe at the responses ("Why do I tell people what I do?"); other times I defend my turf ("Actually I rather like hormones."); occasionally, I agree ("Why do I work with these people?"). But most of the time I recognize that those outside the middle school circle simply fail to understand what those of us in this circle know so well: there simply is no other group as interesting, exciting, and challenging to teach.

Adult in many ways, yet children at heart; independent, yet seeking guidance, support, and love; full of confidence, bravado, and spunk, yet shy and tentative inside, middle school students are a walking set of opposites. Peers are their most important advisors, yet young teens are certain that they are alone in their feelings. They want to dress like, walk like, talk like, and

3

look like their friends. The kiss of death is the wrong hairstyle, clothes style, or book bag. "But, Mom, everyone . . ." is the middle schoolers' national chant. At the same time they constantly (and loudly) proclaim their individuality. No one knows how they feel; no one can understand them.

As I stand in our school hallway and watch the students change classes, I am reminded of a herd of zebra moving across the Serengeti Plain: the zebras move in the same direction, at the same speed. Then, without any overt signal, all turn and move in another direction. The strength and beauty of the herd comes from the conformity of their behavior. But when still, close observation reveals that each zebra carries its own pattern of stripes, its fingerprint on individuality. Likewise, middle schoolers feel strongest when in the midst of their peers, work hard to fit in and move with the group, yet possess characteristics that mark each an individual.

Early adolescents are at the same time alike and different. Understanding this dichotomy is key in moving toward an understanding of middle schoolers as a group and as individuals. Understanding takes more than reading about them; it takes living with them for an extended period of time, probing to understand what makes them act and react, listening to their comments, watching their movements, and feeling their triumphs and tragedies. And sometimes it means simply accepting what we don't—and perhaps can't—understand.

Ten years ago, when I became a middle school principal, my district started the school year with an inservice presentation by a speaker who was an expert on brain research. He began his talk by sharing research that pertained to the kindergartner's brain development, moved to the first and second grader's, and so on. I anxiously awaited the information he would offer about the young adolescents in my middle school. When he began to talk about the 11-, 12-, and 13-year-olds, he talked about the physical changes that take place at this age. He went into great detail about the body and changes related to puberty. Eventually he concluded that the body demands so much attention with all its changes that the brain goes into hibernation during this growth period. Then he moved on to the next age group.

I was nearly in tears. I was expected to go back to my campus, meet with my faculty for the first time, and inspire them to teach students whose brains were in hibernation. As I recall, I ignored the speaker, went on with the details of opening school, and hoped that most of my staff hadn't heard what he had said.

It took me some time to synthesize his information. I now realize that what he said is accurate to a point, and I have incorporated the term *hibernation* into my own vocabulary as I explain to new teachers the uniqueness of middle schoolers. At any given moment in my school, some of the students are in mental hibernation. At the same time, others are not in hibernation. Teachers can't tell by looking at their classes if students are in or out of hibernation. However, one clue is whether or not they do the work that you have assigned. Students flip in and out of this hibernation for weeks at a time. Some move in and out several times in an hour. What is important is that teachers and parents understand the developmental pattern and plan accordingly. Yes, teachers might have to repeat the directions three or four or five times. A student might not read one book assigned yet chew up the next. It is okay to regive a test. A student who bombed a test the first time but earned a 100 on the retake can receive the 100 that he really made. He was hibernating the first time around.

Each year I search for ways to improve our middle school. My vision is a school where every child belongs and each finds his or her niche. The Carnegie Council on Adolescent Development established a task force in 1986 to "place the compelling challenges of the adolescent years higher on the nation's agenda." Their report, *Turning Points: Preparing American Youth for the 21st Century*, has guided me. It opens with this passage:

> Young adolescents face significant turning points. For many youth 10
> to 15 years old, early adolescence offers opportunities to choose a path
> toward a productive and fulfilling life. For many others, it represents
> *their last best chance* to avoid a diminished future. (p. 8)

I cannot think of a more powerful reason to seek to understand middle school students better than to know that it is quite possibly "their last best chance." To meet their developmental needs, middle school teachers and administrators must consider each student's physical, cognitive, social, and emotional development.

Physical Development

During the adolescent years, many physical changes take place. "Physical development, in which diversity is the rule rather than the exception, is of great concern to middle schoolers" (George, p. 6). Changes in physical development can take place as early as age 9 or as late as age 15 or 16. They can occur over a period of several years or be completed in a matter of months. Changes in girls occur sooner than those in boys, but as a group, teens of today mature sooner than teens of earlier generations. Some of these changes are obvious, and some are much more subtle.

When I attend a swim meet of middle school students, I am always amazed at the variation in physical development among the participants. Some of the boys will stand close to 6 feet tall on the block, ready to dive with shoulder muscles bulging, bodies narrowing at the hips, lips bristling with fuzzy mustaches. Others look like little boys, standing barely 5 feet tall, skinny ribs poking out. Similarly, some of the girls look more like young coeds with shaved legs, trim waists, rounded hips and developed breasts.

They stand next to their best friends who often have flat chests, no curves, and nary a thought of shaving their legs.

Physical changes, occurring more rapidly during puberty than at any other time with the exception of early infancy, are an all-consuming concern for adolescents. The need to be *normal* is strong, and each worries about everything and anything from nose shape to penis size and breast measurements. Students need to be educated about what is happening to their bodies and must constantly be reassured that whatever stage of development their bodies are in, they are okay just as they are.

While adults can tell these young teens that all is normal and they are fine, they often look at us with skepticism. After all, we are adults who certainly haven't been young in many years. How would we know? When physical change happens, these teens look to other sources for affirmation. Often these sources include young adult novels that have characters who are also worried about their bodies. Two books fast becoming classics in this category are Judy Blume's *Then Again Maybe I Won't* (mostly read by boys) and *Are You There God? It's Me, Margaret* (mostly read by girls). In the latter book, Margaret and her friends have formed a secret club. Each girl has to think up a rule.

> Nancy's rule was we all had to wear bras. I felt my cheeks turn red. I wondered if the others wore them already. I didn't think Janie did because she looked down at the floor after Nancy said it.
> Gretchen's rule was, the first one to get her period had to tell the others all about it. Especially how it felt. (p. 33)

Margaret wants to be like everyone else. That night in bed, she has her regular conversation with God:

> Are you there, God? It's me, Margaret. I just told my mother I wanted a bra. Please help me grow God. You know where. I want to be like everyone else. (p. 37)

To understand the degree of change that is occurring, consider these statistics. On average, teens grow 2 to 4 inches per year and gain between 8 to 10 pounds. Between the ages of 10 and 15, this means an average growth spurt of 10 to 20 inches and 40 to 50 pounds (Van Hoose & Strahan, 1988, p. 3). This rapid growth is accompanied by extreme awkwardness since muscle development does not keep up with bone growth. A ravenous appetite often appears during this time, and eating disorders often begin during adolescence. A middle school boy might eat four or five meals a day during his growth spurt. He's always feeling hungry.

Hormonal changes during this time cause adrenaline to be released in large quantities when it is not needed. This explains why you often see middle school students squirming in their seats. Many simply cannot sit still for hours at a time in a classroom. These students have difficulty sitting still for more than 10 minutes without grabbing someone else's pen or notebook, twisting in a chair to be able to see a·friend, going repeatedly to the pencil sharpener, dropping to the floor to search through a book bag, stretching legs, hunching shoulders, and flexing muscles. They bite fingernails, make faces, tap their toes, swing a crossed leg, and puff out their cheeks with air which they push out slowly through tightly pursed lips. Then when we ask them to be still, they look at us blankly because they have not realized they have moved.

Teachers of middle schoolers must adopt the strategy of using this energy to their advantage. As they plan their lessons, they must consider the physical needs of their students and try to organize their classes so that adolescents move around from large to small groups and are physically involved with their learning. In reading and language arts classes that means students act out scenes from literature, participate in literature circles, create art, move from the author's chair to peer conferencing corners, and stretch out on the floor or on pillows in the corner for silent or cooperative reading.

However, we must always remember that flexibility is the key to survival. Just as the teachers have created a classroom environment that allows movement, the students become lethargic, with barely enough energy to hold heads off of desks, pick feet up while walking, or raise hands to answer questions. Remember, just as hormonal changes cause adrenaline to surge, they can cause energy to drop. When that happens, energetic, enthusiastic students will sit, stare, and stop. Allowing time for independent work, time for listening to you read aloud to them, opportunities for hearing books on an audiotape, periods for sustained silent reading, and pauses for reflection give students the break they require when their bodies slow down.

As a result of the hormonal changes, complexion problems begin as well. Students worry about the newest zits on their foreheads and struggle to hide the pimples on their cheeks. A wonderful passage in Chris Crutcher's *Stotan* illustrates this concern.

> Anyway, a few nights before the Football Frolics dance up at the gym, during which I had promised myself to ask her to dance—maybe even a slow one—I was visited upon by the first of a forest of pimples yet to come. This wasn't an advance man, an insignificant pimple scout sent ahead to determine whether this peach-fuzz frontier could support a whole pimple nation. This was Sitting Bull. This pimple was red and sore and angry and given to harmonic tremors. Friends asked if I were growing another head. Enemies said it must be my date to the dance. This was a big zit. (p. 72)

Students' moods change with their physical appearance. They are unsure of their looks and unhappy with the image they have of themselves. In one survey of middle schoolers, in answer to the question "What one thing would you change about yourself?" students of both sexes overwhelmingly said that they would change their hair. "Their hair was too long, too short, too curly, too straight, too full, etc.—but it was consistently unacceptable" (Van Hoose & Strahan, 1988, p. 7).

Two years ago, a good friend called to remind me that her oldest son would be coming to my school in the fall. I could tell over the phone that she had some real concerns about his transition to the middle school. We made an appointment for her to bring her son to the school for a visit. When they arrived, it was hard for me not to stare. This young man had grown to over six feet tall and truly fit the description tall and lanky. He looked like a full grown man, and yet this twelve year old was a scared little boy who was terrified of beginning classes at his new school. As we began to tour the school, I realized that this young man had difficulty with directionality. After I pointed out what room he would go to first, then second and so on, he began to cry. We spent two hours that day and several other visits to the school practicing where he would go. The problem for this young man and for many middle school students is that inside the man's or woman's body is a child who still needs adult guidance and support.

Cognitive Development

Just as students at this age vary in their physical development, so too do they vary greatly in their cognitive abilities. Many adolescents are still functioning in Piaget's stage of concrete operations, while others have moved into abstract thinking. Others are venturing into the area of formal operations. Just as you can have two seventh graders who differ in height by two feet, you can have two seventh graders who differ in intellectual development by years. While physical differences are easily seen, cognitive variances are not as easily recognized. Intellectual development does not follow the same growth path as physical development; it doesn't even follow the student from one class to another! Any given student may function at one level in earth science class and another level in English class. This inconsistency is common. Reading teachers may discover in team meetings that students who have been struggling with concepts in a history class can write very effective poems in response to a story they have enjoyed.

Students in the middle school years are beginning to understand how they know what they know. On the positive side, this means they often want explanations from their teachers about why their answers are wrong. On the negative side, due to their lagging social skills, their requests often emerge as demands. In spurts of independence, they often challenge the teacher to prove an answer, rather than quietly asking for an explanation. The best middle school teachers avoid confrontation and remain enthusiastic, positive, and supportive. These teachers willingly explain to students why papers are marked as they are, why certain assignments must be done, and how decisions were reached. These teachers have learned the wisdom in working from the students' strengths. Rather than pointing out what students don't know, they emphasize what students do know. They focus on what is right about students' writing, what is good about an interpretation, what is exciting about their logic. Furthermore, they model the maturity it takes to admit mistakes by congratulating students for finding their mistakes and quickly making corrections. Effective middle school teachers, administrators, and parents avoid becoming defensive with these adolescents who bristle so easily.

Since young adolescents are very egocentric and view the world through their own experiences, learning must be relevant and meaningful to them. They are in the process of developing their own principles and rules for behavior. Therefore, they read and think about situations through their own screen of relevance. They internalize information best when it makes sense to them from a point of view that mirrors their own. Teens who are asked why they like particular books often respond "Because it's just like me."

When I became a principal, grouping by ability levels was a common practice. Most schools had high groups, average groups, and low groups. Some schools took these groupings to five or more levels. Teachers fought over who got the high groups and new teachers often were assigned most of the low groups. The groupings were not necessarily based on *ability* but often were based on *success* in school. In other words, a gifted child could be found in a low group because he had refused to work and frequently failed, or a very average student could be placed in the top group because the student was an overachiever or simply had parents willing to work hard with the child every night.

I had been a principal for 2 years when I visited a professional acquaintance whom I had known for about 15 years. I was anxious to see him. He was a world-renowned neurologist who had seen me through a long illness with my husband. We had grown to respect each other, and I could not wait to tell him that I was now a principal. I was not prepared for his response.

He sat down, looked off into the distance and said, "So what are you doing for kids like me at your school?" He seemed distressed, and I was not sure what he was asking me. All I knew about him personally was that he was a very outstanding physician, married, and the father of two children. He took time to tell me his story.

> My brother and I both had complications at birth. My parents were older and so thrilled to have us they put few expectations on us. When it was time for junior high school, my father, a state's attorney, thought that I should go to a private school. After only a few weeks of school, I overheard the headmaster say that I was the dumbest kid that he had ever had at his school. That night I went home, locked myself in the bathroom, and refused to come out until my parents promised that I did not have to return to that school. The next day they enrolled me in a

public junior high. There I found a coach who recognized my talents in track. The coach moved to the high school with me and kept me under his wing. My father began to realize that I would not be accepted to a university without help, so he gave a large endowment to an Ivy League university. They let me in. I failed freshman English, but scored the highest score to date on the physics exam. The university exempted me from all English courses.

My brother's record was worse than mine. The endowment didn't get him into an Ivy League school. He had to go to a junior college that took students with special problems.

"What does your brother do now?" I asked.

"He's an ophthalmologist at a prestigious medical school."

As I tried to digest this story, I reached across his desk and picked up a medical journal. "Given what you've told me, how can you read this?" I asked as I shook it with some frustration.

"I know what you're asking," he said. "I learned to read in graduate school. But I don't read words like you do, and I still cannot write or spell. I do all of my work by dictation. Now tell me, what you are doing for students like me in your school?"

I did some serious thinking for the next few weeks. From then on, I never saw a student who had a learning problem in the same way again. I saw a doctor, a waiter, a lawyer, a secretary, a mechanic, or a CEO sitting in those seats. I began to make changes in my school so that I was doing something for students like my friend.

The bottom line is that educators must examine their thoughts and practices concerning the cognitive abilities of middle school students. Not only must we believe that all students *can* learn, we must believe that all students *will* learn. Furthermore, we must recognize that learning may not take place in our designated time frames. We need to embrace a process curriculum that offers plenty of time between practice and mastery. For students with learning differences, we need to rethink practices that place low performing students on a low-expectation curricular track. I cringe when I hear about curricula tracks in middle schools and high schools that prepare some students for one type of opportunity and others for another type. Many teens do not become serious students until late in their adolescence or even early adulthood. If we presume that 13-year-old behavior is indicative of a lifetime of ability, we shortchange them and ultimately our society.

We also need to seriously question a school philosophy that puts low-performing students in remedial classes that only emphasize drills. These students also need the stimulation that comes from thinking about ideas. For instance, when we have students in middle school who still have trouble decoding, we should not stop the high-level thinking that comes from discussing Pony Boy's actions in *The Outsiders* or examining Leigh Botts's anger and hurt in *Dear Mr. Henshaw*. If students cannot read a book, we read it to them, help them read it, play it on audiotape, or let them read with a partner. We should not deny them the pleasures and enrichment that come from literature while we are seeking an approach or strategy to teach them to read.

Heterogeneous classes provide opportunities for all students to learn from each other. Higher-level students stimulate those whose skills are not yet developed. At the same time, these better-performing young people often learn more from helping their peers than they do in homogeneous classrooms that pile on extra work. In addition, often students whose skills in reading are less developed have other skills and experiences that enhance discussions and stimulate thinking.

Paul George and Gordon Lawrence in their *Handbook for Middle School Teaching* (1982) identify six dimensions of cognitive development that begin in childhood and continue throughout adolescence. These cognitive changes include a move

1. from concrete into abstract thinking;

2. from an egocentric into a sociocentric perspective;

3. from a limited into a broad perspective of time and space;

4. from a simplistic into a complex view of human motivation;

5. from reliance on slogans toward the construction of a personal ideology; and

6. toward the development of a capacity for forming concepts that stretches from lower order into complex, higher order conceptualizing.

Looking at this list, I am struck at how powerful any *one* of these shifts is and come a step closer to understanding how confusing life is for middle schoolers as *all* of these dramatic shifts occur. As middle school teachers we must be aware of these shifts and see how they affect learning in any given content area.

As reading teachers, we must design experiences that take into account these shifts the students are working through. For instance, as we remember that these students are moving from being concrete to abstract learners, we create the best lessons that reflect that same movement. If students are reading about slave ships in a history class and reading Paula Fox's Newbery Award-winning novel *The Slave Dancer*, they will have a stronger connection to both readings if they first stand together in a space the size of the hold of a slave ship to feel what it must have been like to be crowded into a small space with no air for weeks of seasick travel. From this concrete experience, they then move more easily to understanding the feelings and issues that arise in their texts.

Young adolescents learn best when they work with their peers in cooperative settings where they interact actively with the materials and with each other. Literature circles, paired readings, dialogue journals, creative dramatics, reader's theater, and other strategies that bring students into situations where they learn not only from the teacher but also from each other are the most effective structures for middle school classrooms. These practices, which are often a part of response-centered classrooms, facilitate the students' move from their own limited view of the world to a broader view, encourage a sociocentric perspective, allow them time to practice new reasoning skills, and give them the opportunity to hear one another's thoughts. When they are discussing literature, it is important to ask the kinds of open-ended questions that force them to struggle with ambiguity, with issues of right and wrong, with ethical questions. With those types of questions, they learn that many questions have multiple answers, and they begin to develop their personal set of principles for living.

As students enter middle school some adults believe that these students should stop being childish and embrace the grown-up world. Their bodies often do not look childish, and their insistence that they do not need any help should indicate they are maturing. However, look closer and see 12- or 13-year-old students who are often as interested in their Barbies and Hot Wheels as they are in the school social event or what to wear tomorrow. The girls may arrive at school looking like fashion models one day and come the next day toting their teddy bears; the boys may casually drape an arm around a new girlfriend on Monday and cry at home on Friday when friends won't come to play. One day they understand anything we say and the next day, unless it is written down and acted out, they do not even hear what we are saying. On any given day middle schoolers, while looking like high school students, may actually be cognitively closer to elementary students.

Ask middle schoolers what they remember about a school year. You will hear about the play that they had a part in, the model they built, or the Olympic games that they participated in. No one highlights the worksheets and the lectures. Debates, contests, recordings, videotapings, role playing, artistic creations, and musical interpretations all catch their attention. They love to play—with words, logic, and conflicts. They are curious about the things that are relevant to them. Make your classroom an active, playful learning place.

As reading teachers, it is easy to think of middle schoolers' development in reading in terms of students' growth toward more complex narrative structure, more difficult vocabulary, and more sophisticated responses. These advancements may tell you that the student has the cognitive ability to handle more difficult texts; however, they do not tell you at all where the reader is in his or her development of becoming a lifetime reader with a high degree of appreciation for literature. Instead, to really understand how your students are progressing as lovers of literature, we need to look specifically at reading interests and literary development.

Reading Interests and Literary Development

As in their physical, emotional, cognitive, and social development, middle school students show great variability in their reading development. A student's reading list for seventh grade might include picture books, children's books, young adult books, adult bestsellers, and classics. A serious reader might have a list that includes picture storybooks like *The True Story of the Three Little Pigs* and *Math Curse,* both by John Scieszka; children's books such as *Stuart Little, Dear Mr. Henshaw*, and *Tuck Everlasting*; young adult novels like *Stotan, Lincoln: A Photobiography, One Fat Summer,* and *Hatchet*; as well as adult novels such as *Jurassic Park*, the latest John Grisham novel, and *Gone with the Wind.* Annie's list (found in chapter 8) is another example of the possible range and extent of reading by a serious eighth grade reader. Most of Annie's reading is of young adult novels, but she also read adult books such as *Lily* and *Christy* as well as the classic *To Kill a Mockingbird.* Her comments indicate her own awareness that some books are good simple reads while others evoke more sophisticated aesthetic experiences. Another student in the same class might struggle through a class reading of *The Outsiders* and read two short young adult novels, Jay Bennett's *The Birthday Murderer* and Walter Dean Myers' *Hoops*, independently and feel an enormous sense of accomplishment. Still other seventh grade students may not get to the point of reading an entire novel. The differences in reading development and interest can be huge.

Many middle school students have not yet been hooked on reading. For any of several reasons (for a longer discussion on this, look at chapter 4), these students don't enjoy meeting characters on a page, hearing a good story, or savoring an interesting plot. To connect these students to reading, teachers should expect that the process will take time and anticipate being a part of the process because convincing nonreaders to enjoy reading does not happen with reading kits, worksheets, and drills. It doesn't happen by answering questions at the end of a story, filling in blanks on comprehension tests, or writing book reports. It happens by having a meaningful adult connect them to a meaningful piece of literature. It happens by listening to someone read aloud great stories, by being taken to the library regularly to choose books they like to read, by having lots of time to read, by having time to talk about what they have read, and by having peers share good books with them. Students with negative attitudes toward reading generally have not had these experiences and, not surprisingly, do not see the value in reading. In order to become lifelong readers, students must see reading as an end unto itself, not merely a means to other ends such as finishing assignments or completing tests.

While we can create lifelong readers by helping them find good books and showing them how enjoyable books may be, that alone does not create adult readers who read for some reason other than to escape. Though that is a great reason to read, and the reason that I often read during the summer, appreciating literature to its fullest extent means reading for other purposes than escape. G. Robert Carlsen (1974), building on Margaret Early's work ("Stages of Growth in Literary Appreciation," 1960), defines these purposes by describing the five stages avid readers move through as they become more sophisticated in their appreciation of literature.

In the first stage, which generally occurs between the third and seventh grades, "the reader finds himself unconsciously absorbed" (p. 23) in the book. During this crucial first stage, the reader's satisfaction comes from slipping into the world of the book. Carlsen asserts "I am convinced that nothing else in literature will ever mean very much" (p. 25) if readers don't experience this feeling with books.

Around seventh grade, students who have been given lots of opportunities to read for pure enjoyment begin to read literature with a different purpose. Now readers, while still enjoying the story, also read for vicarious experiences. When this happens, readers have moved into the second stage. Readers vicariously live the character's life, learning about the world as the character learns about the world. Carlsen says this focus continues as the main purpose for reading until ninth grade when "reading literature is suddenly [about] meeting ourselves, encountering situations similar to our own, rediscovering our own emotions and relationships" (p. 25).

Now into the third stage, the reader's goal is to read about someone who represents him or herself. Day to day, these 14- and 15-year-old students are thinking mostly of themselves, so it isn't surprising that they look for books with characters who resemble them. Realizing what readers want to read during this stage helps us understand why young adult literature appeals to students more than classics. It explains why *The Scarlet Letter*, though about peer approval and sex—certainly two topics teens think about—will never be as popular with teens as Chris Crutcher's *Running Loose*.

As students who continue to have lots of reading experiences move into their junior year in high school, they shift again in their purpose for reading and move into the fourth stage of literary development. Now their focus in reading literature, Carlsen explains, is to grapple with the philosophical issues that have confounded people throughout history. They read to come closer to understanding life's mysteries about love and greed and right and wrong. They read a novel about war and focus not on the battles, but on the issue of war itself: Is war ever the right choice? Are the deaths and losses worth the victories? Are causes more important than people? At this stage, literature becomes the vehicle that carries readers toward philosophical speculation.

Finally, as they move from this stage, they read to experience a well-crafted piece of literature. This stage, generally not seen as the prevalent purpose for reading until mid-college years, represents the most mature stage of literary appreciation. Here, the purpose for reading exceeds the need to be absorbed into the story, to vicariously live another's life, or to ponder man's inhumanity to man. Instead, the purpose is to have an aesthetic experience with the texture and resonance of the written words. At a conscious level, the reader anticipates the beauty of the words and finds satisfaction in that.

Carlsen emphasized that these stages are not separate and discrete units but rather are *overlapping satisfactions* in which one satisfaction from reading is more prevalent at one age than another. Middle school students could be in any of the first three stages quite easily. That means that some middle school readers will primarily want to read to lose themselves in the pages of a book. I look back on my own reading development and see myself at this stage spending hours between the covers of a Nancy Drew mystery or a horse book, oblivious to the world around me. That kind of unconscious delight in a story is what young teens experience today while pouring through novels by Judy Blume, Gary Paulsen, or Gary Soto, or series books such as *Goosebumps* by R. L. Stine or *The Baby-sitters' Club* books by Anna Martin. Hundreds of books are read during this stage. This is the critical time where readers fall in love with books. Margaret Early (1960) reminds teachers of the importance of a period of unconscious delight:

> The stage of unconscious delight is the beginning of literary appreciation; it cannot be by-passed. Before readers are willing to work for a higher level of delight, they must be convinced that literature affords pleasure. . . . Unfortunately, many persons are denied even unconscious enjoyment by having literature forced upon them before they are ready. Teachers should remember that a reader of trash has the chance of improving his taste; a nonreading pupil has no taste to improve. (p. 164)

So while some middle school students continue reading at the unconscious delight level, others will have moved on to reading to enjoy vicarious experiences, while still others are seeing themselves in the situations and characters in the book. These readers consciously place themselves in the wild with Brian in *Hatchet* or think through what they would do if they were given a gun to hold like Jamal in *Scorpions*. They expand their experiences and store information from their reading. Urban teens learn about nature and wilderness survival with Julie in *Julie of the Wolves*, about farm life and baseball with Billy Baggs in *Striking Out*, or about World War II in Denmark with Ellen and Anne Marie in *Number the Stars*. Finally, other students will read not to test themselves against the main character, but rather to contemplate the larger thematic issues they see in the book.

Like our students, at any given time in our lives, we may be reading different books for different purposes. The mystery or romance we read before we go to sleep each night may be read for vicarious experiences while we are reading the latest National Book Award winner at other times during the day to consider some of the philosophical issues involved in the development of the plot. At the same time we might be involved in one or more professional texts that increase our understanding of pedigogical issues.

Understanding how a reader's purpose for reading shifts as she becomes a more mature reader helps teachers understand their students' reading behaviors. For instance, an eighth grader may choose to reread *Stuart Little*, a book she read in unconscious delight as a third grader, but she will now read it aesthetically to analyze how E. B. White created his characters and established a believable fantasy. It explains how two students reading Rodman Philbrick's *Freak the Mighty* might respond to the question "What did you like about this book?" so differently that a teacher might wonder if they had read the same book. One student, reading the book at the unconscious delight stage, might recount the funny adventures the two main characters had, while the other student might never mention any specific instances but instead discuss why bad things happen to good people. If the teacher understands that different facets of literature emerge as important to the reader depending on the reader's purpose for reading, then the teacher will understand why responses vary and not judge one student's response against the other. Instead, this teacher will watch each student's responses to books over time for hints that the reader is moving on to the next stage of literary appreciation.

Social Development

During adolescence, a young person will ask "Who am I?" "What will I become?" and "How did I get this way?" A child's perception of himself or herself undergoes a tremendous reorientation during the move from childhood to adulthood. Middle school students begin to try on roles as they develop their own social behavior. When a 3- or 4-year-old puts on a cape and flies off the couch screaming "Superman," we recognize the behavior as a developmentally appropriate one. Likewise, 13- and 14-year-olds will wear strange clothing, walk with a different swagger, and say things they have never before said. Reactions to their role-playing will determine whether or not they will incorporate some of this role into their routine behavior.

Students at this age begin to try on adult roles. As children, they played dress-up, and we knew what they were doing and understood the change in voice, the change in facial expressions, and the acting out that went on. As young adults, they begin to do the same thing, only in a more serious manner. Often, as teachers, we have no idea what they are doing. We may ask a question and get a response we never expected from this child. Whether imitating a friend, another teacher, or a coach, the student is trying on a role. It's important not to make fun of these attempts to find an identity. Feelings of rejection from adults often drive students to the seemingly safe haven of their peer group. As teachers we must respect the risk-taking and help guide students in a positive direction. Perhaps more than at any other time in their development, teens in middle school need teachers to be honest, attentive listeners and advisors.

When a 13-year-old girl comes to school with green fingernails and a pink streak in her hair, we can get excited, make a fuss, and insist that she go home and change her appearance. More likely, we can ignore her temporary appearance. This is the time of life when they need to break away from dependence on adults, and sometimes that rejection can take an extreme form.

More important than our response is the response of the student's peers. Middle school is the social meeting place for these students. While all people have social needs, the need for social interaction with friends is particularly strong for middle school students. In *Transforming Middle Level Education* (1992), Irvin discusses the importance of friends:

> Friends represent an important act of choice for young adolescents. . . . Friends serve a number of purposes for us—one of which is that they help expand our world. Friends allow us to compare families, contrast values, and take risks. Their reactions to our dress, our jokes, our athletic ability, and our appearance allow us to measure our ability in these areas. (Irvin, p. 19)

During the teen years, the peer group becomes the focus for the student. Hours spent on the phone to "see what everyone is wearing" can easily result in tears if she is not wearing the same color shirt or shorts. Boys, too, get caught up in the need to look like the group (remember the zebras?) and insist on a $100.00 pair of tennis shoes because "that's what everyone is wearing." The pressure to conform is strong. Student groups will often isolate those who were "part of the group" only yesterday because they failed to conform to the *rules* of the group today.

During this time, middle schoolers appear to reject their family members and instead turn to their peers for support. They will argue with parents over what to wear, when to go to bed, and who to choose as friends. They will question the assignments we give at school, the books we read, and the clothes we wear. In spite of these battles that occur because they think they know everything about social behavior, they actually often feel embarrassed, awkward, and confused in social settings. For that reason, we continue to sponsor dances at our middle school.

Many schools have abandoned social gatherings of this kind because the students seem out of control; some principals complain that their students aren't mature enough to handle a dance, while others worry that they are too mature and the dance could lead to all sorts of trouble. Yes, some of the students are immature and some are too mature, but I believe that the social development of our students is also part of our responsibility. If we want our students to learn appropriate behavior in less structured situations, then we must give them the opportunity to practice.

At the school dances, as with all other aspects of dealing with adolescence, we see all levels of social confidence. While some teachers take on the task of making sure that hands are in appropriate places and that bodies are not too close for too long, other teachers worry about the ones who won't budge from their chairs. Some teachers work to find a student just one friend with whom to talk, while others corral the more boisterous ones who only know how to relate to others by running around the room, grabbing something from one person and passing it off to another.

Just as students move quickly from one dance partner to another, they also change friends and social groups repeatedly during the teenage years. The transition from elementary to middle school generally brings several schools together or sometimes splits elementary schools into various middle schools. The merging almost always results in changes in a student's peer group. Then as the students move on to high schools that are much larger and often comprised of several middle schools, they may shift peer groups again. During the middle grades, as students begin to select courses of study that interest them, they will find new friends. If a girl makes the volleyball team and her two best friends do not make it, the time required to be successful in the sport may pull on the old friendships. She may look at the girls on the volleyball team to find new friends.

During this transitional stage, socially and emotionally, a student will one minute be like a child and the next minute be like an adult. A girl will "hate" someone one morning and the next day will want that same person to spend the night. Deciding which friend to sit with at lunch or who to meet at the locker are questions that can be traumatic for some students. While the student is trying to develop a sense of self, the student knows that, in part, some of the answer will come from peers.

Sometimes they seem to realize that adults can also help them answer who they are. At those times, they will ask for advice. But then they promptly discard any advice as "ridiculous." They want our help, but they flaunt the power to reject it. They do not recognize their need to have someone listen to them so they can discover what it is they believe. They develop trust with adults slowly and are critical of adults who do not show sensitivity to their needs. As students sit in my office and relate an incident within a classroom, I am often amazed at how accurate they are in their perceptions of how the teacher feels about them. If they have a low-trust relationship with a teacher, the student will either pull back and not participate in the class or he will challenge the teacher at every opportunity. Neither approach leads to a successful learning experience. I admonish the middle school teachers I work with to remember that their students goad them to watch their reactions. The students want to check their thoughts about adulthood by watching how adults act. They need us to be calm and reasonable, compassionate yet resolute. We must be in control but not be controlling.

Once middle school students see their teachers in that light, then they will open themselves to them. Saundra Kelley (1996), a sixth-grade teacher in Houston, explains what happens as they accept you:

> They bring you their baby pictures, pictures of their siblings, their mailman, Aunt Jessie Rae, their best friend of the current two weeks. They bring you presents. They ask you every Monday morning, 'Did you miss us?' They will see you way-y-y-y down the hall and call out your name very loudly, 'Hi, Miss Kelley! I'm here!' They admire your jewelry, clothing, acne, shoes. 'Miss Kelley, I like your shoes. Did you get them at Payless?' This is not a put down; they want you to know that they are aware of current market offerings. These same students, next year, in seventh grade and experiencing terminal cool might merely give you a circumspect nod.

Emotional Development

Just as students in the middle school years flip in and out of mental hibernation, so too do their emotions switch from calm to volatile. Often, their hormonal changes are so swift and strong that even the students do not know what is happening to them. Girls cry unexpectedly and boys fly into rages for no apparent reason. In the time it takes to change classes and discover they weren't invited to Friday night's party, they plummet from feeling assured to feeling inferior. Bravado is replaced by fear and confidence is replaced with rejection.

Students at this age tend to exaggerate. What appears to be a small problem becomes an overwhelming one. The wrong pair of socks ruins the entire outfit. A parent arriving 5 minutes late destroys them for life. A younger sibling "totally" embarrasses them, and they will never live it down. They are never happy with themselves. "Ask the students you consider the most talented, healthy, skilled, artistic, and wholesome in your school whether they are happy with themselves. Their answer will almost assuredly consist of a hundred things they believe are weird, unacceptable, barely adequate, or just plain wrong with themselves" (Schurr, Thomason, Thompson, 1995, p. 11).

Perhaps because of their insecurity about themselves, if they trust you they will tell you more than you ever want or wish to know about them.

They will tell you about their families, their friends, the bus driver, the kid sitting next to them ("Danielle's not doing her work, Miss."). One middle school teacher told me, "Sixth graders do not understand the concept of the rhetorical question. There is no question for which there isn't an answer. Ask them nothing you do not wish to have answered right now and in vibrant detail" (Kelley, 1996). Sixth graders are still enthusiastic about volunteering for anything. However, don't be confused when you see these same teens in eighth grade. Chances are that by then they are much too worldly to spend time with you and much too cool to enthusiastically participate in class discussions. They are trying out different personalities and expect that you will understand this and not question it.

In fact, we must understand it because they certainly don't. They are searching for an identity against a backdrop of insecurity. Seeing everything about the world and themselves in absolutes gives them little room for mistakes. Nurturing middle schools offer wide but definite boundaries and become places where students can try a variety of roles, change their minds, make mistakes, and grow.

Conclusion

As this school year came to a close, one seventh grader mailed me a letter thanking me for the extra attention I gave her during some trying times she put us all through this year. The very fact that she wrote and mailed a letter as well as the letter's form itself indicated maturity: typed, inside address, paragraphs, typed signature with a space for her handwritten signature. While I was filled with pride at this level of adulthood she was moving toward, what made me smile was the rest of the letter: crayon and marker drawings of hearts, rainbows, and teddy bears that filled the borders of the page. A smiley face was drawn after her pencil-signed name and the P.S. asked me to please "WB!!!!!" (write back). Her letter captures the dichotomy of middle schoolers. They are grown-up children who do not want to need us but desperately need us to want them.

I suspect that those of us who choose to work with this special group make that choice because we remember a bit more than other adults about being this age. I'm counting on that because I agree with the Carnegie report—middle school may indeed be these students' "last best chance."

References

Atwell, N. (1987). *In the middle*. Portsmouth, NH: Boynton Cook Publishers.
Carlsen, G. R. (1974). Literature is. *English Journal, 63*(2), 23–27.
Carnegie Council on Adolescent Development. (1989). *Turning points: Preparing American youth for the 21st century*. Washington, D.C.

Early, M. (1960). Stages of growth in literary appreciation. *English Journal, 49,* 161–167.

George, P., & Lawrence, G. (1982). *Handbook for middle school teaching.* Glenview, IL: Scott, Foresman and Company.

George, P., Stevenson, C., Thomason, J., & Beane, J. (1992). *The middle school and beyond.* Alexandria, VA: Association for Supervision and Curriculum Development.

Glatthorn, A. A., & Spenser, N. R. (1986). *Middle school/junior high principal's handbook.* Englewood Cliffs, NJ: Prentice Hall, Inc.

Irvin, J. L. (Ed.). (1992). *Transforming middle level education.* Boston, MA: Allyn and Bacon.

Kelly, S. (1996). *They came from sixth grade.* Unpublished manuscript for Greater Houston Area Writing Project Summer Institute.

Muth, K. D., & Alvermann, D. (1992). *Teaching and learning in the middle grades.* Boston, MA: Allyn and Bacon.

Schurr, S., Thomason, J., & Thompson, M. (1995). *Teaching at the middle level: A professional's handbook.* Lexington, MA: D. C. Heath and Co.

Swanson, G. L. (1988). *Adolescence: The confusing years.* Lancaster, PA: Technomic Publishing Co.

Van Hoose, J., & Strahan, D. (1988). *Young adolescent development and school practices: Promoting harmony.* Columbus, OH: National Middle School Association.

Trade Books Cited

Babbitt, N. (1975). *Tuck everlasting.* New York: Farrar, Straus & Giroux.

Bennett, J. (1977). *The birthday murderer.* New York: Delacorte.

Blume, J. (1970). *Are you there God? It's me, Margaret.* New York: Dell/Yearling.

Blume, J. (1971). *Then again, maybe I won't.* New York: Bradbury.

Bonner, C. (1992). *Lily.* Chapel Hill, NC: Algonquin Books.

Cleary, B. (1983). *Dear Mr. Henshaw.* New York: William Morrow and Co.

Crichton, M. (1991). *Jurassic Park.* New York: Ballantine.

Crutcher, C. (1983). *Running loose.* New York: Dell.

Crutcher, C. (1986). *Stotan.* New York: Greenwillow.

Fox, P. (1973). *The slave dancer.* New York: Bradbury.

Freedman, R. (1987). *Lincoln: A photobiography.* New York: Clarion.

George, J. C. (1972). *Julie of the wolves.* New York: Harper & Row.

Hinton, S. E. (1967). *The outsiders.* New York: Dell.

Lee, H. (1960). *To kill a mockingbird.* New York: Lippincott.

Lipsyte, R. (1977). *One fat summer.* New York: Harper & Row.

Lowry, L. (1989). *Number the stars.* New York: Houghton Mifflin.

Marshall, C. (1976). *Christy.* New York: Avon.

Mitchell, M. (1936). *Gone with the wind.* New York: Macmillan.

Myers, W. D. (1981). *Hoops.* New York: Delacorte.

Myers, W. D. (1988). *Scorpions.* New York: HarperTrophy.

Paulsen, G. (1987). *Hatchet.* New York: Bradbury.

Philbrick, R. (1993). *Freak the mighty.* New York: Scholastic.

Scieszka, J. (1989). *The true story of the three little pigs*. New York: Viking.
Scieszka, J. (1995). *Math curse*. New York: Viking.
Weaver, W. (1993). *Striking out*. New York: HarperCollins.
White, E. B. (1945). *Stuart Little*. New York: Harper & Row.
White, E. B. (1952). *Charlotte's web*. New York: Harper & Row.

Chapter 2
VOICES OF MIDDLE SCHOOL READERS

Hollis Lowery-Moore

The Middle Grades Slump

I'm sure you know folks who believe that there is a special place in heaven for junior high/middle school teachers and librarians. And I'm sure you've met other people who don't believe heaven is enough of a reward to work with this group of young adolescents! Most of us who work with middle schoolers easily understand why people believe we are slightly off-center for working with—and enjoying—these students. They can be flaky, forgetful, and frustrating.

Yes, those of us who choose to work with this age group certainly do find them challenging; however, we also see them as eager, spontaneous, and interesting. Furthermore, we see these students as people who are interested in various topics, are humorous, stimulating, and creative, and, in the right circumstances, are even willing to read, write, and learn. Like older teens and adults, they worry about the environment, care about the elderly, delight in wit, anguish over war, cry over lost loves, hesitate in new relationships, and spend countless hours enjoying friends. They also know that as a group they are often considered social misfits, and they cringe at the names they are called. James Beane (1991) reminds us that while the names they are called—often by adults—seem humorous ("hormones with feet" and "brain dead"), these labels demean early adolescents and encourage low expectations (p. 10).

While no adult purposefully intends to demean middle schoolers or intentionally does anything to encourage poor academic performance, halting the name-calling addresses a minute part of the problem. The fact remains that there are some behaviors of this group that cause concern among educators and the population in general. This concern is so widespread and great that a recent report by the Carnegie Council on Adolescent Development, *Turning Points* (1989), reveals that school and society in general have deemed young adolescents almost unmanageable and have "more or less ignored" them. Unmanageable behavior is only a part of the problem as educators and parents continually worry about a decline in middle schoolers' academic performance, particularly their reading ability. Test scores and reading surveys indicate that many middle school/junior high students hit an academic reading slump as well as a recreational reading slump somewhere between the fifth and eighth grades. The 1988 National Assessment of Educational Progress (NAEP) report on *Learning to Read in Our Nation's Schools* indicates how widespread this problem is. Note the following major findings from the report:

- Students reported doing very little reading in school and for homework. At all three grade levels assessed, approximately half of the students (47 to 61 percent) reported reading 10 or fewer pages each day for schoolwork across the curriculum.

- Not all students are "hooked on books," and their interest in books seems to decrease as they progress through school. Three-quarters of the 4th-grade students reported reading for fun at least weekly, but only half of the 12th-grade students reported doing so. (p. 7)

Other parts of the NAEP report indicate that as students progress through middle school and into high school, they read for pleasure less and watch television more, own fewer books, and visit the library less. Many students report that they rarely discuss books in small groups. My informal observations of middle school students confirm the information in the NAEP study. Middle school students read less than they did in elementary school.

Recognizing that the students read less is easy. Now the important question becomes why. Why do these students read less? Certainly, middle school students are in transition, in the midst of a confusing swirl of biological changes, new school settings, and confusing social choices. But does less reading mean less interest? If so, what happens to their desire to read and how does that affect their reading ability? Do middle schoolers read less because they care less? What is this slump?

To answer these questions, my first thought was to look for the most recent reading interest surveys, but I knew what the surveys would say even before I read them: most middle school students don't enjoy reading, some hate to read, some love to read, many name as a favorite book any version of

Goosebumps and list Shel Silverstein as their favorite poet, most hate to do book reports, and more dislike oral reports. These surveys tell us much and at the same time tell us little as they provide broad brush strokes that create outlines of the portraits of middle school students. These outlines are useful. As Ken Donelson (1994) explains, surveys give librarians and teachers insight into the books young people like, describe something about current tastes, hint at students' interests, and recommend activities to attract stubborn readers. Donelson is correct that they create some boundaries within which to work. But the danger of surveys is that the resulting outline is incomplete. The outline lacks the substance that creates the essence of the portrait—the individual features. To manufacture that substance and complete the picture, we often take the outline created from the survey and try to fit our own students' faces into the space created—whether the face is too small for the outline and leaves gaping areas or is too wide and extends beyond the boundaries. In essence, we make the student fit the outline whether the fit is right or not.

Donelson (in Sherrill, 1994) clarifies the role of surveys as he discusses G. Robert Carlsen, a pioneer in the study of adolescents' reading interests and author of the benchmark work, *Books and the Teenage Reader* (1967). "Bob had no sympathy for English teachers who wanted young adults to fit into certain molds. He believed that one of our most important jobs—maybe the most—was to find out where our young people were in their reading and to start with them at that point" (p. 5). Linda Rief (1992) reiterates the importance of seeing students as individuals when she calls for teachers to "listen to their unique voices and ask how they have come to be" (p. 10), and Nancie Atwell (1987) concurs as she discusses the need to continually examine and analyze each student's literacy development.

I decided to listen to what individual adolescents say about themselves through their reading autobiographies, much as Carlsen did for three decades as he collected reading autobiographies from his students in his college class *Literature for Adolescents*. Over several years I collected hundreds of auto-biographies from students in grades 4 through 8. In those autobiographies I found the individual voices that provide the texture to complete the outlines. I found voices that belie the sudden sinking of reading abilities and inter-est, voices that stress personal reading development during the middle years, voices that indicate a strong dislike of *school reading*, and voices that verify that for some reading is not a chosen activity, but rather a nec-essary evil.

As a reading specialist and the mother of a high school sophomore and a seventh grader, I expected that I would know what the students would say in their autobiographies and would know how they would say it, but I was surprised. The honesty of these students, some categorized as special education students, others identified as academically gifted, and many somewhere in between, jolted me from smugness to awareness. I was amazed at their honesty and shocked at what they said about reading. I was heartened to find that out of hundreds of reading autobiographies, the number of students claiming to like or at least value reading was greater than the number of students who said they dislike reading. And I was convinced that listening to their voices is mandatory if we want to understand how to connect the middle school student to reading.

Voices of Those Who Like to Read

Teachers, librarians, and parents can have hope. There are some middle school students who genuinely enjoy reading. Seventh-grader Julie's comments capture an avid reader's love of books best: "I still have all of my books and I still read them. I love reading and I will love reading until I'm rotting in my grave. In fact, I will probably be reading while I am rotting." Sarah, a sixth grader, doesn't extend her love to the grave, but she does recognize that it fills most of her time at home: "My parents don't have any trouble getting me to read, but they have trouble getting me to do something else around the house." Blake, a sixth-grade avid reader, reminds us that readers know what they like, know why they like it, and know their literary tastes change:

> In fifth grade I read for a grade and did not appreciate certain writing styles until now. Now I read for fun and more writing styles appeal to me, like *The Hobbit, Avalanche, Nolan Ryan*, and *Old Yeller*. My appreciation toward reading has rapidly grown and I hope it continues to grow.

Blake's mixture of fiction and nonfiction, fantasy and realistic fiction is a reminder of how eclectic middle school students' tastes can be. Other avid readers also show a strong awareness of their reading development. Jeany tells us that

> . . . now that I'm in seventh grade . . . I'm very much into novels. Sometimes it takes weeks to finish a book, other times it takes a matter of hours. I read constantly now, even though I went through a stage where I barely read, and only when I had to. . . . Now I seem to be able to balance school, fun, family, and friends, and still reserve time to curl up with a good book.

Other readers recognize that their attitudes toward reading change over time. Tara writes,

> When I was six, I hated to read. My mom would make me read for 20 minutes and I would just sit there. But as the years passed the books got more interesting.

Some students know the importance of finding the right book. Bill reports:

> Ever since fifth grade all I've read are magazines. But lately a friend
> of mine has been supplying me with a new type of book which I have
> liked more than any kind at all, mysteries/horror. Now I'm starting to
> pick up my old reading habits and am enjoying reading.

The autobiographies provide insights into why these students who like reading are willing to invest the time and effort. The opportunity to use the imagination is the key for Catie, ". . . as my parents say, [reading] opens up a whole new world—and it's true." John writes, "so I think reading is swell because you have to picture what's going on in your head. . . ." Jimmy explains that what he likes are books that ". . . scare you and make you feel like you are in the adventure or horror." Other students report that they read to identify with the main character. Peter says, "Each time when I read a book, I imagine that I'm the main character and I have his adventures." Brandon remembers, "I was dreaming that the main character, Jeff [from *Rifles for Watie*], died and I woke up from my slumber and noticed I was crying." Brandon and Peter connected with their books through the main characters.

Some students' comments remind us that students read for more than entertainment. Some read to learn. Lizzie, a fifth grader, writes that "I read because I want to and not because I have to. . . . I think reading is important because it teaches people to understand life more and understand themselves." Jason reads because he believes "that I need it because most of my information comes from reading." Julie echoes Jason's sentiments when she says, "I can learn stuff from the books I read," and Luke concludes, "When I read now I read to further my knowledge on things." Ryan states, "If you read a lot it will help you write better, because you have seen how the author would write it in that situation." Bill preaches, "Everyone should read something once in a while, be it a magazine or a book, you need to keep your intelligence up." A number of students agree with Michelle, "I think reading is one of the most important parts in education, because if you can't read well then when you get a job you may mistake something for something that's not really that. So read and be smart!" Elisha adds, "You learn many things from books, at least I have. Everyone should read all the time, it is good knowledge for the brain. You should always feed your brain new words." (Place all these comments from the previous two paragraphs against the stages of literary development that Carlsen (1974) outlines. Linda Robinson discusses these in Chapter 1. When you review their statements with the stages in mind, you easily see which students are reading for what purpose.)

Occasionally, readers recognize the importance of having parents who enjoy reading. Betsy writes, "I don't feel right unless I'm reading a book. That's how my Mom is, too. Whenever I come home from school she's reading a book." Anne says, "I come from a long line of educated readers. I guess I inherited their skills." These comments remind us that as parents model their own reading habits they also promote reading in others.

Some students read because their personal connection to what is happening provides them with the intrinsic motivation and reward to continue reading. These students read to identify with the main character, to find information, or to enjoy the imaginary world of the book. Those reasons are the motivation to read, and the pleasure that comes from the reading is the reward. However, other middle schoolers are blatant in their conviction that reading is not motivating and if they are to do it, they need an extrinsic reason to read. Sometimes that external reason is the teacher: Tony writes, "I still love to read. My English teacher loves to check what books I'm reading to find out whether I've slacked off on the big things. So far she's been impressed." Sometimes the external reason is a peer's reaction: Heather explains, "As I got older I started reading big books which I didn't understand. I just read them because I look somewhat intelligent." Sometimes the motivation is parents and grades. Stacy writes, "The encyclopedia contest we are having, *Surf*, and my parents motivate me to read." Wesley concurs, "My parents and my grades motivate me to read. On my personal reading inventory I got a failing grade, so now I'm reading a book every two days to keep up."

Voices of Those Who Don't Like to Read

While some plan to read as they rot, others would rather rot than read. Their reasons for *not* reading range from frustration over tiny print to claiming they have no time to read. James, a student who has always hated reading books with "little tiny words that have no pictures" claims that he "probably won't enjoy reading a real book until I pass 20 years of age." Sometimes students explain that reading itself isn't the problem, but finding the time to read seems impossible. These students, ones who view reading as important and plan to return to reading someday, have little time for it now. Labeled as dormant readers by Beers (1996), this group of students stop reading as school activities, sports teams, and other interests consume much of their time. Seventh grader Pat closes his autobiography, "I don't like reading as much as I used to because I don't have time for it with algebra, projects, and baseball plus drawing and Nintendo!" Heather, also a seventh grader, says, ". . . I don't read as often now. I have other interests so reading is not as important to me."

These students with negative attitudes remind us that like readers who know why they like to read, nonreaders know why they don't. We may not agree with their logic, but as we listen to their voices we come closer to changing their minds about reading.

Favorite Choices

In "Literature and the Teenager" (in Sherrill, 1994), Carlsen states that "For over 50 years studies have shown that reading tastes develop through predictable stages" (p. 64). Although Carlsen's essay was written in 1958, recent interest studies still support this statement. The reading autobiographies I collected indicate few surprises about what students are reading. Of course, there are those few individuals with very unique tastes, and their autobiographies provide a great resource for teachers and librarians who need to be sensitive to teens' idiosyncratic choices.

Overwhelmingly, mystery and horror books are the favorite choice of the middle school students who wrote reading autobiographies. This was true for both those who said they liked to read and those who said they hated reading. Katie, who says she would much rather be outside playing sports than reading, goes on to add, "Now I read mysteries, romances and scary stories. I don't know why, I just think them best." Homer writes, "I really do not like to read very much but I still do. Now one of my favorite books is written by Stephen King. I especially like *Children of the Corn (sic)*." Aaron says, "My type of book: scary or funny ones." Leigh explains, "I usually don't read very much now unless I'm really bored. I really like books by R. L. Stine." The message to teachers is obvious: If you want readers in your middle school classrooms, make sure Stine, King, and Pike are in attendance, too. Then, when students tire of those three (and they will, just keep chanting that to yourself), recognize that they may not have tired of the genre. So also have books by authors such as Lois Duncan, Caroline Cooney, and Wendy Staub. These authors move students up the mystery/horror reading ladder while still honoring their desire to vicariously enjoy fear. For specific titles and authors see Figure 2.1.

Sports books and books with humor were cited most after mystery and horror by the students who didn't like to read. It is always amazing to see the student who wants to be scared also want to be tickled. Figure 2.2 provides you with a list of books about sports, while Figure 2.3 is a list of books with humor.

Those students who expressed a love of reading

Figure 2.1   Beyond Stine, King, and Pike

Cooney, Caroline. *The Cheerleader.*

Cormier, Robert. *Fade.*

Duncan, Lois. *Daughters of Eve.*

Klause, Annette Curtis. *The Silver Kiss.*

Mahy, Margaret. *The Changeover.*

Nixon, Joan Lowery. *The Dark and Deadly Pool.*

Nixon, Joan Lowery. *Whispers from the Dead.*

Peck, Richard. *Ghosts I Have Been.*

Westall, Robert. *Gulf.*

Yolen, Jane and Greenberg, Martin H. (Eds.). *Vampires.*

listed a greater variety of types as their second and third favorite categories. Romance appeared on many autobiographies as did historical fiction, nonfiction, and magazines. These students who enjoy reading remind us that avid readers read a wide range of material and enjoy nonfiction as well as fiction. Barbara says:

> Now I like all kinds of books. I used to read all *Baby-sitter's Club* books in the sixth grade but as I got into seventh they were too childish so I moved onto the *Sweet Valley High* books in seventh, but now in eighth they are beginning to become too cheesy to me. So I try to go for new types of books like mysteries or books on true life experiences. But even sometimes those are disappointing. By next year, Who knows?

While the girls enjoy the series books, boys often mentioned nonfiction as a favorite type of book. John writes, "Every once in a while I enjoy reading car manuals." Luke is also a nonfiction reader, writing that as he got older he "started reading about things I liked like helicopters and jets." These two boys remind us that nonfiction is important to readers. The important point

Figure 2.2   Books about Sports

Brooks, Bruce. *The Moves Make the Man.*

Dueker, Carl. *Heart of a Champion.*

Klass, David. *Danger Zone.*

Knudson, R. R. *Zanballer.*

Lewin, Ted. *I Was a Teenage Professional Wrestler.*

Lipsyte, Robert. *The Contender.*

Littlefield, Bill. *Champions: Stories of Ten Remarkable Athletes.*

Lynch, Chris. *Shadow Boxer.*

Rivers, Glenn and Bruce Brooks. *Those Who Love the Game: Glenn "Doc" Rivers on Life in the NBA and Elsewhere.*

Weaver, Will. *Striking Out.*

Figure 2.3   Books with Humor

Brooke, William J. *Teller of Tales.*

Cleary, Beverly. *Dear Mr. Henshaw.*

James, Mary. *Shoebag and Shoebag Returns.*

Jukes, Mavis. *Expecting the Unexpected.*

Kormon, Gordon. *The Chicken Doesn't Skate.*

Naylor, Phyllis Reynolds. *All but Alice.*

Parks, Barbara. *Skinnybones.*

Paulsen, Gary. *Harris and Me.*

Robinson, Barbara. *The Best School Year Ever.*

Scieszka, Jon. *The Stinky Cheese Man and Other Fairly Stupid Tales.*

Silverstein, Shel. *A Light in the Attic.*

Spinelli, Jerry. *Maniac Magee.*

Wrede, Patricia. *Dealing with Dragons.*

to remember is that nonfiction interests are varied and dependent upon students' individual tastes. For a list of romance novels and historical fiction see Figures 2.4 and 2.5.

Not Hearing the Message

In "Literature and the Teenager" (in Sherrill, 1994), Carlsen discusses the flexibility and variety of young teens' reading choices. He describes an interview with one girl who was asked about her favorite book. After some thought, the girl said, "Well it depends. I have favorite children's books, favorite teen age girls' stories, favorite Gothic romances, and favorite serious books" (p. 63). In commenting on her progression of enjoying children's books to preferring "serious" books, Carlsen notes the importance of letting students' interests guide their reading development:

> Fortunate is the adolescent who either on his own or through the encouragement of an understanding adult has been allowed to experience each of these stages of reading interest without being

Figure 2.4   Romance Novels

Bonner, Cindy. *Lily.*

Bridgers, Sue Ellen. *Home Before Dark.*

Burns, Olive Ann. *Cold Sassy Tree.*

Byars, Betsy. *Bingo Brown and the Language of Love.*

Conrad, Pam. *What I Did for Roman.*

Kerr, M. E. *If I Love You Am I Trapped Forever?*

Kline, Suzy. *Who's Orp's Girlfriend?*

Levy, Elizabeth. *Cheater, Cheater.*

McFann, Jane. *Nothing More, Nothing Less.*

Mills, Claudia. *Dinah in Love.*

Nelson, Peter. *Sylvia Smith-Smith.*

Spinelli, Jerry. *Jason and Marceline.*

Stanek, Lou Willett. *Katy Did.*

Voigt, Cynthia. *On Fortune's Wheel.*

Figure 2.5   Historical Fiction

Curtis, Christopher Paul. *The Watsons Go to Birmingham—1963.*

Cushman, Karen. *Catherine, Called Birdy.*

Lasky, Kathryn. *Beyond the Burning Time.*

Lowry, Lois. *Number the Stars.*

McKissack, Patricia C. & McKissack, Fredrick L. *Christmas in the Big House, Christmas in the Quarters.*

Nixon, Joan Lowery. *Ellis Island Trilogy.*

Nixon, Joan Lowery. *The Orphan Train Adventures.*

Paulsen, Gary. *Nightjohn.*

Rinaldi, Ann. *In My Father's House.*

Salisbury, Graham. *Under the Blood-Red Sun.*

made to feel inferior in his tastes or perceptions for doing so. For traditionally, American schools have negated this sequential pattern. (p. 63)

Some students' comments indicated that some teachers must not agree with Carlsen's position that teens need to be encouraged to follow their own tastes and not be criticized for their selections. These are the teachers who require certain books, forbid others, and often condemn an entire genre. For instance, Colin explains that as a fourth grader he preferred to read nonfiction, and "today I read mostly the same thing [at home] except I can't [at school]. I have to read fiction which I hate and has no point in my classification of it." Another student, Katherine, echoes the same frustration of teacher control in her reading selection as she says, "Now I like horror books, but my teacher won't let me read them." When students give us direct messages about what they want to read and we continually push them in other directions, we are moving them further from reading and convincing them that their needs are unimportant.

Acting on Their Voices

When we listen to what students tell us about reading, however, we discover that a lack of choice is not the only thing that bothers them.

First, look at what they say about reading and assignments. Sarah says, "Reading is okay except when we have to answer questions on the book. . . ." Tiffanie writes, "My favorite point of reading was in fourth grade because I had no assignments to read books. I got to read them freely and any time I wanted." Mark, an eighth grader, discusses how his teacher's assignments have encouraged him to dislike reading:

> I learned to read when I was in first grade and read pretty well in second. In fourth and fifth grades we had to do a lot of book reports. BORING! I usually didn't even read the book. I always relied on my abundance of imagination and creativity to fool the teacher. I haven't read totally through a book from start to end since *Hunt For Red October*. That was two years ago. I still have book reports due. Just last week in Mrs. M's class I never read any books and made one up. I got a 96! Pretty good! I think.

Next, review their comments about reading from trade books versus reading from textbooks. John describes three years of school time reading this way:

> In fourth grade I started reading literature in novels instead of a reading textbook. We read books such as *Sarah, Plain and Tall, Pinballs* and in the fifth grade we read *The Cay, The Witch of Blackbird Pond, Fantastic Mr. Fox,* and *Island of the Blue Dolphins.* In sixth grade I went back to a textbook called *Elements of Literature.* I learned all about plot, gods, and goddesses, anthropomorphism, and many other literary forms.

Another student, Pratesh, is more direct in his comments about textbooks: "I hate, absolutely hate basals and home readers."

Third, notice what middle school students write about having time to read. Over and over again students noted the importance of giving them the opportunity to read during school. This is an interesting point since many reading and reading improvement teachers give students plenty of time to drill on reading skills, complete worksheets, take computerized tests, practice taking minimum competency state-mandated tests, but rarely give students time to read for large blocks of time. However, the following comments remind us that if we want students to read, we must let them read. Kendra's statement may be one of my favorites: "Now since we read during reading, I enjoy reading a lot more. It's like once you start reading, you read a lot." Joseph had the same experience after he "accidentally enrolled"(!) in a reading enrichment class: "I really don't like to read, and normally I didn't until last year I accidentally enrolled in a reading enrichment class where I actually read books for about the whole semester and I really enjoyed it sort of. Sometimes I loved it though."

These thoughts provide clear direction. Students need to be given time to read, provided with an assortment of reading materials from which to choose, asked to do few answer-the-questions-in-the-packet assignments, and offered trade books rather than reading or literature anthologies. When teachers make these adjustments to their curriculum, they can have an enormous impact on students' reading interests and attitudes! In *Side by Side* (1991), Nancie Atwell writes about the importance of teachers:

> As parents, there may be no greater gift we can give our children than a literate household to grow up in. But as teachers, we have to work from the premise that all students, no matter their household, will read and talk about literature as if it is their daily bread. In my life I had just two teachers who invited me to become a reader. Two was enough. . . . Time and Choice are important, but for these kids the teacher's individual responses to them, their tastes, and their troubles will be another key. (p. xviii)

One student, Andy, who wrote to me made a comment that mirrors what Atwell was saying. He recounted several years of reading classes revealing the importance of teachers:

> Fourth grade was a huge changing period, for about half of the year I didn't change but in about the middle of the year a new teacher was introduced into the fourth grade. The [administrators] gathered at random a handful of kids including me. This new teacher's name was Mrs. M—and she was nice. She taught in alot [sic] of new innovative ways. One thing was the book rack loaded with books, and I don't know what possessed me but I read just about every book in there. The book that stands out the most is *Wrinkle in Time* which is a very, very,

very good book. In sixth grade (fifth was so boring I'm going to skip it) I read alot. I had Mrs. S.—and she read alot including *Hank the Cow Dog.*

Andy tells us that teachers do make a difference. They inspire, support, and convince students that they are readers and that reading is valuable. These teachers listen to their students' voices and from their words they know what to do. Some of the things these teachers often do include the following:

- Increase reading time in the schools and stress silent reading.
- Take time to find out what students want to read and let students read those books.
- Balance free choice and curriculum requirements.
- Use tradebooks rather than basals and literature anthologies as often as possible.
- Model for students how experienced readers and writers plan and accomplish their goals.
- Allow students to read nonfiction as well as fiction. They recognize that not all readers prefer fiction. Many students want informational books, how-to books, magazines, and other nontraditional reading material.
- Encourage response discussions by asking open-ended questions that elicit answers requiring critical thinking rather than yes/no answers. These teachers model the importance of creating meaning through discussion.

In her book *The Other Way to Listen*, children's author Byrd Baylor reminds readers that listening takes practice and takes patience, but as we practice, listening becomes the most natural thing in the world. As junior high/middle school teachers and librarians, let us listen to the unique voices of the students, respond to their voices with diverse materials, and embrace teaching practices that nourish their interests, abilities, and habits. Let us do these things until they become the most natural things to do in our classrooms. Let us listen to their voices so that as these middle schoolers reach new turning points, we hear their concerns and can help steer them in the direction that will turn them toward books.

References

Atwell, N. (1987). *In the middle.* Portsmouth, NH: Heinemann.

Atwell, N. (1991). *Side by side: Essays on teaching to learn.* Portsmouth, NH: Heinemann.

Beane, J. (October 1991). The middle school: The natural home of integrated curriculum. *Educational Leadership, 49:2,* 9–13.

Beers, K. (1996). No, time, no interest, no way! Part II. *School Library Journal, 42.3*, 110–113.

Carlsen, G. R. (1967). *Books and the teenage reader*. New York: Harper & Row.

Carlsen, G. R., & Sherrill, A. (1988). *Voices of readers: How we come to love books*. Urbana, IL: National Council of Teachers of English.

Langer, J. A., Applebee, A. N., Mullis, V. S., & Foertsch, M. A. (1990). *Learning to read in our nation's schools: Instruction and achievement in 1988 at grades 4, 8, and 12*. Princeton, NJ: Educational Testing Service.

Rief, L. (1992). *Seeking diversity: Language arts with adolescents*. Portsmouth, NH: Heinemann.

Sherrill, A., & Ley, T. C. (Eds.). (1994). *Literature is . . . : Collected essays by G. Robert Carlsen*. Johnson City, TN: Sabre Printers.

Trade Books Cited

Baylor, B. *The other way to listen*. New York: Charles Scribner's Sons.

Byars, B. (1980). *The pinballs*. New York: Harcourt Brace.

Clancy, T. (1984). *The hunt for Red October*. Annapolis, MD: Naval Institute Press.

Dahl, R. (1970). *Fantastic Mr. Fox*. (1988). New York: Knopf.

Erickson, W. (1988). *Hank the cow dog*. Houston, TX: Gulf Publishing.

Facklam, H., & Facklam, M. (1991). *Avalanche*. New York: Crestwood House.

Gipson, F. (1956). *Old Yeller*. New York: Harper & Row.

Greenberg, K. (1993). *Nolan Ryan*. Minneapolis, MN: Lerner Publications.

Keith, H. (1987). *Rifles for Watie*. New York: Trophy Keypoint.

L'Engle, M. (1989). *A wrinkle in time*. New York, Dell.

MacLachlan, P. (1985). *Sarah, plain and tall*. New York: Harper & Row.

O'Dell, S. (1990). *Island of the blue dolphins*. Boston, MA: Houghton Mifflin.

Speare, E. G. (1958). *The witch of Blackbird Pond*. Boston, MA: Houghton Mifflin.

Taylor, T. (1963). *The cay*. New York: Doubleday.

Tolkien, J. R. R. (1990). *The hobbit*. Oxford, NY: Windrush.

Chapter 3

Choosing Not to Read: Understanding Why Some Middle Schoolers Just Say No

Kylene Beers

Understanding Aliteracy

Consider what some reading researchers have to say about reading and reading instruction:

> Learning to read is a rather fruitless activity if it is not utilized beyond school assignments. (Culliton, 1974, p. 183)

> We are creating *school* time readers rather than *life* time readers. (Trelease, 1989, p. 12)

> I believe a lot of children leave school without ever suspecting that reading can be a pleasant activity. (Smith, cited in Sabine & Sabine, 1983, p. 134)

> The consequences of not reading although you are able to are only marginally less frightening than those arising from illiteracy itself. (Crompton, 1980, p. 80)

> If we teach a child to read, yet develop not the taste for reading, all of our teaching is for naught. We shall have produced a nation of "illiterate literates"—those who know how to read but do not read. (Huck, 1973, p. 305)

> Young people who cannot read at all are far outnumbered by young people who can read (poorly or well) but won't. The latter, who choose not to read, for whatever reason, have little advantage over those who are illiterate. (Holbrook, 1983, p. 38)

Plainly, reading experts recognize that some students leave school with the ability to read, but without the desire. However, like many things in education, we don't need researchers to tell us what we see every day. Secondary school teachers are well aware that every year it is harder and harder to connect students to texts. We can all easily conjure up the image of avid readers. How do they sit in class? Slumped? Heads down? Jacket hoods pulled over their heads? Hardly! These students sit up, lean forward, smile, volunteer to answer questions, nod their heads. And they read! We can also visualize the reluctant reader. You know these students. They pull up their jacket hoods, slump into their chairs, roll their eyes, and look bored. These students read only under great duress and often fake it at that. Indeed, middle school teachers know it is more the norm to teach students who don't enjoy reading than those who do.

Additionally, we don't need statistics to show us that the less students read, the poorer the readers they become. The poorer the readers they become, the harder reading is for them, which validates their negative attitudes toward reading. We also know that many of these students who dislike reading become parents who dislike reading. Consequently, they spend little time reading to, with, or in front of their own children. This in turn creates a new generation of students who often, taking their cues from home, see little use for reading beyond completing their school work. This downward spiral is difficult to break especially as state-mandated minimum competency tests force many teachers to think they should focus more on reading skills than on reading pleasure. Maracek (1978) reminds us that "when skills take over . . . and word recognition becomes an end in itself, there is a greater dislike for the whole reading process. Instead of opening up the world of literature as a source of pleasure, reflection, and insight, we close the door to enjoyment and exploration—the primary goals of reading" (p. 32). Skills alone do not produce readers.

If we want to do more than teach reading skills, if we also want to instill in students a desire to read, then we must do as Teale (1983) suggests and "pay special attention to the extent to which the taste for reading is being fostered" (p. 14). Without this special attention, aversion to reading may develop, for as Frank Smith (1988) explains:

> Reading can become a desired activity or an undesirable one. People can become inveterate readers. They can also become inveterate nonreaders, even when they are capable of reading. One of the great tragedies of contemporary education is not so much that many students leave school unable to read and to write, but that others graduate with an antipathy to reading . . . despite the abilities they might have. (p. 177)

Agreeing that this antipathy to reading is a great tragedy leads me to wonder why: Why would a child who can read, choose not to read? Why do some youngsters enter school excited about reading (Holdaway, 1979), but then leave school caring little for it? Why in a time of more children's and young adult books being published, why in a time of more being known about the nature of reading, why in a time of increased spending on reading programs are some students turning away from reading? Why won't Johnny (and Jenny) read?

Whether called "literate non-readers" (Nell, 1988), "illiterate literates" (Huck, 1973), "nonreaders" (Smith, 1988), "reluctant readers" (Chambers, 1969), or "aliterates" (Beers, 1996a&b; Boorstin, 1984; Decker, 1986; Mikulecky, 1978; Ohanian, 1989), this group of people who can read but do not is truly one of the "great tragedies of contemporary education" (Smith, 1988, p. 177). They are found throughout all age groups of our society (Winkle, 1988) and cross all socioeconomic and educational boundaries (Decker, 1985). External reasons—too much television, too little parental modeling, too much emphasis on a skills approach to reading—offer some insights as to why students dislike reading. These insights are crucial because these nonreading students have the potential to create, as William Baroody (1984), President of the American Enterprise Institute explains, a two-tiered society:

> Aliteracy reflects a change in cultural values and a loss of skills, both of which threaten the processes of a free and democratic society. Literacy . . . knits people together, giving them a common culture . . . and provides people with the intellectual tools used to question, challenge, understand, disagree, and arrive at consensus. In short, it allows people to participate in an exchange of ideas. A democratic nation is weakened when fewer and fewer citizens can participate in such an exchange. Aliteracy leads inexorably to a two-tiered society: the knowledgeable elite and the masses. It makes a common culture illusory or impossible; it erodes the basis for effective decision making and participation in the democratic process. (p. ix)

Obviously, this tragedy of choosing *not* to read reaches far beyond affecting state-mandated minimum competency test scores. The first step in curbing aliteracy is finding reluctant readers who are willing to talk about their dislike of reading with responses that move beyond the typical "it's boring" explanation. Luckily for teachers, those students do exist. What follows are some excerpts of many hours of conversations with several aliterate students (Beers, 1991). While their names are pseudonyms, their comments are real, straight from their hearts, filled with honesty that can certainly guide us toward an understanding of why some choose not to read.

What the Students Said

Steve

I don't like it when people think I'm not real smart. I'm real smart. I used to be in the gifted class. Did you know that? I got in in second grade, in November, and I was in until two years ago. I was in sixth grade then. See, I had to do sixth grade twice. That wasn't a very good year—the first year for sixth grade. Last year was better. I think I'm probably still gifted, but I just got sorta lazy. I mean everything started taking so much time. And like for everything, they wanted all this effort. Lots of time I just didn't have the energy. I'd rather do my Nintendo. . . . I don't do much reading now. Well, you know how it is. I just got real busy. I read a lot in fifth grade. And I still like to read. I just can't find any good books anymore. I just don't do it much. . . . I don't know. I'm just not into it right now. My friends are real important to me, and I'd rather hang out with them than read a book. You know, you can read a book any time but you can't always be with your friends, and if you aren't there when they say, "Let's go to the mall" then you don't go. . . . I like to read, it's real good for you and all, but I just need to be with my friends now, okay?

Geoffrey

I don't read much now. . . . I mean like you have to know how to read to get a job and stuff. And if it's a good book, like I really like those like *Skinnybones*, then it can be real relaxing. You sorta forget everything else, and it's like I just become that person and do what he's doing. . . . I just don't read much now. I like to read, but I just don't have time for it. I've really decided that gymnastics is something I want to concentrate on right now. [Reading] will just have to wait. Once you are a reader, that's just what you are. I just don't have time to be doing it right now.

Burt

I'm not one of "the ones," you know, the ones who get elected to everything, the ones who are the teacher's favorite, the ones who wear the right clothes, the ones who go to the parties. I don't like to read too much. It doesn't hold my interest very well. I just read slow. Most of the books I know are boring. . . . I'm not really someone who enjoys reading—nothing really happens when I read, so I guess I don't see much use for it. Most of the stories are pretty dumb. . . . Some people are just always having to do some-thing. Like my mother never only watches TV—she watches TV and reads a book or does this sewing stuff. I don't have to always be busy. Sometimes I just sit, and I just don't think about doing something. If I wanted to do something, I guess it would be like watching a movie. I just don't have the same level of going out and doing things that other people have.

I don't like to read. [My teacher] keeps telling us about how some books are about kids our ages doing the same kinda things we're doin'. Why's that good? . . . Don't tell me you can help me find books about kids like me. Why would I want to read about someone like me? I'm boring. I don't have many friends. I don't like

me in real life—why would I like me in a book? . . . It's just that
sometimes I don't know what's going to happen to me. I try really
hard. I don't know—maybe someday I might like to read. Maybe if I
do it enough, I'll learn to like it. But I don't know. I think maybe I
first gotta learn to like me. . . .

I just don't like to read. It's boring and nothing happens. Then
I just lose interest, and then when I try to start it again [a book],
then I don't remember what is happening, and so I just give it up. I
don't get any feelings from reading a book. Reading is just like just
figuring out words and meanings and comprehension.

Angie

I wish I liked to read more, but reading just never really
interested me. Reading makes me frustrated. I worry all the time
"What is the teacher going to ask? What am I supposed to know?"
and then all the names of all the people just get all mixed-up and
then we have a test, and then what if I don't do very good? Then
sometimes I have to read it over again, and then I get mad. Getting
frustrated about not understanding and worrying about what the
teacher will ask make me not like to read.

I don't read like that [for entertainment] too much. I learned
that the best way for me to stay ahead of my comprehension
problems is to constantly ask myself "What's the author saying
here? What does the teacher want me to know?" So when I read, I
am constantly thinking about what I'm supposed to be knowing.
But [reading] is okay for people who like to do it. I mean I guess I'm
pretty uncommitted about reading. I haven't really made up my mind.

Kii

I wouldn't actually say that I don't like to read. Some things
don't really interest me for me to read. So, I like reading, but it has
to be something interesting. Like, if it is some sort of scary novel or
it is fun or something. I rather prefer novels that have something to
do with a mystery or something. I'm not against [reading] or
anything like that. I just don't do it enough to be called a reader. I
mean, like, I'm not hating reading, [but reading] means you can't be
doing something else like going to the mall.

Paul

Reading is boring. It's a do nothing. You open the book. You
look at the words. You close the book. Big deal. Reading is hard
because you have to concentrate. . . . All the time I have to keep
saying to myself what is happening, and then I forget to say it, and
so the next thing I know, I've turned all these pages and I don't
know what happened. Why should I read? I mean what's it going
to get me? Is there like a reward out for being the best reader of the
year? And they [students who like to read] are still boring.

While those students' comments about reading were valuable, two particular interviews clarified some ideas for me. I want to share them with you.

Katy

"I never liked reading. It's boring. And I don't like it. You just sit there and nothing happens."

"What would you want to happen?" I asked.

"I don't know. What could happen? Nothing. It's just words and you just read them. Nothing happens."

"Do you think nothing happens to everybody that reads?"

"I don't know. Some kids in here are really into reading, and they talk about the people in the books like they are real or something. That's pretty strange, if you ask me. . . . They are like strange, always going around with a book and going emotional over it. . . . Why would anyone go emotional over a book?"

"Could you ever go emotional over a movie?"

"Yeah. I saw *Beaches*. My friend and me. It was so sad when that mother died."

"Did you cry?"

"We both did. We just sat there and cried and cried."

"So you went emotional over a movie?"

"Very."

"What if that had been a book instead of a movie? Would you still have gone emotional over it?"

"No, I don't think so."

"Why not? The same things would have happened."

"Maybe, but the book doesn't have any pictures. I couldn't see it, so I wouldn't know what was happening."

"So, Katy, did you ever see pictures in your mind from reading?" I continued.

"Elementary school."

"What about elementary school?"

"Well, those books had pictures, and so I could see what was happening."

"So you liked reading then?"

"Yeah."

"When did you stop liking it?"

"Around fourth or fifth grade. The books got really longer and no pictures."

"So what if you had books now with pictures?"

"That would be okay if they weren't baby books."

"What about magazines? They have pictures."

"That's not reading."

"What's not reading?"

"Looking at magazines."

"Well, maybe not if you are just looking at pictures. Do you ever look at the pictures and read the words?" I asked.

"I do with *Sassy*."

"So why wouldn't you say that is reading?"

"I would, maybe."

"Yeah?"

"Teachers wouldn't."

"Why wouldn't they, Katy?"

Katy took a long pause, then tried her best to explain why she thought teachers wouldn't call reading a magazine reading.

"It has to be something for reading. Oh. [pause] It is reading for you to learn about comprehension things. You study like prediction and fact and opinion. You can tell that is what it [reading] is because of the, like, questions you always get asked.... Usually when I read something, it's just to answer the teacher's questions about it. I guess I've never thought about a book being something that I might think about, you know, emotionally. The teacher's always told me what to think.... [Reading] seems pretty boring, pretty useless. I just don't feel any motivation to do it."

"So, Katy, what should I tell teachers to do so that they can help students like to read?"

"Tell them to ask the students what they thought. No teacher ever asked me what I thought. And when I start to tell them what I thought, they say, 'We all have our opinions, but what does the story tell us?' and you know what that really means? That really means what I think isn't important. But maybe it is; maybe it was important to me."

Martella

"How do you feel about reading?" I asked.

"Hate it."

"Do you ever read anything?"

"Well, sometimes I read the labels on cans at a grocery store if I'm shoppin' with my mom."

"How about magazines?"

"Sometimes I read the captions under the pictures. That's all."

"Do you read your school assignments?"

"No. Sometimes. Don't have to read in math. Science usually has a film. In here [language arts], I can usually just listen to what everybody else says and then just agree with someone."

"What do you do instead of read?"

"TV."

"How many hours of TV would you say that you watch?"

"When I get home, I do my homework, and then I watch TV, and then I talk on the phone, and then I watch some more TV, and then I take my bath, and then I watch some more TV, and then I go to sleep."

"Why do you like TV?"

"Don't know. You start watchin' it and then you can't stop."

"Could reading ever be a way to be entertained?"

"No way."

"Why not?"

"Borin'. All you do is sit."

"You sit when you watch TV."

"Not really. You could be doin' somethin' else. And anyways when you watch TV, it's like you are there. If they laughin', you just start laughin' too."

"Funny books—wouldn't you laugh at those?"

"Not at a book. Nothin' happens. It's just words. . . . I'm never gonna like it, no way."

Types of Aliteracy

As these students told me their thoughts about reading, I realized that these students chose not to read for a myriad of reasons. But within that myriad, after listening closely, I saw that there were patterns of responses. Those patterns led to categories of types of aliteracy (see Figure 3.1). To understand those categories, I used avid readers as the anchor from which to move. The students who identified themselves as avid readers during this study tend to do the following:

1.   Enjoy reading.

2.   Read often.

3.   Make time to read.

4.   Approach most reading events, those at school or at home, with an aesthetic stance, but read with an efferent stance if necessary.

5.   Define reading as an experience, "a way of life," an activity that "takes me places I've never been before."

6.   See the purpose of reading as providing entertainment.

7.   Like being identified as readers.

8.   Have positive feelings about people who enjoy reading.

9.   Plan to read in the future.

Most telling about these avid readers, and perhaps the trait that determines what type of reader all students will become, is the fourth point: they approach most reading events, those at school or at home, with an aesthetic stance, but read with an efferent stance if necessary.

Rosenblatt (1978) explains that readers approach any reading event with a stance that is either more aesthetic or more efferent. Students who read efferently are "focused primarily on what will remain as the residue after the reading" (p. 23), while students who read aesthetically are concerned "with what happens during the actual reading event" (p. 24). Put into the context of middle school classrooms, students who read *The Cay* by Theodore Taylor efferently will read to answer questions about such things as setting, dialect, causes of the war, reasons Philip's mother wanted Philip to return to America, how Philip changed on the island, conflict in the story,

Figure 3.1 Types of Readers

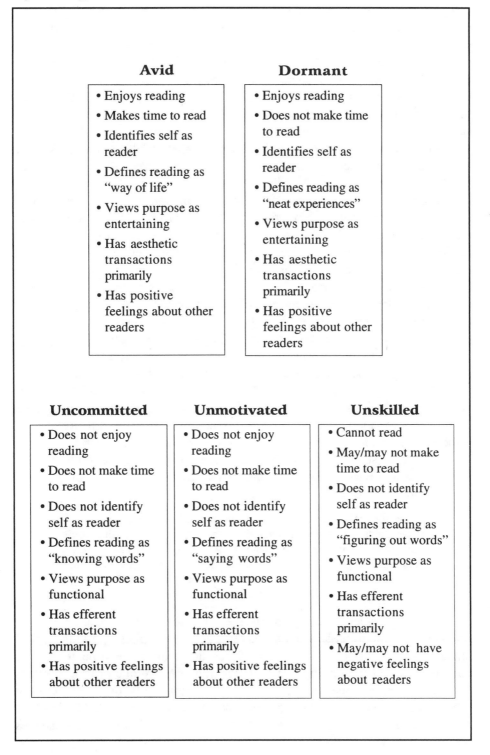

Avid
- Enjoys reading
- Makes time to read
- Identifies self as reader
- Defines reading as "way of life"
- Views purpose as entertaining
- Has aesthetic transactions primarily
- Has positive feelings about other readers

Dormant
- Enjoys reading
- Does not make time to read
- Identifies self as reader
- Defines reading as "neat experiences"
- Views purpose as entertaining
- Has aesthetic transactions primarily
- Has positive feelings about other readers

Uncommitted
- Does not enjoy reading
- Does not make time to read
- Does not identify self as reader
- Defines reading as "knowing words"
- Views purpose as functional
- Has efferent transactions primarily
- Has positive feelings about other readers

Unmotivated
- Does not enjoy reading
- Does not make time to read
- Does not identify self as reader
- Defines reading as "saying words"
- Views purpose as functional
- Has efferent transactions primarily
- Has positive feelings about other readers

Unskilled
- Cannot read
- May/may not make time to read
- Does not identify self as reader
- Defines reading as "figuring out words"
- Views purpose as functional
- Has efferent transactions primarily
- May/may not have negative feelings about readers

and to explain the author's theme. Rosenblatt explains that when this response occurs then the reader has directed his attention "outward . . . toward
concepts to be retained, ideas to be tested, actions to be performed after the
reading" (p. 24). However, if the reader's "attention is centered directly on
what he is living through during his relationship with that particular text" then
"he pays attention to the associations, feelings, attitudes, and ideas that these
words and their referents arouse within him" and "synthesizes these elements into a meaningful structure" (p. 25). Simply put, with an efferent
stance readers read focusing on what happens when they are done, while
with an aesthetic stance they live the adventure that unfolds in the book. (For
a more thorough discussion of efferent and aesthetic response, see Chapter
7, "Reader Response in the Middle School.")

The stance readers adopt affects the type of transaction they have. For
example, a wonderful poem could evoke an efferent transaction if the
readers are concerned with identifying the meter when they are finished
reading. Likewise, the same poem could evoke an aesthetic transaction if the
readers are allowed to focus on their emerging responses—feelings,
emotions, ideas, associations—to the ideas or images in the poem. I found
that avid readers automatically approached the texts in their language arts
class with an aesthetic stance. Other types of readers, though, did not.

Once I understood avid readers' behaviors, then all other readers'
behaviors could be typed. These readers, the aliterates, begin to fall into two
distinct groups. One group said they liked to read, but they did not have the
time to do it right now. The second group said they didn't read because it
wasn't enjoyable. As I studied these differences more carefully, I saw that the
first group, even though they were not presently reading, viewed themselves as
readers; the second group, however, did not see themselves as readers.

An earlier study (Beers, 1988) had identified a group of students who
enjoyed reading but did not read. One student from that study labeled such a
reader a *dormant reader*:

> Sometimes you get so busy that you don't have time to read. Like
> those plants we've been talking about in science, the ones that don't
> grow in the winter, dormant plants, they don't grow because the time
> isn't right. Well, right now with everything, it isn't the right time for me
> to read. But when it's summer and I don't have school and volleyball
> and all, then I'll have time to read. I'm dormant right now. (p. 18)

Dormant readers identify themselves as readers, enjoy reading, but do
not have the time to read. (I think this term not only applies to middle school
students, but to all of us who sometimes don't have the time to read. I
certainly find myself "going dormant" when grades are due or term projects
have come in. As one teacher told me, "I'm basically dormant between
September and May—but look out summer, I bloom with books!") Geoffrey
and Steve fit this category. Both boys like to read, both call themselves

readers, yet both realize it is not a part of their routines at this time. Dormant readers, such as these students, are inclined to do the following (the italicized items highlight this group's variance from the previously discussed group):

1. Enjoy reading.
2. *Not read often at this time.*
3. *Not make time to read.*
4. Approach most reading events, those at school or at home, with an aesthetic stance, but read with an efferent stance if necessary.
5. Define reading as "neat experiences" that sometimes "take up a lot of time."
6. See the purpose of reading as providing entertainment.
7. Like being identified as readers.
8. Have positive feelings about people who enjoy reading.
9. Plan to read in the future.

Notice, all their reading behaviors look the same as avid readers' behaviors except for reading often and making the time to read. They still like it, approach texts aesthetically (where a reader connects emotionally with the text) rather than efferently (where a reader connects cognitively, to carry away information, with a text), interpret reading as an experience for entertainment, call themselves readers and like people who do read. What is critical to remember with these students is that just like dormant plants will become dead plants if the growing conditions fail to materialize, dormant readers will become nonreaders if they go too long without reading. This speaks strongly to the need to create time for students to read. Furthermore, dormant readers explain that they don't like being confused with readers who have negative attitudes toward reading. They want the teacher to talk to them about books, like she does with avid readers. To keep from confusing dormant readers with other types of reluctant readers, we must remember that lack of a behavior (reading) does not always indicate a negative attitude. Spending time talking with individual students about their attitudes toward reading and administering reading attitude surveys certainly helps avoid this mistake.

While dormant readers have positive attitudes toward reading, students such as Angie, Burt, and Kii did not see themselves as readers. Burt continually stated, "I don't like to read," while Angie said, "Reading just never really interested me," and Kii admitted he couldn't be called a reader because "I just don't do it enough to be called that." However, unlike Katy, Martella, and Paul, these students would not speak negatively of those who did like to read. Furthermore, they each suggested that they might find reading enjoyable in the future. Concerning reading, they were, as Angie offered, uncommitted. *Uncommitted readers* from this study are likely to do the following:

1. Not enjoy reading.

2. Not read at this time.

3. Not make time to read.

4. *Approach most reading events, especially those at school and perhaps ones at home, with an efferent stance, but have read and can read with an aesthetic stance.*

5. *Define reading as a skill, as "knowing words and what they mean."*

6. *See the purpose of reading as functional;* however, admit that under certain conditions it might be enjoyable (e.g., if there were pictures accompanying the text).

7. *Not identify themselves as readers.*

8. Have nothing negative to say about students who do enjoy reading.

9. Not know if they will read in the future.

These uncommitted readers definitely have negative attitudes about reading and their view of it shifts from enjoying the process to focusing on what is due when they finish the text. For them reading is a functional skill. However, because there has been or occasionally is some sort of aesthetic transaction with texts, they haven't totally disconnected from reading. Most importantly, they haven't adopted a peer group that encourages negative thoughts and comments about students who do enjoy reading.

That is in fact what the aliterates with the most negative attitudes toward reading have done. These extremely *unmotivated readers* not only have negative thoughts about readers, but they surround themselves with peers who harbor the same feelings. These unmotivated readers call readers "strange" and "nerds" and "book boys." These students are certain they would not read in the future. They talk about never "going emotional" over a book and reading being "just words" or "figuring out words and meanings and comprehension." Reading is "boring" because they don't see the action of the words in their mind's eye. Few images are formed when they read, so reading remains the skill of word-calling. Their purpose for reading is to be able to answer the teacher's questions, an efferent purpose. They don't read because they "just don't feel any motivation to do it." Unmotivated readers in this study are prone to do the following:

1. Not enjoy reading.

2. Not read at this time.

3. Not make time to read.

4. Approach most reading events, especially those at school and perhaps those at home, with an efferent stance, but have read and can read with an aesthetic stance.

5. Define reading as a skill, as "saying words, looking at sentences, answering questions for the teacher."

6. See the purpose of reading as strictly functional.

7. *Not identify themselves as readers and not wish to be identified as readers.*

8. *Speak negatively about students who do enjoy reading.*

9. *Not plan to read in the future.*

These unmotivated readers have none of the same traits as avid readers. Their view of reading, their inability to connect emotionally with the text, their negative attitude toward reading in the future, and their unwillingness to associate with those who do like to read make this an especially difficult group to reach.

To complete the contrast of avid readers to other readers, I must include those who don't read because they cannot read. While this study did not focus on disabled readers, students talked about them. They suggested that some students have reading problems because "they can't tell the words" or "they don't know what things mean." Several students pointed out that once students learn to read, they may choose to become readers. Angie, though, felt that if reading problems persist too long, reading might never become pleasurable:

> I was having a lot of trouble with reading. . . . Probably if that had kept on going on and on, well I maybe wouldn't ever like to read because it would have always been so hard.

Lack of reading skill, in her mind, could lead to lack of desire to read. After interviewing students in this study, I talked with seventh graders who read two or more years below grade level. I asked them how they felt about reading, how they viewed themselves as readers, and how they felt about others who enjoyed reading. I saw that these unskilled readers tend to do the following:

1. Not be able to read.

2. Not read often, unless it is to practice skills.

3. Not make time for reading, unless they are highly motivat-
    ed to learn to read.

4. Approach most reading events with an efferent stance,
    especially those at school and perhaps those at home, but
    have read and can read with an aesthetic stance.

5. Define reading as a skill, as "figuring out words, sounding
    them out and all."

6. See the purpose of reading as functional.

7. Not identify themselves as readers as they recognize they
    lack the ability to read.

8. Have either positive or negative feelings about those who
    can read.

9. May or may not choose to read in the future. (Continued
    lack of success with reading may lead them to choose never
    to read.)

Analyzing Their Differences

Basically, the distinguishing attributes among these types centered on three areas: time spent reading voluntarily, identification of self as a reader, and feelings about others who enjoy reading.

Avid readers valued the time to read so much that they would make time to read. Anita reported "staying up late if I have to so I can read," and Maria said, "I'll find the time somewhere." As busy as these students were, reading was so integral to their lives that they made time for it. Dormant readers, uncommitted readers, and unmotivated readers did not make the time to read. The commitment to read voluntarily easily divides readers from nonreaders.

Additionally, another distinguishing attribute is their identification of self as reader. Avid readers called themselves readers and took pride in their love of reading. Adam put it this way:

> I'm a reader, an avid reader, like some people are avid sports fans.
> It's what I do. I'll always do it. I don't care if anybody else thinks
> it's nerdy or anything.

They valued reading and, therefore, valued the identity of being readers. Similarly, dormant readers identified themselves as readers and were pleased when they were labeled as such. Uncommitted and unmotivated readers, however, did not reference themselves as readers. This label was of no value to them. They did not encourage the term, and unmotivated readers in particular were offended when I asked them if they were readers.

A final differentiating characteristic was students' reactions to students who liked to read. Avid readers and dormant readers had positive reactions to other avid and dormant readers. They thought reading was "neat" and didn't see anything wrong with students who liked to read. Interestingly, un-committed readers also had favorable comments about students who enjoyed reading. They were quick to point out that they did not enjoy it, but that did not imply that others should not like it. Furthermore, they didn't mind working on projects with them and often would act interested in a book if a friend who was a reader recommended it. This willingness to be associated with students who *do* like to read is very helpful in convincing uncommitted read-ers to read. Unmotivated readers, however, did not respect those who en-joyed reading. They called them "strange ones" and "really weird." They did not value the act nor did they value the students who partook in the act. They did not want to sit near these students, work with them, or listen to them. Their distance—both in physical proximity and in personal interests—makes connecting these students to books even more difficult. These unmotivated readers surround themselves with other unmotivated readers and together they create an anti-reading community that continually supports each student's decision to disconnect from the reading.

Why They Disconnect

As I have listened to students, I continue to see that avid and dormant readers remember many reading/storytime experiences as youngsters. These students continually talked about joining book clubs, attending reading groups, visiting libraries, and participating in play groups that included a story hour. They had concrete items such as library cards, reading certificates, their own books, and homemade reading logs to help make the intangible joy of reading real for them. They also talked about being read to almost every day "for as long as I can remember" and "every day that I was little" and "all the time—everywhere we went."

These students' parents confirmed their children's recollections, ex-plaining that they read to their children all throughout their childhood years, from birth through age 7 or 8. They read at least four times a week and often every day of the week. And they read for long periods of time, so that by age 4 or 5, they might read to a child for 30 minutes at one sitting and up to an hour over the entirety of the day.

Second, these parents explained that they not only read often, but read aloud to their children at different times during the day and kept books throughout the house and in the cars. When these parents placed their children in day care, they made sure that reading to children often and throughout the day was a number one priority for the school. If they saw that the day care center or preschool had a bigger video library than book library, they left.

Uncommitted and unmotivated readers do not share these memories. These students' parents, when pushed to recollect their own child's early childhood year by year and not just see it as a single time between birth and age 6 or 7, realized that they didn't read aloud for many years. Many recognized that they didn't start reading aloud to their child until around age 2 and stopped reading aloud by age 4. When urged to think of how often they read each week, these parents often recollected two to four times a week, while others remembered that they only read on the weekends, or maybe on one weekend night. When they had to answer how long they read at each storytime session, the answer ranged from "as long as it took to read one picture book" to "about 15 minutes" or "I really can't remember, but probably not very long."

Next, when asked to name the time of day that they read to their children, most said they read to children at bedtime. Interestingly, some older children who report not liking to read do remember being read to at night. That, they claim, is what convinced them that reading is boring: it was an activity meant to "keep me quiet and make me go to sleep."

These same parents also recollected that they themselves didn't do much aesthetic reading in front of their children. Except for some newspaper reading, most of these parents explained that they did not read in front of the child. They either waited for their children to go to bed or did not like to read themselves. Whichever the situation, their children quickly figured out that reading was something that the parents did for their children, but not for themselves.

The contrast between parents of children who have positive attitudes toward reading and those with negative attitudes is obvious. Children with positive attitudes toward reading had parents who spent a lot of time firmly planting the notion that reading is an enjoyable, worthwhile activity. Most of these parents were creating for their children, without even realizing it, an aesthetic stance toward reading. Though this took a lot of time on their part, it was time well spent.

I believe these early repeated ongoing storytime experiences do two things for children. First, this continual book sharing with children places them in the midst of what Margaret Early (1963) calls unconscious delight. This crucial first stage in the stages of literary appreciation must occur if children are to grow in their appreciation of literature. (See Chapter 1 for further discussion of the stages of literary appreciation.) Second, while in the midst of this unconscious delight stage, these children develop an aesthetic stance toward reading.

Children who came to first grade with an aesthetic stance toward books firmly established remembered being read to long before school began; they remembered specific books, ones they "loved" and "liked the best of all," ones that "really made me cry" or "made me laugh and laugh." They entered school already ensconced into the unconscious enjoyment of literature, knowing how to approach a text with an aesthetic stance. They encountered reading situations at school and expected that the purpose was to be enjoyable, meaningful, and relevant. They expected that school-time reading would be to elicit their personal responses, and so they put themselves into the story as they read it. Their primary stance toward a text was an aesthetic stance. Then, as they encountered a need to read efferently (answering questions at the end of the chapter, comparing and contrasting two characters, identifying the setting, studying for a test, etc.), they learned a second stance that did not subsume the first.

Uncommitted and unmotivated readers entered school remembering few aesthetic transactions with texts. The uncommitted readers recalled more experiences with books prior to formal schooling that might have encouraged the unconscious enjoyment of literature, but these experiences were not repeated often enough to take firm hold. Therefore, when these students entered school they learned the main reading purpose of school-time reading, an efferent purpose, as their primary stance. They learned that reading was to get information, answer questions, finish tests, make Venn diagrams, fill in the blanks, and write book reports. This is not to imply that they never encountered texts that could have evoked an aesthetic response, but lacking a predisposed stance toward reading, they waited for the teacher to set the purpose, and generally, teachers have students read efferently. Even today, with the tremendous push toward using children's literature in elementary schools to teach reading, textbooks and tests continue to ask students to answer questions that value efferent response over aesthetic. Purves (1990) points out that many reading educators, textbook authors, test designers, even those who use the term *transaction* when discussing reading have

> despite their seeming adherence to a view of texts and reading that has been advanced by Louise Rosenblatt, generally missed the point—they would put literature into the primary school curriculum but still focus on an efferent view of comprehension. It is the bottle that has changed, not the wine. (p. 85)

Consequently these students who come to school with no stance toward reading in place learn the predominate school reading stance, efferent, as their primary stance. They occasionally find a text that speaks to their personal response and have the opportunity for an aesthetic response. However, their time in the unconscious delight of reading is shortened, if experienced at all. As Early (1960) explains, this stage "cannot be by-passed" if literary appreciation is to grow.

Avid and dormant readers appear to have the ability to easily shift from an aesthetic stance to an efferent stance and back again. This is seen as they read selections from their reading basals, literature anthologies or science and social studies textbooks. As they move through school, they not only simply enjoy the story or the information, but see themselves in the text, wonder how their reactions would differ from the characters', and ponder the implications of the theme. Then, they can shift and answer the questions that often require an efferent response. However, being told to read a book, or story, or poem and then answer the questions at the end of the selection, redesign the book jacket, write a new ending to the story, find 10 words to look up, find the author's use of metaphor, or any of 1,000 other things we ask students to do when they finish reading just reconfirms the negative attitudes of uncommitted and unmotivated readers.

Lacking the ability to shift easily from an aesthetic to efferent stance, they read the literature efferently, a focus that provides them with little opportunity for personal connection and that reaffirms their belief that reading is "boring." Efferent reading distances the readers from the emotional impact of the words which, over time, distances readers from reading. Smith (1988) explains the result of this distancing: "The emotional response to reading . . . is the primary reason most readers read, and probably the primary reason most nonreaders do not read" (p. 177).

Motivating Aliterate Students to Read

While the remainder of this book is filled with activities that constantly validate for middle schoolers our belief that their responses are important, what follows is a summary of what aliterate students say about what types of reading activities are motivating to them.

Motivating Activities

Motivation, the processes used in arousing, directing, and sustaining behavior (Ball, 1977), is integral to learning. It is that force which compels a student to choose to act, continue the action, and move to completion of the task (Wlodkowski, 1984). Just as motivation affects all aspects of learning, it affects reading. Mathewson (1985) states "if children are to read, they will need not only a favorable attitude toward reading, but also an appropriate motivation" (p. 842).

Rupley, Ash, and Blair (1983) emphasize that activities labeled as reading motivational activities should be used carefully with students. They explain that often teachers perceive an activity to be highly motivational if the students react with active participation and positive comments. In reality, although the activity may encourage interest, it may not actually encourage reading. For example, acting out a scene from a play would encourage high levels of participation. However, very few students may actually transfer the enjoyment of acting out a scene to the enjoyment of reading. Thus, the same activity may not hold the same intrinsic value for all students. They conclude that "it is possible that even though all the students appear interested and motivated by an activity, only a few of them are actually motivated to actively engage in learning the desired reading behavior" (p. 26).

Keeping their point in mind, I was particularly interested in what activities aliterate students in this study labeled as motivational. Again, it was easiest to begin with looking for the activities that students with positive attitudes toward reading enjoyed (see Figure 3.2).

It quickly became evident what kinds of activities avid and dormant readers found to be motivational. Their preferences (column one of Figure 3.2) reveal that avid and dormant readers desire activities that encourage a connection with what was read. For these students, reading is an intensely personal activity. They want to make their own selections, keep a journal about their reading, talk in small groups, and meet the author. They connect at a level that pulls them into active participation with their thoughts, the author's thoughts, and their peers' thoughts. For them, reading becomes a

Figure 3.2   Motivational Chart

Avid and Dormant Readers	**Uncommitted and Unmotivated Readers**
They do want to	They do want to
1. Choose their own books	1. Choose their own books from a narrowed choice
2. Have teacher read aloud a few pages	2. Have teacher read aloud an entire book
3. Meet the author	3. Compare movie to book
4. Buy books at a book fair	4. Read illustrated books
5. Keep a reading journal	5. Do art activities based on books
6. Go to the library	6. Read nonfiction material (comics, handbooks on sports, drawing, cars, fashion, makeup, magazines)
7. Participate in panel debates, and small group discussions, or share books with friends	

Activities move from motivating to unmotivating

They don't want to	They don't want to
1. Write book reports	1. Meet the author
2. Do many art activities	2. Buy books at a book fair
3. Hear the teacher read aloud an entire book	3. Go to the library
	4. Read for a charity
	5. Keep a reading journal
	6. Participate in panel debates, and small group discussions, or share books with friends

way to learn more about themselves; furthermore, it becomes, in Bloome's (1987) term, "a social process—a means to participate in and establish a community or social group" (p. 123). Reading begins as a solitary act between the reader and the text and then becomes an opportunity for interacting with a group, taking part in discussions, swapping favorite stories, or arguing over themes. Therefore, to keep these students motivated, we need to offer them, first, a chance to connect personally with the story, and second, a chance to connect with others.

The same can't always be said, though, for students with negative attitudes toward reading. In fact, sometimes the very activities that encouraged avid and dormant reader s to keep reading discouraged the nonreaders. Activities that avid and dormant readers preferred doing did not motivate students with negative attitudes, but instead the activities intimidated them and confirmed their anticipated feelings.

So what activities did these students see as motivating? In reality—very little. The standard first response to the question "What would encourage you to read more?" was "Nothing." However, observation of their actions coupled with observation of their reactions to their teacher's assignments showed that these students did see some activities as slightly motivating (see column two of Figure 3.2).

First, these students said that if they were going to read a book, they would want to be able to choose what it would be. Interestingly, though, for some, total freedom was frustrating as they had little ability to find good books.

Consider what usually happened to these reluctant readers when they visited the library. They often walked in and immediately sat at a table, not looking at books at all. When they did occasionally go to the shelves, they wandered aimlessly up and down aisles. I asked them if they liked going to the library and if they ever checked out books from there. Their responses revealed that they felt uncomfortable in the library, that it was "too big" and had "too many books" so that "I wouldn't know where any of the good ones were." An experiment with placing about 30 books in a box labelled *Good Books* revealed that these students were much more comfortable hunting for books when their area for choice had been narrowed (Beers, 1996).

Second, these students want to read books with illustrations. Initially, I thought this was because these students were lazy readers and wanted the pictures to provide meaning that they were not taking time to get from words. However, after listening to Martella and Katy talk about not seeing pictures in their minds, I changed my beliefs. I was reminded of an avid reader from a previous study (Beers, 1988) who compared reading to a VCR. She said that reading was like having a VCR in her mind—she could hear the words, see the action, replay exciting passages, fast forward, and pause to savor ideas. When I asked her if she liked books with pictures, she replied negatively, saying "they ruin what I've created" (p. 42).

The avid and dormant readers in this study agreed with that student. Uncommitted and unmotivated readers, though, time and time again said that they liked many illustrations. The few materials they did read corroborated this preference for illustrations: Paul's Nintendo magazines were filled with illustrations of video screens, charts, and graphs. Angie's intramural rule book had pictures of the basketball court layout, proper stances for ball shooting, and examples of referees' hand signals. Katy's teen magazines were packed with photographs and illustrations. Judy and Judy (1979) support this finding, explaining that some readers need materials with illustrations to help them bridge the gap between print and meaning. Looking at these materials, it is obvious that not only do these students want illustrated texts, they want informational texts. In fact, many reluctant readers prefer nonfiction over fiction. Whether it is because the topics offer an immediacy to their lives that fiction does not or that the format of the book aids in their comprehension is of little consequence. More important is the fact that these students appeared to read their selections aesthetically. Paul saw himself getting the highest scores playing Nintendo as he read about new techniques; Angie saw herself playing basketball; Katy saw herself in the clothes being shown on the pages of her magazines. Their willingness to look at these texts reminds us that we must expand our definition of acceptable reading to include what interests them.

Third, they want to compare the movie to the book. They want to see the movie and then read the book. Burt suggested that by seeing the movie first, he could "get what was going on in my head." By contrast, when avid readers mentioned comparison of film to book as motivating, they wanted to read the book first and then see the movie. As Anita explained, "Movies always leave out too much. I'd rather read about it first and then I'll know what got left out."

Fourth, these students want the teacher to read an entire book aloud. Avid readers also mentioned that they enjoy this practice. Amy clarified this when she said, "But not the whole thing. That would take up too much of the time when I could be reading." Chris concurred: "What I like is when she reads just a little bit and then we get to finish it." These readers with positive attitudes wanted her to read aloud, but only for a few pages—just enough to tease. Again, when reluctant readers want the teacher to read the entire book aloud, it is not only because they do not want to do the reading. Instead, they mention how the teacher's inflection, hand movements, and explanations of what is happening combine to help them to understand the story.

Fifth, some of the reluctant readers want to do art activities. "I guess I would like to do a poster on what I read. You know, like read something and then draw it. I'm pretty good at drawing," Kii reported. The students, especially those who saw themselves as artists, wanted to draw the setting, do a puppet show of a scene, act out a scene, or make models of characters. Whether these activities help them make the abstract words concrete or give them the opportunity to do something (drawing) they do well, I don't know. Regardless, repeatedly, connecting reading to art was important for these students. On the other hand, avid and dormant readers from this study did not favor art activities. "I'd rather get to talk about it," Christopher explained.

Much more revealing is to look at what students do not find as motivational. Avid and dormant readers in this study find very few activities as unmotivational. They like to read so much that one must work hard to dampen that enthusiasm. However, their least enjoyable activities included the following: writing book reports, doing art activities based on the books, and listening to the teacher read aloud an entire novel. By contrast, the unmotivated and uncommitted readers of this study had a long list of activities that were not motivational.

These students do not view reading as a positive activity, a process that goes beyond decoding; they view it as a skill. However, the absence of interaction is the very factor that interested uncommitted and unmotivated readers. Activities they did not want to do included exercises that connected them to other people. They did not want to meet the author, have panel discussions or small group talks, share books with friends, or read for a charity. Trips to the library were overwhelming and purchasing their own books offered them little enticement. They did not want to connect with the text or themselves in the form of reflection or keeping a journal. Since they usually have efferent transactions with the text, they have little personal response to write about, hence the common complaint "But what do you want me to write about?" Furthermore, since these students were not comfortable with their own responses to literature, they were not at ease sharing those responses with others. In the words of one student, "Sometimes [it's] really embarrassing because it's like I don't have anything to say." Continually facing embarrassment, these students convinced themselves that they were right not to like reading.

Because reluctant readers do not recognize reading as a positive social experience, they have little motivation to move into a community of readers. To help reluctant readers move into a community of readers, we must first convince them that their reactions to a text are important and that in sharing their responses and listening to others they will enlighten others and learn from others. To do this, consider Moffett's (1968) thoughts on becoming a writer. Moffett tells us writers first write for themselves; later, they write for a known audience; finally, they write for an unknown audience. I believe that avid and dormant readers follow the same progression. First, they read for themselves; after they have gained confidence in their own responses to texts, they feel comfortable joining a small, trusted community of readers; finally, after feeling comfortable interacting with others about their reading, they are prepared to join a larger community of readers.

Uncommitted and unmotivated readers do not follow the same progression. We see that every time these aliterate students refuse to participate in group discussions, act out in literature circles, fail to keep their reading journals, and make snide comments about other readers' responses. But if we think about their actions in light of Moffett's stages, we can see why they sabotage their own participation within a community of readers. These students have not yet formed responses to literature for themselves other than believing "it's boring" or "it's dumb." Consequently, they have had no time to gain confidence in their own responses to texts. Lacking that confidence, they are uncomfortable interacting with a small group of readers, much less the larger class group, many of whom they may know only by name. Middle school students judge much of their lives on how well they fit into the larger group. For students who fear their responses may set them apart, it is much safer to play the role of not wanting to participate than to try and fail. Teachers might consider structuring reading events for uncommitted and unmotivated readers that enable them to progress comfortably from self as audience, to intimate known audiences, to a large community of readers. For that progression to occur, the disconnected readers must connect with texts in a way that they have not yet done.

So How Do We Reconnect Disconnected Readers?

Wouldn't it be nice if once we recognized disconnected readers (perhaps they could arrive with that loud, obnoxious beep-beep that uncradled telephone receivers emit), we could simply put them back on their hooks and the connection would be made? In fact, these students do arrive in middle school emitting a warning signal, though the signal is usually withdrawn silence rather than purposeful noise. But if we recognize the signal, the connection can be reestablished. However, (let's stay with the phone metaphor a while since the phone is where most middle schoolers live!) something caused the student's reading receiver to fall off the hook in the first place, so the reconnection must be made carefully.

To restore service, the right equipment with the right service technician must be utilized. Too much static and interference will result in another disconnection. Depending on how good the original connection was, new and better installation may be in order and stronger wires might be required. And probably, there needs to be a switch in long distance carriers. Let's start there.

Long Distance Carriers

If you are thinking that your students' reading connection is poor, then you might be doubting the long distance carrier you've been using. Perhaps that carrier service has not placed enough emphasis on its customers' needs and satisfaction. Attending to readers' needs means choosing a carrier service whose philosophy is to encourage the user to actively work to respond on a personal level as a way to forming stronger connections among the reader (the person answering the phone), the text (the telephone), the caller (the author), and the message (how the reader interprets the caller's words). For too long secondary school reading and literature pedagogy has embraced a carrier that put the telephone (the text) and the caller (the author) at the top of the priority customer list. With that carrier service, improved connections are the readers' responsibility as they are expected to listen harder to the caller and decipher the caller's words, phrases, and tone. If they don't hear the caller, or someone (the teacher?) says they got the wrong message, it is their fault, and the carrier service recommends redialing and listening to the same recorded message again. With this service, after the call is finished, the listener checks his receiving ability by answering efferent questions and completing efferent activities.

The contributors to this book, *Into Focus*, subscribe to a different carrier service, a different philosophy, from the one described above. All the contributors in this text put the reader at the top of the priority list; we all believe that the strongest connections are made when the reader is an integral part of the loop—not an outsider listening in, but an insider, creating the message with the caller. Futhermore, we value the aesthetic response.

Purves et al. (1990) describe what happens to a student who responds aesthetically to a work:

> She understands what the words say to her.
>
> She translates the experience she has read about into her own context.
>
> She has a feeling about the experience.
>
> She has attitudes about the experience and the poem.
>
> She reaches conclusions and makes judgments. (p. 48)

Purves (1990) explains that this reaction to a work is facilitated by a teacher who encourages response, encourages students to explain their responses, and encourages students to try new things. In a response-centered approach, teachers read aloud and then talk about their responses to what was read; they explain how they translated the experience on the pages into their own life's experiences; they explain their feelings when they read; they explain how they reached their attitudes, conclusions, and judgments about their reading experience.

The comments and actions of reluctant readers would suggest that moving students into the unconscious enjoyment of literature requires more than sharing books with them. Prior to their school experiences, sharing may be sufficient. At that time, the focus is generally on enjoyment, which leads to aesthetic experiences. However, once school has planted firmly the notion that reading is an efferent experience, reluctant readers may need more than exposure to good books to change their approach to reading. They may benefit from a literature program that

- recognizes that they are not comfortable sharing their responses in a group setting,
- recognizes that what motivates them to read is different from what motivates students who like to read,
- recognizes that they may prefer nonfiction over fiction,
- encourages response-centered literature classes, and
- recognizes that teachers must model for these efferent-oriented students how to read aesthetically.

Students with negative attitudes toward reading do have emotional responses toward reading: negative. These students do react to reading: negatively. They do believe their responses have value: none. Changing those perceptions, though difficult, is possible and is, to a large extent, dependent on what we as teachers do in the classroom. We must convince these students that their responses are important and valued. Katy, the nonreader who claimed she would never like to read, explained this point perfectly as she offered her advice for teachers. Her words are worth repeating—and remembering:

> "So, Katy, what should I tell teachers to do so that they can help students like to read?"
>
> "Tell them to ask the students what they thought. No teacher ever asked me what I thought. And when I start to tell them what I thought, they say, 'We all have our opinions, but what does the story tell us?' and you know what that really means? That really means what I think isn't important. But maybe it is; maybe it was important to me."

References

Ball, S. (Ed.). (1977). *Motivation in education.* New York: Academic Press.

Baroody, W. (1984, September). Foreword. In N. Thimmesch (Ed.), *Aliteracy: People who can read but won't.* Conference sponsored by the American Enterprise Institute for Public Policy Research, Washington, DC. (ERIC Document Reproduction Service No. ED 240 543)

Beers, K. (1988). *Middle school avid readers talk about reading: An ethnographic account.* Unpublished manuscript, University of Houston, Houston, TX.

Beers, K. (1990). *Choosing not to read: An ethnographic study of seventh-grade aliterate students.* Doctoral dissertation, University of Houston, Houston, TX.

Beers, K. (1996a). No time, no interest, no way! Part I. *School Library Journal, 2*(2), 30–33.

Beers, K. (1996b). No, time, no interest, no way! Part II. *School Library Journal, 42*(3), 110–113.

Bloome, D. (1987). *Literacy and schooling.* Norwood, NJ: Ablex Publishing.

Boorstin, D. (1984). *Books in our future* (Report No. S-PRT-98-231). Washington, DC: U.S. Government Printing Office. (ERIC Document Reproduction Service No. ED 253 243)

Chambers, A. (1969). *The reluctant reader.* Oxford: Pergamon Press.

Crompton, J. (1980). The politics of not reading: Writing for power. *Children's Literature in Education, 11*(2), 76–81.

Culliton, T. (1974). Techniques for developing reading interests and attitudes. In   G. Duffy (Ed.), *Reading in the middle school: Perspectives in reading no. 18* (pp. 183–196). Newark, DE: International Reading Association.

Decker, B. (1985). *Aliteracy: What teachers can do to keep Johnny reading.* Paper presented at the Southeastern Regional Conference of the International Reading Association, Nashville, TN. (ERIC Document Reproduction Service No. ED 265 528)

Decker, B. (1986). Aliteracy: What teachers can do to keep Johnny reading. *Journal of Teacher Education, 37*(6), 55–58.

Early, M. (1960). Stages of growth in literary appreciation. *English Journal, 49(3),* 161–167.

Holbrook, H. (1983). Motivating reluctant readers: A gentle push. In J. Thomas & R. Loring (Eds.), *Motivating children and young adults to read—2* (pp. 29–31). Phoenix, AZ: Oryx Press.

Holdaway, D. (1979). *The foundations of literacy.* New York: Ashton Scholastic.

Huck, C. (1973). Strategies for improving interest and appreciation in literature. In A. Beery, et al. (Eds.), *Elementary reading instructions: Selected materials* (2nd ed.). Boston, MA: Allyn and Bacon.

Maracek, M. (1978). Silver sandals and golden tassels: Enriching language experiences for young children. *Language Arts, 55,* 30–40.

Mathewson, G. C. (1985). Toward a comprehensive model of affect in the reading process. In H. Singer & R. B. Ruddell (Eds.), *Theoretical models andprocesses of reading* (3rd ed., pp. 841–856). Newark, DE: International Reading Association.

Mikulecky, L. (1978, May). *Aliteracy and a changing view of reading goals.* Paper presented at the annual meeting of the International Reading Association, Houston, TX. (ERIC Document Reproduction Service No. ED 157 052)

Moffatt, J. (1968). *A student-centered language arts curriculum, K-13.* Boston, MA: Houghton Mifflin.

Nell, V. (1988). *Lost in a book*. New Haven, CT: Yale University Press.

Ohanian, S. (1989). Creating a generation of aliterates. *The Education Digest, 54*(6), 29–32.

Purves, A. C. (1990). Can literature be rescued from reading? In E. Farrell & J. Squire (Eds.), *Responding to literature: A fifty year perspective*. Urbana, IL: National Council of Teachers of English.

Purves, A. C., Rogers, T., & Soter, A. O. (1990). *How porcupines make love II: Teaching a response-centered literature curriculum*. New York: Longman.

Rosenblatt, L. (1978). *The reader, the text, the poem: The transactional theory of the literary work*. Carbondale, IL: Southern Illinois University Press.

Rupley, W. H., Ash, M. J., & Blair, T. R. (1983). Motivating students to actively engage in reading. In J. L. Thomas & R. M. Loring (Eds.), *Motivating children and young adults to read—2*. Phoenix, AZ: Oryx Press.

Sabine, G., & Sabine, P. (1983). *Books that made the difference: What people told us*. Hamden, CT: Library Professional Publication.

Smith, F. (1988). *Understanding reading: A psycholinguistic analysis of reading and learning to read*. Hillsdale, NJ: Lawrence Erlbaum.

Teale, W. (1983). Assessing attitudes toward reading: Why and how. In J. Thomas & R. Loring (Eds.), *Motivating children and young adults to read—2* (pp. 3–6). Phoenix, AZ: Oryx Press.

Trelease, J. (1989). *The new read aloud handbook*. New York: Penguin Books.

Winkle, A. (1988). Research on aliteracy: Why Johnny doesn't read. *Ohio Reading Teacher, 22* (2), 40–47.

Wlodkowski, R. J. (1984). *Motivation and teaching: A practical guide*. Washington, DC: National Educational Association.

Trade Books Cited

Park, B. (1982). *Skinnybones*. New York: Knopf.

Taylor, T. (1963). *The cay*. New York: Doubleday.

Chapter 4
CALL ME ISHMAEL: A LOOK AT GIFTED MIDDLE SCHOOL READERS

Barbara Baskin

"Call me Ishmael," was the answer Steven, 6 1/2 years old, gave when asked for a sentence using a short "i" sound. Startled, the alert teacher (who discovered he had actually read *Moby Dick*!) ran to the office saying, "I have a problem." The principal, however, didn't believe in giftedness nor did other administrators in that district: poor or inadequate adaptations for that extraordinarily gifted boy were made in his education. He eventually dropped out of college.

That example of tragic indifference is neither surprising nor unique. Although some fortunate primary youngsters have modifications made for their reading "problem," attention to giftedness often vanishes during the middle school period, then reappears at the high school level.

Textbooks designed for prospective middle school teachers rarely include information about the reading needs of highly able children. *Secondary Reading, Writing and Learning* (Tonjes, 1991), for example, contains fewer than three pages on gifted youth. Even among many texts on giftedness, reading issues focus on the early years: rarely can "reading" even be found in the indexes! This topic is equally scarce in administrative journals. That dearth of information is exacerbated in states like New York where giftedness courses are not prerequisites for teachers' or administrators' licenses. Reform-minded critics state that senior administrators nationally are uninformed on the subject while the "current staff has little idea of how to adequately differentiate curriculum" (Gallagher, Coleman & Nelson, 1995, p. 73). Tomlinson (1995) adds that often teachers' decisions about how to deliver instruction to gifted students are also misguided. Some teachers offer more unchallenging assignments, while others prepare more rigorous tasks, but neither appropriate, specific, nor consistent differential planning is undertaken. Even the founder of the middle school movement admits "[we] have not attended . . . to gifted students" (Council for Exceptional Children, 1995, p. 15).

In the national (N=46 sites) Classroom Practices Observation Study, Westberg, Archambault, Jr., Dobyns, and Salvin (1993) found that gifted children got less attention, received less "wait time" when questioned, and had few chances to respond to demanding questions. Even when teachers grouped the students by ability level in other subjects, they did not do so during reading periods! Appallingly, instead of receiving reading instruction themselves, gifted pupils often acted as teacher surrogates. While we as teachers ourselves know that there is no better way to learn something than to teach it, surely we can also provide differentiated instruction aimed at challenging our gifted students.

Some educators opt for packaged material or, more devastatingly, use basals. One investigator reported that teachers "would not be allowed to teach reading without basal readers and workbooks" (Woodward, 1986, p. 28). Clark (1988) studied heterogeneous settings, reporting that "the same basal series . . . used with the nongifted was used with the gifted reader" (p. 337). Using basals sabotages reading for advanced readers whose prior knowledge of vocabulary, story structure, etc. resulted in a boring, passive (Weaver, 1990), and unproductive experience. Basals typically "dumb down" language and condense the efforts of masterful writers. Tomlinson (1994a) points out that there are no admonitions against utilizing under-challenging material. Halkitis & Hoffman (1992) contend that gifted children "need to learn early that language is whole, that it can fulfill a need for creative expression, and that a literary work is complete, not simply an excerpt used to fulfill [an] artificial curricular structure" (p. 4). In spite of those admonitions, many schools still use basals with gifted students. Baskin and Harris (1980), Vacca, Vacca & Gove (1991), and Woodward, (1986) among others, are unanimous in criticizing basals, claiming that their content is inane, and their decoding exercises, reinforcement activities and controlled word lists are antithetical to advancing reading competency for gifted readers. The Commission on Reading of the NCTE has strongly rejected basals (Weaver, 1990), yet they continue to be used despite their severely limited concept of literacy. In middle school, how appropriate would such insipid material have been for Steven (who at 6 had begun a project of reading both the Old and New Testaments)?

How should gifted readers be more fairly and fittingly guided in the middle grades? To probe this quandary, I address the following: aspects of middle school philosophy and practice that particularly impact on this group; attributes of gifted youngsters and implications for reading; non-recommended responses for gifted readers; criteria for book selection; strategies for teachers; and special classroom adaptations that promote cognitive development among advanced readers.

Middle School Philosophy and Practice Regarding Gifted Readers

Although a stated objective of middle schools is to customize instruction, Tomlinson (1992) examined the professional literature and argues that awareness of, intent to serve, and plans to deliver differentiated curriculum are largely absent in middle school journals. Indeed, heterogeneous grouping is actively promoted. She claims numerous studies have extensively documented that schools consistently display a tendency to "teach to the middle," so that highly able children undoubtedly get exposure to content they already know. Vacca et al. (1991) agree that "teachers hold gifted readers back" (p. 517) and that grouping them with above-average pupils is an inadequate adaptation.

The more students diverge from the norm, the more differentiation is needed (Kulik & Kulik, 1992). While above average students should be heterogeneously grouped, exceptionally gifted middle school youngsters need special attention. Differentiation means "consistently using a variety of instructional approaches to modify content, process, and/or product in response to learning readiness and interest of academically diverse students" (Tomlinson, 1995, p. 80). Clark (1988) contends *both* differentiation and individualization must be in place, describing the latter as "the process of adapting the curriculum to the needs and interests of a particular gifted child" (p. 305). Postponing the introduction of complex and demanding ideas until high school may result in diminished potential (Bloom, 1956). Halstead (1988) argues, "If their environment provides enough stimulus, they may experience the elation of the insights and awareness that their giftedness makes possible" (p. 4). Equitable and evenhanded treatment requires that gifted children be served responsively throughout the school experience. This means implementing practices in middle schools such as:

- designing beneficial settings,
- selecting suitable and challenging reading materials,
- de-emphasizing grades to focus more on process than product,
- reassessing the implications of accountability (with its stress on minimum standards), and

- enriching instruction to reverse the underachievement of some gifted students.

Attributes of Exceptionally Able Readers

Often our children's introduction to the world of ideas begins with literature, and their intellectual growth "depends on their access to and regular involvement in the reading process" (Dyer, 1994, p. 37). They need frequent opportunities to hear and read excellent literature. Though we know that reading tapers off for most students at middle grade levels, gifted children go against that trend (Carter, 1982). Ley & Trentham (1987) discovered that these students tend to hold more favorable attitudes towards reading than their agemates. But simply giving these children more to read is not the answer, nor can it be presumed that [gifted children] will automatically select intellectually stimulating reading material (Archambault, Jr. et al., 1993; Baskin & Harris, 1980). How should a middle school reader and book best be matched? An examination of the attributes of both provides direction.

Among gifted students, Piechowski & Colangelo (1994) consider intellectual excitability as common. They explain that such children ask probing questions, typically enjoy problem solving, display curiosity, concentrate easily, display independence of thought, and enjoy inquiry into moral issues. Further, they relish intellectual effort, are comfortable with theoretical or abstract matters, and have a wide variety of interests. Gifted students also retain an extraordinary quantity of information, demonstrate unusual retentiveness and advanced comprehension, show advanced levels of language development and verbal ability, reveal unusual capacity for and pace of processing information, disclose flexible thought processes, show ability to delay closure, integrate ideas from different disciplines, demonstrate heightened capacity to see unusual and diverse relationships, and use and develop conceptual frameworks. They reveal such thought processes as thinking in alternatives, making generalizations, and comprehending figures of speech (Clark, 1988). These attributes affect teachers' guidance of their reading choices. In no real-life situation (like the classroom) does one size really fit all. Quality of the experience is the key issue. Teachers must learn how materials can best be exploited to advance the cognitive growth of their already excellent readers. Since these pupils show exceptional comprehension, higher level books (sometimes even at an adult level) should be made available; since they have the capacity for sustained effort, longer books are reasonable options; since they can understand symbolic material, books including such components are possibilities. Conversely, mediocre books that stress "message and overemphasize or distort life" (Karl, 1987) should be avoided. Abilities and interests should control the reading curriculum.

Gifted students are a heterogeneous group, ranging from students like Steven to those having difficulty in the language arts despite their assessment as being highly intelligent (Whitmore, 1980). Further, as this cohort ages, developmental rate varies even more widely, interests mature and differ, and group divergence increases. Even more within-group individualization and differentiation are necessary in middle school than in elementary classrooms. As with other children, reading serves other purposes such as social and psychological growth. Henjum (1983) concurred: "All too often academically gifted . . . students receive neither positive intellectual stimulation nor emotional and social support which they need" (p. 23). Sometimes overlooked, personal issues may arise directly from special abilities. Gifted children have "heightened sensitivity to the comments and actions of others so that being misunderstood or rejected is a more painful experience for them than for most" (Halstead, 1988, p. 2). As a result, material below their reading level but dealing with age-related issues may, at times, be fitting. Perceptive teachers are aware that individuals, including gifted students, are seeking books for a multiplicity of purposes, some of which reflect quandaries typical of this age group. Middle school gifted students, for example, may be drawn to the conflicts about being different in such varied young adult books as *Catherine, Called Birdy* (Cushman, 1994), *Words by Heart* (Sebestyen, 1979), and *The Moves Make the Man* (Brooks, 1984). Concerns for both academic and psychological divergence cannot be overstressed. Although they are capable of reading complex and sophisticated adult texts, middle school gifted students may need to read about young adults like themselves.

Non-recommended Practices with Gifted Middle School Readers

Clearly, whole-group use of basal readers is not an effective practice for gifted middle school readers. In addition, Shore, Cornell, Robinson, and Ward (1991) reported that Junior Great Books (JCB), frequently used with gifted readers, might also have problems associated with its implementation. They argue that JGB is highly dependent upon the intelligence and ability of teachers who are often untrained in individualizing work for the intellectually gifted. While the titles in the JGB have merit, the program's structure might be altered to make it less teacher-directed. Instead of following a routine in which the teacher always poses questions supplied in the teacher's manual and students respond, other approaches could be developed to encourage questioning by the students themselves. Varying the structured discussion after reading experiences can be more stimulating for gifted students.

Reading specialists have long urged reductions in oral questioning following book completion. Indeed, Rosenblatt (1978) condemned inquisition models, cautioning teachers to curb questions. Eeds & Peterson (1991) suggest student-centered literature discussion groups in which the teacher avoids predetermined probes, but asks "only those questions she or he genuinely wonders about" (p. 119). This clearly suggests that the quantity and quality of questions should be contingent upon circumstances, not foreordained by text. Responsiveness is an essential in any curriculum, a criterion that obviously cannot be met by prepackaged programs or even difficult JGB stories. Allowing gifted students to raise their own questions raises concerns specific to the students' needs.

To assume that acceptable strategies for average readers will be equally productive for advanced readers is erroneous; indeed, Tomlinson (1994b) asserted that acting on such beliefs can be harmful. She adds that "middle school literature warns of the dangers of 'overchallenging' adolescents" (p. 52) and that teachers in heterogeneously grouped classes "tend to concentrate on students in academic peril, assuming that their advanced learners will muddle through on their own" (p. 53). Such assumptions—that gifted children must wait while others catch up, that they do not need guidance and can teach themselves, that rigor and challenge are to be minimized—are patently discriminatory. When students must sit through lessons on content and structure that they have already mastered, valuable instructional time is being usurped.

Reading Materials for Gifted Middle Schoolers

Language is the single most significant component to be considered in selecting engaging and stimulating material for gifted students. It should be rich, varied, accurate, precise, complex, and exciting, for "language is the premier instrumentality for the reception and expression of thought" (Baskin & Harris, 1980, p. 46). Gifted students love to play with the sounds of words and the imagery of figurative language. Materials containing such attributes as language patterns from other eras and cultures, literary and historic allusions, symbols, sophisticated vocabulary and powerful imagery are captivating for this cohort. Through language, these readers enjoy exposure to microcosmic and macrocosmic views as well as multiple world perspectives: Plotz's *Imagination's Other Place* (1955) and *The Gift Outright* (1977) are among the best examples in poetry.

For gifted readers, theme is a more important element for exploration and discussion than plot. Major motifs might be prospected within a genre or by combining fiction and nonfiction titles. Philosophical, moral, or social issues could be explored through science fiction, fantasy, historical fiction, and history books. Paul (1990), implying that some reading assignments are trivial, suggests critical questions about content: "What is worth thinking about for an extended period of time? Is there personal meaningfulness for readers in the text? Is the subject robust and does it have societal significance?" (p. 10). Both classic and contemporary works should be analyzed for these ingredients. Academically able readers enjoy exploring issues such as the nature of heroism, boundaries, and relationships. In a Piagetian sense, the reader grows as accommodations are made to novel content, meaning is constructed, and the potential for even more profound understanding is generated. As Weaver (1990) has emphasized: "Meaning is not *in* the text itself but rather is constructed as the reader transacts with the text" (p. 202). But when the material is sufficiently demanding (Baskin & Harris, 1980) and strategies are employed congruent with the best practices in gifted education, the likelihood of finding deeper meaning in those reading interactions is maximized.

"Content determines what readers think [about] . . . but structure determines how they will think about it" (Baskin & Harris, 1980, p. 47). When books have time manipulations, parallel plots, interdisciplinary content, metaphorical as well as realistic elements, etc., the reader is challenged to deal with these complex components. Poetry is particularly fruitful because of its ambiguous nature. Almanacs, dictionaries, and other such references provide endless pleasure for other highly competent readers.

Exposure to breadth is vital. In classrooms of gifted readers, teachers should offer a selection of different trade book titles to students. Advanced readers are likely to choose books with topics similar to those chosen by average readers but with more sophisticated treatment. In a study of mythology, for example, advanced readers might delve into Garfield & Blishen's (1973) "The God Beneath the Sea" while others read various grade-level tales. All can participate.

Since middle schoolers often read nonfiction (Abrahamson and Carter, 1991), reading guidance should include introduction to a wide variety of genres, such as drama (Beaumier, 1993; Dixon, 1994), poetry (Nodelman, 1992), autobiography and biography (Stewart, 1985), and others. Biographies that feature role models who have faced adversity and overcome resistance to their ideas are particularly recommended. If students have pursued hobbies for some time, their knowledge is often extremely advanced and they legitimately benefit from adult journals, particularly in scientific publications. A sense of humor is noted frequently in these children; therefore books responsive to their comic bent are also legitimate choices (Ziv & Gadish, 1990).

Figure 4.1 is a list of young adult trade books gifted students might find interesting. Positing such a list is always a risk as some may think all gifted students should read all the books or that only these books work for gifted students. Neither supposition is accurate. Instead, this list should be viewed as a starting point or a resource that might benefit some gifted readers.

Academically able middle school students benefit from additional research opportunities beyond what is traditional for their peers since independent utilization of reference books facilitates their drive to discover. Being characteristically independent learners, gifted students need ready access to atlases, encyclopedias, thesauruses, and dictionaries, as well as newspapers and magazines. For youngsters who have immersed themselves in particular hobbies from an early age, only sophisticated nonfiction will provide them with material they do not yet know. Indeed, many children are already readers of adult materials. These books and journals are excellent options when a

Figure 4.1   Some Books for Middle School Gifted Children

The Abracadabra Kids. S. Fleischman. Greenwillow Books, 1996.

Bad Man Ballad. S. R. Saunders. Bradbury, 1986.

Best Intentions: The Education and Killing of Edmund Perry. R. S. Anson. Random House, 1987.

Bull Run. P. Fleischman. HarperTrophy, 1993.

The Confidence Man. L. Garfield. Viking Press, 1979.

Dateline: Troy. P. Fleischman. Candlewick, 1996.

Emergence. David R. Palmer. Bantam, 1984.

Enchantress from the Stars. S. L. Engdahl. Atheneum, 1978.

Eva. P. Dickinson. Delacorte, 1989.

A Fate Totally Worse than Death. P. Fleischman. Candlewick, 1995.

Father's Arcane Daughter. E. Konigsburg. Atheneum, 1976.

Go Hang a Salami! I'm a Lasagna Hog! J. Agee. Farrar, 1991.

I Am the Cheese. R. Cormier. Pantheon, 1979.

It's For You. J. Talbot. Dutton, 1995.

Make Lemonade. V. E. Wolfe. Holt, 1993.

Motel of the Mysteries. D. Macaulay. Houghton Mifflin, 1984.

The Mysteries of Harris Burdick. C. Van Allsburg. Houghton Mifflin, 1986.

Searches in the American Desert. S. Cowling. McElderry, 1989.

Slake's Limbo. F. Holman. Scribners, 1974.

So Many Dynamos! J. Agee. Farrar, Straus & Giroux, 1994.

Some Small Stones. G. Strauss. Knopf, 1990.

Star Walk. S. Simon. William Morrow, 1994.

Tell Them We Remember: The Story of the Holocaust. S. D. Bachrack. Little, Brown, 1994.

3 NBs of Julian Drew. J.M. Deem. Avon, 1996.

Tulku. P. Dickinson. Dell, 1995.

child has a particular interest in science or history, for example, and has developed deep and sophisticated knowledge in the discipline. If students are not yet reading adult magazines, such excellent magazines for young people as *Calliope*, *Cobblestone*, or *Odyssey* are valuable resources. When the school's library is limited, the teacher can borrow magazines from high school libraries or provide other access opportunities. Weaver (1990) emphasizes that a print-rich environment could also include such reading matter as theater scripts, jokebooks and book reviews written by students, as well as their stories and poems. Availability is equally important for mixed classrooms, since faster readers will finish assignments quickly and often need to seek out other advanced or intriguing material.

Internet connections offer a wide range of research possibilities for gifted middle school students. Often experts at surfing the web by the time they reach middle school, students should be encouraged to engage in computer searches to read in depth about subjects of particular interest to them. They might then compile their information and use presentation software to enhance public sharing of their product.

One goal in curriculum development is to achieve an engaging and meaningful match between materials and users. Contents should be accessible but simultaneously provide for intellectual stretch. Reading materials for gifted students ideally must harmonize with their reading abilities and interests. (See Section IV in this book for further discussion of materials.)

Strategies for Teachers of Gifted Readers

When they are working with a homogeneous group of gifted learners, teachers are freer to go beyond curriculum mandates and customize reading, emphasizing themes, raising metacognitive awareness, calling attention to certain linguistic or structural features, hypothesizing about story events, or involving readers in evaluative or analytical activity. Indeed, Cushenbery and Howell (1974) suggest that gifted readers "evaluate material in terms of truth, authority and value" (p. 69). The writers' work, the vocabulary employed, and the theme emphasized are all expressed in ways that differentially engage readers. This implies that youngsters, because of differing backgrounds, bring disparate perceptions to the literary encounter, responding to different narratives dependent on past literary history, emotional status at the time, and other idiosyncratic factors. Since readers extract personalized meaning from texts (Goodman, Smith, Meredith, & Goodman, 1987), their understandings and interpretations must differ, often on a profound level. Assessments of student work must accommodate these inevitable variations in responses.

In student-centered curricula, gifted children are often involved in determining when, how, and sometimes even if they should respond to questioning after reading (VanTassel-Baska, 1994). Weaver (1990) adds that able readers should also schedule and choose assignments. Although some assignments are not negotiable, Clark (1988) says that when there is choice, there is perceived control, an outcome she claimed to be significant in terms of achievement and self-concept. She adds that research indicates that choice produces quality and retention. To explore what children have absorbed from their reading, ask gifted students open-ended, more demanding questions, expecting, accepting, even welcoming divergent responses or relevant digressions. While recognizing the importance and legitimacy of selective inquiry, teachers must refrain from excessive questioning and testing. A preferred option would be to eliminate formal testing of literature altogether and instead offer a menu of diverse response alternatives from which readers could select preferences. These outcomes should be conceptualized not as exercises for monitoring student work, but as productive or creative opportunities to demonstrate that students have responded to the information.

One common option involving synthesis is a writing experience. For example, some gifted fifth and sixth graders heard (and read) work by Whitman, Emerson, and Thoreau and subsequently "published" a book of poetry inspired by those writers (Schulkind & Baskin, 1973), demonstrating their comprehension of content and style. After such an experience, which required higher level thinking skills and literary knowledge, testing would have been superfluous.

Parker (1994) suggests using individualized reading contracts and small group discussions, based on differentiated reading materials. Suppose that six children all read biographies of individuals who had proposed new ideas rejected by the public. They all analyze the respective problem-solving strategies of their subjects. The subsequent discussions about lack of societal acceptance of innovations, historical context, resources—personal, physical, and financial—are all fruitful, relevant topics. Another suggestion is that books grouped thematically, i.e., good vs. evil. After some modeling experiences, children could come to the discussion with such questions as: What moral questions were being asked? Were the themes dealt with realistically or metaphorically? If the latter, what symbols were used by the author to illustrate those positions? As the protagonist, what questions would you have been weighing as you decided to act? How is this issue similar to any contemporary event? How were these books similar or different? If so, what patterns exist? Pattern finding is of particular intellectual utility. Robert Cormier's novels offer unusually rich opportunities for such analyses. (Elizabeth Poe addresses classroom literature discussions in Chapter 9.)

Halstead (1988) also suggests discussion that analyzes authors' decisions, i.e., Why was that format chosen? How does the writer make characters seem real? Not only does she label the process used by the children in their commentaries, e.g., analyzing, synthesizing, evaluating, but sometimes requests that they bring specific examples to book discussions. When students become book discussion leaders, analytic, social, communication, and leadership skills readily come into play.

Slaughter (1994) describes a literary club model. (For a thorough discussion of literature circles in the classroom see Chapter 10 by Judith Scott and Jan Wells.) Slaughter claims that comprehension of text is enhanced as a result of collaborative analysis and discussion" (p. 86). Flack (1991) also emphasizes analytic activity, promoting the use of detective fiction for gifted readers. Dixon (1994) details how seminars with advanced material could be used.

Revamped literature instruction for gifted readers should aim to guide students to think critically about their reading and to fulfill the following objectives:

- "to develop prediction strategies and schemas for anticipating meaning . . . ; to develop inferential strategies using text" (Goodman, Smith, Meredith, & Goodman, 1987, p. 249);

- to use the same methods of inquiry as real scholars (Clark, 1988);

- to make students more aware of literary devices used by writers and to attempt to use these devices in their own writing;

- to sensitize readers to symbolism and other abstract devices used in storytelling;

- to facilitate looking at rationales for decision making; and

- to provide opportunities for drawing analogies between theme and contemporary issues.

Special Adaptations in the Classroom

Many educators have suggested revisions or modifications of common practice to improve the instructional milieu for gifted students. Clinkenbeard (1991) reports that gifted sixth graders deplore cooperative learning arrangements since they often assume the major burden of work and also believe teachers hold unreasonable expectations of them. Instead, differentiation through practices such as enrichment, ability grouping via clustering or homogeneous groups, and acceleration (Kulik & Kulik, 1992; Tomlinson, 1994b) have the largest effects and are the most beneficial to learning for these students. Such adaptations for gifted pupils may run counter to current practice, but consistent, constructive outcomes should persuade administrators and teachers that this organization is needed. These recommendations should be taken seriously since they are important in preparing the context for optimum learning experiences.

The emotional milieu of the classroom is also of crucial concern. Excellent readers must feel they are not about to become social pariahs if they are excited by ideas and express themselves in mature ways. It is up to the teacher to insure a healthy climate in which respect for these children and their thoughts is in place. These gifted students have been used as models or as unpaid tutors in mixed classrooms, but when those classes do not contain a critical mass of their intellectual equals, their own learning time has been squandered. When they are the only ones with an unusual grasp of a subject or advanced vocabulary, they may contribute significantly to class discussion, but they will not have an opportunity to grow themselves. They need opportunities to speak with others who challenge their ideas, thereby helping to refine them. It is detrimental for children to believe they "know it all" and to be seen as significantly dissimilar from their peers. Schools reinforce such harmful views when gifted children are isolated from intellectual counterparts. Without the benefits of challenges or criticism, these pupils are apt to grow lazy and coast in class. Such children often retrogress into "yellow bus scholars" finding that a modicum of effort, expended on the way to school, is enough to earn them passable grades.

These discussions about setting are critical to the discussion of a reading program: when such middle school enabling structures and procedures are not formally in place and supported by the administration, differentiated strategies may become solely the responsibility of a few conscientious teachers (hence subject to change) rather than school policy.

Recently, representatives from middle schools and educators of the gifted have examined their mutual concerns through observation of current practices (Council for Exceptional Children Today, 1995). A series of site-based studies revealed barriers in educating gifted children as well as clear-cut evidence that the interests of such middle schoolers have not actively been addressed. Five schools with admirable programs were reviewed and the following components were evident:

- administrative leadership;
- faculty and administrative autonomy;
- availability of a resident expert in gifted education; and
- attitudes of enthusiasm, trust, and commitment to educating gifted students. (Council for Exceptional Children Today, 1995)

Improvement in all aspects of the school lives of gifted children, including their reading programs, is inextricably tied to such reorganizational changes in the schools. Meanwhile, caring reading teachers, impatient with the likely lag time for reform and motivated by the observation that gifted children are being grossly underserved, have reorganized their classrooms so reading instruction may be more responsive. They have prescriptively selected reading material congruent with reading profiles of gifted children. These teachers have adopted an old maxim in gifted education—"Be a guide on the side, not a sage on the stage"—as updated by Coleman and Gallagher (Council of Exceptional Children Today, 1995) to state: "Have teachers serve as facilitators of learning rather than disseminators of knowledge" (p. 48). Further, they are reconsidering their goals and behaviors in order to emphasize higher level thinking skills, developing more sensitivity to the emotional, social, and academic needs of students, all the while emphasizing the exquisite and satisfying pleasures of growing by reading.

References

Abrahamson, R. F., & Carter, B. (1991). Nonfiction: The missing piece in the middle. *English Journal, 80*, 52–58.

Archambault Jr., F. X., Westberg, K. L., Brown, S. W., Hallmark, B. W., Zhang, W., & Emmons, C. L. (1993). Classroom practices used with gifted third and fourth grade students. *Journal for the Education of the Gifted, 16*, 103–119.

Baskin, B. H., & Harris, K. (1980). *Books for the gifted child*. New York: Bowker.

Beaumier, T. (1993). A Shakespeare festival in the middle grades. *English Journal, 82*, 49–51.

Bloom, B. S. (Ed.). (1956). *Taxonomy of educational objectives: Cognitive domain*. New York: David McKay.

Carter, B. (1982). Leisure reading habits of gifted students in a suburban junior high school. *Top of the News, 38*, 312–317.

Clark, B. (1988). *Growing up gifted*. Columbus, OH: Merrill.

Clinkenbeard, P. R. (1991). Unfair expectations: A pilot study of middle school students' comparison of gifted and regular classes. *Journal of Education for the Gifted, 15*, 56–63.

Council for Exceptional Children Today. (1995). Gifted symposium unites middle school and gifted educators. *Council for Exceptional Children, 1*, 15.

Cushenbery, D. C., & Howell, H. (1974). *Reading and the gifted child: A guide for teachers*. Springfield, IL: Thomas.

Dixon, F. (1994). Literature seminars for gifted and talented students. *Gifted Child Today, 17*, 12–16.

Dyer, S. K. (1994). Literature for the gifted reader. *New England Reading Association Journal, 30*, 37–47.

Eeds, M., & Peterson, R. (1991). Teacher as curator: Learning to talk about literature. *Reading Teacher, 45*, 118–126.

Flack, J. (1991). Sherlock Holmes meets the 21st century. *Gifted Child Today, 14*, 15–21.

Gallagher, J. J., Coleman, M. R., & Nelson, R. (1995). Perceptions of educational reform by educators representing middle schools, cooperative learning and gifted education. *Gifted Child Quarterly, 39*, 66–76.

Garfield, L., & Blishen, E. (1973). *The golden shadow: A recreation of the Greek legends*. New York: Pantheon.

Goodman, K. S., Smith, E. B., Meredith, R., & Goodman, Y. M. (1987). *Language and thinking in school: A whole language curriculum.* New York: Owen.

Halkitis, P. N., & Hoffman, M. (1992). Shakespeare in the intermediate grades. *Gifted Child Today, 15,* 2–6.

Halstead, J. W. (1988). *Guiding gifted readers: From preschool to high school.* Columbus, OH: Ohio Psychology Pub.

Henjum, A. (1983). Summer programs: One way to provide for the gifted. *Middle School Journal, 15,* 23–24.

Karl, J. E. (1987). What sells—what's good? *Horn Book, 63,* 505–508.

Kennedy, D. M. (1995). Glimpses of a highly gifted child in a heterogeneous classroom. *Roeper Review, 17,* 164–168.

Kulik, J. A., & Kulik, C. C. (1992). Meta-analytic findings on grouping programs. *Gifted Child Quarterly, 36,* 73–77.

Ley, T. C., & Trentham, L. L. (1987). The reading attitudes of gifted learners in grades seven and eight. *Journal for the Education of the Gifted, 10,* 87–98.

Li, A., & Adamson, G. (1992). Gifted secondary students' preferred learning style: Cooperative, competitive, or individualistic? *Journal of Education for the Gifted, 16,* 46–54.

Nodelman, P. (1992). *The pleasures of children's literature.* New York: Longman.

Parker, J. P. (1989). *Instructional strategies for teaching the gifted.* Boston, MA: Allyn & Bacon.

Paul, R. W. (1990). From lower order to higher order learning. *Understanding Our Gifted, 2,* 1, 12–14.

Pearson, P. D. (1985). Changing the face of reading comprehension instruction. *Reading Teacher, 36,* 724–738.

Piechowski, M. M., & Colangelo, N. (1984). Developmental potential of the gifted. *Gifted Child Quarterly, 28,* 80–88.

Rosenblatt, L. (1978). *The reader, the text, the poem—The transactional theory of the literary work.* Carbondale: University of Southern Illinois Press.

Schulkind, C., & Baskin, B. (1973). Impaled on a wild entanglement of lace: Poetics for the young gifted child. *Elementary English, 50,* 1209–1214.

Shore, B. M., Cornell, D. G., Robinson, A., & Ward, V. S. (1991). *Recommended practices in gifted education: A critical analysis.* New York: Teachers College Press.

Slaughter, J. P. (1994). The readers respond—a key component of the literary club: Implementing a literature based reading program. *Reading Improvement, 31,* 77–86.

Stewart, E. D. (1985). Social studies. In R. H. Swassing (Ed.), *Teaching gifted children and adolescents.* Columbus, OH: Merrill.

Tomlinson, C. A. (1995). Deciding to differentiate instruction in the middle school. *Gifted Child Quarterly, 39,* 77–89.

Tomlinson, C. A. (1992). Gifted education and the middle school movement: Two voices on teaching the academically talented. *Journal of Education for the Gifted, 15,* 206–238.

Tomlinson, C.A. (1994a). Gifted learners: The boomerang kids of the middle school. *Journal of Reading Research, 16*, 177–182.

Tomlinson, C. A. (1994b). Making middle schools work for gifted kids. *Principal, 74*, 52–53.

Tonjes, M. J. (1991). *Secondary reading, writing and learning*. Boston, MA: Allyn and Bacon.

Vacca, J. A., Vacca, R. T., & Gove, M. K. (1991). *Reading and learning to read*. New York: HarperCollins.

VanTassel-Baska, J. (1988). *Comprehensive curriculum for gifted learners*. Boston, MA: Allyn and Bacon.

Weaver, C. (1990). *Understanding whole language: From principles to practice*. Portsmouth, NH: Heinemann.

Westberg, K. L., Archambault, Jr., F. X., Dobyns, S. M., & Salvin, T. J. (1993). The classroom practices observation study. *Journal for Education of the Gifted, 16*, 120–146.

Whitmore, J. R. (1980). *Giftedness, conflict, and underachievement*. Boston, MA: Allyn & Bacon.

Willard-Holt, C. (1994). Strategies for individualizing instruction in reading classrooms. *Roeper Review, 17*, 43–45.

Woodward, A. (1986). Overprogrammed materials: Taking the teacher out of teaching. *American Educator, 10*, 26–31.

Ziv, A., & Gadish, O. (1990). Humor and giftedness. *Journal of Education for the Gifted, 13*, 332–345.

Trade Books Cited

Brooks, B. (1984). *The moves make the man*. New York: Harper & Row.

Cushman, K. (1994). *Catherine, called Birdy*. New York: Clarion Books.

Plotz, H. (Ed.) (1955). *Imagination's other place: Poems of science and mathematics*. New York: Crowell.

Plotz, H. (Ed.). (1977). *The gift outright: America to her poets*. New York: Greenwillow.

Sebestyen, O. (1979). *Words by heart*. New York: Little, Brown and Company.

Chapter 5
REACHING STRUGGLING READERS

Margaret Hill

> How can I teach middle school children who do not read above the first or second grade level?
>
> How do students reach sixth grade while reading at a second grade level?
>
> What happened to these struggling readers in elementary school?

These are all questions that middle school teachers ask when large numbers of students reach middle school with low literacy skills. The question becomes, how do teachers accelerate these children so that when they leave middle school, they will have the promise of a successful secondary education?

Perhaps Jason has some of the answers. Jason told me one day, "I don't know where I've been for five years. I just tuned out of school and stayed tuned out." Then, in sixth grade, Jason tuned back in and decided he wanted to learn. He admitted to me that he did very little during his primary school years and often missed school. Then when he reached fourth grade he realized that he didn't know how to read as well as his friends.

"So," he said, "I just avoided it! I learned to do anything else but read. While others were practicing reading, I was doing other stuff—mainly messing around with my buddies. I copied a lot. I asked questions a lot. And I made the teacher mad a lot."

Sarah told me that she just wasn't in school very much because her mother kept moving. "My mom had to move us a lot because she could not afford rent. Apartments give 3 months free or cheap rent. Mom moved us every 3 months 'cuz she couldn't afford regular rent. We never lived in a place over 3 months. I just had to keep startin' over. After a while, I gave up on reading."

Alex indicated that his family, while living in the same place for a long while, did not think that reading and writing were important. His parents had both learned to survive with minimal levels of literacy skills. "Neither of my folks read or write. They were both in special education classes and promoted. I think because they don't read or write, the school 'spects the same from me. I've always been in special education classes."

Jesus revealed that neither his mother nor his father spoke English. They speak Spanish at home, but neither read nor write in Spanish. "I was in ESL (English as a Second Language) for a while, but I never learned to read. We talked and we looked at Spanish words, but I never learned what it was to study and practice reading and writing. Actually, I love to draw. My drawing tells stories."

Students reach middle school with a score of reasons for failing literacy requirements. They are also aware of their inadequacies. Most of these students have resigned themselves to finishing school at eighth grade or 16 years of age. They are patiently spending time searching for ways to cope with academia, but they do not believe that they will ever graduate from high school.

Middle school teachers say they never realized that they would have to teach beginning reading in the middle schools. Most indicate they don't know where to begin with these low-level readers. In addition, many worry about perpetuating reading problems by constantly reading content material to their low readers, relying too much on audiotapes and videotapes, or always having them read with peers just to cover the curriculum. To reach that goal, they remove students from the very practice they need most: reading. Instead of practicing reading and writing, low-level students spend most of their time practicing listening.

These low-level readers know they are below level and develop sophisticated methods of avoiding real reading and writing. They misbehave in class, out-wait their instructors, beg others to help them complete their work, or choose not to do the work. Reading and writing are so painful that they avoid these tasks at all costs.

In addition, many have parents who read and write with minimal skills. One sixth grade girl smartly reported that her mother told her she didn't need to learn to read or write. Her mother explained that what was really important was to "look pretty and take care of a man." And so, while the teachers expend tremendous amounts of energy trying to build in reading and writing practice, students often work at cross purposes. Perhaps our first campaign must be the promotion of literacy. It is through literacy that we can maintain a free and democratic country. We must convince our youth, first, of the importance of literacy, and then it must become a necessary goal for their own survival.

Illiteracy among youth cuts across gender, race, and culture. Julian Middle School (a pseudonym), where I worked last year, was a school balanced racially among Anglos, Asians, Hispanics, and African Americans. Ten percent of the student body was reading at the first/second grade level and was struggling with basic high frequency words. These low-level students were distributed equally by gender and race. For these middle school below-level readers, the miscue analyses from their informal reading inventories indicated that they were good at decoding, yet they had very little understanding of what they read. These students rarely read to the end of the sentence for predictions and seldom reread passages they did not understand. Reading, to them, was the arduous task of pronouncing words. In fact, most said that reading was "sounding out hard words." Where would teachers start with these students? How could teachers help these students move toward grade level reading?

The Plan: Independent Practice, Guided Practice, Shared Reading

As the teachers at Julian Middle School struggled with these questions, they kept coming back to the same answer. They wanted their readers who struggled the most to have more time to read independently, to have more time to read with guided instruction, and to have more time to read and write in shared reading and writing settings. Consequently, they designed a reading program based on independent reading, guided practice, and shared reading/writing. Practice became the number one priority for these non-readers.

Independent Practice

Independent practice immediately became a problem! Teachers complained that their students didn't know how to choose books, couldn't read with help much less on their own, and would rather sleep than read.

Keeping students focused, practicing, and aware of their reading became the major objective. Thus, independent reading practice took on many forms: silent to oral, solo to partner to group, aided with tapes or CD-ROMs to unaided. Teachers brought in many types of reading to practice: lists, directions, sports statistics, information pieces, human interest stories, horror books, mysteries, folk literature, and poetry. Reading varied by interest, level, and genre. The objective was to get students to read and enjoy reading.

During this independent reading time, teachers initially thought that they could read with the students and/or conference with them. They were wrong! They were able to read with them and therefore model for a short time. But they also needed to serve as cheerleaders, circulating by each reader to question, probe, add information, suggest reading strategies, help with vocabulary, help develop background knowledge and all the time cajole them into reading, thinking, and questioning.

One way the students practiced silent reading was through the game charades. This highly motivational game captured the interest of the most unmotivated readers, put a focus on comprehension, and gave students practice reading texts silently. Students were given cue cards and told, "Read silently. Act out the command." Gradually, cues were lengthened and then transformed into small paragraphs of information about a subject of high interest to the student. After some time and practice, students understood that they could read silently. In addition to a short focused passage to read, students were given a clear focus and purpose for reading.

Instructors modeled strategies for varying reading rates, from skimming and scanning, to slow and careful, to moderate and rapid. Articles were scanned for specific information such as finding facts about fish or whales or volcanoes. Students skimmed for favorite jokes and then read them slowly and carefully. Favorite lines were shared from their *Goosebumps* or other formula novels. Passages were read and reread during the independent practice. Because sociability is so important at this middle school level, all responses were tied to the larger group. Reading was not just for self or between teacher and self, but instead, information and thinking were always shared with a friend, small group or the entire class. However, students were not made to share before they were ready. Beers's research (see Chapter 3) found that students with negative attitudes often did not like to participate in group discussions, as they lacked confidence in their ability to add anything to the conversation. The below-level students also were hesitant to join conversations until they were convinced of their ability to say something that would not embarrass them. Reading and writing then became the acceptable social avenue for students to achieve recognition.

Teachers stressed the importance of practicing reading and writing in many environments both at home and at school. Students competed for the types of places where they read and wrote outside of class as well as the different kinds of reading and writing they did. Teachers introduced many different genres, levels, and a variety of organizational formats. They allowed students to work singly, with partners, or in small groups. Students slowly began to find that practicing reading was motivational as their practice led to success. With reading materials that were highly motivational, students quickly began gaining automaticity through practice. They learned which books could be read quickly, which books helped to entertain, and which books helped to solve problems. How to expand this practice time became the focal point for the school.

Paula not only showed her students that she valued reading/writing practice, but she tried to build in times when she could work toward that end. During lunch, Paula invited students to share readings. One day a week was R. L. Stine day, where students brought Stine books to her room with their lunch and read. Paula read the same books the students read. They discussed scary plots and compared them with other books they'd read. With lunch trays on the floors and bodies sprawled across beanbag chairs, pillows, and carpets, munching while reading became the milieu for the hour.

R. L. Stine was not the entire focus, however. Each day had a different focus based upon theme, author, or genre, from poetry, to jokes, to mysteries and science fiction. Through this diversity, Paula demonstrated her respect for the readers and their choices and offered them additional time to practice.

In her lunchtime classroom, Sue encouraged students to bring a buddy and read. Every day she opened her classroom to those students who were serious about reading and reading practice and wanted to share their interest with a friend. She asked that buddies read the same or similar books so that they could read and discuss their books. Thus, her classroom consisted of students reading and eating or quietly talking about books.

Teachers encouraged reading whenever possible. While students waited for the bus, teachers conducted short book talks. They asked for the best book of the week, for reviews, for suggestions, for comparisons. Teachers were seen with their own books in their hands as they roamed the lines of readers seated on the concrete aisles waiting for their buses.

Even outside of class, teachers encouraged their students. Paula turned movie connections into social book events. After students read *Jumanji* (Van Allsburg, 1981), they came to her house one Friday afternoon for a pizza party. Then she took a group to see the movie. Always, Paula helped students to build ties from one type of media resource to another.

Teachers learned that for these children who came with reading levels far below their classmates', extra time, extra resources, and extra encouragement must become the standard. As their classmates had practiced reading for the prior 6 years in school, these students for many reasons had not. How to build in 6 years of practice within 1 year of time became their challenge.

Guided Practice

Although teachers wanted to encourage reading practice as much as possible, students could not just spend all their time practicing on fun and easy books. They had to learn to read more difficult materials. During the time for small group guided practice, reading strategies and skills became the focus so that comprehension and vocabulary could be developed. Teachers discovered quickly that most of these students thought that reading was pronouncing words accurately. Comprehension suffered because thinking was not a part of reading.

In fact, Julia said one day, "I can not think while I read out loud. I can think while Maria is reading. But when I read, I concentrate on how to say the words." To Julia, reading was pronouncing words orally. She never practiced reading silently during her years of schooling. And, she had never realized that reading was thinking.

Think-Alouds

Teachers began to strengthen students' comprehension by explaining that while readers read, they are always thinking to themselves. Readers ask themselves questions, they make connections, they picture what they are reading in their minds, and they note if there are parts in the passage that don't make sense. Davey (1983) suggests that Think-Aloud is a powerful comprehension strategy. A Think-Aloud requires a reader to read a text either orally or silently, pausing to make statements about what was read. These statements become the oral thoughts that help the reader focus on thinking about the text and help the teacher hear where comprehension fails. Tierney, Readence, and Dishner (1995) suggest five goals to include in the Think-Aloud process: *picture, predict, "like-a," problem,* and *fix-up.* Each of these key words indicate things good readers do as they read. For instance, good readers *picture* a scene, *predict* what will happen next, *compare* text structures to each other, *recognize problems* in comprehension, and do something to *fix-up* those problems.

In addition to doing those things, the students at Julian discovered that as they read they also made *comments* about the texts. In other words, they didn't always picture or predict, but sometimes just responded to the text with a comment such as, "Oh, that makes me sad," or "That was so funny." Comments like these are spontaneous and important reactions from the reader. In addition, we found that as students thought aloud about their reading, they often added a great deal of background knowledge to the content. This knowledge seemed to go beyond simple *"like-a"* connections. So, to their list of things that good readers do, they also added *gives background information.*

As students listened to each other and to their teachers think aloud about a text, they listened for comments in these categories. They tallied the times they heard each trait on a rubric. Sometimes one response received more than one tally. For example, picturing might turn into a prediction: "I picture a tree hanging low over the road and it is dark, and it might be like grabbin' him."

As one student named Cindy read *The Ghost-Eye Tree* (Martin & Archambault, 1985), she worked her way through the text making Think-Aloud comments. As you read part of the transcription from her Think-

Aloud, remember, she's been taught how to think aloud, and her teacher has constantly modeled Think-Alouds. You'll see that Cindy uses some of the Think-Aloud language in her comments:

> I picture myself and my brother in this poem walking down a road. It sounds like my brother talking to me. And I can picture where I used to live and my mama always used to pick me up and walk to a place to get water. (*Picturing* and "*Like-a*")

> I predict that his brother says, "My hat does not look dumb on me." (*Predicting*)

> I like this. I like the sister saying, "What's the matter?" (*Commenting*)

> The problem is she is saying what she is afraid of, but I know that might be wrong. I am wondering what that means. Is she afraid or isn't she. I don't know if this is supposed to be scary or funny. (*Identifying problems*)

> I guess that sometimes things can be both funny or weird and scary at the same time. I still wonder what the author meant. (*Fix-up, commenting and identifying problems*)

As Cindy worked with her Think-Aloud, she combined many of the traits that Davy (1983) mentions good readers do. Cindy was able to verbalize pictures that she imaged in her head, compare them to things that were familiar to her, and predict what might come in the text. In addition, she was also able to ponder the author's intent. Was it scary? Was it funny? She seemed to settle the matter in her own mind, but still questioned the author's intent. She did not come back to that question throughout the rest of her Think-Aloud. This could be a teaching point for the teacher who might use the discussion with all her students.

Another student, Jimez, did Think-Aloud while reading a passage about a deer hunting trip. Jimez paused a long time at a picture of a boy dragging a deer along a snowy trail bloodied from the deer carcass. He finally responded to the text by offering background information, which is an extended "*like-a*."

> This is like the deer hunting trips that I go on. But we don't drag the deer on the ground. We have to cut up the deer and carry it out in parts. The hind quarters are always the heavy part. Sometimes I have to walk a long ways with that heavy hind quarter hangin' over my shoulder, blood streaming down. Deer hunting with my dad is the best, but it sure is work when you kill your deer.

Jimez connected to the text he was reading with more than a simple "like a" as he described his own experience. He continued to make comparisons with his own hunting experiences and the feelings that he had for hunting. Clearly, his background knowledge about hunting helped him make a stronger connection to the reading. It is important for teachers to recognize this strong and important connection to background knowledge.

Obviously, good readers think all the time they are reading. However, struggling readers often say they do *not* think about what they read because they are working so hard to pronounce the words. Many also report that they never picture or visualize a story as they read. Think-Alouds, they say, force them to create an image of the action in their minds.

After practicing Think-Alouds, most of the students visualized regularly and described their visualization process. Once Think-Alouds were firmly planted with independent-level reading, teachers began to apply Think-Aloud strategies to more difficult content materials and finally to test-taking strategies. Teachers found that Think-Alouds were an excellent way for students to practice test taking because they helped teachers monitor the test-taking behaviors of each student. In fact, they believed that Think-Alouds impacted readers the most, enabling them to make the jump to silent reading, to comprehending at deeper levels, and to initiating metacognitive strategies. Judy Wallis offers additional examples of Think-Alouds in Chapter 12 and discusses a modification called Think Silently.

Retelling

Teachers also used Retelling as a way to build silent reading fluency and to measure comprehension. Retellings (Mitchell & Irwin, 1983) give teachers a way to assess how much a student understands what was read. By studying a student's Retelling, teachers gain insight into how that student organizes information, into what that student views as important, and to what information from the text stands out as important and noteworthy to the student. Have a checklist as to what is expected to be covered as the student retells the text. Several Retelling forms already exist (Irwin & Mitchell, 1983; Morrow, 1988). Using a checklist helps both the teacher and student determine if the student can identify main idea, make inferences, identify concepts, make generalizations, and connect personally to the text. In facts, readers are encouraged to respond with their own personal connections. At Julian Middle School, as the reading materials changed, teachers modified their rubric for Retellings in order to be specific to the materials read. They also simplified the scoring using the following degrees of involvement: none, few, some, and many. Again, students scored teachers and discussed the scores before they rated themselves. They tape recorded their Retellings and scored themselves and their partners.

When students at Julian Middle School first began giving Retellings, they lacked detail, lacked order, and indicated only surface-level responses. There was little elaboration, and this indicated that students had no understanding of main idea and supporting detail. Students only responded to isolated events within the story. Look at what Evan, a struggling sixth grader, said in his first retelling of an R. L. Stine book: "The girl found a mask at the man's store. And they asked like where was this sort of thing? And she finds a mask that look like a beast."

This Retelling made little sense. Seeing how this child organized what this book was about gave his teacher a real insight into why reading made little sense for him. For Retelling to become an effective strategy for Evan, his teacher had to combine modeling Think-Alouds with modeling Retelling. She distributed a checklist for students to use as she retold her story (see Figure 5.1). She occasionally gave a poor Retelling so students could identify what she should have done better. Most importantly, she gave them the opportunity to practice retelling text. Students gave Retellings to one another, to the teacher, and sometimes into the tape recorder. At intervals, the teacher scored the students' Retellings just to see what kind of growth the students were showing with Retellings over time.

Figure 5.1 Retelling Guide for Fiction

	0 None	1 Few	2 Some	3 Many
Does this Retelling				
1. have a good beginning that explains where and when the story takes place?				
2. tell the characters' names?				
3. explain the main points of what happened?				
4. give some supporting details?				
5. make sense?				
6. sound organized?				
7. keep the story in the right sequence?				
8. tell what was the main problem in the story?				
9. tell how the problem was solved?				

Total points earned _____

Student's name _____

Retelling of _____

Date _____

Not surprisingly, as students heard their teacher think aloud, as they scored her Retellings, and then as they used Think-Alouds and Retellings after their own readings, they became better retellers. As they gave more Retellings, they began to use terms like *main idea*, *the most important thing*, *first*, *the setting took place*, and other terms that indicated students were organizing the story by literary elements, by order of events, by main idea and supporting detail.

Look at this transcription of a Retelling, again by Evan, from the same R. L. Stine book. This Retelling came after the teacher spent time modeling what a good Retelling has in it:

> This is about a little girl named Annabelle and she needs to find a mask for Halloween. She finally found a mask at a man's store. It was a mask that looked like a beast with monstrous ears and sharp teeth that looked like it was drooling. . . .

Now Evan starts his Retelling by introducing a character and describing the basic plot. He moves through the story in sequence providing details along the way. Evan wasn't the only student to show that type of growth. Figures 5.2 and 5.3 show the growth that one sixth grade girl, Guadalupe, had in her Retelling between September and February.

These typed transcriptions of two of Guadalupe's Retellings reflect tremendous growth for this student. This sixth grader began the year barely able to talk about any books she had struggled through. However, after repeated modeling of Retellings by the teacher, Guadalupe began to understand how to organize her thoughts. Look at Guadalupe's September Retelling (Figure 5.2). This one barely makes sense; however, the February Retelling (Figure 5.3) indicates a sense of audience, an organization of story events, the ability to label the setting, and an understanding of the main idea. The italicized sections of Figure 5.3 have been added to show you the places Guadalupe is trying to use the literary terms she has learned. For instance, she begins with a statement about the children in the story and then abruptly stops and begins again. "OK, it was a cold, November day, and the kids are bored." Obviously Guadalupe has learned that good Retellings have a beginning that recognizes that the audience needs a setting and a conflict. That alone is a major step from her September Retelling. As she works her way through the story we see that Guadalupe has not only learned to add detail, but she is also using language like "main problem" and "second important thing" and "main thing."

As students learned to elaborate, to distinguish main idea from supporting detail, and to summarize, their oral Retellings clearly showed strong growth in oral fluency, comprehension, and response. Similarly, students' written responses to the reading passages changed dramatically. Students first wrote sentences like, "This is a good book because it is exciting and scary."

Figure 5.2 Guadalupe's September Retelling

It's about wolves, and um how much they eat and how they're related to the dogs. Um, they can eat 20 pounds of meat. That's like eating the whole pound of 100 hamburgers. And in order to them to be like a king or something, the other wolves have looked that man dog. . . . ?

Figure 5.3 Guadalupe's February Retelling

Well, it all happened whenever the two little kids. *OK, it was a cold, November day,* and the kids are bored. And their momma and their daddy, they went, you know, they went I think to work. And they told Peter and Judy that, not to make a mess or anything because they were expecting company. And so, um, and so, um, and so they left and stuff and Judy and them were getting out their toys, and it wasn't funny anymore because they were laughing and they made a big old mess, and they decided that they were going to the park. And so they went to the park and stuff, and they seen a game and so they picked it up and thought they were going to play it, so whenever they went back home and picked the thing, it said read instructions first. And the instructions were the game is going to end as soon as one winner gets to the golden city. *The main problem* was they played the game and the animals came to life, because it was about a jungle thingy. OK. So they started to play the game and stuff. And so Judy, she said "go back" she said because Peter rolled the dice and it was seven and seven was the lion. And so, um, and so Judy said go back two spaces. And there was a lion on the piano, and Judy goes look slowly, slowly, slowly turn around and look. And Peter saw the piano and the lion was running after Peter. And then monkeys started showing up and stuff. In then a stampede came and they had a rain storm in the house—only in the house because the game was in their house and stuff. And then they had a real, real hard time because all these animals started coming to life. And snakes started coming and stuff, and monkeys and all that. And there's a snake that has the same, same exact . . . the snake looked exactly like the couch, and if the snake was laying on the thing, a kid would've sat down, they wouldn't know if there was a snake or not. *And this whole entire story started happening at their house. And the second important thing* was they started to play it and they weren't supposed to play it, and stuff appeared and stuff started to happening. OK, the girl finished the game and said, "Jumanji." And they opened up the windows and the doors and everything disappeared. *But the main thing* about it was they shouldn't have played the game because, because animals and stuff, they start happening you know, and that's why.

One way teachers got students to expand their writing was to encourage them to draw pictures of what they had read and then write about the pictures. These pictures not only helped students visualize the characters and the action, but also served as graphic organizers of the plot's development. Through diagrams, designs, and pictures, students developed elaborate ways to communicate what they had just read and what it meant to them. Figure 5.4 shows what one of Paula's students designed as he read the story *Young Merlin* (San Souci, 1990).

This particular student found this technique highly motivating. Though a poor reader and a transitional speller, the young man has obvious artistic talent. Allowing him to use his artistic ability as a means of organizing his thoughts encouraged him to keep reading.

Figure 5.4 Mark's Picture Map of *Young Merlin*

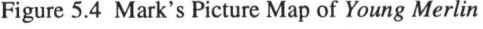

Reciprocal Teaching and ReQuest

As students at Julian Middle School improved in their reading abilities, teachers moved to less teacher-directed strategies such as *Reciprocal Teaching* (Harris and Sipay, 1990) and *ReQuest* (Manzo, 1969). Teachers asked students inferential questions and required, in turn, that students follow up with their own inferential questions and responses. Reciprocal Teaching, where students take the role of teacher and explain the reading material, and ReQuest, where partners take turns asking questions, became the most predominant strategies. Students read and then questioned each other and their teacher. Reading stamina grew gradually. Materials were chosen carefully to include short, high interest passages based upon the independent reading level for each student. The independent reading level for a student is the level at which the student needs no help to read the text. This level contrasts with the instructional level in which the student has some fluency but enough difficulty to need help and the frustrational level in which the student understands little of the material.

When the reading material became more difficult, the formats for reading were carefully chosen so that not too many words were on a page. Students could handle harder reading on a limited basis if the passages were short and formatted with illustrations and examples. They started with easy-to-read books such as Arnold Lobel's *Frog and Toad* books, Marjorie Sharmat's *Nate the Great* books, and David Adler's *Cam Janson* books and progressed through the year to other High-Interest/Low-Level books. For a list of these books that students enjoyed, see Appendix 5.A.

Vocabulary and Decoding: "And we don't get hung up on BIG words anymore"

When asked why reading was difficult, all students said reading was hard because of big words. They were hard to pronounce, and even after they could pronounce them, the words meant little to the students. Most of these students had very limited vocabularies; either from homes where parents were illiterate or from homes where English was not spoken, these students had grown up with very limited exposure to rich, varied, oral or written English. Consequently, along with practicing reading, increasing vocabulary became a major goal.

Decoding

During the first week of class, teachers displayed many different kinds of books ranging from Dr. Seuss and poetry to easy-to-read nonfiction and formula narratives. One group of five students kept choosing Dr. Seuss books. In that group, Ken continued to practice the words with strong rhyme patterns from the Seuss books. He explained to me that he was trying to figure how words work. Obviously the rhyme patterns were important to him. These books were helping him learn how words work. After the 10th time through *Green Eggs and Ham* (Seuss, 1960), he began to explain to me how the word patterns were used in other words.

Irene Gaskins' (Gaskins, Downer, Anderson, Cunningham, Gaskins, Schommer, & The Teachers of Benchmark School, 1988) research on onset and rime helped guide these teachers in decoding instruction. For instance, in "cat," "mat," and "bat" they learned that the letters *at* (the *rime*) made the sound /at/ (the *rhyme*). They learned that the c, m, and b of each of those words is called the *onset*. Following Gaskins' program, students worked on finding words that followed the same rime pattern. These words went onto charts that hung around the room. As these older students connected familiar word endings with the syllables of longer words, they began to tackle LONG words with a vengeance. And, they solved the mystery of syllabication!

Anna announced to the class, "I never knew how words worked! Now, I do!" As Anna pronounced the word "reverberate" she applied the following word patterns to help her with the pronunciation. She matched "re" as in "*she*," "ver" as in "*her*," "ber" as in "*her*," and "ate" as in "*late*." Anna's teacher worked with her to use key words which exemplified common rhyme patterns. With multisyllabic words, Anna applied the common word/ rhyme patterns her teacher had taught her. Understanding those onset-rime patterns and knowing that many vowels make the schwa sound helped Anna learn to pronounce multisyllable words.

Vocabulary through Morphology

In addition to decoding, syllabication, and pronunciation, teachers also worked hard to develop strategies to help students learn the meanings of words. Students learned to use analogies, antonyms, restatements, descriptions, and comparisons within the passage to help comprehend key unknown words. Often, teaching students how to use context clues was enough.

But, sometimes, context wasn't enough. Then vocabulary had to be examined from another standpoint also—morphology. Through morphology (roots, prefixes, and suffixes) meanings of words can be determined if their context is not clear. Teachers used a combination of strategies to help students build a solid morphological study that would be both meaningful and enduring. They followed several simple rules:

- Choose words that will be meaningful to the students.
- Teach the morphological roots (or prefixes and suffixes) of the word.
- Provide ongoing opportunities for students to use these words and word parts.

Teachers began the morphology study with common words that all their students would know and recognize. Early in the year, teachers started their morphology study with the root *dic*. They chose this root for several reasons. First, they knew that students would immediately know one word made from that root: dictionary. Second, they knew that quickly the students would reach a part of their history textbook that talked about dictators. Finally, they knew they would be talking to students about predicting what they read. Consequently, they expected that very quickly students could hear, see, and use the root word. As students studied this root, they made an ongoing list of ways to use the root. They found words such as dictation, diction, dictatorial, dictator, dictaphone, contradiction, benediction, predict, and prediction. From these words, students could also study prefixes and suffixes found in those words. For a list of the easiest and most common prefixes, suffixes, and roots, see Appendix 5.B.

From the base word *dic*, students created morphology journals. Morphology journals provide students a place to do the following:

1. list the root, prefix, or suffix they are learning;

2. make record definitions of roots, prefixes, and suffixes;

3. keep vocabulary trees for each root, prefix, or suffix; and

4. keep extension activities that use newly-learned words.

Figure 5.5 is an example of Mark's vocabulary tree. Students at Julian Middle School made vocabulary trees for each root word they studied. These trees were constantly under construction and revision as students added to the branches throughout the year. Mark's tree illustrates the parts of the vocabulary tree.

The trunk of the tree holds the root word and its definition and is a place to list the key word, in this case dictionary. The branches off the tree are added every time the student hears, sees, or uses a word with the *dic* root. Here, Mark found contradict, prediction, and dictator. The main branches list the word and its definition. Smaller branches give the student an opportunity to record where he read it, used it, or heard it. These branches are added all year as the opportunities arise.

In addition to keeping vocabulary trees in their morphology journals, students also recorded any extension or creative activities they did in the journals. Figure 5.6 is an example of one type of creative extension Mark and his buddies did with the root word *dic*. So they could each have a copy for their own journals, the boys wrote the play on the classroom computer, printed four copies, and each stapled it into their journals.

Figure 5.5 Mark's Vocabulary Tree

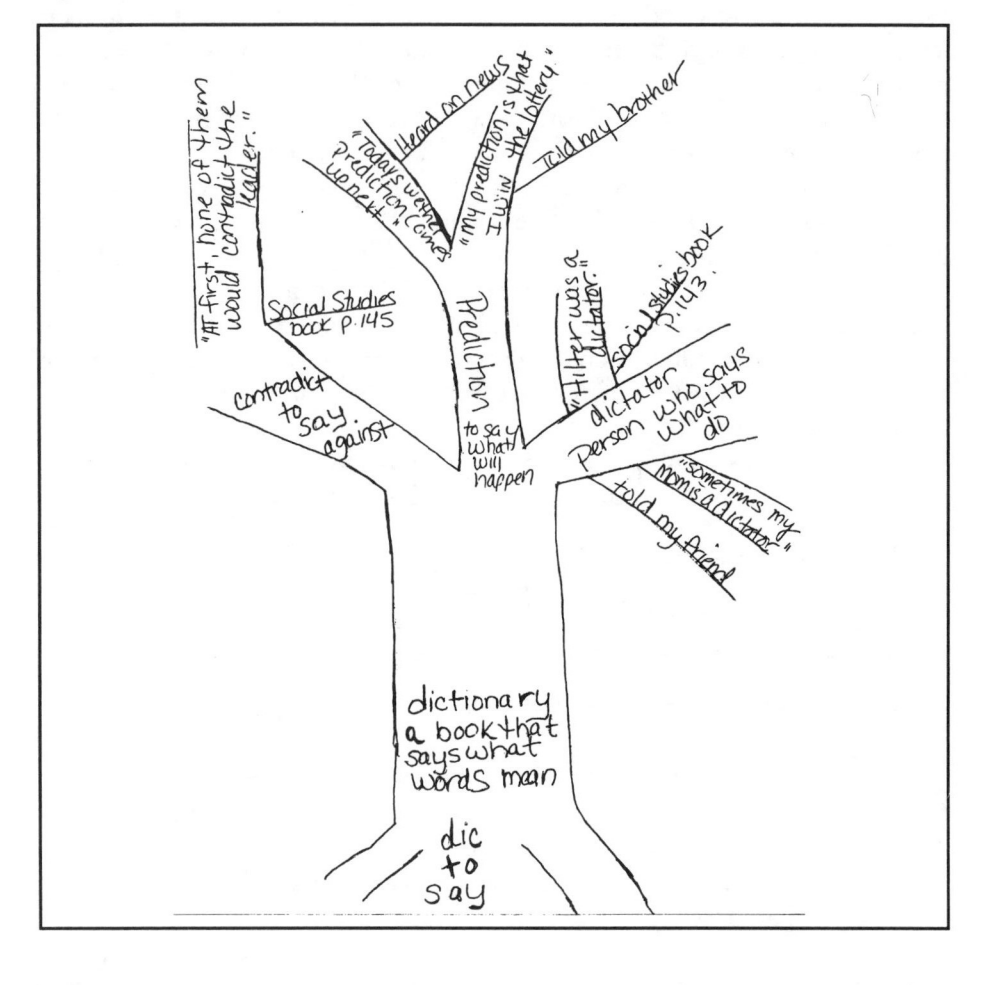

Figure 5.6 The Prediction Play

> **"To Predict or Not to Predict!"**
>
> (Hear thunder in background)
>
> Narrator: (Wearing a raincoat). As your weatherman of the day, I *predict* that it will rain today.
>
> (More thunder)
>
> Narrator: So I brought my umbrella. Children going to the bus stop be prepared for rain today. Do not *contradict* your mothers when they *dictate* to you about what to wear. They usually are right. And I am sure that as you stand in the rain with your umbrellas and rainboots, you will silentyl say a word of thanks to your mom along with a *benediction*. Thanks be to Mom who listened to the weathermans's *prediction* this morning."

Shared Experiences

Much of what has already been discussed certainly may also be called shared experiences. As students work through independent practice and guided practice they are also working within the group and sharing their learning experience. After Paula's students went to see the movie *Jumanji* they returned to class the following Monday to discuss, to write, and to read, making additional connections to the original text. Sue's class tried cooking at least once a week. Sometimes the recipe tied into a theme the class was covering or sometimes into a vocabulary morphemic or semantic structure. She used dried salmon and dried jerky as she read survival stories and discussed sections of *Julie of the Wolves* (George, 1972), *Call It Courage* (Sperry, 1940), and *Hatchet* (Paulsen, 1987). She worked with recipes for corn—bread, hash, and mush—as she discussed the Indian diet in *Sing Down the Moon* (O'Dell, 1970) and in frontier life in *The Sign of the Beaver* (Speare, 1983). She also used apples as she cooked and demonstrated the link of apples to various cultures and legends. Students created a number of apple concoctions from the books on apples.

But beyond these kinds of shared experiences, the teachers also learned that reading techniques could be used during this time to build fluency. Paula worked with her students as they used choral readings with a wide variety of poetry. She also taught her students to change register and voice as she helped them in readers' theater assume the tone of their chosen character. Sue asked her students to keep a diary in the tone of one of the characters in *Where the Red Fern Grows* (Rawls, 1961). Her students also produced a TV show, *You Are There,* to demonstrate how major characters might feel.

Always, there was time left at the end of each class period for brief sharing, whether it was simple book talks, opinions on the story, updates about the story, book critiques, or artistic responses (usually prepared at home). Sometimes there was a large question posed to the entire group concerning their reading. They could come to this question using their own perspective and information from their book. An example for this would be, "What did the author do to make you believe the problem in this book?" Robert Probst's Chapter 7 offers many other examples of fine questions to ask.

Conclusion

Teachers working with struggling readers are constantly searching for ways to help their learners make connections and strengthen their literacy levels. But working with these readers who are just emerging into literacy at the middle school level presents a new set of problems for the teacher. These students are still learning to read instead of reading to learn. And so, many a well-intentioned teacher might say, "But the content is so important, we'll read it for the student." By doing so they make all sorts of adjustments in their teaching to help students learn information and concepts. But this does not help the student practice reading and writing. Unless reading becomes automatic with these learners, the rest is moot. Struggling middle school learners must be given time to grow into literacy, to practice reading many books at their independent level, as well as to practice reading more challenging books. They must be respected for what they can do and what they bring to literacy rather than being disenfranchised through compensations where the teacher reads, peers read, media presents, but the student most in need does not get to practice. The only way to enable these emerging middle school readers is to build time to let them practice what they can read and teach them the reading strategies that will enable them to confront and conquer new and challenging reading.

References

Chall, J. (1991). *The reading crisis: Why poor children fall behind.* Cambridge, MA: Harvard University Press.

Davey, B. (1983). Think-aloud—modeling the cognitive processes of reading comprehension. *Journal of Reading, 27,* 184–193.

Ehri, L. C. (1987). Learning to read and spell words. *Journal of Reading Behavior, 19,* 5–31.

Ehri, L. C., & Wilce, L. S. (1987). Does learning to spell help beginners learn to read words? *Reading Research Quarterly, 22,* 47–65.

Irwin, P.A. & Mitchell, J.N. (1983). A procedure for assessing the richness of retelling. *Journal of Reading, 26,* 391–396.

Gaskins, I., Downer, M., Anderson, R., Cunningham, P., Gaskins, R., Schommer, M., & The Teachers of Benchmark School. (1988). *A metacognitive approach to phonics: Using what you know to decode what you don't know* (Tech. Rep. No. 424). Champaign: University of Illinois, Center for the Study of Reading.

Harris, A. J., & Sipay, E. R. (1990). *How to increase reading ability* (9th ed.). New York: Longman.

Manzo, A. V. (1969). The request procedure. *Journal of Reading, 12,* 123–126.

Morrow, L.M., (1988). *Retelling stories as a diagnostic tool: Re-examining reading diagnosis.* Edited by S.M. Glazer, L.W. Serfoss, and L.M. Gentile. 128–149. Newark, DE: International Reading Association.

Sebesta, S. L., Monson, D. L., & Senn, H. D. (1995). A hierarchy to assess reader response. *Journal of Reading, 38*(6), 444–451.

Tierney, R. J., Readence, J. E., & Dishner, E. K. (1995). *Reading strategies and practices* (4th ed.). Boston, MA: Allyn and Bacon.

Trade Books Cited

George, J. (1972). *Julie of the wolves.* New York: Harper & Row.

Martin, B., & Archambault, J. (1985). *The ghost-eye tree.* New York: Henry Holt.

O'Dell, S. (1970). *Sing down the moon.* Boston: Houghton Mifflin.

Paulsen, G. (1987). *Hatchet.* New York: Bradbury.

Rawls, W. (1961). *Where the red fern grows.* New York: Doubleday.

San Souci, D. (1990). *Young Merlin.* New York: Doubleday.

Seuss, Dr. [pseud.]. (1960). *Green eggs and ham.* New York: Random House.

Speare, E. G. (1983). *The sign of the beaver.* Boston: Houghton Mifflin.

Sperry, A. (1940). *Call it courage.* New York: Macmillan.

Van Allsburg, C. (1981). *Jumanji.* Boston: Houghton Mifflin.

Appendix 5.A
Low-Level High-Interest Books
(These books are in the reading grade levels between 2 and 4)

Series Books

Choose Your Own Adventures. Bantam.
> Best-selling ones:
>> *The Cave of Time* (1982)
>>
>> *Journey Under the Sea* (1987)
>>
>> *Dinosaur Island* (1991)
>>
>> *The Computer Takeover* (1995)
>>
>> *Possessed!* (1995)
>>
>> *Tattoo of Death* (1995)
>>
>> *Typhoon!* (1995)

Choose Your Own Nightmare. Bantam.
> *Island of Doom* (1995)
>
> *Beware the Snake's Venom* (1996)

Ghost Writer. Bantam. *Camp At Your Own Risk* trilogy:
> *Creepy Sleepaway* (1995)
>
> *Daycamp Nightmare* (1995)
>
> *Disaster on Wheels* (1995)

*Graveyard School*s. Tom B. Stone. Skylark Press.
> *Don't Eat the Mystery Meat!* (1994)
>
> *The Headless Bicycle Rider* (1994)
>
> *The Skeleton on the Skateboard* (1994)
>
> *Little Pet Werewolf* (1995)
>
> *Revenge of the Dinosaurs* (1995)

Kids of the Polk Street School, The. Patricia Giff, Yearling. (1988)

Nate the Great. Marjorie Sharmat, Yearling. (1977)

Pee Wee Scouts. Judy Delton. Yearling. (1977)

Pony Trails. Bonnie Bryant. Skylark Press.
        Corey's Pony is Missing (1995)
        Jasmine's Christmas Ride (1995)
        May's Riding Lesson (1995)
        Pony Crazy (1995)
        May Takes the Lead (1996)

Sports Illustrated for Kids. Bantam.
        You Call the Play: Baseball (1994)
        You Call the Play: Football (1995)

Super Hoops. Hank Herman. Skylark Press.
        Crashing the Boards (1996)
        In Your Face (1996)

World of Adventure. Gary Paulsen. Yearling/Bantam.
        Danger on Midnight River (1995)
        Escape from Fire Mountain (1995)
        Hook 'Em Snotty? (1995)
        The Rock Jockeys (1995)

Individual Titles

Adler, D. A. (1996). *Eaton Stanley and the Mind Control Experiment*. Yearling.
Two 6th-grade boys try to control their teacher's mind but find their project getting out of hand when serious things start happening to her.

Bauer, M. D. (1993). *A Taste of Smoke*. Yearling.
While camping with her sister, a 13-year-old finds a ghost.

Burgess, B. H. (1995). *The Fred Field*. Yearling.
Seventh-grade Oren is haunted by his best friend's murder and looks for the murderer.

Dugard, M. (1995). *On the Edge: Four True Stories of Extreme Outdoor Sports Adventures*. Bantam.

Hyppolite, J. (1997). *Seth and Samona*. Delacorte Press.
Funny adventures of two 5th graders.

Kline, S. (1996). *Mary Marony and the Snake*. Yearling.
Mary has funny adventures at school.

Krensky, S. (1995). *The Three Blind Mice Mystery.* Bantam.
Detective Simple Simon must look for Charlie the blind mouse and a ferocious wolf on the loose and two pigs who have lost their homes!

Paulsen, G. (1993). *Dogteam.* Picture Yearling.
Nighttime dogsled run adventure.

Paulsen, G. (1995). *Harris and Me.* Yearling.
Funny adventures of two boy cousins who spend their summer on a farm.

Quattlebaum, M. (1994). *Jackson Jones and the Puddle of Thorns.* Yearling.
Jackson wants a basketball but gets a garden plot of weeds!

Salisbury, G. (1995). *Under the Blood-Red Sun.* Yearling.
Japanese-American boy and family in Hawaii during Pearl Harbor face internment.

Schecter, E. (1995). *Real Live Monsters.* Bank Street.
Combines scientific information and fun facts about real monsters!

Ulrich, G. (1995). *My Tooth Ith Loothe: Funny Poems to Read Instead of Doing Your Homework.* Yearling.
Funny adventure poems.

Woodruff, E. (1995). *Ghosts Don't Get Goose Bumps.* Yearling.
Two friends and a 5-year-old who refuses to talk find ghosts in a factory.

Appendix 5.B

Some Common Roots, Prefixes, and Suffixes

ROOT WORDS

Root	Meaning	Examples
act	do	action, actor, react, transact, enact
aud	hear	audience, auditorium, audible, audition
cred	believe	credit, discredit, incredible, credulous
dic	speak	dictate, predict, contradict, verdict, diction
graph	write	autograph, paragraph, phonograph, photograph, telegraph
loc	place	allocate, dislocate, locate, location
man	hand	manual, manufacture, manuscript, manipulate
mot	move	demote, motion, motor, promote
ped	foot	pedal, pedestrian, pedestal
pop	people	population, popular, populace
port	carry	import, export, portable, porter, transport
sign	mark	insignia, signal, significant, signature
spec	see	inspect, respect, spectacle, spectator, suspect
tract	pull, drag	attract, detract, contract, subtract, traction, tractor
vid	see	evidence, video, provide, providence
volv	roll	evolve, involve, revolve, revolver, revolution

PREFIXES

Prefix	Meaning	Examples
ad-	to	adapt, add, addict, adhere, admit
amphi-	both, around	amphibian, amphitheater
an-	without	anarchy, anesthesia, anonymous, anorexia
auto-	self	automobile, automatic, autograph, autobiography

co-	together	coauthor, cognate, coincide, cooperate, coordinate
de-	down, from	deform, degrade, deplete, descend
dis-	opposite	disagree, disarm, discontinue, disgust, dishonest
for-	not	forbid, forget, forgo
il-	not	illegal, illegible, illegitimate, illiterate, illogical
im-	into	immerse, immigrate, implant, import
im-	not	imbalance, immaculate, immature, immobilize, impossible
in-	not	inaccurate, inactive, inadvertent, incognito, indecisive
ir-	not	irregular, irreconcilable, irredeemable, irregular, irresponsible
mal-	bad	maladjusted, malaise, malevolent, malfunction, malice
mis-	bad	misbehave, misconduct, misfortune
pro-	before	prognosis, program, prologue, prophet
pro-	forward	proceed, produce, proficient, progress, project
re-	again	redo, rewrite, reappear, repaint, relive
re-	back	recall, recede, reflect, repay, retract
sub-	under	subcontract, subject, submarine, submerge, subordinate, subterranean
trans-	across	transatlantic, transcend, transcribe, transfer, translate
un-	not	unable, uncomfortable, uncertain, unhappy

SUFFIXES

Suffix	Meaning	Examples
-ade	action or process	blockade, escapade, parade
-age	action or process	marriage, pilgrimage, voyage

-ant	one who	assistant, immigrant, merchant, servant
-cle	small	corpuscle, cubicle, particle
-dom	state or quality of	boredom, freedom, martyrdom, wisdom
-ent	one who	defendent, resident, regent, superintendent
-ful	full of	careful, fearful, joyful, thoughtful
-ic	relating to	comic, historic, poetic, public
-less	without	ageless, careless, thoughtless, tireless
-let	small	islet, leaflet, owlet, piglet, rivulet
-ly	resembling	fatherly, motherly, scholarly
-ly	every	daily, weekly, monthly, yearly
-ment	action or process	development, embezzlement, government
-ment	state or quality of	amusement, amazement, enchantment
-ment	product or thing	fragment, instrument, ornament
-or	one who	actor, auditor, doctor, donor

Chapter 6

LATINO STUDENTS AND READING: UNDERSTANDING THESE ENGLISH LANGUAGE LEARNERS' NEEDS

Yolanda Padrón

Smith Middle School, a pseudonym, is typical in many ways. When I visited Smith Middle School, my initial impressions were very favorable. Smith, located in a major metropolitan city, is a large middle school that serves over 1,100 predominantly Latino students. The inner-city neighborhood in which this school is located is considered one of the poorest in the city; nearly all of the students come from low socioeconomic backgrounds and about two-thirds of these students receive free or reduced lunch. However, I found the school grounds and facilities immaculate. There were no visible signs of graffiti or vandalism. An efficient school office staff and pleasant, bilingual parent aides greeted me. A tour of the building also gave me a positive impression of a well-run, efficient middle school with quiet and clean corridors and student restrooms.

My positive impressions continued as I met the principal and some of the faculty. The principal, who is Latino and bilingual, seemed to relate well to students, teachers, and parents. For the most part, the faculty at Smith have a great deal of teaching experience. About half of the teachers have been teaching for more than 10 years and about 20% have between 4 and 10 years of teaching experience. Approximately 40% of the teachers have master's degrees. About 60% of the teachers are African American, 30% are Anglo, and about 10% are Latino. The ethnic diversity of the students, however, has dramatically changed in the past few years. As recently as five years ago, Smith's students were predominantly African American. Now, about 90% of the students are Latino and only about 10% of the student population is African American.

At a cursory level, Smith Middle School appears to be an effective middle school, but problems at Smith are like those that exist in many urban middle schools. The difficulties of teaching reading to middle school students whose first language is Spanish are common to middle school teachers throughout the United States. Teachers who have never had training in strategies for second language learners are struggling as they search for ways to build language and reading skills with their students. The purpose of this chapter is to provide strategies and suggestions for middle school reading teachers so that their reading instruction can be more effective for Latino English language learners who are reading text in their second language.

In the past, learners whose primary language is not English have been termed *language minority students* or *Limited-English Proficient* (LEP) students. This description, however, has derogatory meanings because it infers that students are deficient in language rather than the fact that they know one language and are mastering another language. Consequently, the term *English Language Learner* (ELL) has been recently used to describe those students whose first language is not English and who are either: (a) beginning to learn English or (b) have demonstrated some proficiency in English (LaCelle & Rivera, 1994). The construct of ELL helps educators reframe the problem from one of blaming the learners because they have a language "deficiency" or their primary language is not the language of the dominant culture, to a perspective that focuses on the educational needs specific to ELLs because they are learning another language.

The information in this chapter is designed to help middle school reading teachers who have ELLs in their classrooms. Many of these reading teachers at Smith and other schools like Smith face students whose needs are very different from those students they taught 10 or even 5 years ago. ELL students need opportunities to build vocabulary, background experience, and language skills while learning to read.

The chapter is divided into four sections. The first section describes the current status of Latino ELLs. This demographic information is useful to understand the crucial need to identify appropriate instructional strategies for these students. The second section reviews reading strategies used by ELLs while reading English text. Knowledge of the cognitive reading strategies that students currently use can give us some insight into appropriate instructional interventions for ELLs so that they can comprehend text better. This is also important because many ELLs may be transferring strategies used in their first language in order to comprehend English text. Spanish, for example, has a more direct one-to-one correspondence between sounds and letters than English does. Students, therefore, may expect a high degree of correspondence between letters and sounds. They have fewer problems decoding than comprehending text. In the third section of this chapter, we will return to Smith Middle School and examine the instruction in reading classrooms. In the final section of this chapter, specific instructional strategies and suggestions are offered so that middle school teachers can improve their reading instruction for ELLs.

Latino ELLs: How Are They Doing in Schools?

One of the greatest challenges facing educators today is addressing the educational needs of students who come from culturally and linguistically different backgrounds. Students who are from culturally diverse families will continue to constitute a large percentage of the total school population. Projections for the year 2020, for example, indicate that people of color will comprise 46% of the student population (Cushner, McClelland, & Safford, 1992).

Latino students constituted only 9.3% of the student population less than 17 years of age in 1982, but by the year 2020 it is projected that this percentage will increase to 25.3% (Pallas, Natriello, & McDill, 1989). In addition to being the largest growing minority group, Latino ELLs have had the lowest educational level and the highest drop-out rate of any ethnic group (Cardenas, 1990). Latino ELLs from inner-city schools have often been described as one of the groups of students most at risk for academic failure, since they have a lower reading achievement level than other minority and majority students. It is estimated that 40% of Latino students are one grade or more below expected achievement levels by the eighth grade, and only about 50% graduate "on time" (García, 1994). These students are not only less likely to complete high school, but they are also less likely than Blacks and Whites to go to college (Kaufman & Frase, 1990).

Not only will teachers continue to have many students from diverse ethnic backgrounds, but many of the students will also have diverse language backgrounds. The number of school-aged children from various language backgrounds has continued to increase. The ELL population increased 12.6% from the 1991–1992 to 1992–1993 school year, while the overall student population increased at a rate of only 1.02% (Fromboluti, 1994). The projections for the year 2000 indicate that Spanish-speaking students will constitute approximately 77% of the total language minority student population (O'Malley, 1981).

The increasing number of Latino ELLs in our schools today is of concern because most teachers have not received training in English as a Second Language (ESL) or bilingual education, and these ELLs are often mainstreamed into "regular" reading classrooms. There, teachers with no specialized instruction in teaching ELL students are often expected to teach reading and writing to these students. Simultaneously, they are to develop the ELLs' oral language skills. Without doubt, many teachers are overwhelmed by the complexity of this task.

To ease this task and improve the reading achievement of ELLs, teachers must first determine what students are doing as they read a text. That is, what types of strategies are ELLs using when they are reading text in their second language? Knowing the type of strategies that students use provides insight into how to improve instruction for ELLs. If these students are found to be using ineffective strategies, for example, instructional programs can then be developed so that students can learn to use more effective strategies. By instructing low-achieving ELLs to use effective strategies for critical thinking and problem solving, some of the barriers to academic success faced by these students may be removed.

What Reading Strategies Are Used by ELLs?

The reading strategies that ELLs most often report using while reading text in English are: (a) *Concentrating* and (b) *Rereading*. Concentrating is defined as thinking about the story; Rereading is defined as reading the story or parts of the story more than once. Both of these strategies are low-level strategies because they require very little cognitive processing. More sophisticated strategies, such as summarizing or finding the main idea, are seldom mentioned by ELLs. Summarizing has been identified as a more sophisticated strategy because students must read the information and then put that information in their own words. Overall, Latino ELLs have been found to use fewer and less-sophisticated cognitive reading strategies to comprehend text than English-monolingual students when reading English text (Padrón & Waxman, 1988). These findings are especially important since studies have also found that students who use a variety of reading strategies and more sophisticated strategies do better in reading.

One reading strategy that ELLs use is what I call *Predicting-What-the-Teacher-Expects-of-Me*. This strategy is defined as an attempt to guess what the reading teacher might ask or what would please the teacher in terms of an answer. When ELLs who reported using this particular strategy were probed about what they were doing to understand the text, they stated that they were wondering what the teacher might ask them to remember or what kind of answer the teacher wanted. This seems to indicate that ELLs perceived the reading experience as an externally controlled process (i.e., by the teacher) instead of an internally controlled process (i.e., by the student). Since it is important that the reader be in control in order to understand text, the use of this particular strategy may be contributing to poor reading comprehension. Is it possible that ELLs are using this low-level strategy because of the type of instruction that they are receiving? That is, the use of this reading strategy may be attributed to the fact that teachers treat good readers differently from poor readers. Teachers may have perceived that these ELLs were poor readers and thus their reading instruction may have emphasized teacher-controlled activities such as decoding. Consequently, students may have deduced that the objective of reading is to answer questions that the teacher asks. Therefore, students develop and use strategies such as attempting to predict what the teacher expects of them.

Why do ELLs use fewer and less sophisticated strategies? A possible explanation is that they are not being taught stronger strategies. There is evidence that reading instruction for at-risk middle school and upper grade elementary students does not focus on comprehension (Brown, Palincsar, & Purcell, 1986). In other words, one possible explanation for differences in the academic achievement between high- and low-achieving students may be that low-achieving students may not be given the opportunity to learn and practice higher-level thinking skills (Coley & Hoffman, 1990; Waxman, Padrón, & Knight, 1991). One case study of a bilingual reader with a poor reading proficiency (Jiménez, García, & Pearson, 1995) reported that although she recognized the significance of word meanings for comprehension of the material, she possessed few tools for addressing the unknown words when she encountered them in her reading. Reading for her was simply figuring out the meanings of words, and she did not know how to use context or to use her knowledge of Spanish vocabulary to try to figure out the words.

Low-achieving students are perhaps not being exposed to higher-level thinking skills for two reasons. First, it is generally assumed that students must demonstrate the ability to learn the basic or lower levels of knowledge before they can be taught higher-level skills (Foster, 1989). In the case of ELLs, for example, higher-level thinking skills are generally not taught until the student has mastered English fully because it is assumed that students are not able to comprehend until they can speak the language well (García & Pearson, 1991). Second, some teachers have lower expectations for language minority students and consequently teach them less than they are capable of learning (Gersten & Jiménez, 1994). These findings suggest that it may be necessary to change instructional behaviors in reading classrooms where there are large populations of ELLs. It is important that teacher behavior and instructional practices be examined because these factors have been associated with the poor academic performance of Latino students (Padrón & Knight, 1989; Padrón & Waxman, 1993).

Looking into Middle School Classrooms

Outward appearances are often deceiving, and such is the case at Smith Middle School. There the apparent efficiency of the staff, even the cleanliness of the school, seemingly indicates that all is well—including student achievement. However, that is not the case. Student achievement is low and reading teachers' instructional practices with ELLs are inappropriate.

The general achievement level of the students at Smith could be categorized as poor since students' composite achievement test scores in reading on the Iowa Test of Basic Skills were about two and one-half years behind the national norms for all three grade levels (i.e., 6, 7 & 8). Also, only 16% of the students passed the statewide reading achievement test. Approximately 40% of Smith's students failed at least one course the previous year. In addition, there have been serious discipline problems in this school.

As in other urban schools with high percentages of minority students, the major problem in this school is the students' lack of achievement. But can students be blamed? A close inspection reveals serious programmatic and instructional factors that may be hindering these students' academic achievement. First, there were very few ESL classes. Most of the ELLs in this school were mainstreamed into reading classes. After observing all the reading classes at Smith, I concluded that the reading teachers needed help in knowing how to teach reading to students who were learning English.

Nearly all of the teachers at Smith typically lectured or used drill-and-practice techniques in the classroom. Neither basal readers nor whole language approaches were used. Instead I saw needless repetition of previously covered language skills and concepts. There was little group work and no in-depth or authentic learning experiences. Teachers spent very little time working with students in small groups and even less time working with students individually. Students in these reading classrooms were never observed working one-to-one with their teacher or working with another student. During the few times that these students were allowed to work in small groups, these groups did not function very well. Members of the groups were generally uncooperative and tended to work individually. In addition, students were slow at getting started and were generally unsure of the task.

Perhaps the major weakness in the reading classes at this school was that very little time was spent actually reading. Students listened to the teacher lecture or worked on skill sheets. The teaching of higher-level thinking processes was almost nonexistent. Teachers seldom posed open-ended questions for students, asked questions about complex issues, or asked questions where students needed to reason through to a conclusion or explain something at length. I rarely observed teachers ask students to practice critical thinking or relate the content to their past experiences. Teachers were seldom observed allowing students to explore alternative points of view or asking students to explain their thinking processes. Teachers never encouraged the transfer of cognitive skills to everyday life. For example, teachers did not make comments like, "This will help you in your everyday life in this way." In addition, teachers were not observed using "if/then" language or posing "what if" or "suppose that" questions.

Finally, it should be pointed out that there was very little teacher enthusiasm and warmth toward students at Smith Middle School. Stressed teachers seldom communicated to students that they expected them to succeed. Teachers rarely showed any interest in students' work and seldom talked to students outside of class. The saddest observation of all, however, was the fact that there were several monolingual Spanish-speaking students in each of the reading classes I visited, and in every class their reading teachers totally ignored them. The teachers didn't seem to know how to cope with students who needed help with both language and reading skills. The results of these observations indicate that the quality of classroom instruction in these middle school reading classrooms is poor. The reading instructional approaches observed at Smith Middle School provide little opportunity for students to become successful in reading. In addition, the observations indicate that students are not being instructed when or where to use reading strategies or how to evaluate their successful use. This knowledge of strategy use is important if students are expected to use strategies spontaneously in their own reading (Baker & Brown, 1984). Generally, the reading instruction in these classes is very passive.

There are many other implications that can be drawn from the observations in these middle school classrooms. The lack of small-group instruction and cooperative grouping, for example, is problematic given that it has been found to be a very effective instructional strategy and especially beneficial for Latino ELLs. Another critical observation relates to the area of providing students with a positive, supportive learning environment. The reading teachers observed in these classrooms spent very little time interacting with students regarding personal issues, encouraging students to succeed, showing personal regard for students, or showing interest in students' work. These are all areas that have been found to be important for developing positive learning environments where students can become successful learners.

A final area of concern relates to the lack of ESL classes for these middle school ELLs. There is a great need for ESL classrooms for middle school Latino ELLs because many have exited transitional bilingual programs in elementary grades. Their level of English proficiency may not be the level that is required to do more higher-level cognitive tasks. There are also a large number of Latino middle school ELLs who have recently arrived in the United States who similarly have limited English proficiency skills (Faltis & Arias, 1993). Several instructional approaches like *Sheltered Content Teaching* (Krashen, 1985) have been found to be effective for secondary school ELLs who are placed in ESL classrooms, but these methods are generally not suitable for instruction in standard reading classrooms.

What Can Be Done to Improve Reading Instruction for ELLs?

The critical question facing most middle school reading teachers like those at Smith Middle School who have ELL students in their classrooms is what can we do to help ELLs become more successful readers? Viable instructional programs can be developed to help *all* students learn. For example, there is evidence that certain reading comprehension instructional programs can be effective for many at-risk students. The following subsections include some instructional strategies that have been found to be effective for Latino ELLs. At schools where teachers have successfully helped students to build literacy as well as both oral and written language skills, these strategies have enabled all students to learn. These suggestions consider not only cultural differences, but also take into account language differences that the students bring with them. After reading this chapter, if you are looking for further discussions of metacognitive strategies that are effective with at-risk learners see the chapters in this book by Margaret Hill (Chapter 5) and Judy Wallis (Chapter 12).

Learning Environments

ELLs need to be provided with a positive learning environment where they will feel accepted and safe. You can make your classroom comfortable for ELLs by making certain that classroom rules, acceptable behaviors, and activities are explicit. This will help ELLs know what is expected of them.

Establish daily patterns and class activities. Expectations should be clear so that ELLs understand rules for participating in class. ELLs will be less able to focus on instruction when they are concerned about what they should or should not be doing. When there are changes in daily routines or rules, provide as much advance notice as possible and do not rely just on telling students. Find other ways of letting them know about changes, such as through pictures. Language differences may make oral explanations harder to understand.

In a classroom where ELLs feel comfortable and accepted, they will also feel that their participation is valued. ELLs should have opportunities to work on challenging tasks. These students need to be viewed as highly capable and able to take on challenging tasks. It is just as important for ELLs to develop content knowledge and higher-level thinking skills as it is for English-monolingual students. If ELLs are to be successful in academic settings, these skills will need to be developed.

Creating an Environment for Language Use

Learning a second language is a difficult task. Not only is learning a second language demanding, but it also takes time. During the learning process, ELLs are often shy or embarrassed to speak the new language. Therefore, it is important to provide students with an environment where they feel comfortable taking risks with their new language. While some ELLs acquire oral English proficiency very quickly, it may take much longer for the kind of proficiency needed to complete academic work (Cummins, 1981). This type of English language proficiency can take five to seven years to acquire.

To learn a new language, students need to have numerous and varied opportunities to use both written and oral language in a variety of situations. Organize group activities that require small group discussions. Having students work in small groups, student-student dyads, or teacher-student dyads, for example, are effective instructional groupings. When possible, pair ELL students with sensitive English speakers whose language can be a model. ELLs also need to have opportunities to use language for a variety of purposes including dialogues, explaining solutions, formulating questions, and using language for higher-level thinking. Written and oral language, for example, should be used to define, summarize, and report on activities. Seek opportunities for authentic communication with members of the Latino community. Continue to encourage peer conferencing even when students seem to lack the confidence to help each other. Constant modeling of these kinds of interactions is needed. These situations will expose students to a variety of language uses and will also force students to use language.

Most important, focus on *communicating* ideas rather than correcting language errors. In fact, error correction should play a minor role. Regular daily language minilessons can address students' correctness concerns with direct instruction apart from the actual production of communicating situations. If there is constant focus on language errors, ELLs may become discouraged from using English to communicate.

In addition, ELLs need to be provided with the opportunity to respond to higher level questions that require more than a single word or predictable response. ELLs need to be asked questions that require new or extended responses. Ask students to extend their answers by explaining why they feel a particular response is correct. Having the patience to wait for students to frame their responses in English, even if it is not perfect English, is crucial to establishing a comfortable environment for these students.

Building Self-Concept

English Language Learners may have experienced failure in school before they get to your reading class. Their frustrations with academic requirements in school may cause them to develop a learned helplessness. That is, low-achieving students often have a low self-concept and therefore believe that they are not capable of learning. Consequently, reading instruction needs to include techniques that address ELLs' affective needs. If ELLs have low academic self-concepts, this may interfere with their ability to learn. Therefore, reading instruction that does not address the students' academic self-concept may not be suitable for ELLs who are culturally and linguistically different. Give your students meaningful activities that will provide them with opportunities for achieving success.

Introduce students to a variety of reading materials and aim to find readings that tap their particular interests. Read aloud daily from texts with different genres, styles, and topics. For additional information on reading aloud, look at Chapter 13. Then encourage oral and written responses to readings that allow students to express opinions, share ideas, and build on their experiences. When several readings relate to a single theme, students build language about that theme, and their vocabulary grows. Extensive reading helps students become more productive readers as well as sparks ideas for writing (Peyton, Jones, Vincent, & Greenblatt, 1994).

Building writing skills supports reading skills. Teachers of ELLs use the writing process to build language and literacy skills in general while communicating with teachers, community members, or peers in meaningful writing tasks that can help build self-esteem. Involving middle school students in dialogue journals with teachers or with peers can provide an opportunity for modeling in authentic communication contexts. Similarly, letter writing exchanges between ELLs and English-speaking students at another middle school or at a university (prospective teachers) also provides purposeful and responsive opportunities for developing self-esteem while supporting literacy learning. At one middle school I visited, ELL students talked and wrote effectively about photographs they had taken of their family and neighborhood. Pride was evident on their faces as they shared their lives with other students in the class and with their teacher.

Cooperative Groups

Effective reading teachers always provide activities that have ELLs working in cooperative groups. This kind of organization provides for diversity of learning styles. Being in a group may lower the anxiety that some students feel when they have to perform alone. Begin group activities by explaining to students how they are to work together. I have found that I can never depend on the fact that students know how to work in cooperative groups.

Make a list of the group's responsibilities and the role of each student. Maintain the basic structure of the group, so that expectations will be clear even when the task of the group is changed. This kind of instruction in group activities will help your cooperative groups to work more effectively.

Encourage students to discuss their readings in their groups and share their ideas about their texts. Conversations about books makes silent independent reading a significant part of the reading program. Atwell (1987) maintains that these conversations, patterned on conversations readers have around their dining room tables, help create a literate community of readers.

If you are looking for more information about organizing literature discussions or literature circles, see the chapters by Elizabeth Poe and by Judith Scott and Jan Wells in this book.

Prior Knowledge

Prior knowledge is a key ingredient in making sense of text. ELL students, whose cultural background and language may differ from the author's, may have difficulties with texts because they do not have the prior knowledge to understand them. Instructional programs for these students must help them to consider what they already know about a topic as well as to build background when they need it. A student who has grown up in a rural agricultural area, for example, may have no concept of traffic, airplane travel, restaurant dining, or ocean liners. They will need extensive discussion about these topics to build enough background to truly understand them. Use pictures, films, readings, and discussion to help these students. Expert comprehenders, in general, try to relate new material to personal experience (Campione & Armbruster, 1985). Differences in background knowledge or experience due to cultural differences may be an important source of variation for strategy use and outcomes (Steffenson, Joag-Dev, & Anderson, 1979).

If a student has no prior knowledge about a particular topic being discussed, then the student may not be able to understand the topic (Stein, Leinhardt, & Bickel, 1989). In reading classrooms where students are not only of low ability, but also have a culturally different background, teachers need to deal not only with knowledge-base differences, but also with interpretation of issues presented in a text from a cultural perspective different from that of the student. Therefore, if students are from certain populations, especially low-ability or culturally different ones, they may not be able to understand the prerequisite prior knowledge without help, and they may need more teacher-directed activity to help them accomplish the linkage between their knowledge base and the new material.

One strategy that helps ELLs build prior knowledge is *semantic mapping*. Semantic mapping is based on schema theory that suggests that we learn by relating new information to the information we already know. Semantic maps are graphic representations that illustrate concepts and the relationships between concepts (Pearson & Johnson, 1978). For ELL students, semantic mapping is particularly effective in extending vocabulary and thinking. If I were going to share a story about a basketball player with my middle school students, for example, I would ask students to brainstorm a list of related words that might include names of players they know as well as words like *court, hoop, net, foul, jump ball, basket, shoot, key, dribble, guard, forward*, and *center*. As words are generated, they can be categorized into those that are about the playing area, such as *court, basket, net*, and *key*; words that relate to kinds of players, such as *guard, forward*, and *center*; and those that relate to activities in the game, such as *foul, jump ball, shoot*, and *dribble*. The words are mapped on the blackboard or overhead and provide a visual representation of the relationships among the words. Such categorization reinforces the meanings of the words in question as well as the students' understanding of the connections among the words. For more information on semantic mapping, see Karen Feathers's Chapter 14, "Fostering Independent, Critical Content Reading in the Middle School."

Reciprocal Teaching

Studies on strategy training with second language learners have found that when strategies are modeled for students and when students have an opportunity to practice these strategies, their reading comprehension improves (Palinscar & Brown, 1984, 1985; Wittrock, 1991). Showing students the strategies that good readers do automatically, strategies like calling on background knowledge, making inferences, monitoring comprehension, deciding on the main ideas, and creating visual pictures, will help them to learn that there are tools they can use when reading doesn't make sense.

One of the most frequently cited approaches to cognitive strategy training is *reciprocal teaching* (Palinscar & Brown, 1984). This instructional approach incorporates many of the features that were outlined in the sections above. This procedure takes place in a cooperative instructional environment where the teacher and students engage in a dialogue. Students are guided to ask their own reading questions. The students are instructed in four specific comprehension-monitoring strategies: (a) summarizing, (b) self-questioning, (c) clarifying, and (d) predicting. As they read, they are expected to stop after a sentence or a paragraph to summarize and restate what they have just read. They might clarify the information by making a connection to something else they have read. Another time they might predict what the remainder of the material might be.

Don't expect your students to know how to monitor their reading after modeling each of these strategies one or two times. Teachers need to model each of these strategies for the students regularly over a period of time. Gradually, the students take on the role of the teacher, while the teacher takes on a supporting role. This teacher-student dialogue is at the heart of successfully implementing reciprocal teaching. Studies using reciprocal teaching have found that strategies can successfully be taught to low-achieving students and that once these are learned, use of these strategies increases reading achievement (Lysynchuk, Pressley, & Vye, 1990).

The reciprocal teaching procedure provides an important component that can promote the improvement of reading comprehension for ELL students. The text may either be read by the students or the teacher may read the text aloud to students. This technique can be very useful when teaching students who are poor readers or who are just beginning to learn English as a second language (Padrón, 1991). Having the teacher read the text provides the students with the opportunity to learn the four comprehension strategies presented in reciprocal teaching without having to wait until they learn how to decode.

Think-Alouds have also been effective with second language learners. (See the examples in the chapters by Margaret Hill and Judy Wallis in this book.) Block's (1992) study of Think-Aloud strategies with ELLs and English speakers found that less proficient native speakers experienced the same lexical problems as second language learners. Both relied almost totally on semantics for meaning. If they didn't understand a word in a sentence, they immediately decided that they didn't understand the sentence. Block suggests that all learners be taught a four-step process to comprehension using Think-Aloud processes: (1) recognizing the problems they are having with reading, (2) making an action plan to solve the problem, (3) putting the plan into action, (4) and checking their understanding.

Comprehension studies with ELL students suggest that they need specific instruction in the comprehension of content materials (Perez, 1993). In addition to strategies that activate prior knowledge and build background knowledge, students should be introduced to graphic organizers of text structure as well as to study skills such as previewing, setting a purpose for reading, and separating fact from fiction. If you are looking for other ways to teach students about reading expository text, look at the chapter by Karen Feathers in this book. You will find several examples of activities to teach text structure.

Cultural Diversity

Instructional activities should be meaningful and challenging for ELLs. This means that reading teachers should consider students' diversity in developing activities. By incorporating aspects from the ELLs' culture and language, teachers provide social support to the students and validate their language and culture. Incorporating the various cultures and languages of ELLs also provides non-ELLs with the opportunity to learn about cultures and languages. When incorporating culture into the reading classroom, each student should be accepted as an individual. Teachers should not assume that because a student belongs to a particular cultural group they will follow all the customs and beliefs of the culture. Acceptance of the student's culture can provide for a supportive environment. Clearly, it would be difficult for teachers to become experts in every culture; however, teachers need to develop an attitude of interest and learning about ELLs' culture.

One way for teachers to support ELLs cultural background is to seek reading materials that reflect the cultures of the students in the class. Use booklists like *Your Reading* (Samuels & Beers, 1996), *Reading, Thinking, and Writing About Multicultural Literature* (Olson, 1996), *Teaching Multi-*

cultural Literature (Harris, 1994), and articles like "Recent Children's Books about Hispanics" (Schon, 1989) to help you find books and other materials that meet the needs of your students. The Latino population in the United States is very diverse, including Mexican Americans, Cubans, Puerto Ricans, Salvadorans, Nicaraguans, and people from the other Central and South American countries. Unfortunately, there are relatively few books for middle school students about the various Latino experiences. Novels, essays, poems, and novels by Anaya, Cisneros, and Soto form the backbone of available materials in many classes. Make the effort to become familiar with new authors and books as they are published and to seek ways to provide these texts for your students.

Having found a number of texts that reflect students' cultural backgrounds, give your students time to read in class. When you provide time for reading, you convey the message that reading is important and worth spending the time on in class. In addition, just as we need to practice the piano to learn to play piano, time spent practicing reading helps build comprehension processes. Also allow your students the opportunity to choose reading materials from a number of possible text selections. This means that students in a class may be reading a number of different books, magazines, or other materials. Although choice is not directly related to reading comprehension growth, students will choose those books that relate to their interests and backgrounds, which will, in turn, be reflected in their comprehension.

In addition to searching out existing material about your students' cultures, encourage your students to interview their family members to learn about and then write about family stories particular to their culture. Try binding student books from their stories and making them available for all students to read. These stories are particularly interesting to other members of the class.

Concluding Remarks

Reading instruction for middle school ELLs has been characterized as a "pedagogy of poverty" (Haberman, 1991). Haberman suggests that the teacher-directed instructional style that I observed at Smith Middle School leads to compliance and passive resentment among students as well as teacher burnout. Teachers are accountable for *making* students learn, while students assume a passive role with low engagement in tasks or activities that are not authentic. As a result, student achievement is poor.

This chapter has reviewed some issues related to reading instruction for ELLs and has provided some suggestions for improving the process. Reading teachers who have Latino ELLs in their classroom may want to try to implement some of the instructional strategies presented here:

- Create a supportive learning environment where risk taking is encouraged and self-esteem enhanced.
- Create plenty of opportunity for small group discussions and cooperative learning.
- Read aloud.
- Focus on communicating not correcting.
- Ask higher-level questions.
- Encourage oral and written responses.
- Model reading strategies often.
- Build prior knowledge.
- Incorporate aspects of the ELLs' culture into the classroom.
- Share literature that reflects the ELLs' culture.

In addition, reading teachers may want to begin to work more closely with English as a Second Language and/or bilingual teachers in their school. At the school or district level, teachers and administrators may need to specifically focus on the development of bilingual and ESL programs for the middle school Latino ELLs. All children can become motivated, successful, self-directed readers and learners if they are given effective strategies and the opportunity to learn.

References

Atwell, N. (1987). *In the middle*. Portsmouth, NH: Heinemann.

Baker, L., & Brown, A. (1984). Metacognitive skills and reading. In P. D. Pearson (Ed.), *Handbook of reading research* (pp. 353–394). New York: Longman.

Block, E. (1992). See how they read: Comprehension monitoring of L1 and L2 readers. *TESOL Quarterly, 26*, 319–342.

Brown, A. L., Palincsar, A. S., & Purcell, L. (1986). Poor readers: Teach don't label. In U. Neisser (Ed.), *The school achievement of minority children: New perspectives* (pp. 105–143). Hillsdale, NJ: Erlbaum.

Campione, J., & Armbruster, B. (1985). Acquiring information from texts: An analysis of four approaches. In J. Segal, S. Chipman, & R. Glaser (Eds.), *Thinking and learning skills: Relating instruction to research* (Vol. 1, pp. 317–359). Hillsdale, NJ: Lawrence Erlbaum.

Cardenas, J. A. (1990). Texas school dropouts: 1986–1989. *IDRA Newsletter, 7*(3), 1–5.

Coley, J. D., & Hoffman, D. M. (1990). Overcoming learned helplessness in at-risk readers. *Journal of Reading, 33*, 497–502.

120 *Into Focus: Understanding and Creating Middle School Readers*

Cummins, J. (1981). The role of primary development in promoting educational success for language minority students. In *Schooling and language minority students: A theoretical framework* (pp. 3–49). California State University, Los Angeles, CA: Evaluation, Dissemination and Assessment Center.

Cushner, K., McCelland, A., & Safford, P. (1992). *Human diversity in education: An integrative approach.* New York: McGraw Hill.

Faltis, C. J., & Arias, M. B. (1993). Speakers of languages other than English in the secondary school: Accomplishments and struggles. *Peabody Journal of Education, 69*(1), 6–29.

Foster, G. E. (1989). Cultivating the thinking skills of low achievers: A matter of equity. *Journal of Negro Education, 58*, 461–467.

Fromboluti, C. S. (1994). *Mini-digest of education statistics.* Washington, DC: U.S. Department of Education, Office of Educational Research and Improvement, National Center for Statistics.

García, E. (1994). *Understanding and meeting the challenge of student cultural diversity.* Boston, MA: Houghton Mifflin.

García, E., & Pearson, P. D. (1991). Modifying reading instruction to maximize its effectiveness for *all* students. In M. S. Knapp & P. M. Shields (Eds.), *Better schooling for the children of poverty: Alternatives to conventional wisdom* (pp. 31–60). Berkeley, CA: McCutchan.

Gersten, R., & Jiménez, R. (1994). A delicate balance: Enhancing literature instruction for students of English as a second language. *The Reading Teachers, 47*, (6), 438–449.

Haberman, M. (1991). Pedagogy of poverty vs. good teaching. *Phi Delta Kappan, 73*, 290–294.

Harris, V. (1992). *Teaching multicultural literature in grades K-8.* Norwood, MA: Christopher-Gordon.

Jiménez, R., García, G., & Pearson, P. (1995). Three children, two languages, and strategic reading: Case studies in bilingual/monolingual reading. *American Educational Research Journal, 32*, 67–97.

Kaufman, P., & Frase, M. J. (1990). *Dropout rates in the United States: 1989.* Washington, DC: U.S. Department of Education, National Center for Educational Statistics.

Krashen, S. (1985). *The input hypothesis: Issues and implications.* New York: Longman.

LaCelle-Peterson, & Rivera, C. (1994). Is it real for all kids? A framework for equitable assessment policies for English language learners. *Harvard Educational Review, 64*, 55–75.

Lysynchuk, L., Pressley, M., & Vye, M. (1990). Reciprocal teaching improves standardized reading comprehension performance of poor comprehenders. *The Elementary School Journal, 90*, 470–484.

Olson, C. (1996). *Reading, thinking, and writing about multicultural literature.* Glenview, IL: Scott Foresman.

O'Malley, M. J. (1981). *Children's services study: Language minority children with limited English proficiency in the United States.* Rosslyn, VA: National Clearinghouse for Bilingual Education.

Padrón, Y. N. (1991). Commentary. In B. Means, C. Chelemer, & M. S. Knapp (Eds.), *Teaching advanced skills to at-risk students: Views from research and practice* (pp. 131–140). San Francisco, CA: Jossey Bass.

Padrón, Y. N., & Knight, S. L. (1989). Linguistic and cultural influences on classroom instruction. In H. P. Baptiste, J. Anderson, J. Walker de Felix, & H. C. Waxman (Eds.), *Leadership, equity, and school effectiveness* (pp. 173–185). Newbury Park, CA: Sage.

Padrón, Y. N., & Waxman, H. C. (1988). The effect of ESL students' perceptions of their cognitive reading strategies on reading achievement. *TESOL Quarterly, 22*, 146–150.

Padrón, Y. N., & Waxman, H. C. (1993). Teaching and learning risks associated with limited cognitive mastery in science and mathematics for limited-English proficient students. In Office of Bilingual Education and Minority Language Affairs (Eds.), *Proceedings of the Third National Research Symposium on Limited English Proficient Students: Focus on middle and high school issues* (Vol. 2, pp. 511–547). Washington, DC: National Clearinghouse for Bilingual Education.

Palinscar, A., & Brown, A. (1984). Reciprocal teaching of comprehension-fostering and comprehension-monitoring activities. *Cognition and Instruction, 1*, 117–175.

Palinscar, A., & Brown, A. (1985). Reciprocal teaching: A means to a meaningful end. In J. Osborn, P. Wilson, & R. C. Anderson (Eds.), *Reading education: Foundations for a literate America* (pp. 299–310). Lexington, MA: Lexington Books.

Pallas, A. M., Natriello, G., & McDill, E. L. (1989). The changing nature of the disadvantaged: Current dimensions and future trends. *Educational Researcher, 18*(5), 16–22.

Pearson, P., & Johnson, D. (1978). *Teaching reading comprehension.* New York: Holt, Rinehart, & Winston.

Perez, B. (1993). Biliteracy practices and issues in secondary schools. *Peabody Journal of Education, 69*, 1–132.

Peyton, J., Jones, C., Vincent, A., & Greenblatt, L. (1994). Implementing writing workshop for ESOL students: Visions and realities. *TESOL Quarterly, 28*, 469–487.

Samuels, B., & Beers, K. (1996). *Your reading: An annotated booklist for middle school and junior high 1995–96 edition.* Urbana, IL: National Council of Teachers of English.

Schon, I. (1989). Recent books about Hispanics. *Journal of Youth Services in Libraries, 2*(2), 157–162.

Steffenson, M., Joag-Dev, C., & Anderson, R. (1979). A cross-cultural perspective on reading comprehension. *Reading Research Quarterly, 15*, 10–29.

Stein, M., Leinhardt, G., & Bickell, W. (1989). Instructional issues for teaching students at risk. In R. E. Slavin, N. L. Karweit, & N. A. Madden (Eds.), *Effective programs for students at risk* (pp. 145–194). Boston, MA: Allyn & Bacon.

Waxman, H. C., Padrón, Y. N., & Knight, S. L. (1991). Risks associated with students' limited cognitive mastery. In M. C. Wang, M. C. Reynolds, & H. J. Walberg (Eds.), *Handbook of special education: Emerging programs* (Vol. 4, pp. 235–254). Oxford, England: Pergamon.

Wittrock, M. C. (1991). Educational psychology, literacy, and reading comprehension. *Educational Psychologist, 26*(2), 109–116.

A Focus on Response

Chapter 7

READER-RESPONSE THEORY IN THE MIDDLE SCHOOL

Robert Probst

Literary Experience

Picture *literature*. Or better yet, picture *literary experience*. A book, if that's what the word *literature* brings to mind, is easy to visualize—a simple concrete object that anyone can conjure up. So, too, is a reader, though your images will vary tremendously. *Literary experience*, however, is an abstract concept, harder to see.

If you were asked to represent literary experience in a sketch, after the obligatory protests about your artistic limitations, you'd probably draw something that looked like a man sitting in a comfortable wing-back chair, his feet propped up on a footstool, a small pillow supporting his head, a cup of coffee on the light-stand next to him, a pleasant fire burning on the hearth, and a good book in his hand. We'd know it's a good book by the slight smile on his face. Or perhaps you'd sketch a woman in sunglasses, relaxing in a beach chair, basking in the sun or shaded by a beach umbrella, a cool drink propped in the sand close beside her, and a good book in her hand. We'd know it's a good book by her total indifference to the rowdy middle school students tossing a Frisbee in the background, yelling, running around, and making nuisances of themselves as we all know middle school students are inclined to do.

Whatever you sketch, the same theme is likely to emerge. The scene you draw will be calm, comfortable, pleasant. The reader will be quiet, reflective. We'll see escape from the burdens of the day into the pleasures of an imaginary world, or perhaps we'll see quiet contemplation of new ideas, new visions of human possibilities. We may even see excitement over some vicarious adventure, or the pleasant terror of an imaginary danger. But even if the sketch does capture that excitement or terror, it will still be in the image of a solitary reader sitting with a book in hand conjuring experience out of print on paper.

Unpredictable Kids

And that's the problem, or part of it. The middle school students, those rowdy, noisy, sullen, exuberant, caring, inconsiderate, thoughtless, thoughtful kids throwing Frisbees in the background of your drawing—and occasionally straying into the foreground to kick sand into your iced tea—aren't ideally constituted for sitting quietly with book in hand. They are discovering themselves, discovering that they are changing in disconcerting ways, discovering that the species is divided into two sexes (the opposite one of which is both troubling and fascinating), discovering that their parents aren't always right (or always wrong, depending on what they had always been during elementary school days), and otherwise involved in the distractions of impending adolescence. They are erratic, changeable, unpredictable, one moment high-strung and the next unstrung, one moment climbing the walls and the next asleep at their desks. The middle school classroom is not the place for a teacher who likes the calming regularity of an unvarying routine and a placid classroom.

Unpredictable Experiences

There are, of course, other problems. First, the scene you sketch might not remotely resemble the one I predicted, that quiet, contemplative, Norman Rockwell image of the reflective reader alone with a good book. You might, for instance, have drawn a more social scene, perhaps a grandparent with a little child balanced on each knee, all struggling to see the book they're reading together; or perhaps you may have imagined a full class, gathered in the library, listening to the librarian's rendition of a classic. You might have sketched a book group, if you happen to be a member of one, gathered around a coffee table and a bottle of wine, discussing whatever book was chosen for this month. You might have imagined a theater, filled with people watching Shakespeare or Ibsen, or a coffee house with a small crowd listening to an unknown poet. There is no one image of a *literary experience*, as there is no single sketch of the middle school student that could do justice to the confusing diversity that group offers. Literary experience, the actual encounter between a reader and a text, is too complex to allow for reduction to a simple formula.

Efferent and Aesthetic Stances

Occasionally we may, in our efforts to conceptualize readings, oversimplify. We have, for example, tended to view reading as the process of extracting meaning from texts. If we're reading cookbooks or outboard motor manuals, that may be an appropriate conception. When reading that sort of material, our likely purpose is to obtain information—we want to know the ingredients of ratatouille or the proper gap setting for the spark plugs. We probably do *not* go to the outboard manual for the thrill of the narrative, or for insights into the human condition, or to luxuriate in the mellifluous flow of the prose. We want information—facts, instructions, suggestions—so that we can tune it up, crank it up, and go fishing.

Similarly, we read an argumentative essay or a political speech in order to extract, if not information, then ideas. We want to know where the writer stands, what he believes, what he would have us think or do. We are likely to reason with the text, trying to draw inferences, speculate about consequences, or otherwise analyze and interpret. We may try to decide whether or not we agree with the positions offered.

Such reading, the sort we do to learn how to perform a certain task, or to obtain information we need, or to participate in an argument, Rosenblatt (1968) calls *efferent* reading. The emphasis in such reading is on what we carry away with us from the encounter with the text. We read the outboard manual because we want to possess, when we close the book, the information we need to get the machine operating again. If the prose is smooth, pleasant, clever, and amusing, so much the better. If, as we read, we come to feel affection and admiration for the writer and begin to think of him as an old friend, that's fine. But we don't go to the text to be amused or make a new friend—what is absolutely essential is that we find in the text the information and instruction we need.

We don't, however, go to novels, poems, stories, movies, songs, and plays with the same purpose. Here, in the genres we think of as literary, we seek experience more so than information. We hope to participate in the events the novelist offers us, feel the rhythms of the poet's language, hear the melodies of the song, or sense the developing tension of a dramatic scene on the stage. We'd probably be content, working on the outboard, if a friend took the manual out of our hands and offered to read through it, extracting the instructions and summarizing them for us as we handled the wrenches. Fixing the motor, after all, is the point of the reading. If, however, that friend told us about a wonderful movie he'd seen the night before, we'd be less likely to be content with his summary alone. If, in fact, his summary is convincing, and the movie does sound good, then we are all the more likely to demand to see it ourselves. The experience of the movie is the point; the report about it, no matter how good, is inadequate. To know that almost everyone thinks *Jurassic Park* exciting is not the same thing as experiencing the excitement ourselves.

Reading (or viewing) of this sort Rosenblatt (1968) calls *aesthetic*. Essential in such reading is the *living through*, the experiencing of the text, sensitive to all aspects of the encounter—the emotions awakened, the images evoked, the memories elicited, the thoughts aroused. Adopting the aesthetic stance toward a text doesn't, of course, preclude acquiring information, analyzing the logic or design, drawing inferences about the writer's values, assessing his purpose or his logic, or any of the other intellectual activities possible for a reader. The aesthetic stance, however, welcomes attention to matters that go beyond the text and its immediate utility, and the reader who adopts this stance may find himself attending to the music of the language, reflecting on memories of personal experience, even telling his own stories. If efferent reading is purposeful and directed, working toward a defined end, then aesthetic reading is exploratory and responsive, alert to unforeseen possibilities, curious about detours and digressions, playful and experimental, Above all, it acknowledges the uniqueness of the reader. It respects the fact that each reader brings to the text an unduplicated history and the unique perspective that results. The experience of the text, consequently, is unique for each reader. What he makes of it, what it means, depends not simply on the words on the page, but also on who it is who reads them.

Even when there is one short text, the possibilities are virtually endless. Granted, the text may be stable and finite—a poem, perhaps, with so many lines and so many words, no more and no fewer, unchanged since the day it was first printed except for font, surrounding text, and other cosmetic matters. The readers, however, are clearly *not* so stable and finite. They differ from one another in background, ability, interest, maturity, and family circumstance. They even differ from themselves as the days go by, their moods change, and their adolescent fortunes swing from good to bad and back again. Unless we can assume that the poem (or short story, or whatever text we happen to be teaching) contains its meaning and significance, unless we believe that there is one and only one correct and proper way to read the poem, then we have to acknowledge that those differences between students—and within each student—will shape the literary experience.

It's fairly obvious to anyone who has taught young adolescents—or any other group, for that matter—that meaning does *not* reside purely and simply within the text. Words, symbols of any kind, operate only when they enter the mind. Until a mind encounters them, responding to them and making some of the links they suggest and others that our unique individual histories provide, the words are little more than ink on paper. Glance at a poem in Russian (or if you happen to know Russian, try one in Icelandic). What sort of poetic experience results? Is it more closely akin to reading Wordsworth or to reading a page of chemical formulas? Since we are unable to respond to the unknown language, to make any connections, the poem lies there unpoetic and inert despite the immense potential it may hold for someone who knows the language and may be able to make the creative endeavor demanded by the text. The words don't function, not because they are deficient in themselves, but because the reader's mind is unable to make the connections that will yield emotion and image. The text fails to become a poem for the reader, not because it is defective or inadequate, but because the reader isn't able to transform it into a poem. There is nothing of poetry in the experience because the reader is unable to *make* poetry of the text. Those words must enter a mind, and the mind must perform, if a poem is to emerge from the text.

A Small Experiment in Chaos

And if the mind does perform, then the poem that it creates will be unique, because the mind is unique. That, too, is easy to demonstrate, both for ourselves and for our students. Ask them to help you with a small experiment, requiring only pencil and paper and a few minutes cooperation. Tell them that you'd like them to relax, breathe deeply, and clear their minds as best they can. Explain that after a few moments of silence you're going to give them one word, and that you'd like them to concentrate on that word for a short time to see what it calls to mind for them. Tell them that after you've given them the word you'll allow a few quiet moments for them to hold it in mind, and then, when you say "Now," they should write down whatever word, image, or thought happens to be in their heads at that precise moment. They won't have to write much—just a word or phrase or perhaps several if they can't resist.

When they're quiet and ready, run the experiment. Give them ten seconds or so of calm, then state the word. Choose something simple. "Red" is fine, or "car," or "dog." It should be something all will know and will have known since they were three or four. Give them another 5 or 10 seconds before calling time and asking them to write down whatever word or phrase is in their minds at that point. Then collect their jottings and put them on the board. A simple, concrete noun like "car," a word that any 3- or 4-year-old in this country will inevitably and unavoidably know, is likely to evoke from a group of 30 students 20, or 30, or 40 different associations. If your class is in a mood to discuss, ask them what they infer about the nature of language from the variety of terms they see there. They'll likely say that we all know what a car is, and, on the other hand, that none of us knows exactly what another thinks of when he hears that word.

Even with such a simple referential term like "car," meaning does not reside solely in the text itself, those three letters grouped together on the page. What that word means depends, to some degree, upon who reads it. It depends upon the reader's experience—what sort of car he drives, what sort of car he covets, whether he has recently bought a car, wrecked a car, stolen a car. . . . We bring to the text an imprecise agreement about some of the boundaries the term draws for us—trucks and buses are excluded, while convertibles and station wagons are both included—but within the area of agreement there is a great deal of variability. The specific images we each see will be uniquely our own. The memories and emotions awakened by the term will be ours alone, shaped not only by the word but also by our own history.

Complicating Matters Still Further

Now, if that's the case with a term such as "car," a simple word offered up by itself, how much more complicated must the situation be when the word is not simple and concrete? If meaning varies so widely with a word like "car," what sort of consensus should we expect with "love," or "joy," or "right," or "good?" These words don't point to objects sitting in the parking lot, but rather to abstractions drawn from human experience. We may all know what "love" is—at least, we all use the term as if we do—but again, as with "car," we probably have only a vague notion what it means to those sitting next to us. We don't know what happy or painful memories it awakens in our neighbor, what faces and names pass through his mind when he hears the word. Complicate the situation still further by taking one of those short, difficult words out of isolation and placing it in the context of a sentence, with other equally evocative and imprecise words, and the likelihood that we will all understand that sentence in exactly the same way grows slim. Finally, to make matters hopelessly complex, locate that sentence among many others in a poem, or a short story, or a novel. The situation grows complicated very quickly.

Meaning, whether we're referring only to single, isolated words or to such complicated constructions as poems and plays, depends upon the reader. It doesn't exist independently. Consider such a short text as Langston Hughes's *Poem*:

> I loved my friend.
> He went away from me.
> There's nothing more to say.
> The poem ends,
> Soft as it began—
> I loved my friend.

It's an accessible text, not a word in it over two syllables in length, consisting of three direct, simple, declarative sentences and one only slightly more complicated. Yet even with such a simple text the possibilities are infinite. Consider the elements of the child's life that might shape responses to this text. There are children in the middle school—not many, perhaps, but some—who have led charmed lives and may never have lost a friend. For one student, the most tragic loss was a friend's move to Canada, far enough away so that parents would only allow two or three long-distance calls a week. On the other hand, there are also children in the middle school who have lost friends violently. In some schools that may well be the norm. In a classroom in one middle school I visited recently, virtually every child in the room had lost a friend or a neighbor to a knife or a gun, and some had even witnessed the killing.

What will these two different readers—the one who laments a good friend's move to Toronto, and the other who has watched a good friend shot and killed—make of this text? Will they read it in the same way? Should they read it in the same way? Is there a meaning—single, unitary, unvarying—that any reader, despite his own unique circumstances, should be able to extract from these 25 words?

Granted, we can build some arguments for one interpretation or another. Perhaps we could argue that the second line, "He went away from me," indicates volition on the part of the friend. Hughes seems to suggest, we might infer, that the friend left of his own accord. Otherwise, Hughes might have said something like, "He was taken away from me." It's a line of reasoning that seems to exclude violence. The friend left willingly; he wasn't taken away by force or unhappy circumstance. This poem, we might conclude, is not about violence, not about killing, but about some other, quieter loss of friendship.

It's a legitimate, persuasive argument. How persuaded would you be, however, if you had, yourself, recently lost a friend violently? If a teacher said to you, "Your thoughts about violence are irrelevant here because this poem is about something else," would you be inclined to say, on the one hand, "Yes, sorry—I was getting us off track, my own experience intruded and corrupted my reading of this text and I will lay my own memories aside in the interest of more precise and accurate interpretation?" Or would you say, on the other hand, "If I'm not allowed to think and speak about my own loss, which this text called to mind for me, then the poem can shed no light on my experience, and I'll lay the text aside to think about matters more important to me at the moment"?

To deny the reader the opportunity to deal with his own unique responses is to insist that he deny himself, and in so doing is to reduce the reading of the poem to an exercise in extracting or decoding. There may be little that we can extract from this Hughes poem. We can't learn much about his friend, the nature of his loss, even whether or not it is, in fact, Hughes's friend that the poem mourns. But there is much that we can *make* of the text, if we bring to bear upon it our own experiences, our own memories of friendship and loss. The poem is more than the text. Just as the word "car" is more than its dictionary definition, so, too, is the poem more than a single interpretation. As the word "car" is bound up in our experience of cars, so, too, is the poem bound up in whatever aspects of our lives it calls to mind.

Literary works are not simply repositories of information or puzzles to be solved; rather, they are catalysts for complex experiences that involve our minds, memories, and emotions. What the text evokes, what it awakens in the mind of the reader, however unpredictable and unexpected it may be, *is* the poem for that reader at that time. If a quiet and gentle text like Hughes's *Poem* evokes in a student's mind images of violence and brutality, then those images *are* his experience of the text and thus they are the poem he makes of it. To tell him that he's wrong, that his reading isn't allowed by the words, is foolish, unfair, and worse. It tells him not only that he has failed to read well, but also, and more significantly, that he doesn't count. His experience, it says, doesn't matter—what matters is the experience of the poet, or perhaps of the poet's imagined character. Only students who have been sufficiently beaten down by years of such instruction will accept this casual dismissal of their own lives. But if they have any resilience at all, they know that they *do* matter.

So What?

If you accept this conception of literary experience, then the text, immutable and permanent as it is, offers us only an illusory sense of security. Unchanging as it may be, once it enters those diverse minds of its many readers and is transformed by the transaction into a poem or a story it becomes many different things. The single *text*, in our class of 30 students, is suddenly 30 *poems*, each unique, all tied in some way to that single text but also to those 30 different lives. As if we didn't have enough problems— dealing with students in some of the most chaotic years of their lives—this conception of literary experience removes yet another source of stability. Accepting this notion of literary experience has troubling, but also exciting, implications for the middle school classroom.

An Invitation to Talk

One implication, clearly, is that we need to have a broad and inclusive notion of what's appropriate in classroom discourse about literature. We need to redefine talk about literature so that it includes more than interpretation. It is, of course, perfectly appropriate to talk about Hughes's thoughts and emotions as we discuss *Poem*; but it's also appropriate to talk about our own. Talk that seems digressive and off-the-point in a class devoted to finding the one correct reading might be accepted as logical and desirable in a class dedicated to exploring various readings, respectful of the unique lives of individuals and intent upon helping students learn to make sense of their own experiences, both textual and otherwise. Rosenblatt (p. 76, 1968) has argued that a student "can begin to achieve a sound approach to literature only when he reflects upon his response to it, when he attempts to understand what in the work and in himself produced that reaction, and when he thoughtfully goes on to modify, reject, or accept it." If that is true, then the class has to welcome talk not only about the work, but also the reader's response to it, and to what in the reader himself produced that reaction. Thus our own stories are to be welcomed. It may seem a digression, perhaps an indulgence, to spend time telling stories about our own lost friends—the kid next door who moved to Chicago, the kid in the next class who suddenly forgot about us and took other friends, the kindly, elderly neighbor who died, the aunt who went into a distant nursing home. . . . None of those folks, after all, are in the text. Hughes doesn't know any of them. But if they are evoked by the text, then they are part of the reader's *poem*.

Welcoming those stories into the classroom requires a change in our notion of work, our understanding of what it is to be "*on-task*." Those free-flowing discussions of our own experiences are more than just bull sessions, and both teacher and student must come to realize that they are at the core of literary experience. They tie the literature to our lives, and our lives to the literature, and as we talk about those experiences, in the light of the text, we have the opportunity to sharpen our understanding of ourselves and our place in the world. The text gives us that opportunity. Without it, we aren't invited to speak of our own most significant experiences. I can't collar you and say, "Let me tell you about my long-lost friend," without inspiring a certain anxiety and uneasiness. But sharing the Hughes poem invites me to speak of that friend, and it invites you to speak of yours, and thus it enables us to explore an aspect of our lives that might otherwise be neglected. Literature, first and foremost, is an invitation to talk.

And so the classroom discussion must become more than interrogation or recitation. The carefully structured discussion, leading logically, irresistibly, to a conclusion, may be appropriate for some purposes, but it must be balanced with less-tightly controlled designs. The list of the questions that have dominated so much discussion of literature in classrooms must be expanded. In addition to such a question as "What did the author mean by the image in lines 10–12?" we need to ask "What did you see or think when you came to the image in lines 10–12?" As well as asking, "What does the character's behavior in this story indicate that he values most highly?" we need to ask something like "What do you value most highly, and how would you have acted in this situation?" We need to raise questions that will invite the students to reflect on their own experiences, to consider thoughtfully the experiences of their classmates, to notice how the context of the moment shapes their reading, and to observe the strategies and designs of the writer. We need, in other words, to involve them in the creative act of making meaning out of texts.

Though self-direction is the goal, at first students may need a fair amount of teacher-direction. You might try various approaches to setting up discussions, prefacing all with the reminder that if the students have thoughts or responses that arise naturally from the reading, they should pursue them. A diverse repertoire of fairly open questions may help. Myers (1988) suggests these:

1. What character(s) was your favorite? Why?

2. What character(s) did you dislike? Why?

3. Does anyone in this work remind you of anyone you know? Explain.

4. Are you like any character in this work? Explain.

5. If you could be any character in this work, who would you be? Explain.

6. What quality(ies) of which character strikes you as a good characteristic to develop within yourself over the years? Why? How does the character demonstrate this quality?

7. Overall, what kind of a feeling did you have after reading a few paragraphs of this work? Midway? After finishing the work?

8. Do any incidents, ideas, or actions in this work remind you of your own life or something that happened to you? Explain.

9. Do you like this piece of work? Why or why not?

10. Are there any parts of this work that were confusing to you? Which parts? Why do you think you got confused?

11. Do you feel there is an opinion expressed by the author through this work? What is it? How do you know this? Do you agree? Why or why not?

12. Do you think the title of this work is appropriate? Is it significant? Explain. What do you think the title means?

13. Would you change the ending of this story in any way? Tell your ending. Why would you change it?

14. What kind of person do you feel the author is? What makes you feel this way?

15. How did this work make you feel? Explain.

16. Do you share any of the feelings of the characters in this work? Explain.

17. Sometimes works leave you with the feeling that there is more to tell. Did this work do this? What do you think might happen?

18. Would you like to read something else by this author? Why or why not?

19. What do you feel is the most important word, phrase, passage, or paragraph in this work? Explain why it is important.

20. If you were an English teacher, would you want to share this work with your students? Why or why not?

Or you might consider some of these (Probst, 1977):

1. What is your first reaction or response to the text? Describe or explain it briefly.

2. What feelings did the text awaken in you? What emotions did you feel as you read the text?

3. What did you see happening in the text? Paraphrase it—retell the major events briefly.

4. What image was called to mind by the text? Describe it briefly.

5. What memory does the text call to mind—of people, places, events, sights, smells, or even of something more ambiguous, perhaps feelings or attitudes?

6. What idea or thought was suggested by the text? Explain it briefly.

7. Upon what, in the text, did you focus most intently as you read—what word, phrase, image, idea?

8. What is the most important word in the text?

9. What is the most important phrase in the text?

10. What is the most difficult word in the text?

11. What is there in the text or in your reading that you have the most trouble understanding?

12. What sort of person do you imagine the author of this text to be?

13. How did your reading of the text differ from that of your discussion partner (or the others in your group)? In what ways were they similar?

14. How did your understanding of the text or your feelings about it change as you talked?

15. Do you think the text is a good one—why, or why not?

16. Does this text call to mind any other literary work (poem, play, film, story—any genre)? If it does, what is the work and what is the connection you see between the two?

17. If you were to be asked to write about your reading of this text, upon what would you focus? Would you write about some association or memory, some aspect of the text itself, about the author, or about some other matter?

18. What did you observe about your discussion partner (or the others in your group) as the talk progressed?

Of course there are no correct or incorrect answers to such questions as these. They are questions to explore, to play with, rather than measures of the accuracy with which students have read and remembered. They may serve to validate or approve ways of thinking about literary experience. The last question above, for instance, suggests that curiosity about how others have responded to a text is appropriate, and further that literary discussions might lead to sharpened understanding not only of oneself and of the author and the work, but also of other readers. After working with such questions, you might suggest that on some occasions students set themselves the task of formulating their own questions. With some provocative or problematic piece, assign them the task of formulating, as they read or immediately after they have read, one significant question about the reading. By *significant question* I mean one for which there is no easy answer, perhaps no answer at all. A few examples might help them, if they require it, so they understand that "What kind of car did the hero drive?" is a poorer question than "Why was his car so significant to the hero?"

Students need to learn to raise their own questions. If they've had years of waiting for the teacher to ask all the questions this may not be easy. It requires them to accept responsibility for their own thinking, to be assertive and inquiring as they read, to pay attention to their responses and try to catch them. Journals and reading logs help sustain discussion and move students toward this desirable independence. If they haven't had experience with journals, however, they need to be taught how to use them. They need to know that a journal is more than notes on what happened. It is instead a place to record reactions to a reading, to express feelings awakened, to tell stories that come to mind, to articulate and perhaps to answer questions that arise as they read. A journal or log is a tool to make the reader more active, a strategy to transform reading from a passive, receptive act into an active performance. By asking the reader to shape his emotional and intellectual responses to a text, the task of writing entries draws the reader into a collaboration with the text in the making of meaning.

An Invitation to Write

A vision of literary experience that respects the unique responses of readers also places a heavy burden on them. It doesn't offer them meaning ready-made, but requires them to make meaning themselves, and thus demands that they write. Talk serves its purposes—it's exploratory, tentative, probing, free wheeling, and it builds the society of the classroom—but writing allows the private, solitary building of complex personal reactions to texts. Journals are of course a start toward more extensive writing. The immediate and perhaps impulsive and unedited responses that accumulate in a journal or log will serve students as a reservoir, but some of the seeds that gather there need to be cultivated, giving the student the experience of persevering, of staying with a confusion until it becomes a thought, of toying with a thought until it matures into an idea, of working with an idea until it becomes a decision or a commitment. Longer response papers may perhaps wait until high school years, when increasing sophistication and maturity enable students to sustain work on an issue over longer hours and more pages, but middle grade students may be encouraged to hang onto an idea long enough to produce a coherent paper, long enough that it allows its writer to discover something about himself or the text.

The letter is the ideal genre for this writing. It encourages the student to visualize a particular reader, sharpening his sense of audience, and it allows a personal voice, leading gently away from the mechanical, plodding language that is first instilled by the five-paragraph essay and ultimately culminates in the pseudo-objective impersonality of bad dissertation prose. The letter is a link between two people who know each other or would like to know each other. It typically explores something of significance to the writer, perhaps to the reader, too, and so it matters. A real letter, the sort you and I might write, isn't assigned writing, a task imposed by a teacher, and there is a danger, of course, that assigning the letter will drain it of some of its virtues, but the form nonetheless has merit in the classroom. Consider this admittedly fictional letter from Cleary's *Dear Mr. Henshaw* (1984). Leigh has initiated a correspondence with his favorite writer, and here comments on his most recent book:

January 15

Dear Mr. Henshaw,

    I finished *Beggar Bears* in two nights. It is a really good book. At first I was surprised because it wasn't funny like your other books, but then I got to thinking (you said authors should think) and decided a book doesn't have to be funny to be good, although it often helps. This book did not need to be funny.

    In the first chapter I thought it was going to be funny. I guess I expected it because of your other books and because the mother bear was teaching her twin cubs to beg from tourists in Yellowstone Park. Then when the mother died because a stupid tourist fed her a cupcake in a plastic bag and she ate the bag, too, I knew this was going to be a sad book. Winter was coming on, tourists were leaving the park and the little bears didn't know how to find food for themselves. When they hibernated because they had eaten all the wrong things and hadn't stored up enough fat, I almost cried. I sure was relieved when the nice ranger and his boy found the young bears and fed them and the next summer taught them to hunt for the right things to eat.

I wonder what happens to the fathers of bears? Do they just go away?

Sometimes I lie awake listening to the gas station pinging, and I worry because something might happen to Mom. She is so little compared to most moms, and she works so hard. I don't think Dad is that much interested in me. He didn't phone when he said he would.

I hope your book wins a million awards.

Sincerely,
Leigh Botts

The letter demonstrates much that we hope to accomplish with young students in teaching them literature. Leigh begins talking about his responses to the book—it wasn't funny, but he liked it anyway. He reflects upon himself as a reader and demonstrates that he is aware of his own growth—his expectations of texts have changed, so that now he no longer demands that a book be amusing. Then he talks about the text, itself, retelling parts of the story and explaining their effect on him as he read. Ultimately, with little transition, perhaps without quite realizing how he got there, he finds himself reflecting upon his own life in the light of the book. He wonders if the fathers of bears just go away, and then he thinks of his own father, who just went away, and of the consequences of that loss for himself and his mother.

Leigh's one or two pages of writing take him to the verge, at least, of perceptions about his own circumstances. The literature has moved him, compelled him to think about the events it portrays, and led him in the end to reflect upon his own life. The writing of the letter offered him solitude and sustained attention to an idea so his thoughts could take shape, so that he could find the words that enabled him, at least for the moment, to cope with his own experiences.

If the literature, and the activities we design around the literature, do as much for the middle school students we teach, we will have accomplished a great deal. The students in these tumultuous years are beginning to shape their visions of themselves and their possibilities; the literature they read is an invitation to articulate those evolving visions, to consider all the possibilities that lie ahead, to explore the depth and range of their emotions, to question the values and beliefs that will define their character. It is an opportunity and an invitation to begin to take responsibility for becoming the people they will ultimately be.

References

Myers, K. (1988). Twenty (better) questions. *English Journal, 77* (1), 64–65.

Probst, R. (1988). Dialogue with a text. *English Journal, 77* (1), 32–38.

Rosenblatt, L. (1968). *Literature as exploration* (3rd ed). New York: Noble & Noble.

Trade Book Cited

Cleary, B. (1984). *Dear Mr. Henshaw*. New York: Dell.

Chapter 8

THEMATIC UNITS AND

READERS' WORKSHOP:

HOW THE TWO CONNECT

Mary Santerre

Several years ago when I moved to a small town, no high school English positions were available, but there was one opening in the middle school teaching sixth grade reading. Surely if I could teach *Macbeth* and *Great Expectations* I could teach sixth grade, right? Not exactly. I wasn't even finished with the first week of school when I realized my students were not remotely interested in the life of Pip. Not only was the literature I knew too difficult and not age appropriate, but my students wanted to read stories that had something to do with *their* lives. So I was forced to scramble and to search for another way that my students would engage in this act of reading that I had found so pleasurable in my own life.

Here I am, ten years later, teaching eighth grade in middle school, still trying to motivate my students and make them feel the same way I do about wanting to read for a lifetime, not just for a class. In the ten years of my reading/writing process I've participated in writing projects, taken young adult literature classes, finished a master's degree in English and read Rosenblatt, Probst, Atwell, Rief, and others to help me become a more effective reading workshop teacher. If there's one underlying message that I can relay to the aspiring workshop teacher, it is that the process of building a workshop classroom does not happen by chance. Instead, transforming a classroom into a student-centered/teacher-assisted workshop is like putting together a puzzle; numerous attempts at making the pieces fit require patience, hard work and extensive risk-taking before the puzzle starts to fit together, but the rewards are incredibly worth the effort when you start to see the picture taking form.

Before I put the pieces together, I had to know what the pieces are and what they mean in building this classroom where students find learning *relevant*. The first important piece of information that I learned about middle schoolers is that the reading must be relevant to their lives; they must relate to the characters they are reading about, and they must be able to travel down those characters' roads of experience. What is key about this piece of the puzzle is that not every book will be relevant to every child; therefore, choice is mandatory in reading workshop. Students need to read about characters with whom they find a connecting cord of experience. Consider Stephen's response (see Figure 8.1) to Sarah Byrnes in Chris Crutcher's *Staying Fat for Sarah Byrnes*:

Figure 8.1 Stephen's Response to *Staying Fat for Sarah Byrnes*

When Maggie read of Stella's depression in *Home Before Dark* (Bridgers), she could very easily relate to Stella's having to get along with a stepmother (see Figure 8.2).

When Rachel read *Katy Did* (Stanek), a book in which Katy, the protagonist, gives away part of her physical, psychological and emotional self to another human being's control, Rachel responds on an even more universal level of how a book like this one relates to the lives of many modern teenagers (see Figure 8.3).

Figure 8.2 Maggie's Response to *Home Before Dark*

I was surprised that Maggie and James Earl got married after only a short time of really knowing each other as adults and the frankness of James Earl and his feelings for Maggie was hard for me to conceive. But frankly I was very happy of the outcome. At first when Stella would not move into Maggie's home I was depressed because I once was in the same situation. Both my parents are remarried and like Stella I had to start again almost like I had a new family. When my dad remarried he married an attractive young woman by the name of Natalie. It was hard for me to accept the fact that would have to share my dad with another. Ant I think it was hard for her as well that she would have to love me as well as her own children. At first I tried to ignore the fact that I was actually living with her but as soon as I loosed up I realized that she was great. She taught me to have fun and most of all how to love and how to accept love, just like Maggie and Stella.

[Handwritten marginal notes: "Wow! This is what I call writing from the heart!" and "I love your comparison"]

Figure 8.3 Rachel's Response to *Katy Did*

I think that this is a really good book for kids to read as a choice novel. It has a lot of strong topics but I think that eighth graders who feel they can handle it, can. I've never thought that some things could disturb kids, because (sad to say) the subjects this book deals with do happen. Death of a friend, teenagers having sex, these are all things kids deal with. I feel that this book should be put out as a choice novel and recommended to the future eighth grade. I think that kids will enjoy reading this book and it will touch them, like it does me. The writing in it is fabulous. Every scene is so clear and so vivid in my head because of the way she illustrates every thing. It is a great book and I think it should be read by kids.

Very Sincerely,
Rachel

Finding the relevant topics in the literature is just the beginning. Sources such as *Your Reading* (Samuels & Beers, 1996) and sessions at conventions provide the starting points to find books. What I have found is that I read extensively during the summer and add titles gradually each year. Figuring out how to structure the reading workshop and still teach the English elements of the class have been my challenge.

What works well for me is a thematic structuring of books. At my school, we are on the quarter system that allows for four 9-week thematic groupings. We generally read a text in common for 3 weeks of the quarter, and then students are allowed to choose other books in that theme for the remaining 6 weeks of the quarter. My most recent thematic groupings include: *A Light at the End of the Tunnel, Victims and Heroes, Other Times and Other Places,* and *Rebels With and Without Causes.* (See Appendix A for specific literature titles for each unit.)

In *A Light at the End of the Tunnel* we look at a variety of nonfiction, particularly people who have overcome personal obstacles in their lives. This year Gloria Estefan and Captain Scott O'Grady were two people whose life stories were enjoyed by my students. This common text experience allows me to include different cultures and different life experiences, which is part of the multicultural requirement of my curriculum. Students then went on to select other books about individuals who triumphed over adversity.

Moving from the personal experience to the more universal conflicts of man vs. society is the goal of the second quarter's *Victims and Heroes.* Our in-common text is Robert Cormier's *After The First Death.* In the wake of the Oklahoma City terrorist attack, a book about global terrorism seems not only timely, but logically relevant. Students choose a variety of books in order to further examine the topic of heroism and victimization. During the third quarter study of *Other Times and Other Places* common reading of myths and fables comprise the core reading shared by all students and historical fiction, science fiction and fantasy are genres from which students select their choice reading. During the last quarter as we focus on *Rebels With and Without Causes,* we read film text. This provides a different medium to which students may respond. Choice selections for the fourth quarter include books, short stories, and poetry about rebels. In this unit, students are forced to ask themselves two questions: Can there be a rebel without a cause? How do rebels relate to personal and societal adversity, thereby contributing to the heroism and victimization of a person?

In describing how thematic structuring is done, I'm often asked how I decide the thematic divisions and which books fall into which categories. Arne Sippola, in "When Thematic Units are Not Thematic Units," asserts that the "true thematic unit will focus on a literary theme—an underlying idea that ties the characters, the setting and the plot together" (Sippola, 1993). I tend to keep the basic literary conflicts (i.e., person vs. self; person vs. society, etc.) in mind when devising my broad categories. Then the selections of the literature that make up choice books and stories are designed to extract different thematic threads relevant to that conflict. In the *Light at the End of the Tunnel* unit, Kate comments on the theme of Ouida Sebestyen's *Out of Nowhere* and how it more specifically ties to the thematic grouping for the quarter (see Figure 8.4):

Figure 8.4 Kate's Response to *Out of Nowhere*

There is one paragraph that I believe really relates it this book. The "theme" of the book, Singer, is talking about her mother, who is dead, but is still with her. "She is dead. But I mean I feel her. Always close. People don't stop loving you just because they leave." This quote relates to his whole book in that everybody has to go. Harley is left, Singer's mom left, Harley starts to leave Ish, and Singer leaves. At the end of the book, Singer is moves on to be with her dad, and she says to Harley, "Remember on the picnic, what I said about my mom?" It just all makes me want to sigh. Although this book maybe a "hunkey dorey" ending, or be funny, yet sad, it has a lot of depth in it. May wanted to put a huge garden in her back yard, and Singer leaves a package of seeds for May when she left. It seems as though everything has significance in the novel.

What a wonderful image of the double rainbow in the end of the book to unite them all. Bill says to Harley and May, "Dang, I never get over that," he said. "How raindrops and light come together and make that." YES! This is the theme and direction! I take this as the raindrops being Bill, Harley, and May. The light being Singer. How amazing it is that raindrops and light can come together to form that wonderful rainbow! Ms. Santerre, talk about the light at the end of the tunnel Well, I enjoyed this book, and I do think that the author did a nice job putting the extra depth in the book. I hope that I will be able to read another humorous book like this and enjoy depth and character as much as I did in this book.

very!
true.

Sincerely,

Kate

The major points I try to remember when using thematic groupings are: 1) Keep the categories broad enough that a variety of literature can fit into the category; 2) Know that the books many times overlap in categories and can move from one category to another; and 3) Constantly add and delete books to the thematic groupings. No list is ever static. In addition to those points I also always look for some in-common reading. This is necessary because it is during the in-common reading that I teach literary elements. For example, if I'm trying to teach narrative structure, I use a specific piece of text from Cormier and then ask my students to be looking for those same elements as they read their individually-selected titles. Then when a student such as Billy points out the way Chris Crutcher relates his story, that response becomes the basis for another direct teaching lesson that would explain a literary element (see Figure 8.5):

Figure 8.5 Billy's Response to *Ironman*

> Undisputedly, my favorite part of this book are the letters to Mr. Larry King. I think that just the idea of writing a book like that is an accomplishment, but to actually write a book like that is increditable. I have just realized that he is not sending these letters, but just writing them and putting them in a folder to be sent at a later date. Did you know this? Also the letters are so in depth that to me they are the "highlights" of this book. I grin every single time that I see and read these wonderful accounts of Bo and the other's life. The letters, of course, do only tell what Bo thinks of a situation, but I think that it is a creative way to show what he is thinking instead of using the common way of just including the character's thoughts in to the subject matter of the book. I always like to know what the characters are thinking, but in a book that is poorly written this many times confuses me and many other readers.
>
> Well said! Narrative Structure is important!!
>
> the content is too mature?

The critical difference in teaching literary elements in reading workshop format is that I provide the initial schema when we read texts together, and then as the students begin their individualized reading I ask that they find evidence from their reading that helps them understand whatever literary element we are studying. A typical minilesson for a day might be for the entire class to look at Billy's observation and comment on Crutcher's narrative structure.

When I began to understand how the curricular piece of the puzzle could be put together, I started to face the intricate pieces of my puzzle, the pieces that needed to fit so that the seamless presentation of the picture would be complete. That is when the nitty-gritty questions just kept coming. How do I structure the days of the week in reading workshop? How do I decide which classics and which pieces of young adult fiction and nonfiction will be read? How do I get in all the curricular elements that need to be taught? How do I teach grammar in reading workshop? And—most importantly the question that continues to haunt me—How do I get it all covered?

To really understand how reading workshop works for me, you need to understand my role as a teacher. I no longer stand in front of the students for 45 minutes and deliver knowledge from my brain to theirs. Rather, each 45-minute class period consists of genuine reading/writing time for the students. If I do direct teaching to the entire class, I try to limit it to 15 minutes and cover a single literary element, or I try to cover an editing exercise such as punctuation or usage rules. Some days I do not do any whole-class teaching; rather, students are reading and writing, and I am conferencing with a group or with individuals.

One aspect of classroom management that bothered me the most when I first began to use a workshop approach was ensuring that the students were on task. The first 2 weeks of independent reading are critical; the students must know that their reading time is not "goof-off" time; reading quietly (in his or her own area) must be seen as a very important part of the instructional process. Consequently, in the beginning I don't individually conference as much as I do later. Instead, I model, model, model. I read with my students, and I respond. I share my thoughts with the students as I read, and I try to convey to them each day the passionate caring I have about words . . . the ones I am reading and the ones I am writing.

Gradually, as the students move into the books they have chosen, they are usually quite interested. If, however, I see that students are not getting into their selected books, then I get involved and suggest that they change books or change locations or whatever it takes to get them interested in reading. If I've done my book-talking job well, I've enticed most students to books that match both their interest and reading levels. Sometimes, though, the match isn't there, and we must together find a solution. Many times the adjustment will require that I drop the reading level of the novel in order for the student to experience the successful enjoyment of connecting to something that she reads. The most important principle I've found in guiding students to books is that I have to listen to what they are telling me and then go to my arsenal of possible books. Of course, inherent in this process is my having read the choice books. I must know the books in order to pique a student's interest; therefore, I am always reading and searching for the very best books possible!

If I were to describe myself now as literature teacher, I would characterize myself as a teacher who has shifted from a traditional authoritative keeper of knowledge to a tour guide on the vicarious journeys my students take in their reading experiences. I try to point out some memorable sights, answer questions about the terrain, and listen to their voices of observation regarding the scenery.

As tour guide, however, I still have the very traditional job of assessing my students. I have had to realize that the workshop model of reading and observation is quite individualized and what a student learns during the process can't necessarily be evaluated on a traditional 50-item objective test. Rather, assessment must come from their written response to the literature that they are reading. Recently I asked my students what they thought about reading and taking tests over what they had read. Mary's journal entry reveals her perspective of test-taking the *facts* of a book versus getting what the content of the book is about when she says (see Figure 8.6):

Figure 8.6 Mary's Journal Entry

Everyday I look forward to coming in and reading during sixth period. There is nothing I hate more than reading a book and knowing I will be tested on it. It is so distracting! I concentrate more on remembering facts rather than what the book really means.

As a literature teacher, my primary concern is that Mary understands what a book means. Isn't that critical interpretative analysis; isn't that thinking?

I have struggled with many methods during the last few years, but what I have concluded is that true response involves a variety of modes—letters, poetry, expository writing, drawings, book chat groups, and critical analysis to name a few. Deciding how to structure my students' responses during the year depends on my curricular objectives; I study my curriculum guide to see that in eighth grade I am required to teach a character sketch, a critical analysis paper, a poetry unit, etc. Then I decide how to expedite those objectives in student response. Is it easy? No. What I have found, however, is that all of the writing modes, the grammar usage through editing, and a high level of critical thinking can happen in a workshop classroom; it's just that the way the students get there is different from the way they would get there in the traditional classroom.

During my early days of teaching high school, my students' literary responses were guided by the traditional thesis essay that had guided my responses as a student. However, as a student I found this form restrictive, and as a teacher I discovered that was still true. After reading Kathleen Andrasick's *Opening Texts* (1990) I understood why. Andrasick argues that a response to literature should include a variety of modes, not just the traditional thesis-controlled essay. I could not agree more. The issue is not whether a thesis essay is a viable way to respond to a piece of literature; instead the question is whether students are capable of getting to that level of abstraction without prewriting informal responses and oral book discussions. I don't think eighth graders are ready. Therefore, our reading workshop begins with response letters intended to have students examine and explore text. They are not allowed to discuss plot summary; they are invited to dig in and explore character motive, the way the author tells the story, the author's use of figurative or symbolic language, etc. They write letters in a conversational tone that addresses traditional literary topics.

When I first begin the year, students write four letters during the time they are reading their choice novels: a daily letter about 30 pages into the book (which counts as a daily grade counted twice), a midpoint response (which counts as a quiz grade), a first draft final letter that is conferenced one on one, and then an edited and revised final letter. The revised and edited final letter counts as a test grade, but I also average all four responses as a process grade. In effect, in response to a given novel, students will receive two daily grades, one quiz grade, and two test grades: one product grade for the final letter and one overall process grade. All of the grading is done holistically based on a 4-point scale with specific criteria depending on the instructional objectives.

Early in the process, modeling what makes a 4-point versus a 2-point paper is critical. Also, another important part of my assessment process with the letters they write is that I don't grade the daily and quiz letters until they turn in their entire portfolio packet of responses. I do, however, keep informal notes in my own notebook that reminds me of the strengths and weaknesses of the initial responses. During the first three drafts, my goal is to build their confidence at analysis with my comments and to ask them to look further into what they are exploring in their analysis. Most importantly, on the daily and quiz drafts I do not grade grammatical and usage issues, although I may use an example from a student's paper to teach a minilesson if I see a usage problem many students are displaying. Students know that if I circle errors at this stage that they are to take note of them, but that my major assessment is based on their thinking and analysis.

In order to get a picture of a daily progress letter, let's return to Mary's response journal. (Incidentally, we have 12 word processors in our writing centers so students type their responses and save them on disks.) Mary chose Elizabeth Berg's *Durable Goods* as her first choice book during the first quarter. Her first daily response looks like this (see Figure 8.7):

Figure 8.7 Mary's Response to *Durable Goods*

9/15/95

Dear Ms. Santerre,

I am reading DURABLE GOODS by Elizabeth Berg. I am on page
thirty and I already know this will be one of my favorite books
ever. I like the way there are no chapters, just short
paragraphs. There are so many parts that I can just relate to.
Like the part when Katie shaves her legs. I can just remember
the time I first shaved my legs, and when I got out of the
shower, I was dripping blood everywhere. It just about scared me
half to death. The subject of puberty and growing up is just so
humorous. I don't like the way that Katie's dad handles things.
It disturbs me to think that kids like me would have to be scared
all the time about their parent abusing them. This book has
already made me wake up and smell the coffee. I now realize how
hard life can be living in such poor circumstances. I am so
lucky to live in a stationary place and have such loving parents.
This book is not like any other book I have ever read. It is as
realistic as a story gets without being true. The characters are
so likeable. When I think about Katie having to ask herself if
this would make her dad angry every time she does something, it
makes me so frustrated that no one can help her, no one can make
her life easier. I wish I could help Katie, I want her to have a
normal childhood and be carefree. I wish everyone could be
carefree. I'm hoping that this book will teach me lessons about
life. Lessons that I need to learn, lessons that reveal truth.

Sincerely,

Mary

Mary's daily response reveals her initial thoughts, observations, and questions about the book. She is commenting about the style of Elizabeth Berg when she is noticing that there are no chapters, she is examining a character when she makes the definitive statement that she doesn't like the way Katy's dad handles things, and she's beginning to focus on the theme of the novel in what she says will be "lessons of truth." It is now my job to respond to her in writing with questions meant to probe to the next level. Note that I am asking her to examine the details that make the book realistic to her, and I am urging her to continue with the ideas of these lessons she is learning. Mary will continue with this discussion in her progress letter about halfway through the book; I will comment back to her and ask her to elaborate in another direction that she has begun to explore. During this process of writing back, I also individually conference with her to discuss my comments as well as to get her to ask more questions.

When Mary finishes the letter, she writes the first draft of her final paper of response. This draft is usually three pages typewritten and is the draft that we call the edit draft. I respond to this draft and conference with Mary before she does her final letter, a second draft of the final paper in which she revises content and edits. When she turns in this fourth letter, she will also turn in her other drafts for assessment in what we call a portfolio packet with a cover sheet (see Figure 8.8):

Figure 8.8 Mary's Portfolio Packet Cover Sheet

Choice Book 1

DURABLE GOODS

LANGUAGE ENRICHMENT

Daily response: 4 Excellent thoughts

Quiz response: 3+ Brief - Remember - a full 2 pages to discuss thoughts

Final (Test) Response

1st draft 4 - a bit brief and edit!

2nd draft 4 Very, very nice writing!

Conference ✓

Comments: Your final P.S. has such strong ideas and feeling!

[illegible] 92

This four letter process requires students to answer direct questions from me on the subsequent drafts and demands that they dig a little deeper into text the next time they write. This drafting process is highly dependent on conferencing and editing techniques employed by the writing process. The reading and writing process is so intertwined in the response to a novel that it is impossible to separate the reading and writing workshop. The response-centered classroom is one big language workshop.

What I have learned about responding to literature is that these letters are only one piece, albeit a very important starting piece, to the response puzzle. When I was a neophyte reading teacher several years ago, Nancie Atwell's *In the Middle* (1987) was the invaluable starting point. Another important source that has influenced me to vary my response teaching is Andrasick's *Opening Texts*. Andrasick contends that letter writing, response journals, poetry response, and imitating text are all ways to respond to text. What I try to do is to begin with the letter approach and then branch out.

I encourage my students to vary their response patterns by asking them to keep a response journal. The fundamentals for responding in journals are similar to those for responding through letters. Students are asked to respond to the literature that they are reading. Sometimes I ask them to respond after a certain page number or chapter number. A typical chapter response in a journal might resemble Whett's response to Chris Crutcher's *Running Loose* (see Figure 8.9):

Figure 8.9 Whett's Response to *Running Loose*

> ## Chapter 5, "Take Him Out!"
>
> I haven't read past this point, but my guess is that this will be the precipitating event of the novel. Unlike my previous response, I think this was excellently written, almost downplaying the event. I absolutely hate racism, and this made my blood boil. Aren't people from Idaho supposed to be peaceful? I can't wait to keep reading.

As part of this response process, students make observations, judgments, and assertions just as they do in the letter process. Or, consider Bill's response journal to *Pierced by a Ray of Sun*, a poetry anthology edited by Ruth Gordon (see Figure 8.10).

Bill's response represents a conscious attempt by our class to read more poetry and respond to that poetry in similar yet different ways than we do to the choice fiction.

Figure 8.10 Bill's Response to *Pierced by a Ray of Sun*

This has some good poetry! One great line of many in the poem "End of the Beginning" is "Who knows why the Creator thins the herd." This line is so true because so many people wonder this. I think that God "thins the herd" so that we can come to be with God in heaven. This poem brings up many of "life's little wonders," and it is made very real by those things. Another reflective poet is Mary Sarton. She talks so much of nature that I think she has a large bond with nature in some way....

The poem "Aids" is also an example of a great comparative poem. It makes the comparison between fear and love very beautifully. I think that it is easily one of the best comparisons that I have EVER seen or read. Emily Dickinson writes of hope being like a bird and does it quite well.

Figure 8.11 Annie's Web

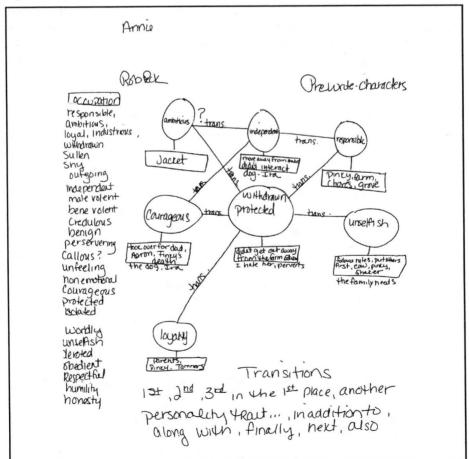

Response journals also serve as a repository of teaching and thinking ideas. When we begin to work toward structuring a more formal paper about character (that generally starts in letter or informal response), Annie's response journal illustrates how we would brainstorm and web about characters so that text can be used to support Annie's assertions about Rob Peck in *A Day No Pigs Would Die* (see Figure 8.11).

I introduce a wide variety of prewriting strategies including letters, journals, note-taking and webbing to generate the thoughts that are used in building a trained critical literary eye. As a high school student in the 1970s, I was expected to formulate this thesis or critical assertion without being given these opportunities to "scratch around" with my initial responses to what I was reading. What response theory and practice have done for me is to give the methodology to the thinking process that results in a higher level of interpretive processing and thus a written piece that has substance, voice, and meaning.

In addition to letter writing and journaling, I particularly enjoy asking students to engage in what Andrasick calls imitating and transforming text, bringing understanding to an even higher level of abstraction. When Emily read *The Diary of Adrian Mole* (Townsend) and *Go Ask Alice* (Anonymous) it seemed only natural for her to respond by creating her own diary (heavily fictionalized) that reflected her own adolescent eating disorder (see Figure 8.12):

Figure 8.12 Emily's Diary

September 10

Dear Diary,

This weekend was great Jenny and I spent the whole weekend together and I think we are going to be best friends. On Friday night we just did girl stuff like pig out and give each other makeovers. On Saturday Jon and his friend Mark took Jenny and me out to dinner and then we went to a movie. We had so much fun. I am so glad I was able to make such great friends. By the way Jenny taught me how to purge. Now I can eat all I want and not get fat! Isn't it great!

September 13

Dear Diary,

I have lost three pounds and I am still losing. Isn't that great. I think I am going to try eating lunch and dinner only. It is great to be thin! This weekend Jenny and I are going to go to the mall to buy new wardrobes. I have decided that my has become too drab.

Or when Sarah was reading Virginia Euwer Wolff's *Make Lemonade*, her response letter was intended to imitate Wolff's style (see Figure 8.13).

Figure 8.13 Sarah's Response to *Making Lemonade*

> Jolly is seventeen LaVaughn is fourteen
>
> Jolly's babies are Jeremy and Jilly
>
> Jeremy is older.
>
> I cannot imagine having two babies
>
> at such a young age
>
> LaVaughn is only three years younger
>
> than Jolly.
>
> She is shocked at how Jolly lives
>
> and that she has no education,
>
> and lives with two babies.
>
> This are my feelings exactly.

When students are asked to imitate text, they are asked to study the style, mood, and structure of the author's wording in a way that far exceeds the typical literary analysis exercise, one more way of getting students into the text in a nonsuperficial manner.

One favorite way of my students to analyze character is to transform the prose into poetry. When a student like Kate transforms the protagonist Valerie Michon in Norma Fox Mazer's *Out of Control*, she tells the story of sexual assault from Valerie's point of view; she, in effect, becomes that young, tortured girl trying to survive and cope with her loss of innocence (see Figure 8.14). Poetry succinctly captures the inner conflicts of character; students who choose to write poetry to express character (or other aspects of the novel) write at a level of synthesis that goes beyond the topic sentence or thesis classificatory writing of the traditional character paper. To explore another approach to using journal writing and transforming text, read the chapter by Sandy Robertson on using dialectical journals.

The reality of English class, however, includes teaching students to write formal papers that they will encounter in high school, college, or graduate school. As an eighth-grade teacher I must teach my students how to write for a variety of audiences using a variety of purposes; the critical analysis paper must be included in that teaching. The difference in the way I teach formal critical analysis now in a response classroom and the way I once taught it is simple; before students ever get to the formulating stage, they have had opportunities to engage with the text in an informal manner.

Figure 8.14 Kate's Poetry Response to *Out of Control*

Magnolia

I am a flower of brilliant white

although I have not opened to my full extent

my petals glimmer in the sun

quite before I have fully bloomed

my petals are touched and picked

shouldn't I be able to keep my color

and keep my petals?

many of the outside petals are brown

though I am still not fully opened

a rain shower brings life to the tree

I soak up the energy

I begin to open more and more

to let my real fragrance, my real

colors be known

I opened up so that all may see

my outside petals will remain a stained

and ugly brown

but since I have opened to the world

my magnificent white

my magnificent fragrance

will prevail in me,

the delicate magnolia flower.

Remember Mary's four letter process experience with Elizabeth Berg's *Durable Goods*. Mary's thinking exercise became the basis of her final exam topic in which she adapted her thoughts to a more formalized mode of discourse, a character sketch (see Figure 8.15):

Figure 8.15 Mary's Character Sketch

Kate

Many barriers slow us down in life. Kate climbs over many of these barriers. When Kate lives through all of these obstacles, she gains many likeable traits. Those traits are what make Kate such an interesting character. In Elizabeth Berg's novel, *Durable Goods*, Kate is a character who is courageous, optimistic, and persistent.

In the beginning of the novel the author reveals that Kate is courageous. Her abusive father is not very understanding to complaining or nagging. In the car ride home from her adventurous journey with her sister, Kate, for the first time in her life, stands up against her father. Disagreements were not something her father was a fan of. Kate knew what the consequences were, and she faced them head on. Taking those kinds of chances takes bravery, and that is something only courageous people possess.

Of course, Mary's letters do not just magically transform themselves into this kind of writing. I model webbing and grouping thoughts and use the basic funnel paragraph to teach a thesis paper. I spend time showing the entire class how to take the webbing ideas and mold them into a thesis idea. Mary's beginning essay is simplistic, but it is a beginning point; the important point is that Mary has the basis for the paper; what she is doing now is putting different clothes on her mannequin of ideas. If she continues to have time to respond to literature, if teachers continue to ask questions about her responses, if she continues to write and conference, then the thesis paper will become as natural to her as journaling or letter writing.

Another effective way to have students engage in response to text is through the use of film, which comprises a large part of our fourth-quarter study. Robert Probst asserts that "visual literature is as value-laden as the written. Dealing with human life as it does, it cannot be otherwise. It continually reveals its values in its choice of some subjects—crime, violence, romance—rather than others—philosophy, art, scholarship" (Probst, 172).

In our reading workshop we use film as the basis of analyzing at a different level—but central to that analysis are the same literary elements we have addressed in our fiction, poetry, and nonfiction. Consider Mark's first draft of his paper on *Citizen Kane* dealing with the character of Kane (see Figure 8.16):

Figure 8.16 Mark's Draft of a Critical Analysis Paper

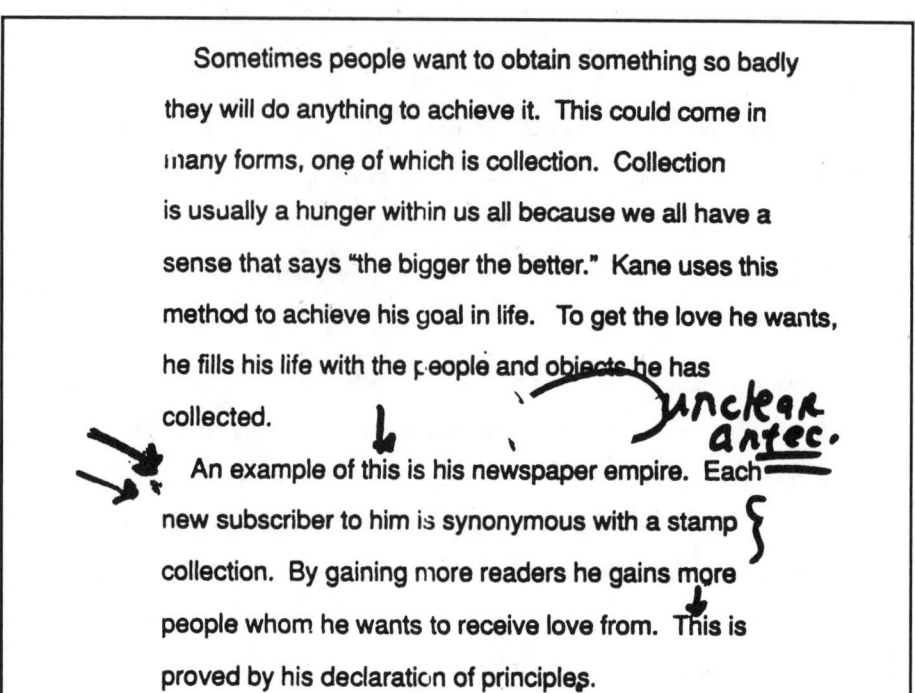

This example of critical writing based on film became the basis of a lesson on unclear antecedent. No doubt that this particular essay seems formulaic and somewhat artificial, but it is another way to practice writing for a certain purpose. As an English teacher I must prepare my students to have the thesis-paper format in their writers' strategies of purpose and audience, but I stress to them that the formal paper is just one mode that serves a specific audience.

Sometimes letters stay letters; sometimes they become letters to authors or critical analysis formal thesis papers. Sometimes they evolve into other pieces of writing. Perhaps the most important kind of writing that I try to expose my students to is real-life publishable writing that includes contests, magazine writing, and book reviews. We have had winners in *The Houston Chronicle* Writing Contest, The National Council of Teachers of English Promising Young Writer's Contest; we have had students' stories published in *Merlyn's Pen;* and we have had book reviews published in *Writing Magazine* as well as *Voices in the Middle*. Our students write to other teachers and students about books in our school and outside of our school. I have my students write to university students. Student responses about books take so many forms—we are just beginning to participate in the book clubs at North Carolina University through the use of the Internet. What possibilities technology will offer our students of the future when they are responding to what they read by communicating with other students all over the world who are reading the same stories or poems!

As the puzzle continues to come together for me as teacher, I am convinced, however, that the shape of the design will only continue to change. One area that I am actively trying to expand is the involvement of our parents in the reading-response classroom. We have formed a reading committee of parents from each grade level in our middle school (fifth through eighth grade) to read new books and to help find new titles. Another task of the reading committee is to help us with any concerns over content in young adult literature. We have a process in place for any censorship concern that is brought to our attention, and the reading committee is a vital part of that process. Also, I invite parents to the conference I have with their students and ask the parents to read novels that children are currently reading. Recently we had a lively discussion on Ernest Gaines's *A Lesson Before Dying* with two students and their mothers and me. We sat around a conference table at lunch and had a wonderful book discussion. Remember Rachel's letter about *Katy Did*? I invited her mother to come and discuss the book after she read it. I loved the reflective comments that Rachel's mother sent me a few days after the conference (see Figure 8.17):

Figure 8.17 Rachel's Mother's Reflection

Reflections on a three-way conference on <u>Katy Did</u> with

Mother, Daughter (14) & English teacher

I can't help musing on how I got from changing diapers to conferencing with an adolescent and her teacher about a novel which deals with issues such as pre-marital sex, death and major life choices . . . it all happened so fast. The latest growth spurt from "happy go lucky" eleven year old to serious, moody often angry, woman-child of 14 went by in a flash!

The conference setting was a great forum for exploring ideas and values and giving me a chance to actually listen and hear Rachel's thoughts and feelings about important issues. I found myself so impressed with the depth she exhibited in exploring the issues presented in the book. She clearly had understood the book, liked it, and had thought about the subject matter. Because it was dealing with some of the hard issues of real life for adolescents she was empathetic toward Katy and seemed to have explored in her mind how she might have reacted in a similar situation. She also was impressed with the writer's craft in the novel and appreciated how it was put together to make its points.

Having students and their parents share in a reading community is a great way to share the richness of responses that I want to continue to develop and to experiment with in future reading workshops. At the end of the eighth grade year I want the student puzzle to begin to come together. When I ask my students at the end of the year to build their portfolio, I want to know that they have had a wide choice of reading material and a wide choice of response to that literature. I want their reading lists to have variety and to hold interesting memories for the students. Annie's reading list in her portfolio illustrates such a wide variety of interests and experiences as a reader (see Figure 8.18):

Figure 8.18 Annie's Reading List

P.S. hope you can read, they're just quickie thoughts, the first that came to me. This is a more complete list of the books I read this year. I was highlighting when I was writing my letters for the finals.

Annie
5/21/94

♥ always ANNE

List of books read during eighth grade school year

284	Mrs. Mike	I don't remember many details, just seems that I enjoyed
183	The Twisted Window -- Lois Duncan	ok, my story
294	The Sword Bearer -- John White	good Fantasy
139	A Day No Pigs Would Die -- Robert Peck	
312	Gaal the Conqueror -- John White	good Fantasy
148	Trapped in Pharaoh's Tomb -- Peter Reese Doyle	
	Stalked in the Catacombs -- Peter Reese Doyle	} dinky, Fluff books
	Ambushed in Africa -- Peter Reese Doyle	
380	Rebecca -- Daphne Di Maurier	every class needs to read it
393	The Iron Scepter -- John White	good Fantasy
	April Morning -- John Mazzio	I just wanted to hug the poor boy!
170	Leaving Eldorado -- John Mazzio	good book!
220	Sabrina -- Candice Ransom	I enjoyed it! Good to read with April Morning
181	December Stillness -- Mary Downing Hahn	not too good
349	Mrs. DeWinter -- Susan Hill	ruins Rebecca
150	Home Before Dark	good book, vivid images
260	The Good Earth -- Pearl S. Buck	Not my favorite, but I'm glad I read
182	The Rain Catchers	love it, love it, love it!
181	Taming the Star Runner -- S.E. Hinton	pretty good
336	Lily	Wonderful
150	Incident at Loring Groves -- Sonita Levitin	ok
	Cold Sassy Tree -- Olive Ann Burns	I loved every moment
132	Woodsong -- Gary Paulsen	a good, quick read (mostly for guys)
233	Homecoming -- Cynthia Voigt	I stopped reading at p.233, it goes blah to page 818) BORING!
	Don't Care High -- Gordon Korman	icky book
174	Seventeen Wishes -- Robin Jones Gunn	} easy, but enjoyable reads
175	Starry Night -- Robin Jones Gunn	
202	Bruchko -- Bruce Olson	interesting, captivating, action packed
135	The Dolphins and Me -- Don C. Reed	4th grade read
	Warwyck's Woman -- Rosalind Laker	Loved it!
	Gentlehands -- M.E. Kerr	Loved it!
	When Angels Appear -- Hope MacDonald	short stories
240	Shabanu -- Suzanne Fisher Staples	Go Shabanu!
501	Christy -- Catherine Marshall	can I cry, sing, and dance for joy
564	To Dance With Kings -- Rosalind Laker	excellent writing
	That Was Then, This Is Now -- S.E. Hinton	blah, depress me
158	The Pigman -- Paul Zindel	I enjoyed it
224	Spring's Gentle Promise -- Janet Oke	
220	Love Takes Wing -- Janet Oke	} easy, ok reads
303	Too Long a Stranger -- Janet Oke	
227	The Hero and The Crown -- Robin McKinley	wa-hoo! Wonderful
281	To Kill a Mockingbird -- Harper Lee	obviously a classic. I love Scout!
	Sing Down the Moon -- Scott O'Dell	good quickie read
	Baby (I wrote a letter to myself... just thoughts)	

⬛ = choice w/letter

Although Annie's list may be a longer example than the average reader's list, she is an example of a person who, if given the opportunity to grow and experiment with literature, can become someone who will read long after our reading class is over. Choice, books relevant to adolescence, a variety of writing responses, and open discussions all help Annie and other students like her to have a pleasurable experience as readers. It is our responsibility and our privilege as middle school teachers to make our reading classes havens of pleasurable reading moments. Building good, strong reading communities takes effort and time, but it makes teaching and learning so much more enjoyable. Watching the rough edges of that puzzle come together makes me want to stay in teaching and most importantly with middle school readers. Yes, I want my students to critically analyze literature and be able to write to a variety of audiences, but most importantly, I want my students to see me in years to come and sit down over a cup of coffee or a coke and tell me about the latest book they've just read; that's when I'll really know I've done my job!

References

Andrasick, K. (1990). *Opening texts: Using writing to teach literature.* Portsmouth, NH: Heinemann.

Atwell, N. (1991). *Side by side: Essays on teaching to learn.* Portsmouth, NH: Heinemann.

Probst, R. E. (1988). *Response and analysis: Teaching literature in junior and senior high school.* Portsmouth, NH: Boynton/Cook.

Sippola, A. (1993). When thematic units are not thematic units. *Reading Horizons, 33* (3).

Trade Books Cited

Anonymous. (1976). *Go ask Alice.* New York: Avon Books.

Berg, E. (1993). *Durable goods.* New York: Random House.

Bridgers, S. E. (1976). *Home before dark.* New York: Bantam.

Cormier, R. (1979). *After the first death.* New York: Dell.

Crutcher, C. (1995). *Ironman.* New York: Greenwillow.

Crutcher, C. (1983). *Running loose.* New York: Delacorte.

Crutcher, C. (1993). *Staying fat for Sarah Byrnes.* New York: Greenwillow.

Gordon, R. (1995). *Pierced by a ray of the sun.* New York: HarperCollins

Mazer, N. F. (1993). *Out of control.* New York: Avon Books.

Peck, R. N. (1972). *A day no pigs would die.* New York: Knopf.

Sebestyen, O. (1994). *Out of nowhere.* New York: Orchard.

Stanek, L. W. (1991). *Katy did.* New York: Avon.

Townsend, S. (1982). *The secret diary of Adrian Mole, aged 131/2.* New York: Avon.

Wolff, V. E. (1993). *Make lemonade.* New York: Scholastic.

Appendix A - Thematic Units
Victims and Heroes

Core Reading:

After the First Death. R. Cormier. Bantam Doubleday Dell, 1991.

Choice Reading:

California Blue. D. Klass. Scholastic, 1996.
Danger Zone. D. Klass. Scholastic, 1996.
Driver's Ed. Caroline Cooney. Delacorte, 1994.
Eva. P. Dickinson. Bantam Doubleday Dell, 1990.
Fallen Angels. W. D. Myers. Scholastic, 1989.
Freak the Mighty. R. Philbrick. Scholastic, 1993.
The Giver. L. Lowry. Bantam Doubleday Dell, 1994.
Make Lemonade. V. E. Wolff. Scholastic, 1994.
Night. E. Weisel. Bantam, 1982.
Nightjohn. G. Paulsen. Dell, 1995.
Out of Control. N. F. Mazer. Avon Flare, 1994.
The Postman. D. Brin. Bantam, 1986.
Staying Fat for Sarah Byrnes. C. Crutcher. Dell, 1996.
A Taste of Salt. F. Temple. Orchard, 1992.
The Things They Carried . T. O'Brien. Viking Penguin, 1991.
To Cross a Line. K. Ray. Puffin, 1995.

Other Times and Other Places

Core Reading: Selections

The Beggar. A. Chekov. Amsco School Publications.
Beowulf. B. F. Huppe. Pegasus Press.
Jane Eyre. C. Bronte. Viking Penguin.
Madame Bovary. G. Flaubert. Oxford University Press
My Uncle Jules. G. de Maupassant. Amsco School Publications.

Choice Reading:

Across Five Aprils. I. Hunt. Silver Burdett, 1993.
Beauty. R. McKinley. HarperCollins, 1993.
Beyond the Burning Time. K. Lasky. Scholastic, 1996.
A Break with Charity. A. Rinaldi. Gulliver/Harcourt Brace, 1994.
Catherine, Called Birdy. K. Cushman. HarperCollins, 1995.
The Endless Steppe. E. Hautzig. HarperCollins, 1987.
The Glory Fields. W. D. Myers. Scholastic, 1994.
The Hero and the Crown. R. McKinley. Greenwillow, 1984.
Magic Kingdom for Sale. *SOLD*. T. Brooks. Ballantine, 1986.
Othello. J. Lester. Scholastic, 1995.
Redwall. B. Jacques. Avon, 1990.
The Ruby in the Smoke. P. Pullman. Knopf, 1988.
White Lilacs. C. Myer. Gulliver/Harcourt Brace, 1993.

Rebels With and Without Causes

Core Reading of the Movies:

"Citizen Kane"
"On the Waterfront"
"A Rebel Without a Cause"

Required Core Reading:

To Kill a Mockingbird. H. Lee. Warner, 1988.

Choice Reading:

The Chocolate War. R. Cormier. Bantam Doubleday Dell, 1986.
Ender's Game. O. S. Card. Tor, 1994.
Grab Hands and Run. F. Temple. HarperCollins, 1995.
Katy Did. L. Stanek. Avon, 1992.
Lily. C. Bonner. NAL/Dutton, 1994.
Little Little. M. E. Kerr. HarperCollins, 1991.
The Moves Make the Man. B. Brooks. HarperCollins, 1996.
Shadow of a Hero. P. Dickinson. Delacorte, 1994.
Selections from *Visions: Nineteen Short Stories*. D. Gallo (Ed.). Bantam
    Doubleday Dell, 1988.
Warriors Don't Cry. M. P. Beals. Archway, 1995.

A Light at the End of the Tunnel

Core Reading:

Standing Tall: The Stories of Ten Hispanic Americans. Scholastic. (Gloria
    Estefan selection)
Who Do You Think You Are? H. Rochman and D. McCampbell (Eds.). Little
    Brown, 1993. (Tobias Wolff selection)
One More River to Cross: The Stories of Twelve Black Americans. Haskins
    (Ed.). Scholastic, 1992. (Malcolm X selection)
Famous Asian Americans. Cobblehill Books. (Maxine Hong Kingston selection)
Peeling the Onion. R. Gordon (Ed.). HarperCollins, 1993. Poetry anthology
    featuring such poems as Cassian's "A Man."

Choice Reading:

Crazy Horse Electric Game. C. Crutcher. Dell, 1988.
Durable Goods. E. Berg. Avon, 1994.
Heart of a Champion. C. Deuker. Avon, 1994.
Home Before Dark. S. E. Bridgers. Bantam, 1985.
Ironman. C. Crutcher. Bantam Doubleday Dell, 1996.
A Lesson Before Dying. E. Gaines. Random House, 1994.
Lucy Peale. C. Rodowsky. Farrar, Straus & Giroux, 1992.
Out of Nowhere. O. Sebestyen. Puffin, 1995.
The Rain Catchers. J. Thesman. Avon, 1992.
Weeping Willow. R. White. Farrar, Straus & Giroux, 1992.
Wrestling with Honor. D. Klass. Scholastic, 1996.

Chapter 9
PROMOTING LITERATURE DISCUSSIONS

Elizabeth A. Poe

Just as reading can be a lifetime pleasure, so can discussing books provide a continuing source of satisfaction. But because not every type of book discussion is pleasurable or satisfying, learning how to discuss a book is an important part of middle school reading/language arts programs. Whether book discussions occur between two readers, within small groups of readers, or in a whole-class setting, certain principles and practices foster the development of book discussions in which middle schoolers become readily engaged. The following discussion of Lois Lowry's *The Giver* (1993) exemplifies the type of literary transaction that can transpire when an entire class is fully engaged in a student-centered discussion.

Sample Student-Centered Discussion

Mrs. Hadley: All right. Now that each of your literature circles has finished reading and discussing *The Giver*, let's talk about it as a whole class. So—what are your thoughts on the book?

Jeremy: I thought it was a really cool book!

Alice: So did I!

Jake: Yeah, it's the best book I ever read.

Sharon: I think so too. Does Lois Lowry have any other books like that?

John: Well, I think it su—, I mean I didn't like it. It was too confusing. Even after talking about it in our literature circles, I still don't really know what happened. I hate books like that.

Alex: I know what you mean. The ending was hard to understand, but after our group talked about it, it started to make sense to me, and now I think it's an awesome book. I guess I like books that I have to think about to understand.

Sally: I wrote in my journal that the part about the twins gave me the creeps. I mean, if Nancy and I had been born in that society, one of us would have been released. That's terrible.

Several students at once: Yeah, that's terrible!

Mrs. Hadley: OK, great. I can tell we've got a lot to talk about. Where shall we start? Maybe we should start with John's comment.

John: Good. Did anyone else find any part of the book confusing?

Ingrid: Well, now that you mention it, I had a hard time figuring out what was going on at first, but after awhile it started to make sense.

Many students agree with this.

Mrs. Hadley: Just to make sure we've got all the confusion cleared up, would some of you like to reconstruct the story for us?

Alice: Sure. It's about a boy named Jonas who lives in a different type of society, probably in the future sometime. His community has very strict rules which everyone follows without questioning. The children do not live with their Birthmothers, but in assigned family units. The Council of Elders assigns each person a role after eleven years of schooling and trying out different jobs. Jonas is special and is appointed to become the Receiver of Memories.

Simon: So in order to become The Receiver of Memories, Jonas has to be specially trained by the Giver of Memories. The Giver is the only one in the whole community who knows about life as we know it. He is the only one who experiences emotions. No one else has any idea what it's like to feel pleasure and pain. He also learns all that goes on in the community.

Maria: Well, as Jonas receives the memories from the Giver, he begins to question his community. For example, he realizes that his father killed the weaker twin baby because that was his job. He decides he wants to leave the community and takes a baby, Gabriel, who also has the power to be a receiver, with him.

John: Now this is the confusing part—after they are outside of the community. I still don't know what happens.

Mrs. Hadley: What are the possibilities?

Sarah: Well, I think they get to another community, the Elsewhere that has colors and music and feelings.

John: But it doesn't say they do.

Andrew: I think they die.

John: How do you know?

Inez: Maybe we should read the last chapter over.

Inez reads the final chapter aloud and the class members find clues that support the varying points of view. They agree to disagree about what happens to Jonas and Gabriel since several possibilities seem feasible. Each reader can end the story in the way that makes sense to him or her personally.

Mrs. Hadley: OK. Now, what about some of the other comments made about the book? Sally, you were upset by the fact that twins were not allowed in the community. I can understand your reaction.

Sally: Yes. Up until they released the weaker twin, I thought the community was kind of neat—like it was someplace I would like to live. When that happened, I changed my mind.

Maria: Yeah, I wanted to live there until that happened too.

Alex: So did I because I liked all the rituals they had. They each had to say the same thing when they made a mistake, and they each had a chance to talk at dinnertime. I would like that because at my house I never get a chance to talk; no one ever seems to listen to me. Here they all seemed to care.

Anna: *Seemed* is the key word here. The more we learned about the society, the more we saw that the people did not really care. They were just acting the way they were taught to behave. They had to or they would be punished.

Alex: Yeah, I know what you mean, but I still wish my parents would listen to me once in a while.

Stephen: I know, my parents are like that too, but I wouldn't want to live in that community. All that Sameness would drive me crazy.

Many students agree with this.

> *Mrs. Hadley*: This is really interesting. Many of you who did not like the community in *The Giver* thought this was a wonderful book. Why is that?

> *Jeremy*: Well, I liked it because it described everything in such detail. It's like I could picture it in my mind. Here is the passage I copied into my journal the day you asked us to select an impressive passage: 'The colors of the carnage were grotesquely bright: the crimson wetness on the rough and dusty fabric, the ripped shreds of grass, startling green, in the boy's yellow hair.' It's from a battlefield that is described on page 119. I feel like I'm right there.

Several others eagerly volunteer to share passages they found impressive.

The class continues their discussion of *The Giver* until the bell rings, and they have to go to their next class. Before they leave, Mrs. Hadley compliments them on the lively, thoughtful discussion they have all shared. She reminds them to write a reflection on the class discussion in their journals and to be thinking of ideas for their literature projects for *The Giver*.

Principles Underlying the Sample Discussion

Mrs. Hadley's discussion was student-centered because she believes readers need to begin with their own personal responses to a literary work and then work to understand how and why that piece of literature affected them as it did. Real learning, she believes, occurs when readers make their own connections among themselves, their extended worlds, and a literary work. She encourages emotional responses because they are important in and of themselves, and often lead to readers' aesthetic and intellectual connections with a work. Because she believes it is neither possible nor desirable to cover every important aspect of a literary work, she takes her cues from the students and focuses on what is important to them.

She carefully structures their experience with the book to include opportunities for writing about it in response logs, talking about it in small literature circle groups, and extending their learning with related literature projects. All of these activities prepare students for learner-centered literary discussions. Mrs. Hadley sees herself as orchestrating literary discussions and learning along with her students as they explore the books they read. She loves literature and wants her students to develop a relationship with the printed word that will lead them to become lifelong readers and learners. She intends for students to model their small group or individual discussions after the type of discussions they have with her individually and as a whole class. Her belief system is quite similar to my own, which has evolved over many years of teaching and learning from my own students.

Evolution of a Book Discussion Facilitator

I have worked in school settings where literary elements and knowledge about literature were stressed and teacher-centered teaching was the standard pedagogical mode. When I first started in a school of this ilk, I did what my colleagues did. We gave daily quizzes and an objective test at the end of the unit to make sure the students read and understood the assigned novel. Every day after the quiz, we discussed the assigned reading. I would read the quiz question; the students would answer it with the concrete information required; and I would elaborate, hitting all the important points contained in those pages. I thought the discussions went well: The students were involved, did well on the quizzes and test, and seemed to enjoy the book. And I felt the heady exhilaration that comes from a whole day of espousing literary thoughts and enlightening young minds. I was really teaching. But were they really learning? Probably not.

Needless to say, I soon grew uncomfortable with this approach. In the years that followed, I gradually developed an approach to discussing literature much like that exemplified by Mrs. Hadley. I started offering students choices in what they read, had them work in small groups, and replaced a teacher-dominated discussion format with a student-centered reader-response approach. None of these techniques were used by other teachers in my school, but I was studying Louise Rosenblatt's theory of reader response as part of my doctoral work and liked what I was reading. I slowly incorporated her suggestions into the way I discussed literature, and my students responded positively to the changes I made. Literature discussions are now one of my major teaching strengths.

Much of what I read in Rosenblatt's works reinforced some basic beliefs I had already developed about life in general and more specifically the study of literature. Working with a wide array of students from preschool to college age had shown me the importance of the individual in all educational settings. The juvenile delinquents I worked with in group homes and detention centers helped me see the necessity of respecting all points of view. The low-ability language arts students I taught led me to see the value of choice in reading materials. The gifted students in my after-school book club showed me what can happen when we develop our students' intellect and neglect their emotional capacities. The many, many average students I had in class made it clear that literature discussions are a vital part of any classroom. Along with my experiences in traditional and nontraditional teaching situations, facilitating group counseling sessions at the school for pregnant teenagers where I taught underlined how essential it is that adults remain nonjudgmental when working with adolescents.

My Beliefs About Teaching Literature

The outcome of all this is the belief system that undergirds every literature discussion in which I become involved.

1. Each reader has a unique experience with a literary text. This is the main premise of Rosenblatt's work, and my own experience with many readers certainly supports her theory. In addition, my dissertation research showed that three pregnant teens could read the same novel and have completely different ideas about it based on their own decisions concerning their pregnancies.

2. Each reader's transaction with the text is important, interesting and worthy of respect. All responses to a literary work have value. Discovering similarities in readers' transactions with a text can create bonds between readers; exploring the differences in transactions can promote understanding of oneself as well as others in the learning community. Respect for all readings of a text is essential for honest, constructive literature discussions.

   A corollary to this belief is that people are more important than books. As much as I love reading and literature, I love people more. People, especially students, can easily feel inadequate because they do not see the same thing in a book as someone else, namely the teacher, does. Teachers have the power to devastate readers by denigrating students' tastes in literature or their personal responses to a text. Other students also have this power. It is the teacher's responsibility to see that individual responses to books are used as a bridge between readers rather than a means for intimidating or putting down fellow readers.

3. Emotional responses to a literary work should be encouraged and acknowledged. Overlooking or minimizing the emotional connections readers have with a piece of literature cuts off an important reason for reading fiction. Starting with emotional responses can lead to multidimensional literature discussions as readers explore what in the text caused them to respond as they did. Long after the content of a book is forgotten, the feelings associated with reading it often remain.

4. Inductive learning is true learning. When readers make connections for themselves about why a literary work holds power for them or they extend their own learning based on something

in the text that interests them, the discoveries they make are more likely to remain than if readers are told directly about the text or information and materials related to it. Much of what the teacher must do involves setting the scene so inductive learning can occur. This approach is particularly important when studying literary elements.

Book Discussions Come in Many Shapes and Sizes

These underlying beliefs come into play whenever a discussion of literature takes place. Book discussions can take place in a variety of situations.

One-to-One Literature Discussions

Often a student who has read a book he or she really liked will mention this, and it will lead to a one-to-one chat about the book. Most teachers love these spontaneous discussions because they occur with students who enjoy reading and talking about books. They are frequently sources for the mutual recommending of books to read. Sometimes one-to-one conversations occur more formally when students and teachers schedule conferences to discuss independent reading. This might happen in the type of readers' workshop setting made popular by Nancie Atwell and Linda Rief. Students may also confer with a partner about a book read in common or tell each other about different books.

Small Group Literature Discussions

Literature circles are small autonomous groups in which students collaborate as they read a common text or individual texts that are somehow related. Literature circle members talk a lot about what they are reading; they also share their written responses and develop group projects. In *Literature Circles: Voice and Choice in the Student-Centered Classroom*, Harvey Daniels defines, describes the history of, and explains the use of literature circles in the classroom. He points out that literature circles involve true collaboration among students as they work together to construct meaning from texts (p. 49).

Whole Class Literature Discussions

Sometimes the entire class can discuss a book it has read or heard read aloud. When literature circle members have read a variety of books connected by an overarching theme or concept, the whole class can become involved in a discussion about what the books have in common even though class members have only read one of the books discussed (Poe, "Intensifying Transactions Through Multiple Text Exploration," pp. 160–162). These large group conversations can be fascinating and inspire students to read beyond the books read for their own literature circles. But no matter the number of books being discussed, as Richard Beach and James Marshall point out in *Teaching Literature in the Secondary School*, "orchestrating successful classroom discussions is an art that requires study, planning, skill, practice, and often, a fair amount of timely intuition" (p. 49).

Book Discussions Outside Classroom Settings

Outside the classroom setting, similar configurations for literature discussions occur. Librarians are quite familiar with the one-to-one conversations that take place about a book an excited reader just has to talk to someone about—now. Parents who share books with their middle schoolers also experience these rewarding conversations. Book clubs generally involve small group discussions about one or more books. In the book club I worked with, some of our liveliest discussions occurred as each member lobbied for the book he or she wanted the group to read next. Teachers and librarians who have participated in teachers-as-readers groups, adult book clubs, or adult literature circles are generally enthusiastic about them because they foster personal and professional growth in an enjoyable social context.

Practices that Promote Book Discussions

Establishing an Atmosphere Conducive to Discussion

In any situation involving literature discussions, it is imperative to create an atmosphere in which readers feel comfortable expressing their thoughts on books. Trust is an essential ingredient in such an environment, and a discussion facilitator can help members develop trust for one another by frankly discussing the importance of respect for all readers and their responses. The model the leader provides is, of course, vital to the health of the group.

When I am working with a new group of students, we generally read a short story together and talk about it (Poe, "Student Responses to *Sixteen*," pp. 68–70), but a group read-aloud of any sort can accomplish the same purpose. I lay the groundwork by stressing there are no wrong responses, just those which are more considered or thoughtful than others, and that we can all learn from the responses of each other. I guide them through their first discussion by complimenting students who make encouraging comments and pointing out the positive aspects of dissimilar transactions with the story. Because students develop trust for the teacher and each other at individual rates, consistency and a true belief in a democratic classroom are essential. It's just as important to stick to the ground rules as it is to establish them in the first place.

Defining Our Roles

It is difficult for students to accept that a teacher or adult does not have a *right* or *preferred* answer/response that he or she is looking for. Once in an essay test, I asked students to write about passages that had been important to them. Several students paraphrased a passage I had mentioned as my favorite and gave reasons similar to those I had expressed in class. Realizing that imposing, sometimes even just mentioning, my own thoughts about a literary work can be detrimental to students' individual relationships with the text, I am now careful to minimize my personal input and to focus on helping readers clarify their thoughts about the work and explore them with one another.

Hearing that their answers are as valued as mine and that what I want is for them to read and think for themselves is usually disconcerting at first, but generally it is appreciated before too long. Because I see myself as a discussion facilitator, the few questions I ask to elicit responses from students are open-ended, like Mrs. Hadley's "What are your thoughts on the book," or posed to encourage readers to find connections with the text or other readers. Asking "Why?" and suggesting a reader return to the text to help explain or understand a response can assist in the clarification or deepening of a response. I hope that students will internalize these questioning strategies and ask questions of themselves as well as of other readers with whom they converse. Mrs. Hadley's student Inez did this in *The Giver* discussion when she suggested that they return to the text for illumination.

Choosing Materials and Format

Selecting appropriate literature is paramount for facilitating student-centered literature discussions. Young adult literature frequently elicits positive responses from readers who might otherwise not become engaged with reading materials. But just using young adult literature is often not enough because forcing students to read or talk about *anything* frequently has ill effects. However, the more choices middle schoolers have in terms of what young adult literature they read, the more likely they are to engage with the text, and the better the potential for strong, lively discussions becomes. Even when the entire class will be reading the same novel, it is helpful to let them vote on, as Mrs. Hadley did, which novel that will be. Choice becomes more possible if teachers do not insist all their classes read the same book at the same time.

In addition, offering readers a choice between traditional teaching methods and readers' workshop, or literature circles, or student-centered whole-class discussions can help ease the tension between teacher and students because students are generally more cooperative and responsible when they have had initial input into the discussion format to be used for their literature study. This type of student-centered approach includes allowing readers to set their own reading schedule and decide whether they want to discuss a book in sections or after the whole book has been completed. Making decisions throughout the school year encourages students to be actively responsible for their own learning and not passively expect the teacher to make all the decisions.

Preparing for Discussions

Having readers write out their initial responses to a work before discussing it provides a written rehearsal that helps to get the conversation started; offers security against unintended, potentially embarrassing, remarks; and generally encourages more thoughtful discussion. Written responses are kept in a response journal or reading log, like the one Sally mentioned in the sample discussion, and must be completed before students can participate in individual, small group, or class discussions. This requirement helps insure students have read and thought about the material before discussing it with their peers.

Encouraging During the Discussion

The teacher's task is to gently guide the students' exploration of the text and help them to learn to do this for themselves and each other. This is done by asking open-ended questions, encouraging readers to question when they do not understand, and fostering interaction between and among discussants. Active listening is an essential skill for all who participate in literary conversations. Ideally, everyone taking part in the discussion should listen carefully and reflect the speaker's words back to him or her when clarification is necessary for understanding. This technique, which benefits both speakers and listeners, can be taught directly or modeled by integrating it into the discussion smoothly and naturally. Because it is important to hear from everyone, students who tend to dominate are gently encouraged to give others a chance to speak; shy students are also kindly urged to share their thoughts.

Sometimes students working in literature circles are assigned specific tasks as they learn how to function in small groups. One student may function as the encourager, another may be the summarizer who reflects others' ideas, another might be the discussion leader, and another might serve as group recorder. Ideally, these functions will become internalized so that students will perform whatever task is needed naturally and spontaneously despite the size of the discussion format.

I have discovered that everything I would have once covered in a lecture format can be worked into reader-response-based discussions. By carefully listening to and drawing upon students' statements and questions about a text, it is possible to weave in many important aspects about a piece of literature. Students frequently have the background, perceptions, and insights to collectively delve into a text. When they do not, they can reread, research, or rethink before regrouping and continuing the discussion. Again, the teacher can help them learn how to do this independent of an adult. For example, the students in Mrs. Hadley's class had been encouraged to respond aesthetically to a text because she had asked them to record words or passages in their journals that impressed them and to think about why these lines created the effect they did. Discussing his aesthetic response was a natural part of Jeremy's discussion of the text, and the other students enjoyed doing so as well because they were encouraged to look at passages that touched them personally in some way.

Ending the Discussion

Leave 'em laughing or know when to fold, because developing lifelong readers is the goal. Too often students say they hate a book, poem, or short story because it was "analyzed to death in a language arts class." I don't want that to happen in my class. It's a fine line to walk, but I try to gauge how much literature talk my students can absorb and quit while we're all ahead. An unanswered question or an unpursued thought may result in a future rereading of the text. Also, talking about what they have read may have helped readers clarify thoughts or may have raised more questions they want to commit to writing, so I, like Mrs. Hadley, ask students to write reflective comments following literature discussions.

Studying Skills through Literature Discussions

Literature discussions require readers to do much writing in conjunction with their reading. And the writing they do is purposeful with personal significance, the type that students usually do most successfully. Informal writing assignments can provide raw material for more formal writing assignments that provide opportunities to polish writing skills. Speaking skills are also enhanced through frequent opportunities to talk about matters of personal importance to readers. Listening and thinking skills are similarly improved through challenging discussions based on student-selected readings. Literary analysis skills can be incorporated into discussions by introducing literary elements after students have read and discussed a work and asking them to identify and discuss examples from the text.

Assessing the Discussion

Authentic appraisal of personal contributions and achievements rewards readers for being constructive discussants. Outside the classroom, the energy generated from a spirited discussion is its own reward. In a classroom setting, I find that awarding a participation point each time a student contributes to the discussion encourages reluctant speakers to join the conversation. By placing a check mark next to the student's name who contributes any constructive comment, I let them know the class and I really do want to hear what they have to say. These participation points become part of the student's grade for the course and greatly help with classroom management.

Students also earn participation points for staying on task during literature circle meetings and for making positive contributions to the group's progress on projects. Participation points provide concrete evidence of students' involvement in literature conversations, and earning them becomes part of the pleasure of the discussion. After a while they become unnecessary, but I still use them to be on the safe side of student evaluation and classroom management matters. Of course compliments to students about both in-class and out-of-class discussions reward readers for taking an active part in literature discussions. I frequently tell them how pleased I am to be privy to the wonderful thoughts they express about the books they read. I mean this sincerely, for taking part in literature discussions is one of the true joys of life.

Managing the Classroom during Discussions

But it's impossible to have a successful discussion if the classroom is out of control. The participation point system does a lot to help with classroom management during reading workshop conferences, literature circle conversations, and classroom book discussions. It is essential to stress each reader's responsibility to contribute to the group, be it large or small. Peers can also be quite effective in making this point. Middle schoolers often want to be part of the group and will work to please their group members by contributing when they might not have when working with the whole class.

Conclusion

Although there are some specific techniques that can enhance student-centered book discussions and make them run more smoothly and efficiently, the most important ingredient for success is understanding the underlying beliefs upon which this approach is founded. Teachers who embrace reader response as a part of their belief system are continually adapting and refining strategies that respect the individual's right to his or her own transaction with a text. These teachers are ingenious about discovering ways to offer students a choice in reading materials, and they are constantly devising methods for helping students share in the education of everyone in their learning community. They also encourage students to be responsible for their own education. As is the case with any art, learning to skillfully facilitate a reader-centered literature discussion is a lifelong process. But, as those engaged in this process know, there is much satisfaction in honing the necessary skills because the resulting discussions can be so deeply gratifying for all concerned.

References

Atwell, N. (1987). *In the middle: Writing, reading, and learning with adolescents*. Portsmouth, NH: Heinemann.

Beach, R. W., & Marshall, J. D. (1991). *Teaching literature in the secondary school*. San Diego, CA: Harcourt Brace Jovanovich.

Daniels, H. (1994). *Literature circles: Voice and choice in the student-centered classroom*. York, ME: Stenhouse.

Poe, E. A. (1992). Intensifying transactions through multiple text exploration. In N. J. Karolides (Ed.), *Reader response in the classroom: Evoking and interpreting meaning in literature*. White Plains, NY: Longman.

Poe, E. A. (1986). *Reader-responses of pregnant adolescents and teenage mothers to young adult novels portraying protagonists with problems similar and dissimilar to the readers'*. Unpublished dissertation. University of Colorado.

Poe, E. A. (1988). Student responses to Don Gallo's *Sixteen. English Journal, 77,* (1), 68–70.

Rief, L. (1992). *Seeking diversity: Language arts with adolescents*. Portsmouth, NH: Heinemann.

Rosenblatt, L. M. (1983). *Literature as exploration* (4th ed.). New York: Modern Language Association.

Trade Book Cited

Lowry, L. (1993). *The Giver*. Boston, MA: Houghton Mifflin.

Chapter 10

READERS TAKE RESPONSIBILITY: LITERATURE CIRCLES AND THE GROWTH OF CRITICAL THINKING

Judith Scott and *Jan Wells*

The middle school years are a critical junction in the lives of children. Their bodies are changing, they are trying to discover who they are, and they are struggling for independence. In this struggle, it seems reasonable that they would turn to literature for guidance. Instead, there is abundant evidence that, although they are capable of reading, many students in grades 5 through 12 choose not to read on their own (Early, 1984; Anderson, Wilson & Fielding, 1988). By the time students reach middle school, most of them are able to deal with literal aspects of comprehension, and they can connect details that are obviously related (Early, 1984). On the other hand, as a group, they seem to have difficulty in responding to the more demanding critical and creative aspects of reading comprehension (Pikulski, 1991). For instance, in the 1987 NAEP (National Assessment of Educational Progress) reading assessment (Applebee, Langer, & Mullis, 1988), seventh graders were reported as able to read with surface understanding, but they had difficulty when they were asked to think more deeply about what they had read, or when they were asked to defend, elaborate or write about their ideas.

Oldfather (1995) links diminishing motivation for literacy learning in the middle grades to fewer opportunities for self-expression in their learning environments. According to Oldfather, authentic self-expression is linked to becoming "part of a community of learners that enriches and extends mutual thinking and ideas, and enhances their motivation for further engagement in reading and writing" (p. 422). Creating an effective learning environment where students think deeply about their reading, with the ability to defend or elaborate their ideas, and where they read for enjoyment, is a central task for middle school teachers. This chapter describes how one grade 5 teacher used a variation of literature circles to create such a community of learners.

The authors of this chapter are part of a teacher/researcher group that has been looking at issues related to language awareness and vocabulary development for the past 4 years (Scott, Jones, Blackstone, Cross, Skobel, & Hayes, 1994; Scott, Blackstone, Cross, Jones, Skobel, Wells, & Jensen, 1996). In particular, we have been looking for ways to help students develop an appreciation for words and to experience enjoyment and satisfaction in their use (Baumann & Kameenui, 1991). A central concept in this work is the idea of instructional scaffolding where the teacher's task is to provide temporary support for children's efforts until they can complete a task on their own (Bruner, 1974; Langer & Applebee, 1986). As the teacher/researcher group was looking at the power of language in the classroom, specifically the development and enhancement of word awareness in children, Jan decided to investigate what happens when this focus is integrated into literature circles during novel studies.

Jan's Journey

In May, after following my new approach for the year, I asked my class of ten- and eleven-year-olds to write their reflections and to discuss whether they liked working in novel study groups. Here are some of the replies.

Alison: Yes, because it makes me think harder. If I don't understand something the other people help me understand. It's a responsibility.

Amanda: Yes, because you get to tell the others what you think and they can say what they think. Also you get to see if everyone agrees or if they have other opinions.

Jaqueline: Yes, I like it because you can tell other people what you think and they can tell you what they think and if you don't understand something they can help you.

Charlotte: Yes, because it makes you understand the book more. Also, because it is funner. It also gets you to think about the book more.

Brett: Yes, because there is only four people and not the whole class and you get to choose the book.

Lyndsay: Yes, because you have all sorts of opinions. I also like it because it is demanding for you and you do your work.

Janette: Yes, because you get to read a book and share your opinions with friends and not in front of the class and you can tell someone about what you felt.

Robbie: Yes, because it makes you not just read—you get to express your reading.

The themes that emerge relate clearly to self-expression and deeper understanding. But to get there, I had to examine my role as a teacher. Organizing novel study groups was a departure for me and a risk-taking exercise. I had to let go of my control of the ideas being discussed. I had to trust that the class, divided into "book-groups," would actually read and engage in discussion. I had to let go of assigning activities that develop comprehension and believe in the power of talk to generate new meanings. These responses confirm that my hunch was right. Young readers will develop and grow together when the power of the peer group is harnessed for learning.

As a teacher of reading over many years, I have tried various structures to provide successful learning experiences for my students with the goal of developing positive and thoughtful readers who know that picking up a book is a good way to spend time. Yet as I observed my classroom over the past few years, I felt a need to do something more, to take the ideas I have about student choice and ownership in reading even further. It seemed to me that usually it was me who set the reading agenda, either by choosing the material to be read or by demanding assignments that would demonstrate the students' understandings. I was offering open-ended ways for the children to tell me about the literature in their own words, but I sensed that often they were floundering to discover what it was I expected of them. While believing in reader-response theory, I was not facilitating the sort of enthusiastic sense of engagement with the literature that I wanted for my students. Their journal writing was too often vague and devoid of real interest. They did not own the response; they were trying to do an assignment for the teacher. And these students were, with one or two exceptions, enthusiastic readers who willingly engaged in silent reading and who enjoyed reading for pleasure.

The missing piece seemed to be the talk in the classroom that builds a sense of a community of readers. To be sure it was there when we all read a novel together, but that was when I directed the activity and when I asked the questions. I wanted to devolve responsibility for the discussions from myself to the students. I wanted them to become members of book clubs who meet to enjoy a book together and feel a sense of belonging. I believe that our understanding of what is happening in a novel is best explored through talking to others, adding to our own insights by comparing our ideas with those of other readers. I wanted my students to learn that there are many ways to respond to a text and that different people often have different reactions as we read. What speaks to one reader may not be significant to another. Yet I knew that I must provide some structure or "scaffolding" to help facilitate these discussions. They would not happen without some teaching on my part.

I have often had the children keep reading journals, asking them to write about the things that they think about as they read. My guideline for journal writing exhorts them to record their feelings, to comment on what they like and dislike in a book. They are encouraged to connect the book to their own lives and to comment on the questions that they have in respect to the story. I have tried through my responses in their journals to push their thinking further. "Why do you think this happened?" "What is the reason for this do you suppose?" Somehow our dialogue never seemed to go any further and the constraints of time meant that my reading and responding in the journals never seemed to be fast enough—by the time they got them back they had read the whole book and were on to the next one! So I knew that I needed to find a way to improve the method I taught the students to write and think about books without taking away from them their ownership of the response.

As we entered this school year I decided to try a new way of organizing our reading groups. Inspired by Harvey Daniels (1994), I wanted to organize literature circles where each student would have specific responsibilities. In his book *Literature Circles: Voice and Choice in the Student-Centered Classroom*, Daniels describes how high-school students discussed literature by adopting one of a number of lenses and focusing for each discussion on the aspect of response that they had chosen. Instead of being faced by the overwhelming instruction to respond to the literature, each student was to be responsible for a different aspect of the response. Roles were created and described, which between them added up to the bigger picture. Over time every student would take a turn at every role so that by the end of a novel they had covered all aspects of reader response, and by working collaboratively with their group had fully explored the text. The idea of roles seemed so simple and yet so effective! I felt sure that this would work for my fifth graders. It also offered me an opportunity to create the role of Word Hunter, thereby directing one child in every group of four to focus exclusively on the language of the novel. In this way I would be able to see if word awareness, the focus of our teacher research group, could be enhanced through the literature program. I decided to implement these ideas, adapting them to meet the needs of my class.

Learning to Respond in Role Through a Read-Aloud Novel

Learning how to do literature circles was introduced in phases. First, in September, I read a short novel aloud. As I read I stopped and orally asked the children to respond. I taught them to be Discussion Directors. This role

demands that the reader ask questions about the selection read and make predictions. Together we brainstormed the big questions arising from each section as I read it and together we sought answers. Why were characters taking
the actions they were? What would happen next? Was there anything we
didn't understand? What puzzled us about the chapter? Discussion Directors
raise issues and try to answer questions. They also act as "chairpersons" for
their group, directing the conversation. I wrote the responsibilities of Discussion Directors on a chart and posted it on the classroom wall.

Next, I taught them to be Friends of the Characters. In this role we pretend that the main characters are friends of ours. We try to decide how they
are feeling at the moment. Are things going well or badly for them? What
are they doing and why? What advice might we give them? What kind of
people are these characters? Do we recognise them and understand them?
Do we like them as people? What do we like and dislike about them? There
are often times when the Friends of the Characters respond to the same issues that have been raised by Discussion Directors; the roles are not in reality discrete. Keeping them separate is merely a device for organizing and
making manageable the whole business of discussing a book.

The next role was Connector. Through this lens we think about the
story in relation to our own experience. How do we feel as a reader about
what is happening? Does it make us happy, sad, angry, or leave us un-
moved? What experiences have we had that we can remember when we have
felt the same as the characters in the story? Again, there is an overlapping of
ideas here with those of the other roles, especially Friends of the Characters.

Finally, we learned how to be Word Hunters. In this role we pay attention to the word choice of the author. We look for examples of particularly
rich or expressive language. We seek powerful adjectives and adverbs, unusual turns of phrase, and deliberate imagery. We called these Gifts of
Words because it is as if a writer has given us something special, a gift of
language used uniquely. In asking the students to focus on words in this way
I hoped to develop their sense of the power of language to express ideas and
move the reader. I also hoped to see some transference of this awareness to
their own written expression and in their ability to look at the author's craft.

Learning to Work in Small Groups

Once we had explored these roles through the read-aloud novel in September, we were ready for the second phase during which the students read a
book together. They each had a copy of the novel *The Sky is Falling* (1989)
by Kit Pearson, a Canadian novel set in World War II concerning two
children who are evacuated from London to Toronto for the duration of
the war. This is a popular novel with both girls and boys and had the
added attraction for us of being written by a local author whom some of
the children had met.

I divided the book into sections, typically two or three chapters, and posted these on the blackboard. We met twice a week, on Monday and Thursday, to discuss the sections. The book took 6 weeks to complete. My goal in organizing the whole class to read the same book in this way was to reinforce the responsibilities of the four roles and to get the children used to working in groups. The children signed up in groups of four to be Discussion Directors, Connectors, Word Hunters, and Friends of the Characters.

Figure 10.1 Grade Five Novel Study Unit

The Sky is Falling
by Kit Pearson

- You will be reading this novel together with your classmates during the next six weeks.

- You are required to do the following assignments:

  1. Read the chapters assigned by the dates posted on the homework board. You can read in school and at home but *you must have your book in school for discussions*. Some chapters may be read aloud in class by your teacher.

  2. Keep a reading journal with entries written chapter by chapter and be ready to share in discussions on the dates posted. You will have different roles for different chapters.

     The roles are:

     > Discussion Directors
     >
     > Connectors
     >
     > Word Hunters
     >
     > Friends of the Characters

  3. Bring your reading journal to class and be ready to talk about the chapters with your group. You will first meet with other people who have had the same role as you. Then you will meet with people from other groups or with the whole class.

How will you do a good job in this unit?

- Be ready on time with the chapter read.

- Do your responses in time for the discussion.

- Bring your journal to class with the entries up to date.

- Be prepared to talk in your group.

Each member of the group of four would have the same role. In their journals they wrote responses in role that they brought to their group to share. In class they read to each other from the journals, comparing what each had decided to write about. When the small group discussions ended, the class met as a whole and shared the ideas of all the four roles. We heard from each group the main ideas that they had discussed. This is the guideline that I gave to the students outlining the project.

Figure 10.2 Guideline For Keeping Your Reading Journal

At the end of each chapter take out your journal and write! You will have one of the following roles.

DISCUSSION DIRECTORS: Write about one or more of the following things:

Any questions you have about what is happening in the story.

Any predictions you might have.

Anything of importance that you think your group should discuss about this chapter.

CONNECTORS: Write about any connections you make between the events in the book and your own experience.

Have you ever felt like the character in the book? Discuss these feelings.

Have you ever been placed in a situation similar to the one faced by the character in the book? Write about it.

How do you feel about what's happening? Does it puzzle you, make you mad, sad or happy?

WORD HUNTERS: Write any words or phrases that jump out at you as evidence of the writer's craft or seem to you to be a Gift of Words.

Describe what it is you like about these words. Why are they special?

FRIENDS OF THE CHARACTERS: Write about the characters in the novel.

What is happening to them? How are they feeling?

What sort of people are they? Why do they behave the way they do?

During the reading of *The Sky is Falling,* I noticed a number of things about the process that I thought were interesting. The journal writing was some of the best I had ever read—the focus provided by the clearly defined roles helped these young readers organize their thinking. They didn't write vast amounts, in fact the opposite, but what they did write was pertinent and text-specific. I could tell by reading the journals that the reading had been done and that understandings about the book were emerging. Here's a sample from Katannya's journal. She is one of the Friends of the Characters:

> Norah feels weird because she is going into a very big house and it is mostly boys things. But she feels happy because she is going to sleep in the tower. Gavin feels happy too because he got lots of lipstick all over his cheeks and mouth. Norah is acting that way because she just came to move to a new house with new people she doesn't know. Gavin is acting that way because he got a new toy, a model aeroplane. They are acting the way they are because it's like going to a classroom with no one you know. (Of course they are going to a school.) She had to leave and they only wanted Gavin. That's why too.

Although there are some cryptic references here to the way the characters are acting, Katannya shows me that she has understood the essential dynamic of the story. Norah is unhappy at leaving her friends and family in England and feels rejected by the family in Canada who clearly prefers boys. Her somewhat gauche behaviour is explicable once we understand her feelings. Katannya shows that she understands the dramatic tension in the novel and demonstrates her empathy for the child in the story by analogy to everyday experience ". . . It's like going to a classroom with no one you know." In the discussion group with other Friends of the Characters students would have an opportunity to flesh out these ideas.

My role during these discussions was to visit each group briefly, to see that all was going well, and to check the status of the class. I had kept the evaluation criteria very simple—to do well all you had to do was participate! Of course, remembering to have the book and the journal in class at a specific time is not easy for fifth graders and one of the biggest learnings for them as a result of this process has been that of organization of time and materials. When a child comes to class without the work done and with no journal to share, the whole group has a problem. As a class we talked about what we could do when this happened. The students were far harder on the miscreants than I would have been! They decided that a person who didn't do their work would have to take notes during the discussion. They would also have to have their response ready for next time and read it first before the business of the day. No getting away with not doing it! As Lyndsay said, "I like it because it is demanding for you and you do your work." The peer pressure to be responsible to the group was an aspect of this that I had not predicted. No one wants to let the group down by being unprepared. This was particularly important once we moved to the third phase in which each student represented one of the four roles in a group. If one person forgot their journal then one of the roles was missing and the others gave them a hard time.

I also noticed that the quality of the group work was steadily improving. I could sit back and watch the groups get to work without there being a lot of fuss or management issues to deal with. These students liked the work and looked forward to the discussions. I attribute this to a number of factors. First, they worked in friendship groups. Middle school students want to work with their friends and are often most productive when allowed to do so. One of the perennial problems of the classroom is the wide range of interest and ability in any group of students. I didn't want students to be grouped by ability, but grouping by friendship patterns did in fact lead to the creation of fairly homogeneous groups. Students who choose to work together are often like-minded people. Of course, there are in any classroom those individuals who are hard to place in cooperative groups, but over time we have worked at various compromises and combinations of students to be as equitable and harmonious as possible. By and large, this system of book groups taps into the inherent sociability of the students at this age.

Another reason for the success of the discussions is the preparation for talk that has taken place through the writing of the journal entries. These literally provide a text for talk. If nothing else, each group has to listen while four people read aloud their writing. The Discussion Directors are in charge of organizing turn-taking and asking such questions as, "Do you have any more to say?" At best the journal entries provide a mere springboard for wider-ranging talk that goes far beyond what has been written. Through the coming together of four readers the ideas blossom, and new insights are revealed in discussion—new ideas actually created when four minds share their perceptions.

Finally, I think the literature itself had a role to play. When the book is engaging and the students really like it, then the group work is successful. During subsequent phases I saw this work in reverse—a group who had chosen a novel that did not engage their interest had a difficult time staying on task during discussions. Choosing rich literature at an appropriate reading level is crucial, and I enlisted the help of my school librarian in looking for titles.

Developing Independence in Book Groups

In the third phase, the book groups became independent of me and organized their own schedules. I provided sets of four novels that represented a range of readability and interest. In groups of four they chose a book that they all agreed they wanted to read. I gave book talks to whet the appetite for many of the titles, but my recommendations did not always sway the choices. The students then divided up the novels and assigned each person a different role for each discussion. Figure 10.3 is a sample of how this was done from Lyndsay's journal.

So Lyndsay, reading *Bridge to Terabithia*, will be a Friend of the Characters for Chapters 1, 2, and 3. She will be the Discussion Director for Chapters 4, 5, and 6. For the third response she will be the Word Hunter and for the final response she will be the Connector. Her three friends also write the schedule in their journals and ensure that for every discussion there is someone responsible for each role. Now when they meet they address the questions raised by the Discussion Director; they discuss the events of the story and what is happening to the characters; they make connections from the story to their own experiences; they discuss the Gifts of Words chosen by the Word Hunter. I encourage them to add to their writing during the discussions. They annotate their entries jotting down the answers to questions and adding more Gifts of Words. Figure 10.4 is the guideline that I gave to the children for this phase of the study.

The class read three books in this way in the same groups. After three novels were read in these book clubs, we decided it was time to reflect on what was happening and decide on some modifications. We watched a video of our group work taking place and listened to our discussions. We created a list of those criteria that make the process very successful and posted these on the wall. At this point I decided to have the groups reform so that everyone could work and meet with completely different people. Some children were more successful in this system than others, and I wanted to share these more able readers and writers equitably throughout the groups to help less reflective readers engage in deeper discussions. The original groups read at different rates. Some children are faster readers, some were reading longer books. The system is flexible enough to allow for the differences between the types of novels and the different needs of the groups but it demands refinement and fine tuning as you go along. Every class will be different and adjustments need to be made to make it as successful for everyone as it possibly can be.

What criteria for success did we come up with? The students decided that to be a really good Discussion Director you had to find really important questions that don't have immediately obvious answers—questions that give the group something to talk about. An open question such as "Why do their parents think something is going to happen if they play together?" gives more scope for opinion than a closed question such as "What is the dog's name?" Yet it is important to be able to ask those specific questions such as "Is this book set a long time ago?" because these are the details which are the necessary building blocks of comprehension. Friends of the Characters need to be able to write about the character such that "you would know them

Figure 10.3 Sample from Lyndsay's Journal

Feb 6 Bridge to Terabithia

        1st Response-chap 1, 2, 3 = Friends of the characters

        2nd Response chap 4, 5, 6 = Disscusion Director

        3rd Response chap 7, 8, 9 = Word hunter

        4th Response chap 10, 11, 12, 13 Connector

Figure 10.4 Grade 5 Novel Study Spring Term

This term you will be studying novels together with a group of three other students. You will be called a NOVEL STUDY GROUP.

Your novel study group will discuss the book you choose and work together to reach an understanding of the book. You will tell the rest of us about the book when you have finished it.

This is what you will do.

1. Choose a book that you all wish to read.
2. Divide the book into six to eight manageable chunks, 20 pages or so. List these in your reading journal.
3. Decide on a role for each person in the group for the first reading response. You must have one of each role; (Discussion Director, Connector, Word Hunter, Friend of the Characters). Make a note of the date of the first discussion.
4. During the discussion in class everyone will share what they have written and discuss predictions, problems, connections, interesting words, etc. You can add more to your journal during the discussion.
5. Decide on your role for the next reading response. You must have a new one each time. Make a note of the date of the next discussion.
6. To do well in this unit you must keep up with the reading and responding, bring your journal to every class, and be ready to talk in your group.

---

if you met them." They also "bring them to life." To be an effective Connector you have to show that you have understood how people in the book are feeling and talk about the significance of those feelings, remembering times when you have felt the same way. You can then tell your own stories, which are triggered by the events in the book. Most of all Connectors "show empathy." Word Hunters do a good job when they choose words and phrases that appeal to the ear. Often we can't say why we like them—we just do. The children will say "because it paints a picture in my mind" or "because I can see it clearly." The journal writing in all the roles is improved by everyone who remembers to include headings and page numbers and to use quotation marks when quoting from the book.

This year of novel study has been the most successful for me that I have ever taught, and I have seen enormous enthusiasm for reading. When I suggested that maybe we might change it and do something different an outcry erupted.

The students have developed a vocabulary for talking about books that is inclusive of a range of opinion, precise in its textual reference, and that clearly demonstrates their ability to find the details to support a main idea. Here is the transcription of conversation between four girls who have read a book called *The Baby Project*. In this novel, by Sarah Ellis, Jessica's mother has a baby, a surprise for the already grown-up sons and 10-year-old Jessica. Very shortly after her birth, however, Lucy dies an unexplained crib death and the family is plunged into grief. In their different ways they deal with their loss, and the readers in this discussion group are trying to establish how exactly everyone is reacting and why. To set the context, Simon and Rowan are the two brothers, Charlene is a neighbour and Margaret is Jessica's school friend. I have annotated the transcript with my interpretation of each turn in the conversation.

Student		My Reflections
Lyndsay (Connector)	Their parents are weird. Like, um, in chapter 11, page 115, um, (reading from the book) "She ripped off. . . Mom grabbed Simon by his jacket and slammed him against the wall. She ripped off his headphones and threw them on the floor."	Makes proposition and quotes from text citing page reference in support.
Alison (Friend of the characters)	She. . . I think she is more embarrassed or confused. Yeah.	Interprets character's behaviour by suggesting feelings.
Lyndsay	No, she's sort of fed up I think.	Makes a counter suggestion.

Student		My Reflections
Janette (Word hunter)	Confused I think. Actually, I think she is more angry because she's trying to like, she's trying to get over, um, from losing Lucy, plus she has Jessica, and then there is Simon and he's just not doing anything, he's just being a smart alec, and. . .	Agrees with Alison; then making another suggestion to explain the Mum's behaviour.
Lyndsay	Yeah, like he's swearing at his Mom.	Agrees with Janette and cites example.
Alison	Okay he is not saying like "I miss her so much" and he is not offering to comfort her, he's just sitting there like a jerk.	Agrees and gives more evidence in support of the idea.
Amanda (Discussion Director)	Yeah	Gives affirmation.
Janette	He is not going like we haven't hurt her	Gives further example.
Amanda	Okay, do you have anything else?	Discussion Director moves the conversation to a new topic.
Alison	Okay, well, Charlene and Jessica make up because it sounded like they were in a little bit of a fight . . .	Friend of the characters reports events.
Lyndsay	Yeah because Jessica was really unhappy.	Agrees and gives reason.
Janette	And she is like, "Oh, okay" and when her Mom came out she was like "Do you need anything at the local store?" "No" but then when the Mom came out he said "Yeah" but from the store further away.	Adds more detail by citing an incident.
Alison	That's not true.	Disagrees.
Janette	Yeah, it is.	Disagrees.
Alison	They were all at the table and then, um, he said, "Aah", and he looked at her eyes and said "Okay." She didn't come into the room.	Supports her opinion with details from the book.

Student		**My Reflections**
Lyndsay	Yeah, she said she needed apple juice from the far away store.	Agrees with Janette.
Amanda	Yeah	Agreeing.
Janette	I think it was because they wanted to talk about her.	Offers a reason for the father and mother's behaviour.
Amanda	Yeah, they did because, you know, you could get the same kind of apple juice at the other store and it was closer.	Agrees and supports the idea with detail.
Alison	And you know what . . . Jessica is kind of feeling like "Oh, well I'd better leave them alone" but in a way I think she is feeling kind of left out or something . . .	Describes and explains Jessica's feelings.
Amanda	Yeah	Affirms.
Alison	. . . because she can't do much to make the baby come back, and they are doing all that, and they are planning the funeral and she is just kind of like . . . oh	Continues her thoughts.
Amanda	Yeah, I know, and usually like her Mom has talks and all that kind of stuff, but now she is just sort of feeling "I don't want to be around her."	Agrees and clarifies by adding further evidence.
Janette	Yeah, well, she hasn't talked to Margaret after the funeral.	Agrees and introduces new idea.
Amanda	Yeah.	Affirms.
Lyndsay	After the funeral party sort of thing?	Seeks clarification.
Janette	Yeah, after they have . . .	Begins to give clarification.
Alison	She doesn't talk to Margaret again. That is the last time she talks to Margaret.	Interrupts to give more information.
Janette	Is it?	Seeks clarification.

Student		**My Reflections**
Alison	Yeah, I read the whole book.	Gives clarification.
Lyndsay	Oh, well don't tell us then!	Request.
Amanda	Okay, Lyndsay, do you want to go now?	Discussion Director moves the discussion along by turning to the Connector.
Lyndsay	Okay, I'm the Connector and I think that Jessica is sad but I don't think she'll, I don't think, I think she is exaggerating when she says she'll never be happy again.	Offers opinion based on own feelings.
Alison	Well in a way . . .	Tentatively agrees.
Amanda	Yeah.	Affirms.
Alison	. . . 'cause she feels she told Charlene that she feels bad about having so much fun and thinking about Lucy when she is dead and . . .	Adds a reason by citing evidence from the book.
Amanda	Yeah	Affirms.
Alison	. . . she's trying to, um, and Simon is kind of like trying to feel sorry for her but it's kind of not working	Tries to clarify her thoughts about Jessica.
Lyndsay	Yeah, but like, I don't really get it because I mean she is not that big a part of the story, Lucy, she is not that big a character in their family . . .	Offers own opinion based on evidence from the book.
Alison	She makes the disaster.	Sees the bigger picture—the role of the baby in the story.
Lyndsay	. . . I would be sad, but I wouldn't think that I would never be happy again.	Connecting—giving own opinion based on knowledge of self.
Amanda	Yeah except the thing is, the thing is . . .	Disagreeing.

Student		My Reflections
Janette	You'll always be sad but you will be happy again	Agreeing—reformulates the idea.
Lyndsay	Yeah	Affirms.
Amanda	. . . the thing is that she was just like, she was just born so it is kind of sad because now she doesn't have a life	Continues her train of thought; brings a new idea.
Alison	Yeah and you know for the heredity or whatever it's called, they never did find out and Simon says to Jessica in one part that they never found out what colour her eyes were going to be or what she is like and stuff because that was part of the heredity	Agrees and adds on with more evidence.

As they talk I can see these girls contributing equally to the development of the thinking. They analyze incidents in the story seeking their significance—why did the parents send Jessica to the far away store for apple juice when it could have been obtained nearby? How is Jessica feeling as a result of all the strange adult behaviour? How does she react to the baby's death and why does she feel guilty for laughing with Charlene? Why doesn't she see her friend Margaret again? How would you feel if your baby sister died? These questions are generated by the readers here, not by their teacher. They pursue what interests them, and at the end of the novel they are prepared to make an informed judgment as to its success for them as readers. Alison wrote (see Figure 10.5).

Literature circles using roles in reading journals have opened a world of literary discussion in my classroom that is thoughtful and respectful, specific and yet wide-ranging, personal and yet text-related. I know that the majority of the readers in my class have become more thoughtful readers, more sensitive to the nuances of characterization, more finely tuned to notice cause and effect. And they are particularly more aware of words and the writer's role in choosing particular words for particular purposes.

Conclusion

Over the year, Jan created an environment where children could develop ownership in their literacy learning, where discussion brought out different interpretations, and where students learned to clarify and justify their thoughts. Applebee (1991) describes five dimensions of effective environments for teaching the English language arts: Ownership, Appropriateness,

Figure 10.5 Alison's Response to *The Baby Project Journal*

Feb. 15, 96.　　　✳ evaluation of The Baby Project ✳

At the start of the book Jessica was a normal girl with a family, but when her Mom tells Jessica that she's pregnat that is a bit of a shock.

I think that Sarah was trying to get to us that babies do die even if you love them. I think Jessica was not expecting anything to happen to Lucie. You know what?. It's true that babys bring back old memories that no one talks about. At the end of the book Jessica was a little bit more aware of things. For a moment I actually thought Jessica didn't believe Lucie was dead. It was like a nightmare to Jessica. What I think Sorah is trying to tell us is; a normal person's life can change fast! Out of a 100 I rate the book 80 there were no gifts of words (barley any) and It wasen't exiting. It was a fairly good book and I recomend it.

Collaboration, Support, and Internalization. Ownership occurs when students are encouraged to develop and defend their own interpretations of their reading as Alison, Lyndsay, Janette, and Amanda do in lines 2 through 8, rather than accepting the teacher's predetermined view. Taking responsibility for their interpretations and defending their positions becomes an expected reality instead of an anomaly.

The materials that students use are appropriate because they are choosing books that they will read in social groups. The books available cover a range of levels, and children quickly learn that reading a book together with friends may make a difficult book manageable. It became noticeable that the books that generated the best discussions were ones that posed some hermeneutic challenges. When they had to struggle to understand what was happening, they worked at it together and enjoyed a sense of discovery. *The Giver* (1993) was a tough read for some groups, and students who might have abandoned the book in an individualized reading program were rewarded by perseverance as their group began to clarify the story together. In contrast, books that were too easy, or written to a formula, did not offer enough substance for discussion. Connectors would often say "You can't really identify with it," and Word Hunters would complain that there were "No gifts of words." Working in this way has really helped the students to see that "you can't judge a book by its cover." Asked what was learned about reading this year by doing discussion groups, Lyndsay replied, "You sort of compare books. You become so aware that each book is different— say that book had the most questions but this book had more gifts of words." Janette agreed with her: "So you're more aware. One book has this, and one book has that. You see them on the library shelf and you think they look the same but they're not. They're, like, totally different." These young readers are discovering intertextual similarities and differences that are the beginnings of critical response.

Evaluation was replaced by collaboration. The criteria for success was laid out in a simple and straightforward manner: To do a good job in the unit, students had to keep up with the reading and responding, bring their journals to every class, and be ready to talk in their groups.

The structured progression from whole-class read-aloud to independent group work exemplifies the gradual release of responsibility that is a central tenet of instructional scaffolding. In the beginning, Jan provided the framework and modeling that guided the students toward eventual independence. As the students became more competent in their roles and self-expression, she stepped further and further out of the picture. They, in turn, internalized the mode of discussion that was expected, and were able, later in the year, to reflect on and modify the way in which the roles contributed to the group discussions.

Reading and discussing good books can help middle school students through this unsettled period in their lives. Characters in books often face issues that students may face, or they may experience similar feelings. The Friend of the Characters and Connector roles allow the students to explore these feelings or issues in a low-risk environment. Students know that talking with others helps them learn (Oldfather, 1995). As Marcel, a seventh-grade student, commented in an interview with Oldfather (1995): "Talking is a very important part of learning for me. In talking with friends, you mix ideas and build ideas. We need schools where talk is possible."

Let us echo that sentiment—We need schools where talk is possible. If we want middle school children to become intrinsically motivated to read, to handle the critical and creative aspects of reading comprehension effectively, and to think more deeply, we need to provide opportunities for them to do so. This chapter has provided one model that worked with one teacher in one environment. We would like to invite others to use it as a frame, a scaffold, for providing opportunities for students to talk and to take charge of their own learning.

References

Anderson, R. C., Wilson, P., & Fielding, L. (1988). Growth in reading and how children spend their time outside of school. *Reading Research Quarterly, 23*(3), 285–303.

Applebee, A. (1991). Environments for language teaching and learning: Contemporary issues and future directions. In J. Flood, J. Jensen, D. Lapp, & J. Squire (Eds.), *Handbook of research on teaching the English Language Arts* (pp. 549–556). New York: Macmillan.

Applebee, A., Langer, J., & Mullis, I. (1988). *Who reads best? Factors related to reading achievement in grades 3, 7 and 11.* Princeton, NJ: Educational Testing Service.

Baumann, J. F., & Kameenui, E. J. (1991). Research on vocabulary: Ode to Voltaire. In J. Flood, J. Jensen, D. Lapp, & J. Squire (Eds.), *Handbook of research on teaching the English language arts* (pp. 604–632). New York: Macmillan.

Bruner, J. (1974). *Beyond the information given: Studies in the psychology of knowing.* London, England: George Allen and Unwin.

Daniels, H. (1994). *Literature circles: Voices and choice in the student-centered classroom.* Markham, ONT: Pembroke Publishers.

Early, M. (1984). *Learning to read in grades 5-12.* New York: Harcourt Brace Jovanovich.

Langer, J., & Applebee, A. (1986). Reading and writing instruction: Toward a theory of teaching and learning. In E. Z. Rothkopf (Ed.), *Review of research in education, 13,* 171–194.

Oldfather, P. (1995). Commentary: What's needed to maintain and extend motivation for literacy in the middle grades. *Journal of Reading, 38*(6), 420–422.

Pikulski, J. (1991). The transition years: Middle school. In J. Flood, J. Jensen, D. Lapp, & J. Squire (Eds.), *Handbook of research on teaching the English language arts* (pp. 303–319). New York: Macmillan.

Scott, J., Jones, A., Blackstone, T., Cross, S., Skobel, B., & Hayes, E. (1994, May). *The gift of words: Creating a context for rich language use.* Presented at the 39th Annual Convention of the International Reading Association, Toronto, ONT.

Scott, J., Blackstone, T., Cross, S., Jones, A., Skobel, B., Wells, J., & Jensen, Y. (1996, May). *The power of language: Creating contexts which enrich children's understanding and use of words.* Presented at the 41st Annual Convention of the International Reading Association, New Orleans, LA.

Trade Books Cited

Ellis, S. (1986). *The baby project.* New York: Bradbury.

Lowry, L. (1993). *The Giver.* Boston, MA: Houghton Mifflin.

Paterson, K. (1977). *Bridge to Terabithia.* New York: Harper & Row.

Pearson, K. (1989). *The sky is falling.* New York: Viking Penguin.

Appendix

A short list of suggested novels for literature discussion groups for middle school students.

Aiken, J. (1981). *The Wolves of Willoughby Chase*. Dell.

Babbitt, N. (1975). *Tuck Everlasting*. Farrar, Straus & Giroux.

Bell, W. (1990). *Forbidden City*. Doubleday.

Byars, B. (1968). *The Midnight Fox*. Viking.

Cooper, S. (1968). *Over Sea Under Stone*. Puffin.

Creech, S. (1994). *Walk Two Moons*. Macmillan.

Doyle, B. (1978). *Hey Dad!* Groundwood.

Doyle, B. (1984). *Angel Square*. Groundwood.

Ellis, S. (1986). *The Baby Project*. Groundwood.

Fleishmann, P. (1980). *The Half-a-Moon Inn*. Harper & Row.

Garrigue, S. (1985). *The Eternal Spring of Mr. Ito*. Macmillan.

Holm, A. (1974). *I am David.* Puffin.

Kogowa, J. (1988). *Naomi's Road*. Oxford.

Lawson, J. (1993). *White Jade Tiger Beach*. Holme.

Lewis, C. S. (1950). *The Lion, the Witch and the Wardrobe*. Macmillan.

Little, J. (1989). *Different Dragons*. Puffin.

Little, J. (1986). *Mama's Going To Buy You a Mockingbird*. Puffin.

Lowry, L. (1990). *Number the Stars*. Dell.

Lowry, L. (1993). *The Giver*. Houghton Mifflin.

Lunn, J. (1985). *The Root Cellar*. Puffin.

MacLachlan, P. (1985). *Sarah, Plain and Tall*. Harper & Row.

Magorian, M. (1981). *Goodnight Mr.Tom*. Harper & Row.

Naidoo, B. (1986). *Journey to Jo'Burg: A South African Story*. Harper & Row.

Park, R. (1984). *Playing Beattie Bow*. Puffin.

Paterson, K. (1977). *Bridge to Terabithia*. Harper & Row.

Paterson, K. (1987). *The Great Gilly Hopkins*. Harper & Row.

Paulsen, G. (1988). *Hatchet*. Puffin.

Pearce, P. (1991). *Tom's Midnight Garden*. Dell.

Pearson, K. (1991). *A Handful of Time*. Puffin.

Yep, L. (1992). *The Star Fisher*. Puffin.

Yolen, J. (1990). *The Devil's Arithmetic*. Puffin.

Chapter 11
USING DIALECTICAL JOURNALS TO BUILD BEGINNING LITERARY RESPONSE

Sandra L. Robertson

The Teachable Moment

What if they say "he" and you don't know who the players are?
Arianna

How come no books start on page one?
Nick

What does "ab or ring gee" mean?
Kristen

In the general shuffle and commotion as we hand out copies of the novel *Walkabout* by James Vance Marshall, these three comments are spoken aloud. We haven't yet begun to read *or* write, but students are responding to the text they have before them, and I am making mental notes about the teachable moments these comments offer. I mentally revise the beginning of my minilesson, thinking about how I can use what Arianna, Nick, and Kristin have said as examples to explain the use of a dialectical journal, my version of Berthoff's (1981) double-entry journal, to record our responses as we read this novel together. My initial response, three times in a row, in fact, and to the amusement of all, is "Write that down in your dialectical journal."

"What's a dialectical journal?" comes a chorus of voices.

"Ah, I'm so glad you asked," I smile back at the class.

We are halfway through the school year, living together for 45 minutes a day in a workshop setting where we have been reading and writing both self-selected and teacher-directed topics and texts. This particular class is a seventh-grade class with a wide range of abilities: many students are reading self-selected books two or three years below grade level and need lots of support to read more challenging selections while others are college bound and reading at or above grade level. Every strategy I use is designed to both support and help students stretch no matter their level. Now, I introduce another stretching strategy, the dialectical journal (DJ). I explain that a DJ is a type of reader's notebook where they will record their thoughts about the novel they read and then share those thoughts with members of their collaborative group. Later, whole class discussions will be guided by the issues students share in these groups.

In using the DJ, as in using all the strategies I choose to include during that all-too-short but precious 45 minutes together, I attempt to create a classroom where language is used for learning and students' questions and responses to texts *are the curriculum* as much as any goal or objective predetermined by curriculum guides or district policy. The DJ provides one of the many places where questions and observations such as the ones from Arianna, Nick, and Kristen can be honored and addressed in a way that builds students' ability to discuss literature in serious ways as well as connect their reading to their writing.

How to Use the DJ

Rethinking quickly, then, I begin my minilesson by asking students to take out a piece of notebook paper and draw a line down the center. I ask them to label the left-hand column *Individual Response*, and the right column *Collaborative Group*. I do the same on an overhead projector and then ask everyone to write *Question* under the words *Individual Response* (see Figure 11.1).

"Who has questions so far, even though we haven't started reading yet?" I ask, and I am quickly told by Nick that we *have* started reading, since checking out the cover of the book is part of getting started, don't I remember that? So goes the daily life in seventh grade. "Yes Nick, you're right, and you did have a question about the page numbering, didn't you? Please write that down under your *Question* section, but ONLY Nick, because that's his question, right?" I also instruct Arianna and Kristen to write their questions, respectively, and then announce that they have already done one-half of their homework: to come up with one individual response to each of the first two chapters of the book. We then talk about the types of responses readers can have other than questions. For instance, besides questions, readers could respond with *Appreciations, Connections, Confusions, Observations,* or *Speculations* (see Figure 11.1).

Figure 11.1   Types of Responses for Dialectical Journal

The following chart of types of responses guides students' use of the DJ. The quote is one that stays on the board and becomes almost a mantra as we try to make visible our problems while reading and accept those *problems* as part of the reading process.

"If anything seems odd, boring, uninteresting, or confusing, it is probably important."

Lorraine Hansen

1. Questions

- vocabulary words
- plot (introduction, conflict, rising action, climax, conclusion)
- where the story takes place and what it's like (setting)
- who are the characters and what are their relationships (methods of characterization)

Who/what is _____?

2. Appreciations

- text rendering: pick a line that stands out for you, write the line, and say why (metaphors, similes, personification)

I like _____ because _____.

3. Connections

- showing your previous knowledge and/or intertextuality

This reminds me of _____ because _____.

4. Confusions

- anything you don't understand, feel lost about, but can't make into a question yet

I don't understand _____.

I feel lost because _____.

I thought I understood _____, but now _____.

5. Observations

- note down what you notice
- pay attention to techniques the author seems to repeat

I notice that _____.

The author always _____.

Figure 11.1 cont'd

---

6. Speculations

- prediction (what might happen next)

- character motivation (why a character acts as they do)

- theme or purpose of story (Why is this story important? What am I learning from it?)

It might be that _____.

It seems that _____.

Summary of instructions given over the course of several minilessons:

1. Read ___ pages (assigned in class/for homework) and record your responses as they occur.

2. Use the vocabulary of plot structure, conflict, show-not-tell writing, and methods of characterization in your responses.

3. Try to answer/respond to your own responses. We are not necessarily looking for right or wrong answers, but for your ideas. Your *wrong* answer may help us all understand something else of importance, which we won't know until we get there!

As we talk about these types of responses, which they have been doing all year, I tell them that as they read the first two chapters of *Walkabout*, they are to write down any question or line that stands out for them.

"Do we answer our questions?" asks Xavier.

"Good question," I respond. " Try to, but if you can't, just guess at what you think *might* be an answer, and we'll work on it together in class tomorrow. For instance, what was Nick's question?"

"Why books don't start on page one," Nick reminds us.

"Right. Can we answer that question by reading this particular book?"

Everyone agrees we can't, and we would have to go to some other person, such as the librarian, who would know more about how books are made, to an find an explanation.

"What about Kristen's question? Did you write it down on your paper, Kristen?"

"Yes," she answers, "but now I know what it means."

"How did you find out?" I probe.

"Emily told me it was *Aborigine*, and I already knew it."

"What was the problem then, why did you have a question about it?" I continue.

"Because I hadn't ever seen it in writing before."

"Terrific," I say and go on to Arianna: "Did you write down your question?"

"Not yet," she responds.

"What made you think of that question?" I ask.

"I was looking at this picture on the cover and I don't know what it is," she answers, referring to the silhouette of the Aborigine on the cover.

"How are you going to get your question answered?"

"I guess by reading the chapters," she replies.

"Yes, I hope so, too," I respond. I continue the minilesson by pointing out to the rest of the class that we have three very different but excellent questions here, each one an example of what each of the students truly wondered: genuine questions, which make the best questions. "Your question," I tell everyone, "is probably different than anyone else's, but by sharing all of our questions and appreciations together, we will get a richer reading of the story." For their homework, they were to read chapters 1 and 2, to self-select a question or appreciation for each chapter, to write them in the Individual Response column, and to bring them to class tomorrow.

I was particularly pleased with the range of the three questions from Arianna, Nick, and Kristen, and I was pleased that they offered a true teachable moment, the chance to discuss the procedures for using the DJ in the context of that particular class. In building the minilesson around their questions, students learn that their ideas are the core of our curriculum. It is in just such details of daily classroom life that we build the atmosphere of a literate community, doing literary work together.

This literary work continues the next day as students return with their completed Individual Response columns. I ask students to divide the page down the middle for several reasons: first, the page then becomes a kind of graphic organizer, enabling us to organize our learning and emerging knowledge so it can be seen as a process. Eventually, the DJ will have four columns, which when opened side by side will reveal to the students the development of their ideas and the growth of their understanding of their issues.

Page one of Arianna's DJ for chapters 1 and 2 of *Walkabout* follows (see Figure 11.2), so we can see the text-rendered line she chose along with her explanation, and her reconfiguration of her initial question.

She has chosen from chapter 1 a fairly sophisticated simile and attempts to explain why it stands out for her. She indicates her appreciation of the author's "thought" that "they" put into the line, indicating her awareness of a deliberate crafting by the author, and then indicates her awareness of audience for her DJ by saying, "You know what I mean." She's writing to the trusted adult: me, as the teacher. With her permission, I would make an overhead of this DJ for a minilesson and while praising Arianna's recognition and explanation of the simile, I would ask that next time she actually

Figure 11.2 Readers' Dialectical Journal *Walkabout* (Student Draft)

Individual Response	Collaborative Groups
Chapter 1 Appreciation: I liked the line. "Random fireflies zigzagged by. their night-lights flickering like sparklets from a rolling toy-sized forge." It stood out to me because of the way they said it like it took them thought otherwise they would probly just have writen "fireflys flying and glowing" you know what I mean. Questions: How many characters where 2 or 3? I got (as in humans) confused? How did his leg get inqured? Chapter 2: Confusion why did he get so afraid of the ants questions: where the ants brown or red? Did Pete know what Ants were. Chapter 3: mixed bag of connection and appreciation: appreciation because I liked how Peter said "I'm hungry Mary. what we going to eat? "Oh, Peter! It's not lunchtime yet!" "when will it be?" "I'll tell you when" It's a connection to me because everytime we go shopping I get hungry and I always ask my mom, if we	

use the term *simile*. If she does, I'll give her extra credit. By giving extra credit, and by using student examples on a daily basis to point out where extra credit is possible, the work of beginning literary analysis is made accessible to students. In order to make a claim about a text and support it, students need to be able to select the appropriate example and use the vocabulary specific to the field of literature to be convincing. I'd also explain that while I, as the teacher, may indeed "know what you mean," to use Arianna's words, the members of their collaborative group might not, and that she should try to write in her own words what she's trying to explain. Even if they think the audience for their journal is just me, the teacher, they should still try to explain their responses as fully as possible. Audience awareness is an important concept in reading and in writing about reading, just as it is in writing.

Arianna's reconfiguration of the question about the characters is an important question for her to ask, and she even qualifies it, indicating that the characters she is referring to are the humans, since there are so many animals introduced in the first two chapters. It's a perfectly logical question to ask, showing an awareness that animals sometimes count as characters. In fact, she's using intertextuality here, a concept we've also developed as part of our language awareness: earlier in the year we've read the animal story *Kavik The Wolf Dog* (1989), by Walt Moray, wherein the main character is the wolf dog. She's connecting her original question about *Walkabout* of who "he" is, assuming that the boy on the cover is one character, but he isn't in the story yet—or is he? Is Arianna asking if the boy on the cover is one of the two children introduced in the first two chapters? The point I'm making is that it is not poor reading on Arianna's part to ask this question; in fact, it is excellent attention to detail. She's trying to match the information on the cover of the book with what she's read, knowing that main characters are usually introduced in the first chapter or so of a book.

The next day, I expand the repertoire of responses by adding *Connections* and *Confusions* as possible responses. As a result, we see Arianna's responses to chapter 2 including these (see Figure 11.2). Spelling errors are not a concern, since DJ writing is considered draft-one writing, or note taking. The question that she lists under the heading *Confusion* should go under the heading *Questions*, but I wouldn't quibble at this point. The difference between a confusion and a question is itself fairly sophisticated, and I have it there for students and texts that warrant it. Some students read an entire book without a confusion, but with many questions. No single type of response is ever insisted upon. However, some students will always take the safe way out and ask only plot-related questions. Those students I will prod. Becky, a student in my gifted and talented class, clearly understands the difference between a confusion and a question, and she helped explain this difference during the minilesson on DJs to her class (see Figure 11.3).

Figure 11.3 Becky's Response

The difference between a confusion and a question is, is that when you have a question you're confused, but you know what you're confused about. That's why being confused isn't the same thing as a question. Being confused is having a question, but you don't know what the question is.

That's why a confusion is a statement (I'm confused about. . . .) And a question is stating what you're confused about (Who? Where? What?, etc.).

In Arianna's individual response we see her voice coming through, something I'm always delighted to see. I see the DJ as part of the bridge between personal narrative writing and more analytic exposition. Seeing personal voice here helps bridge that gap: "mixed bag of connection and appreciation," she writes, and then quotes a fairly lengthy piece to make her point (see Figure 11.2 under Arianna's heading "Chapter 2"). Here we see her personal identification with one of the main characters, his circumstances, and his relationships. One of the reasons for reading literature in general, and this novel in particular, is to provide students with opportunities to identify with and understand people in different cultures, circumstances, and conflicts. Arianna's journal entry shows us her ability to do that (". . . all that reminds me of myself"). I don't know if her level of understanding of Mary and Peter would be as accessible without the specific request to respond in the way that the DJ asks her to. This is only one of the many goals I have for using this method of response.

Setting Up Groups

Now that everyone has their completed individual response, we move into group discussion and complete the *Collaborative Group* column of our journals. Students have been sharing in pairs and fours all year, and they have been participating in both self-selected and teacher-directed groups, but by far the majority of time they've been in self-selected groups. For DJ discussion groups, I want to see a mixture of reading abilities, social skills, gender, and ethnicity. Again and again in group work, I see students who never volunteer in whole class discussion become leaders, both socially and intellectually, in small group discussions. I'll mix students in groups with two males and two females, quiet students with more talkative ones, strong readers with those less likely to complete the reading on time. By this time of year, forming these groups is fairly easy, since I know the students quite well. Sometimes I'll ask students to give me a list of those students with whom they really want to work, and of those they don't feel they can get along with just now. I don't promise, but I tell them I'll try to take their wishes into account as best I can, but that if they end up with someone in their group who is not a social friend, I expect them to be able to cooperate and get the job done. Using myself as an example, I tell them that I am often put on committees by my principal, and even if there is someone on the committee that I would not go to a movie with or have over to my home for dinner, we are responsible and get the job done, and I usually find I learned something from this person as a result of the experience that helps me appreciate them more. Additionally, they know they will have a chance again soon to form their own groups. The vicissitudes of junior high social life present unique problems for group work: best friends one week are at war the next. Despite the best efforts for group work to revolve around mutual respect and tolerance, these circumstances of adolescent development, compounded by the huge range of social classes (some of the wealthiest families in the United States right along with the most impoverished), make group work a special challenge. As with all strategies in the classroom, I find giving the students choices, respecting their social and emotional concerns (without letting them dictate the atmosphere), teaching cooperation, modeling, and using successful group events (always alert to the teachable moment!) as examples go a long way in preventing problems and creating true collaborative learning experiences. In order to help each group gel, I ask them to come up with a group name. Each student in the group has an assigned role, and these roles are posted in the classroom: *Taskmaster* (timekeeper), *Gatekeeper* (makes sure everyone gets a turn), *Praiser* (keeps the group positive), or *Reporter* (presents the overhead and leads the whole class discussion). Warm-ups to build a camaraderie and help group members get to know each others' strengths are used throughout the year. Roles rotate with each completed DJ, but groups remain the same for the duration of study of the text.

As students are in groups, I roam about the room listening in, specifically listening to who is saying what, looking for insight into students' responses that I can use in minilessons, that I can use to support individual learning efforts, or that I can use to begin the whole class discussion. I'll compliment a response or comment that I had a similar question or concern (without giving an answer), doing everything I can to support the group talk that can lead to a successful whole class discussion.

Students share their individual response entries aloud with the members of their groups, trying to answer questions, resolve confusions, decide what element of plot a particular text rendering represents, etc. Each student completes her collaborative group column by writing the name of the student who shared and commenting on that student's issue. Additionally, they are to decide as a group which two or three issues they wish to share with the entire class, prepare an overhead on those issues, and be ready to present to the class at the appropriate time. Arianna's collaborative group column is a bit sparse (see Figure 11.4), showing that she followed my instructions: choose one idea from all the ones shared by your group members and write that in your collaborative group column, trying to resolve any confusions if

Figure 11.4   Arianna's Dialectical Journal *Walkabout*

Individual Response	Collaborative groups
Chapter 1:	Cassie had a question of
appreciation:	"The false dawn." she didn't
I liked the line "Rare	know what it ment. We
fireflies zigzagged by,	either thought it was as
their night-lights flickering	Cassie said IF " it was
like sparkles from a	so pretty, it looked fake"
roving toy-sized forge."	or it's just before dawn
it stood out to me because	and if looks light from
of the way they said it	the moon
like it took them + taught	
otherwise they would	
probly just have written	
fireflys flying and	
glowing" you know	
what I mean.	
questions:	
How many characters	
where there 2 or 3? I	
got confused? as inhumans	
How did his leg get	
injured?	
Chapter 2:	
confusion	
why did he get so afrai	
of the ants	
questions:	
where the ants brown	
or red? Did Pete know what	
ants were.	
Chapter 5:	Matt: we was saying
I think that peter	how he notice the
and mary will	poetry on the begging
become good friends	of every chapter.
when they find	
the bush boy cause	Cassie: Same thing
they will see him as	as last time correcting
him finding their way	their things.
to the uncles house.	
Chapter 6:	Benito: DIDN'T DO
well its mary	ONE
and petter want to	
know what the	
bush boy might say	
then they might have	
to learn his	
language (with body)	

you can. If not, bring it to the whole class. At the least, Arianna's under-standing of the text is improved as she listens to Cassie talk about a descrip-tive passage and hears Matt point out that each chapter begins with the description of the setting. This DJ reflects the first meeting of this group, and it is not atypical of the shyness students might feel in an assigned group during the first meeting. It is worth noting that Cassie, Matt, and Arianna do not socialize together outside of class. In this case, following instructions to the letter, as Arianna has, is an excellent way to begin to build a relationship where more spirited discussion can come, if and when necessary.

Students may take one or two days to complete their sharing and pre-pare the overhead for whole class discussion. Patience and flexibility are the keys here, while trying to stay within some sort of general time line. Experi-ence tells me, however, what general sorts of plot issues, confusions, or in-terpretative problems will arise: that is, eventually I come to know what sorts of texts present what sorts of problems for students—not that I am never surprised, but I can estimate the amount of time needed after several rounds with the DJ. As reporters for each group lead us through the discus-sions, some issues will be repeated. I ask if there is any new input or rethink-ing that anyone wants to contribute, and if not, we move on after acknowledging the importance of similar issues coming up for different readers. In the case of *Walkabout*, and as we see in Arianna's DJ, students are typically taken with the maternal role of Mary toward Peter and are also generally sympathetic to their plight. More individualized are the apprecia-tions, confusions and connections, so this is where many readers help the in-dividual reader gain a fuller understanding of the text.

As students present all these findings to the whole class, the second page of the DJ is begun: with the first group ready to present, I ask students to take out another page of notebook paper, divide it down the center again, and label the left column "Whole Class" and the right column "Second Indi-vidual Response" (see Figure 11.5).

As they listen to the presentation from each group, they are to write the group's name and then select one issue the group has presented to take a note on. They can write down an issue they hadn't thought of, they can write down a piece of evidence that supports an idea they had, or they can write down a different interpretation of an idea they've expressed. Basically, we're looking for similarities and differences of interpretation. In Arianna's whole class column, we see again careful note taking that covers the gamut of response: from each group presentation she's chosen a range of ideas, ev-erything from vocabulary to plot structure to character analysis, with more evidence of Arianna's writing voice seeping in: "I would sertinly think that would be the right thought, where did Mary and Peter get the candy from they said the plain maybe or brought from home." The issue of the candy, on which Mary and Peter survive initially, garnered more attention from every

Figure 11.5 Arianna's Individual Response

Whole Class	2nd Individual Response
The Kookaburra:	Now that I'm halfway threw
They had 3 questions with	the book I have understud
responses. I would sertinly think that	most of my confusions and
would be the right thought, where did Mary	have answered ~~my~~ most question
and peter get the candy from they said	But I haven't answered on
the plain maybe or brought from home	question and that question
The Hikers:	is where the ants brown or
I liked when they said. "we notced	red, I guess it's a gap in
that every chapter starts with a	the book and thats something
setting.	I will have to fill in and I
The Aborigine:	personaly think they would
I liked when they asked what	have to be RED ants'cause
are gang-gangs? Answer: Australian	brown ants don't pick but
bird	as we all know RED ants.
The Quandongs:	
I liked the ?. "How come the parents	
aren't in the story yet" probly they didn't	
go on the trip	
The Pulsating Monkeys:	
I liked their border decorations	
good work !!!	
Dingos:	
I liked their borders and their	
answer for the questions. It'	
like they made them up.	

group this year than in previous years, and I can't account for it. As I mentioned earlier, experience offers me some general guidelines for which issues will come up: the candy had not received such prominent attention in past readings. It became more clear to me what the concern was when the discussion continued with a Quandongs: Noah offered the explanation that if

Figure 11.5 continued

	2nd Individual Response
	I also understud, who Mary was and that she didn't feel comfor table being around the bush boy because he was black. I also understd who Peter was and that he really enjoyed being arrend the bush boy although he did have some fear of him the bush boy seams confiden with mary and Peter but he does have some fear of them cause he hasn't seen people elike then meaning white people. I also found out that the bush boy is the same person as the ~~cxxxxxx~~ tharrigine. One of my confusions were that was there 2 or 3 humans in chapter one and I found that their is 3 characters BUT in chapter I there is only 2 characters an the bush boy didn't one alonen in the story or it

the parents had been along on the trip, there probably would have been other food available for Mary and Peter because when families travel, the mother usually brings more healthy snacks than just candy. Kids on their own would do just what Mary and Peter did: have just candy. The conclusion was quickly drawn that the author has the candy there for an important reason: to make Mary and Peter seem more helpless, ". . . and then we feel more bad for them," concluded Arianna. "The parents were left out of the story on purpose," Selena states.

"That's what we mean when we say the *art* and *craft* of writing, remember?" I add, reminding the class of a recurring refrain from writing workshop and referring back to the Hikers' observation that every chapter begins with the setting. "Why do you think that is, if the author is doing things on purpose?" I probe. Teachable moments abound during presentation time, but I try to skirt in and out, and never take over the discussion or move too far away from the question or issue initiated by the students. I can afford to be patient: it'll all come up again anyway. I want to keep opportunities for making meaning and interacting with the materials of language arts in interesting and provocative ways always before the students, like the onion skin theory of learning. Such interactions form a web of learning that becomes ever wider and more complex as we encounter a variety of texts and create our own throughout the year.

Tim answers my question: "Because Mary and Peter and the Aborigine are always moving around, he [the author] has to let us know where they are now." Again, we see the understanding of the structure of the novel and the crafting involved.

It appears that Arianna maxed her capacity for focused attention as she simply compliments the last two groups' presentations. I asked her individually what she meant by her comment on the Dingos: "It's like they made them up." "Because they couldn't know the answers because it was like a gap in the book so they had to figure it out for themselves with their previous knowledge." I'm thrilled of course, that Arianna is making these connections for herself and demonstrating both her understanding of the concepts we use and her appreciation of the thinking of another group. I would have preferred it if she could have been more specific in recording what the answers and questions were that she liked, but she's obviously worked hard on this column for 2 days of class discussion, and the increments of growth she's shown are significant.

Once presentations for each group are completed, students are to write a second individual response in the right column of the second page. Here, I tell them we're looking for the change or growth in their thinking since their first individual response. By referring to change, I tell them I don't necessarily mean that they have to decide they were wrong or right initially: change can mean that their idea has evolved, become more fully formed. They can cite further examples from the text to support an idea that has not changed. They can write about an issue that someone else brought up that was completely new to them and explain how someone else's reading helped them appreciate or understand the story more completely or in a completely different way. Changes, further development, deepening of thought—these are the qualities the second individual response should demonstrate.

In Arianna's (see Figure 11.5) we see that she's taken the idea of a gap in the text, perhaps from seeing the Dingos use the technique and responded to—finding a gap in the text that she can fill in. Additionally, however, she answers her initial confusion about how many characters there are, and notes her understanding of the relationships among the three and the author's device of ". . . the bush boy doesn't come along in the story yet."

Such reading and discussion continues as we fall into a comfortable rhythm of reading, recording our responses, sharing in groups, and working in whole class discussion. Toward the end of the collaborative group presentations, say during the last third of the book, students begin work on their self-selected projects. These projects should arise from the issues students write about in their dialectical journals and should be projects that demonstrate their understanding of issues in the book that were important to them. Students create a project so that they see that DJs are not the end but a means to an end. The use of a DJ is process, not product. I ask students to go back over their DJs and look for patterns in their response that might help them think of a project: Mary's relationship to Peter or to the Aborigine and how that changes, the influence of the environment, and the powerful descriptions of the environment are frequent responses that give rise to successful projects. Students can work individually, in pairs, or in groups. Projects can be written, artistically rendered, or staged, but in the case of an artwork or dramatic presentation, students also need to do a piece of writing to explain or accompany their presentation. My hope is that the dialectical journal will be full of specific details from the text, so that while the presentations are personal, they are grounded in the text. By so doing, I am hoping to begin to bridge that gap between strong voice in personal narrative writing and the loss of that voice in the still required mode of academic exposition.

The range of projects students select is huge: pieces of writing, in every genre, including the occasional plot analysis (truly!), but more often a continuation of the story of Mary and Peter and the Aborigine; poetry; drawings of Mary, Peter, the Aborigine, the outback, or any of the various scenes from the book; a wooden sculpture of the aborigine which now occupies a cherished position in class (although it doesn't go on display until after the current batch of projects is presented); a dramatic presentation of one of the scenes, more often than not presented on videotape; puppet shows; talk shows; letters to the characters; or letters to the author. If students choose to do any artistic rendering, I also ask that they write a short piece, indicating what scene or character they are portraying, what element of plot this represents, and why this is important: what about this part drew their attention, and what did they learn from it? In this way, students demonstrate their learning actively, playing to their strengths, after having used writing to create their understanding of the text in the dialectical journals.

At the same time, however, I use the reading and writing processes to achieve certain more conventional goals, goals many are worried have gotten neglected or dropped altogether in the process classroom. By using the dialectical journal, students are using reading and writing to construct their own interpretation, but I ask them to read with attention to detail and to record that detail using a subject-matter specific vocabulary. Here is the *content* knowledge in the process classroom. By completing a self-selected project, they are creating a new text, and by sharing it with the rest of the class we create a rich, diverse, and more fully-realized reading. Yet the reading is truly the students' reading. They are developing ownership of the text through these strategies. And in every experience using DJs and student projects, I have seen every element of the plot or theme or any other literary element a curriculum guide would direct us to teach brought up by the students. On the rare occasion when I feel something important has been completely overlooked, I don't hesitate to join in. I've created a classroom atmosphere where I can come in as another reader, contributing my observations. It is not unusual in these instances for one or more students to say, "Oh yeah, I thought of that but didn't write it down." As we see in Arianna's journal, some of her vocabulary to describe those elements is still developing, but she is clearly reading beyond a mere comprehension level. She is beginning to build her own capacity for literary response.

The thread of Arianna's interest in the Aborigine began with her very first responses and culminated in her project: a funeral for the Aborigine (see Figure 11.6).

Figure 11.6 Arianna's *Walkabout* Project Description

My group (Monica, Cynthia & Olwa) decided to do like the bush boy's gravestone. We didn't have any previous knowledge because we didn't know how his culture would have funerals so we decided to do an american funeral. We didn't do this to make fun of him we would like to honor his kindness for taking good care of Mary and Peter.

We did this because we tought he was a beloved friend to Peter and Mary. We also tought that maybe god sent him to them as their gardian angel to protect them on their walkabout and it honor of his thankingness from not just Peter and Mary we decided he gave up an important part of him (actually everything of him) that we tought it was very important to give him a funeral no one like him would ever have. I still think the bush boy is the main character.

During class discussion of her group's presentation, Arianna again made the point that she thinks the Aborigine is the main character, in contrast to many students' position that Mary is the main character. Each position is defended: the reader knows more about how Mary feels; Mary has the biggest conflict and changes the most. Arianna defends her position: the bush boy's conflict is whether to break the rules of his culture by helping them, and his death is certainly a change. "If he's not the main character, then why is it called *Walkabout*?" she asks triumphantly. But Ryan's answer reveals a very thoughtful reading: "Because Mary and Peter end up having a walkabout, too." Arianna listens good-naturedly, willing to let the argument go but not willing to give it up altogether. She gets the last word by inserting the sentence "I still think the bush boy is the main character" after their discussion! Nonetheless, her understanding of the text has been built out of her responses, her interaction with other readers in the class, and finally, her ownership of the meaning that she has created in collaboration with her partners and the whole class.

Another example of a student project from another class and another text will give some idea of the range of projects possible: this piece of writing contains enough reference to the issues noted in the DJ themselves that I've not included them here. The project itself is an example of the extended thinking made possible by the recursive nature of the DJ. The text this class read was a classic of literature and a classic choice in many junior high/middle school curricula, but a choice that some teachers may resist because of its difficulty. What better opportunity for me to see if the level of engagement with this text will be supported by the DJ? The text: *The Red Pony*, by John Steinbeck. The class: a gifted and talented seventh grade, but again the ethnic mix of southern California culture is there. These students overall are typically more willing readers and possess a great deal of independence already. Still, all the resistance to a teacher-selected text, and a difficult classic at that, presented the perfect lab for the DJ, and the results were just as satisfying, as this project from Catilyn will demonstrate (see Figure 11.7).

Granted, Caitlyn is a gifted student, clearly possessing the ability to struggle with difficult concepts, but that in no way diminishes her accomplishment. Her understanding of the pony as a symbol, her creation of an explanation for the theme of death throughout the novel, and her application of her new perspective to life constitute solid examples of her creating new knowledge for herself. Her achievement represents as much growth for Caitlyn as Arianna's does for her.

Caitlyn reported to me that, for her next self-selected book, she wanted to read something more challenging because, "I feel like all the books I've been reading have been too easy for me, so I'm going to try Shakespeare now." Caitlyn began *Macbeth*, and when I inquired how it was going after about a week, she replied, "I have to use the glossary a lot, but I'm getting it."

"Even when I read Shakespeare in college I had to use the glossary a lot!" I told her.

Figure 11.7 Caitlyn's Response to *The Red Pony*

Caitlyn

5/5/96

Period 3

The Red Pony

This book is not like any other I have before. This is the first time that I have ever tried to analyze the plot and try to figure out the whys of things on the first reading. It was difficult, but on the whole I really enjoyed it. This book is also one of the more difficult ones that I have read. I would like to explain why, but if I did, the explanation would be long enough to be my entire project. My partner, (Minka) and I decided to do a sculpture of the red pony for our project. If you just casually reads the book, the red pony would not seem to be very important at all. You'd probably think that the only reason that the book was called the red pony is that he is the first major event in Jody's life. As well as this, you would think that the pony is just part of the introduction that helps give you a feel for what Jody is like, and also how he interacts with the characters around him. However, if you look a little closer and search a little bit deeper, you will find that that is not the case at all.

At first, I thought just the same as the above. Throughout most of the story I didn't really get why the book was called The Red Pony. I really wanted to discard the thought from my mind, because it confused me. I just didn't get it. I was just about to promise myself not to think about it any more when I remembered what Mrs. Robertson said, "If anything seems boring or confusing, it's probably important." So I pondered the meaning more, and finally figured out an explanation that satisfied my question. The Red Pony is a symbol throughout the whole book. He really stands out in surroundings of black, gray and white. It is the first of a string of experiences that Jody goes through, to make him grow up. The pony is the first of four separate kinds of death that Jody experiences throughout the story. The first type of death, is being swept out of the prime of life unwillingly, through a fatal sickness. The second (Gitano old Easter) is the quiet exceptance of death, and the desire to be alone in the place that you are born, when it does come. The third death (Nellie) is the sacrifice of your own life, to give life to another being. The 4rth death (grandfather) is the lonely death among people. This is the most sad of the deaths, and the one that affects Jody the most. The grandfather feels alone in the world full

Figure 11.7 cont'd

of people, and not wanted or needed anywhere. The red pony is the symbol of the starting point of Jody's entrance into the real world of adults.

Although the finished work that you see before you right now probably looks like it was really easy to make, but it wasn't. I'd say that our biggest problem was getting me to succumb to making any large alterations to our block of clay, I was afraid that if we did anything to big to it, we'd ruin it. If it hadn't been for Minka, we never would have gotten it done. Our next biggest problem was deciding how to do it. We began by each drawing a sketch of a pony. Then I drew the basic shape in the block of clay. Next, Minka took a huge knife, and cut out the shape of the pony and molded it into a pony shape. We then both worked on the little stuff like muscle and bones. When we were done with that we left it out to harden overnight. The next morning we put white clay over the gray clay and added a mane and tail. Finally we left the white out to air dry.

Doing this project gave me a lot more time to think about the importance of the red pony in the story. That led into many other aspects, and by the time that we were done, I had reviewed the whole story in my head. I learned a lot more about the story this way, take the four deaths that each help Jody grow in their own way. Also I thought about why the author usually doesn't mention the previous chapter in the current chapter. At first I was puzzled at this, and then I realized that you were supposed to see the difference through Jody. All the things happen to him affect him and make him change in some way. So, even if you skipped a chapter, you would realize that something must have happened to him because he is different. That is also the way it is in real life, if you don't see someone for a while, when you do see them they have changed. In a way this has taught me something about life. Different things change people in different ways, don't expect people to react in the same way. Look for the uniqueness in an individual, and usually you will find a gratifying surprise. Remember that this not only applies to stories but also to people; If something (or someone) is unusual, different or confusing, it (they) are probably important.

Goals: Why Use the Dialectical Journal?

During my struggles to implement a reading-writing workshop based on Nancie Atwell's *In the Middle* for my seventh and eighth grade classes, issues came up that had to be dealt with in order to preserve the integrity of the learning environment offered by the workshop approach for students while preserving my physical stamina, sanity, and the objectives of the curriculum. Some of the most important issues were managerial and organizational, having to do with the fact that I teach five classes of 30 to 32 students per day for one 45-minute period each. Additionally, I wanted to find ways to honor the principles of time, choice, response, and ownership so successful in self-selected writing and reading *even* when the topic for writing or the text for reading was assigned.

Another important factor fueling my modifications of the workshop classroom was my long-term research question of how to bridge the gap between strong personal narrative writing and what may be termed traditional exposition: How can we maintain the level of engagement and strong personal voice evident when students have time, choice, response, and ownership in the writing workshop to develop their own topics as they move on to, in subsequent grades, the other, still required, and (to my mind) still valid necessity of writing expository prose? I also wanted to expand the ways in which students respond to texts with the same variety of writing about texts as we saw in topics for writing when students self-select. After all, in the real world of writing, one way of responding to a text is to write another text that may take some form other than a critical analysis. However, I did not want the option of critical analysis deliberately excluded from my students as a choice, since they would still be required to write in that mode after they left my class—not to mention the fact that there are many students who actually enjoy that mode of writing (many of them become teachers!)—and exposition is still an excellent way to teach critical thinking. I wanted to feel confident that both the direct instruction in exposition as well as the strengthening of personal voice through frequent practice in narrative writing would serve to bridge the gap—or begin to bridge the gap—between personal voice and exposition. More accurately, perhaps, I wanted to be sure that the strong grounding in narrative voice resulting from student self-selection of writing topics would serve them well as they told the story of their reading of any text, whether that text was self-selected or assigned. Bridging the gap then, between strong personal voice in narration and the requirement to write exposition was still part of my role as a junior high school teacher. The DJ has emerged as a tool to begin this process.

An equally important goal was that students learn to develop what Sheridan Blau (1996) calls the "ability for sustained focused attention." A student's capacity to enter into and remain engaged with text is a developmental issue as much as it is an intellectual one. I see part of the teacher's role as helping students engage with text by means of a variety of strategies with a text long enough for the pertinent issues to emerge. By pertinent, I mean those issues that drive the text as a piece of literature as well as the issues that emerge for the reader as he or she, as an individual, confronts and relates to the text. Again, the DJ helps students begin this process by making visible to them their issues as they read.

The first problem I faced as I thought about finding ways to keep students engaged with text was precisely that: how to keep them reading and rereading and interacting with text long enough to go beyond an initial superficial response. I also wanted students to be able to pick out exact details from the text to support their responses and to use the vocabulary of literary analysis (plot structure, character development, conflict, etc.) as they wrote about and discussed their responses. Another goal was incorporating collaborative group work: How could I get students to share their responses in groups over enough time to allow a discussion of depth to develop and to listen carefully to one another? I also wanted students to work in a collaborative manner, so that one point of view did not dominate the discussion and so that no one felt silenced by a strong voice. In other words, I wanted beginning literary discussion in my classroom, but I wanted it to be a classroom where students were engaged, active, and thinking both critically and independently, in a collaborative, supportive environment.

These goals may not sound too different from the traditional goals of any English/Language Arts/Literature classroom, but what marks them as different is that the topics for discussion around the text are generated by the students' responses to the text rather than by predetermined—by the teacher or a study guide—important passages or issues. Vocabulary, sections to be read aloud or discussed in the classroom, even the items on a quiz, because they are selected by the teacher in the familiar classroom scenario, send the message to the students that the teacher is the one who knows what is important about the text. Instead, I wanted to try to build the entire response to the text from the students' active engagement with the text—through their reading, writing, listening, and speaking in their collaborative groups, they would use language for learning rather than to demonstrate that they had learned (by taking a short answer essay quiz, for instance, after reading). I wanted my classroom to be both student-centered and language-centered. Their responses to the reading would become the focus of *all* discussions— and I hoped that the issues I, as teacher, thought were important would find a place in the discussions of their responses. Would I still be fulfilling my responsibility to teach the text if I allowed students to guide the entire enterprise? Would the issues students chose to share be ones worthy of our valuable class time or would I have to step in to make sure the text was honored in the appropriate ways? Yes, I had always considered myself a teacher who believes in and establishes a learner-centered classroom AND I care as much about the integrity of the text as I do about the integrity of the learner. How to meld the two and be true to both has been a driving question as I work and continually revise my classroom organization. A particularly probing question formulated by David Bleich (1988) has given me a perspective that helps me think about this balance between curriculum and student: How does this text help you understand your life, and how does your life help you understand this text? That's the balance I wanted to achieve, and I set about developing strategies to get there.

Problems and Procedures

The students in all my classes represent a cross section of California culture: Latino (including first to seventh generation American), African American, European American, Asian American; every economic segment of the population is also represented. Surfers, skaters, homies, jocks, and soshes—every social class as designated by junior high definitions of status — all converge in English class to share their reactions to texts. Almost from the first day of school, students begin to respond to shared readings in class and their self-selected readings by text rendering, choosing a sentence or line that stands out for them, copying that line in their reader's journal, and then attempting to explain the appeal or intrigue of that line. My instructions include the ideas that a line may stand out because it is beautifully written and paints a vivid picture in the mind's eye; it may be funny; it may be exciting; it may remind a reader of an idea from another text or from real life; or it may make a reader wonder about other issues in the text or in the world at large. I model a response that I have written, and then I set students to work individually. Students then share in partners, move next to fours, and finally, they share their responses with the whole class. These initial responses to text are crucial in building the idea that students' individual responses are central to our discussions and are valued as much if not more than I am, in my role as teacher. Since I see my role as learner-participant in class as well as instructional leader, I want to share my strategies for learning and dealing with difficulties as openly and as often as I can.

The purpose of text rendering is to begin to make quite plain the idea that all of us respond differently to texts, and that all responses can be valid, are informative of either the text or the reader's level of engagement, and are to be respected. Throughout the year, text rendering occupies a central place in our literary discussions as well as serves as a favored response to student written pieces. An additional value of text rendering is that it keeps us engaged with the text: we go back to the text to find our line or to examine the text in order to explain its appeal, and we live with the text again as we hear individual students' explanations for their choices of line. Since students not only read their responses aloud in groups but also read their lines aloud to the whole class before we begin class discussion, the strategy also is a way of rereading the text. I am always amazed at how readily an entire piece can be recalled by the readings of these individual lines. Text rendering is also an invaluable strategy for supporting the goals of active student engagement with text, beginning group work, and balancing the importance and power of the text with the learners' experience of that text—in other words, text rendering gives students a voice right along with the voice of the author. It is a useful technique for giving students a way to enter difficult text, providing students some measure of control over a challenging piece in that a student can respond to at least part of the writing without having to deal with the entirety of it immediately. Text rendering through DJs gives students the opportunity to expand their responses to a text. Clarice sums up what I hope all students learn about using the DJs (see Figure 11.8).

Figure 11.8 Clarice's Comments on DJs

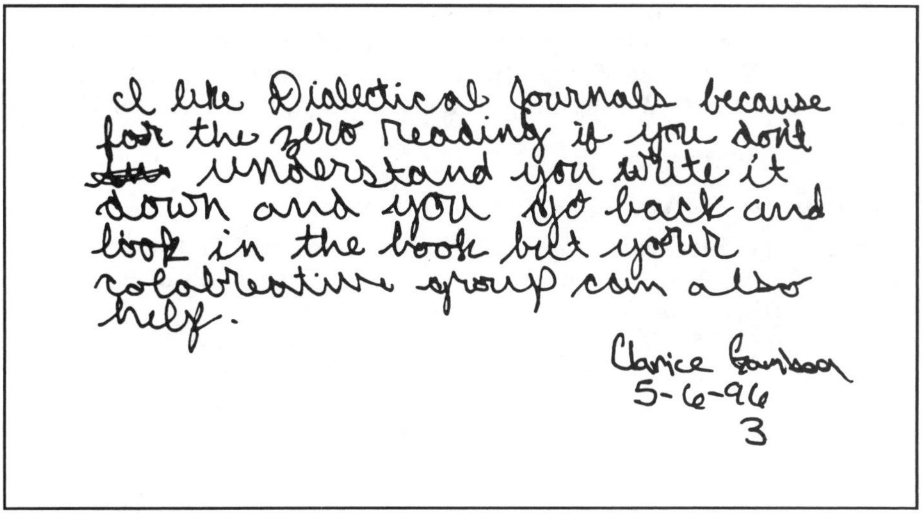

I like Dialectical Journals because for the zero reading if you don't understand you write it down and you go back and look in the book but your colabreative group can also help.

Clarice Bourbon
5-6-96
3

The Dialectical Journal not only keeps students engaged with reading, but it also engages them in writing. Just as students improve as readers when they write, they improve as writers as they read. The two activities are two sides of the same coin, and the DJ itself becomes the coin, so to speak. As students draft their own stories, they model their structures on the structures of the poems, short stories, and novels they have read. If they are consciously aware of the uses of and placements of dialogue, description, action, and humor in the published pieces they have been reading, they are more likely to consciously use these elements successfully in their own writing. But this knowledge of structure won't transfer by simply studying texts in the abstract, by writing reports about the authors, or by taking tests on the plot. By making personal connections and writing about those connections, students are actively engaged in creating their reading, rather than passively allowing the teacher to guide the discussion. In fact, I've come to believe that there is no real learning without a component of personal engagement. The DJ is designed to put that personal engagement up front, and that personal engagement becomes the wellspring for the students to produce their own new texts, their own pieces of writing resulting from their engagement with a piece of reading.

Reference

Berthoff, A. (1981). *The making of meaning: Metaphors, models, and maxims for writing teachers*. Montclair, NJ: Boynton/Cook.

Blau, S. (1993). Humane literacy: Literary competence and the ways of knowing. Presentation to the Conference of the International Federation for the Teaching of English. Auckland, New Zealand, 1990. In J. Milner & C. Pope (Eds.), *Global voices: Culture and identity in the teaching of English*. Urbana, IL: National Council of Teachers of English.

Bleich, D. (1988). Reader response theory and practice, presentation to the National Endowment for the Humanities Literature Institute for Teachers, South Coast Writing Project. Santa Barbara: University of California.

Trade Books Cited

Marshall, J. (1959). *Walkabout*. Littleton, MA: Sundance Publishing.

Moray, W. (1989). Kavik the wolf dog. In L. J. Christensen & E.J. Farrell (Eds.), *Discoveries in literature*. Sunnyvale, CA:

Steinbeck, J. (1965). *The red pony*. New York: Bantam Books.

A Focus on Improving and Assessing Comprehension

Chapter 12

STRATEGIES: WHAT CONNECTS READERS TO MEANING

Judy Wallis

A short lesson about flat and round characters comes to a close. The teacher, Michele, leaves the K-W-L chart that the class created out so the students can use it later. Then she quietly gives directions: "Students, get your books, find your group, and move to your meeting spot." The students make eye contact with group members, dig through backpacks for the novel their group is reading, stretch long arms, fluff long hair, reach for notebooks and pencils, and begin moving into various spots throughout the room. After a moment of clattering noise, the sound diminishes into the steady hum of quiet voices with the occasional laugh or abrupt rise in pitch as someone too vehemently makes a point. Michele moves from group to group listening, prodding, and clarifying.

Confident and articulate, these seventh graders talk seriously about their personal reactions to what they have read. They tell the other members of their group what questions they have after individually reading the two chapters they had agreed to read for this morning's discussion. At times, they search the text for specific passages to read aloud to others in their group. At times, they pose thoughtful questions to one another. Sometimes, they disagree with a peer's opinion.

These students are discussing literature through literature circles. This design is a powerful way to help students become the meaning-makers of what they read. (You can read about how to create literature circles in your class in Chapters 9 and 10.) For most of the students in Michele's class, this design works because these students have read their novels strategically. As they read they predicted what might happen next and stopped to clarify confusion as their predictions didn't match outcomes. Plus, Michele has taught them some strategies to use when meaning-making gets difficult.

What always impresses me about Michele is how selective she is with strategy instruction. She doesn't teach hundreds of strategies to all her students. She recognizes that some students, many times the good readers, need little time in explicit strategy instruction. They've already figured out how to make text meaningful. She knows that poorer readers need explicit instruction in strategies to use when the text overwhelms them; however, she knows that they need 1 or 2 strategies to help them rather than 40 or 50. P. David Pearson said that very thing to me once as he explained that students need less not more; they need a few well-taught and well-learned strategies. As Michele continues circulating throughout the room, she lives out that philosophy.

"Miss, we just don't get it. What is happening here?" one student from a group reading *Tuck Everlasting* (Babbitt, 1975) asks Michele.

"What part is the problem?" Michele asks.

"Here, these two pages, what is happening here?" The students show her the part of the chapter causing problems.

Figure 12.1 The Interactive Nature of Skills and Strategies

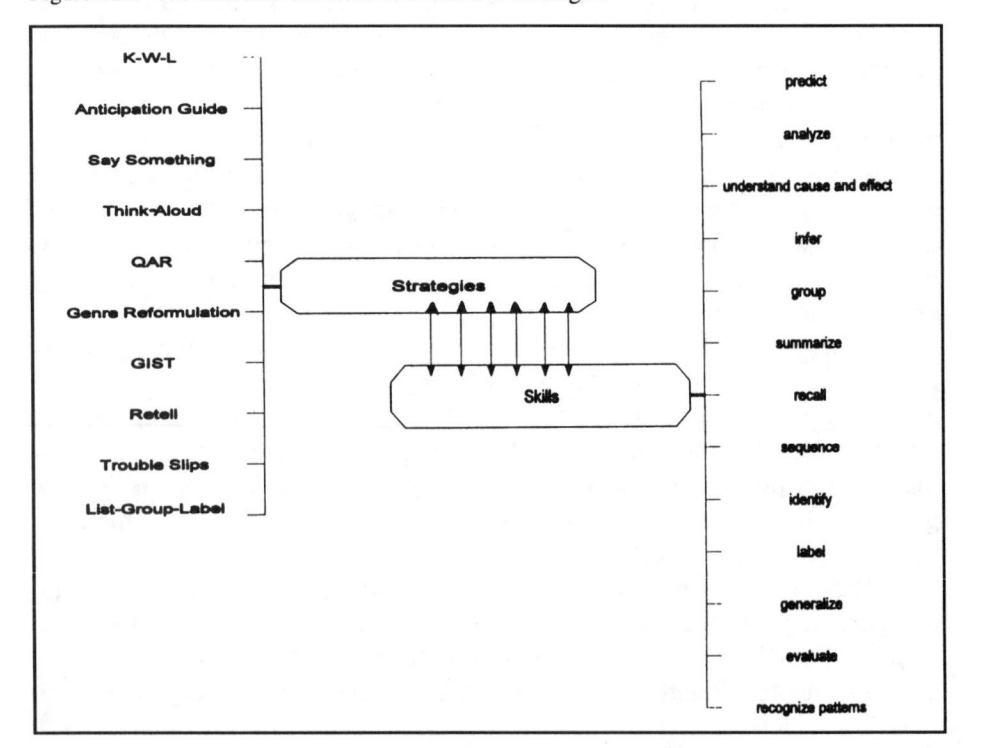

"Well, let's see," Michele says. "What could you do to figure this out? Are all of you confused?" After seeing all four heads nod, Michele asks again what they could do. For a few moments, silence fills this group. Michele doesn't say anything.

"Jason and me, we could do Think-Aloud," Mark finally suggests.

"And me and Orion, we could do Say Something," Christopher says.

"OK," Michele says. "You've got a plan. Call me when you finish and we'll see if you've got a better idea of what is happening on those pages."

Michele's students know some strategies to use when reading doesn't make sense. These strategies require them to use the skills that good readers use automatically (see Figure 12.1). Also, Michele's students know that they don't need to do Think-Aloud or a Say Something all the time. The students understand that these tools are ways to help them when they "just don't get it."

Understanding Strategies

One important goal for teachers is to help students develop into readers who know when and how to use various strategies that help them best understand their texts. Strategies are actions selected deliberately to achieve particular goals or skills (Paris, Wasik, & Turner, 1991). To better understand this difference, look at what a strategic reader does:

- understands the reading task and its purpose or purposes;
- carefully analyzes the reading task in order to establish goals necessary to achieve that task;
- chooses appropriate and useful strategies in light of the assigned task and its purpose;
- uses self-monitoring to determine that comprehension is occurring, and;
- possesses a positive attitude toward reading. (Paris, Lipson, & Wixson, 1983)

Rather than working by trial and error, the strategic reader works deliberately to select strategies that facilitate comprehension. Teachers foster this process by thinking aloud to demonstrate how they select and use strategies themselves. They model strategies for students, demonstrating how a strategy works when used by a more skilled reader. They also help students analyze and refine their own strategy use. Teaching at the strategy level, rather than at the skill level, puts students directly into situations where they are interacting with their texts at the application, analysis, synthesis, and evaluative thinking levels.

Strategies to Improve and Enhance Comprehension

A number of comprehension strategies exist. Some of these are useful before reading, others aid readers during and after reading, while others move students from pre-reading to post-reading. In other words, strategies, like middle schoolers, don't fit neatly into the categories like before, during, and after reading. However, in an attempt to organize strategies, I discuss them within the category where readers would first use them.

Before Reading Strategies

K-W-L Charts

Many teachers have found the K-W-L strategy (Ogle, 1986) a useful tool when preparing students to read or begin a new unit of study. The strategy builds upon the premise that we store information according to categories or schemata. When readers consciously access a category before reading, they know where to connect the new information with the known, thus increasing the potential for learning. The K-W-L strategy involves asking readers to identify what they already know (K) before they read, what they want to know while reading (W), and what they learned (L) in the process of reading. Some extend the K-W-L strategy to include the identification of questions left unanswered by the reading. This strategy highlights the importance of self-questioning. Self-questioning enhances comprehension and keeps the act of reading active and lively.

K-W-L has been widely used as a group strategy with the teacher in charge of recording and monitoring students' comments. However, it has enormous potential when used as a personal reading strategy. Readers learn to access their prior knowledge or schema, identify the information they may lack, and assess what they have learned in light of what they may still want or need to know. Kristen's K-W-L chart (see Figure 12.2) shows us what Kristen knew about the Holocaust before she began reading *Number the Stars* (1993) by Lois Lowry, as well as what she wanted to know and finally what she learned.

Not only did the teacher have Kristen and her classmates complete a K-W-L chart, but she also explained to them the type of thinking that strategy encouraged. In other words, she showed them why it is a strategy and not a skill. Here's a transcript of the conversation Kristen's teacher had with Kristen and her class after they completed the first two columns of the chart.

> *Teacher*: Now let's stop thinking about the Holocaust for a minute and look at, um, what it is that you just did. Now, you filled in this chart called a K-W-L. OK. What did you do to fill this in?
>
> *Students*: No response.

Figure 12.2 Kristen's K-W-L Chart

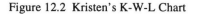

Kristen..

K | W | L

1. Jewish people were put in prison.

2. Hitler was the ruler.

3. This was part of World War II

4. People were killed just because they were Jewish.

1. Why did Jewish people were stars? What do stars have to do with the holocaust?

2. Why did some Jewish people leave Germiny but others stayed?

3. Why did Hitler become King?

Teacher: OK. Let's think about what you had to do to come up with ideas that you put here under the K column.

Student A: You mean like what we had to write first and then tell you to write?

Teacher: Yes, sort of. What did your brain have to do to come up with the things you told me to write?

Student B: Well I had to remember what I knew from other places.

Teacher: Good. [Starting a list on the overhead. See Figure 12.3.] You had to recall information. What else?

Student C: I, uh, I had to know what things were things with the Holocaust.

Teacher: OK. Tell me what you mean by that.

Student C: Well, like, putting people into concentration camps; I thought of that and then had to, uh, think about is that the Holocaust.

Teacher: OK. I see. You had to identify what you knew and then sort it into the right time period. Good. What else?

Student D: Well, like M—said that Hitler ruled the Nazis and I was going to say that Hitler ruled the Germans and then they are the same so I didn't add it.

Teacher: All right. You identified what you knew and generalized it to what someone else said. Anyone else?

This teacher continued this conversation until the students had done the same thing for the W column.

Teacher: In this column (pointing to the W column) you asked questions that you still want to know about the Holocaust that you think this book will answer. Look at the thinking you did. Here (see Figure 12.2, column 2) [Holding up Kristen's K-W-L Chart], Kristen wrote "What do the stars have to do with the Holocaust?" and "Why did some Jewish people leave Germany while others stayed?" What kind of thinking is going on here?

Kristen: I was thinking about what would maybe happen and then in the second one I was, like, wondering why people were staying. I'd have left before anything started.

Teacher: Good. So you were trying to predict and were wondering about causes and effects (see Figure 12.3).

After other students finished discussing other comments, the teacher concluded this part of the mini-lesson saying:

Teacher: OK. Now look at this column I've made up here (see bottom of Figure 12.3). Look at this list: predict, understand, cause and effect, compare, match, infer. These are all skills that good readers use when they read. As you keep these questions in mind while you read and as you answer those questions you have generated, you will be doing what good readers do.

This teacher used K-W-L to not only help students access prior information, but she also used it as a way to get her students thinking about their reading. In that way they see that skills like main idea, predicting, identifying, and cause and effect are arbitrary labels we use to talk about the reading process.

Figure 12.3 Teacher's Overhead Showing Thinking from the K-W-L Exercise

K- W -L

K   W   L

What you did to complete your
     K-W-L chart
   - remembered facts.   W
   - recalled information   - predicted
   - identified what you knew   - looked for
   - sorted information   causes &
   - generalized   effects
   - looked for causes and effects) - asked
                   question

What good readers do   - compared
   - Predict   this book to
   - Understand cause and effect Diary of A.F.
   - Compare   - Think!
   - Match   - Ask questions
   - Infer

Anticipation Guide

An Anticipation Guide (Readence, Bean, & Baldwin, 1995) is similar to the K-W-L strategy in that it helps students activate their prior knowledge and make a personal investment in reading by responding to statements about the reading. Additionally, it acts as a guide for readers as they begin to read (Tierney, Readence, & Dishner, 1995). Having readers agree or disagree with statements prior to reading makes it more likely that they will locate the information in the text and then check to see if their initial predictions were correct.

When preparing an Anticipation Guide, the teacher considers the most important ideas or concepts within the reading in light of what a particular group of students may already know. The teacher creates statements that focus the students on the concepts they will need to understand. After reading, the teacher asks students to return to the Anticipation Guide and evaluate their initial responses to the statements. Anticipation Guides may be used for both narrative and expository text and for books as well as chapters or selections within anthologies. The following Anticipation Guide (see Figure 12.4) was created to introduce *Emily Good as Gold* (1993).

Figure 12.4 Anticipation Guide for *Emily Good as Gold*

Place a "+" beside the statements with which you agree and a "–" beside the statements with which you disagree.

_____ Having a daughter or sister with special needs is more difficult on the family than on the person with the special needs.

_____ People take advantage of people with handicaps.

_____ Growing up means making all your own decisions.

_____ It is good for parents to protect their children from life's problems.

During Reading Strategies

Say Something

Say Something (Harste, Short, & Burke, 1988) is a very simple yet very successful strategy to assist readers in constructing meaning. First, it builds on the social aspect of language. Through the talk, readers gain insights into another reader's thoughts *while* they read. They also become aware of alternate strategies to use when understanding breaks down. Second, it helps readers monitor the process of reading. Poor readers find it especially difficult to know when they are not understanding. In many cases, they discover they need to reread after they have already invested a great deal of energy and time. When students use Say Something, the *lack* of something to say is a sure signal to the reader to go back and reread.

Say Something is most successful when teachers use it after careful modeling with another student. However, the student selected should be a confident reader since the text will be a new and unfamiliar one. Once the strategy is introduced, the teacher needs to continue monitoring the quality of students' statements during the use of Say Something and provide additional modeling if necessary. The procedure is outlined on a task card intended for use with students (see Figure 12.5).

Figure 12.5 Say Something

---

1. Choose a partner.

2. Get a copy or copies of what you are to read.

3. Decide how you will read:

   • silently   • one reader
   • take turns   • share a copy or read from your own copy

4. Locate the first place you will stop and say something about the text.

5. Continue to select additional places to stop.

6. Remember, when you stop to say something, it must be about what you have just finished reading!

An example of two students using Say Something as they begin reading *Flip-Flop Girl* (Paterson, 1994) follows. The students read approximately one page of text before they stopped to comment.

Carol: I think that everybody is very upset in this book. Look at the part about the big ghostly eyes.

Josie: Yes. It sounds like something bad has happened to the dad in the story.

[Students now read until the point for the second break]

Josie: Oh, I see. The dad died. It sounds pretty bad, doesn't it?

Carol: Yeah. Vinnie's pretty mean to her brother. Things are a pretty big mess.

[Students now read until the point for the third break.]

Carol: Vinnie feels lonely, but instead of asking for help, she just keeps being awful to Mason. I'm getting the idea that she's the reason Mason won't talk.

Josie: Weird! Vinnie shouldn't have said that to Mason.

This next example illustrates how two students use the strategy to help them understand some difficult language in a poem:

Jason: I don't get it. What's an epiphany?

Mark: Where?

Jason: Here, on this line. What is this about the epiphany is a baby?

Mark: I think it's like something new 'cause like a baby is something new.

Say Something . . . Silently

After students become proficient in using Say Something with a partner, I extend this strategy to a personal comprehension and monitoring strategy. This variation provides students with feedback in situations where a partner isn't available. Say Something . . . Silently (see Figure 12.6) is particularly helpful as an independent reading and test-taking strategy. Its use keeps readers from reading too far before realizing that they haven't been paying attention to the text.

Figure 12.6 Say Something . . . Silently

---

1. Preview what you are about to read.

2. Notice the location of charts, graphs, or words that seem difficult to understand.

3. Plan where you will stop and say something or write something about what you just read.

Hint: If you have little or nothing to say, you might need to read the part you just finished again.

4. After you finish, make a list of the most important ideas.

Think-Alouds

Think-Alouds (Davey, 1983; Flower & Hayes, 1980; Olshavsky, 1976–77) are designed to extend or support reading instruction, to help poor readers think about their reading, and to help these readers learn to monitor what they *do* and *do not* understand while reading. Strategic readers are generally very aware when text becomes confusing. They stop and try to figure out what to do next. Poor readers generally don't do this. They either don't realize that what they are reading doesn't make sense (remember, they aren't reading for meaning; they are reading for finishing), or they don't know what to do so they just keep reading. This strategy, one especially appropriate for remedial readers, helps them focus on what is happening while they read. (For more examples of this, look at Chapter 5.) Here's how it works.

First, I like to give students a tally sheet of strategies that good readers use as they read. These strategies include predicting what happens next, picturing what is happening in the text, comparing, identifying problems, and finding solutions to the problems (Davey, 1983).

Next, I have to explain what each of those terms means. I show them how they are just words that I use while I am thinking through a problem. I might say, "I predict that such and so will happen next"; or, "Here's a problem," or "This is like another word. . . ." Then I begin reading aloud a piece of text from either a trade book or a textbook. I stop several times throughout the oral reading to think aloud about what I am reading. The students are listening to what I say, keeping a tally of which skill I use. After I've modeled several Think-Alouds for students, they get into pairs and read to each other, thinking aloud as they read. The partner's job is to follow along and keep track of the skill that the reader uses on the tally sheet. Eventually, students do Think-Alouds without partners. Then I have them read into a tape recorder thinking aloud. Then they can go back and listen and identify what they've done, or I can listen to it later. Figure 12.7 is a transcription of Lana's Think-Aloud as she reads a part of *Dear Mr. Henshaw* (Cleary, 1983). Lana is a sixth grader who, at the beginning of the school year, had trouble understanding more than about four sentences of written text, even if the text was at a third grade level. This is her Think-Aloud from mid-November.

Figure 12.7 Lana's Think-Aloud

November 12

Reads . . . "Yesterday after I hung up on Dad I flopped down on my bed and cried and swore and pounded my pillow." So he's like real sad and maybe like real mad. I think that he's mad becuase it says he swore.

Reads . . . "I felt so terrible about Bandit riding around with a strange trucker and Dad taking another boy out for pizza . . . " So I get it. On the phone call with his dad, when he, like, hears someone ask him when they are going for pizza. I get it, that's, like, when he knows his dad is like with another son. That's cold.

Reads . . . ". . . another boy out for pizza when I was all alone in the house with the mildewed bathroom when it was raining outside and I was hungry." Why's he in the bathroom? This is a problem too. What is mildewed? Anyway, this is, like, he's really sad because, I get it, he's not just, not just, like, angry at his dad, he's like, jealousy becuase, because his dad, he took that kid out and left him at home. Yeah, I'd be angry too.

As important as Lana's Think-Alouds are the comments she made about doing them. Her journal entry (see Figure 12.8) indicates that she is aware that Think-Alouds help her stay focused and help her create meaning for what she is reading.

Figure 12.8 Lana's Journal Entry

Students in this class keep a journal to record what strategies they use while reading. When they write in this journal, they know that they are to discuss a particular strategy they have used recently and then they are to discuss why they found it helpful or did not find it helpful.

Lana   Nov 14

English, 4

What strategy helps me?

Think-Alouds help me with my reading. They help me know what I am thinking and what it is when it doesn't make sense. I use think-aloud when I am stuck or the story is a confusing story. That is why I like think-alouds.

To help students adopt Think-Aloud as a personal reading strategy, I give them the Think Silently guidelines I developed (see Figure 12.9). Building on Think-Aloud, Think Silently requires that readers internalize and personalize the process.

Figure 12.9 Think Silently Application of Think-Aloud

After modeling the Think-Aloud strategy, use the chart below to prompt students to use the strategy while reading silently.

Think Silently

What predictions can I make about this text and the content of this text?

What visual images do I have in my mind of the characters, the events, the content or the situation in this text?

What prior knowledge or experiences do I have that would help me better understand this text?

I need to . . .

- reread

- think more about this

- read on

- revise my original predictions

Adapted from the Think-Aloud procedures listed in Tierney, Readence, & Dishner, 1995.

After Reading Strategies

QAR

As Kylene Beers explains in Chapter 3, much of the reading in school is efferent reading. While we want to encourage students to read aesthetically, we know that they must read efferently and often need help doing so. Helping students understand how to more efficiently answer efferent questions not only acts as a morale booster, but it also improves their reading comprehension. The Question-Answer Relationship (QAR) strategy developed by Raphael (1982, 1984, 1986) helps students categorize questions in order to find the answer. Initially, the teacher models, assuming most of the responsibility, but gradually the student uses the strategy independently.

Raphael identified four types of QARs.

- *Right There*: The answer is located in one place in the text.

- *Think and Search*: The answer is located in several places within the text.

- *Author and You*: The answer is not located in the text; the reader must use the author's information in combination with personal knowledge to answer the question.

- *On My Own*: The answer is not located in the text; the reader must use personal experience to answer the question.

The teacher introduces students to the concept that answering questions may require different ways of locating answers. Only one question-answer relationship is introduced and practiced at a time. After initial instruction in all four question-answer relationships has occurred, the students work in groups to identify questions according to all of the question-answer relationships.

In order for students to focus on the strategy rather than on the demands of a text, have your students read short excerpts or abbreviated texts in the beginning. The QAR Activity Sheet in Figure 12.10 was developed for *Timothy of the Cay* (1993).

GIST

Comprehension research suggests that good readers consider the author's intent and purpose for writing while poor readers do not (Graves & Hansen, 1983). GIST (Generating Interactions between Schemata and Text) is a strategy used when students must read efferently to reduce text to a few key ideas (Kintsch, 1977; Dooling & Christiansen, 1977; Anderson, 1978). This strategy helps readers take an analytical approach to their reading. In order to capture the main ideas, the reader must become aware of how a writer constructs a text. The purpose of the strategy is to provide readers a

Figure 12.10 QAR for *Timothy of the Cay* by Theodore Taylor

---

1. Who was Timothy?

Right There _____ Think and Search _____ Author and You _____ On My Own _____

2. What did Philip eat on the island?

Right There _____ Think and Search _____ Author and You _____ On My Own _____

3. Considering the text, do you think Timothy handled his problem very well? Why?

Right There _____ Think and Search _____ Author and You _____ On My Own _____

4. If you only had one badge of courage to award to someone, to whom would you give it?

Right There _____ Think and Search _____ Author and You _____ On My Own _____

5. List some of the obstacles Timothy and Philip overcame during their stay on the is-land.

Right There _____ Think and Search _____ Author and You _____ On My Own _____

---

way to distill a longer text into its most important ideas or concepts. To use this strategy, students must summarize a text they have read. Further, students who use this strategy to produce a summary are more likely to recognize good summaries or main idea statements on tests.

Students initially read a small portion of a text—three to five paragraphs. After reading, they dictate what the teacher should write to capture the gist or summary of ideas in the text. The challenge lies in reducing the passage to just twenty words that capture the gist of the passage. After reading four paragraphs on weather, students dictated the following GIST statement:

Figure 12.11 GIST 1st attempt

LIST 1

Cold fronts or air that
is very cold cause temperature
to drop as colder air
pushes the warmer air up.

The students then read three to five more paragraphs. The students must incorporate the former statement into the new statement. Note that the new statement still has only 20 words.

Figure 12.12 GIST 2nd attempt

LIST 2

<u>Cold</u> <u>fronts,</u> <u>caused</u> <u>by</u> <u>cold</u>

<u>air</u> <u>pushing</u> <u>warm</u> <u>air</u> <u>up,</u>

<u>came</u> <u>from</u> <u>the</u> <u>North,</u> <u>have</u>

<u>dry</u> <u>air,</u> <u>and</u> <u>little</u> <u>moisture.</u>

This strategy can be used in both expository and narrative text. The nature of the task changes slightly, however. In narrative text, students concentrate on theme, plot, and characters' actions while they connect, analyze, and summarize facts and details in exposition.

Recycled Stories

Recycled Stories (Feathers, 1993) requires readers to take a text, summarize it, pull the most important pieces, keep it in sequence, and rewrite it in another text form. For instance, a poem could be recycled as a newspaper item. Giving students a text for them to model their reformulation after is very important. Easy, predictable picture storybooks are great models that students can use as the structure for their reformulation. Start with repetitive text structures such as seen in an ABC book (A is for apple, B is for bear . . .) or in *Brown Bear, Brown Bear, What do you see?* (1983) by Bill Martin, ("Brown Bear, Brown Bear, What do you see? I see a red bird looking at me. Red bird, Red bird, What do you see? I see a. . . .") or cumulative structures such as seen in "This is the House that Jack Built." Then after students know several text structures that they can use as a structure for their recycled story, let them rewrite what they have read into that structure. For some student-generated examples, look at Figures 12.13 and 12.14. In both examples, the first from a seventh grade social studies class and the second from an eighth grade reading improvement class, the students used what they had learned while reading to create these recycled stories.

Figure 12.13 Recycled Story Using ABC Books as a Pattern

Katie, Meredith, Laine   Group 1

Alamo ABC

A is for Alamo which is where the battle between Texans and Santa Anna was fought.

B is for the Battle of San Jacinto which came after the Alamo.

C is for chapel which was a part of the mission called the Alamo.

D is for the determination losing that battle gave the Texans who fought later at another battle.

Figure 12.14 Recycled Story Using "The House that Jack Built" as a Pattern

---

Catherine, Stephen, Drew, Carolyn

The Kingdom Called Fungus

This is the kingdom called fungus.

This is the multi-celled organism
    that belongs to the kingdom called fungus.

This is the mushroom,

    that is a multi-celled organism
    that belongs to the kingdom called fungus.

This is the thing called absorption.
    It is the way the mushroom
    gets food because it is a
    multi-celled organism that
    belongs to the kingdom called fungus.

This thing called absorption
    which is the way the mushroom
    gets its food is because
    multi-celled organisms that
    belong to the kingdom called
    fungus don't have any chlorophyll.

Teaching Text Structure

In Chapter 14, Karen Feathers discusses reading strategies that specifically help students in their content classes. In that chapter, she explains what happens when students read narrative texts as opposed to expository texts. So, what follows is a very brief discussion of text structure. Turn to Karen's chapter for a more thorough discussion of this important topic.

Researchers have found that comprehension increases when students understand the patterns writers use to compose texts. While story maps have been widely used, expository or nonfiction structures have received less attention in the classroom. Comprehension of expository or content area reading is especially difficult for students. It contains specialized vocabulary, complex sentences, and new concepts. In addition, diagrams, charts, and other visual materials challenge middle school readers as they transition into using more expository texts.

Teachers can provide support in content area reading instruction by teaching text patterns or the structures authors use. The goal of such instruction is to assist readers in accessing meaning rather than becoming lost in unfamiliar organizational patterns. Using simple diagrams, along with authentic text examples, helps students learn how to recognize the structure and to use that knowledge to increase understanding. Instruction that focuses on text structure will increase comprehension. In Chapter 14, Karen Feathers describes the differences in narrative and informational texts, while in Chapter 16, Betty Carter and Richard Abrahamson discuss ways to use nonfiction trade books in your classroom.

In addition to providing students with strategies to recognize text patterns, readers need authentic experiences in reading maps, charts, graphs, and other visuals that often accompany informational text. Brown and Cambourne (1990) suggest that students need to learn about different types of texts before being expected to comprehend them. Students need to learn that they should approach reading a diagram differently than they approach reading a story. Identifying the questions students may have about reading visuals provides a useful framework for planning instruction.

- Where do I start reading a visual?

- How do I know when I am finished reading the visual?

- Have I ever seen a similar visual that could help me understand how to read this one?

- For what purpose am I reading this visual? What should I know when I am finished?

- Are there labels or headings that can help me?

- Are there words used that are unfamiliar to me?

- Do I need to use a glossary or dictionary to help me understand?

Instruction that targets the salient features of the different kinds of visual information along with opportunities to see and read a variety of examples will increase both the students' confidence and their comprehension.

A Final Word

It is true that students benefit when teachers take time to teach them strategic behaviors that they can select from and use time and time again. As teachers *show* rather than *tell* students how to utilize these strategies, the benefits for students increase. As teachers demonstrate and model effective strategy use, learners *gradually* accept more and more responsibility for independent use of the strategies in their own reading. Making certain not to short change modeling and the importance of shared responsibility, teachers who consciously provide decreasing amounts of support until strategy use is integrated allow students the time necessary to become successful as strategic readers (see Figure 12.15). The teacher's roles as both co-reader and expert reader continue to surface as we learn more about the social dynamics within the classroom. It is important to note, however, that all of the strategy instruction we can provide as teachers will not make a difference unless students have frequent opportunities to read. Instituting classroom programs

Figure 12.15

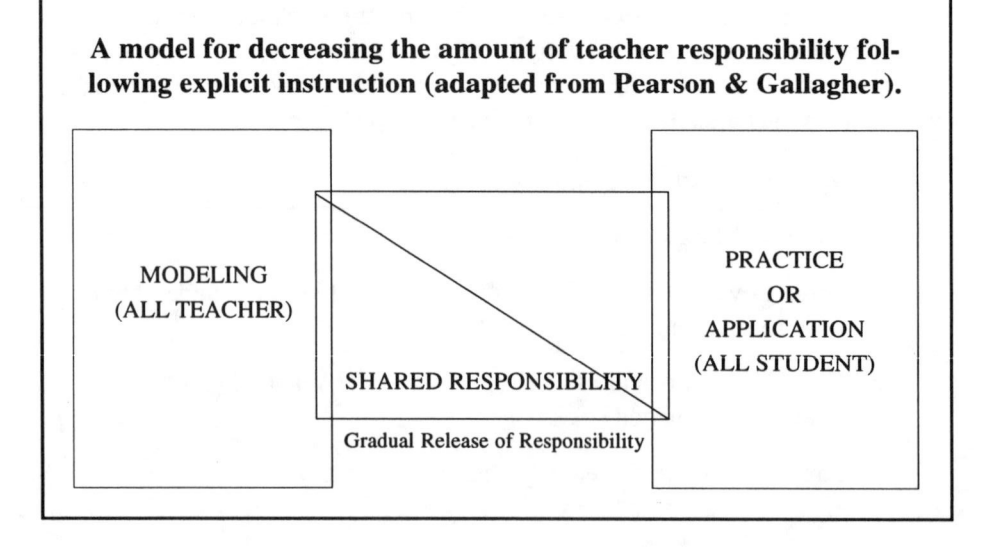

A model for decreasing the amount of teacher responsibility following explicit instruction (adapted from Pearson & Gallagher).

MODELING
(ALL TEACHER)

PRACTICE
OR
APPLICATION
(ALL STUDENT)

SHARED RESPONSIBILITY

Gradual Release of Responsibility

that emphasize voluntary and recreational reading ensures that readers apply strategies in authentic reading events. Real reading along with direct instruction of strategies prepares students to meet any reading challenge. As teachers, we owe it to our students to equip them with the best toolboxes we can provide.

References

Anderson, R. C. (1978). Schema-directed processes in language comprehension. In A. M. Lesgold, J. W. Pellegrino, S. D. Fakkema, & R. Glaser (Eds.), *Cognitive psychology and instruction*. New York: Plenum Press.

Brown, H., & Cambourne, B. (1990). *Read and retell*. Portsmouth, NH: Heinemann.

Davey, B. (1983). Think-aloud—modelling the cognitive processes of reading comprehension. *Journal of Reading, 27*, 44–47.

Feathers, K. M. (1993). *Infotext: Reading and learning*. Portsmouth, NH: Heinemann.

Flower, L., & Hayes, J. (1980). The dynamics of composing: Making plans and juggling contraints. In L. W. Gregg & E. R. Steinberg (Eds.), *Cognitive processes in writing* (pp. 1–50). Hillsdale, NJ: Erlbaum.

Graves, D., & Hansen, J. (1983). The author's chair. *Language Arts, 60*, 176–182.

Graves, M. F., Prenn, M. C., & Cooke, C. L. (1985). The coming attractions: Previewing short stories. *Journal of Reading, 28*, 594–598.

Harste, J. C., Short, K. C., & Burke, C. (1988). *Creating classrooms for authors: The reading-writing connection*. Portsmouth, NH: Heinemann.

Kintsch, W. (1977). On comprehending stories. In M. A. Just & P. A. Carpenter (Eds.), *Cognitive processes in comprehension*. Hillsdale, NJ: Erlbaum.

Ogle, D. (1986). The K-W-L: A teaching model that develops active reading of expository text. *The Reading Teacher, 39*, 564–576.

Olshavsky, J. (1976–77). Reading as problem-solving: An investigation of strategies. *Reading Research Quarterly, 12*, 654–674.

Paris, S. G., Wasik, B. A., & Turner, J. C. (1991). The development of strategic readers. In R. Barr, M. Kamil, P. Mosenthal, & P. D. Pearson (Eds.), *Handbook of reading research: Volume II* (pp. 609–640). New York: Longman.

Raphael, T. E. (1982). Question-answering strategies for children. *The Reading Teacher, 36*, 186–190.

Raphael, T. E. (1984). Teaching learners about sources of information for answering comprehension questions. *Journal of Reading, 27*, 303–311.

Raphael, T. E. (1986). Teaching question-answer relationships, revisited. *The Reading Teacher, 39*, 516–523.

Readence, J. E., Bean, T. W., & Baldwin, R. S. (1995). *Content area reading: An integrated approach* (5th ed.). Dubuque, IA: Kendall/Hunt.

Tierney, R. J., Readence, J. E., & Dishner, E. K. (1995). *Reading strategies and practices: A compendium* (4th ed.). Boston, MA: Allyn & Bacon.

Trade Books Cited

Babbitt, N. (1975). *Tuck everlasting*. New York: Farrar, Straus & Giroux.

Lowry, L. (1989). *Number the stars*. Boston, MA: Houghton Mifflin.

Martin, B. (1983). *Brown bear, brown bear, what do you see?* New York: Henry Holt & Co.

Paterson, K. (1994). *Flip-flop girl*. New York: Lodestar Books.

Rubin, S. G. (1993). *Emily good as gold*. New York: Harcourt Brace & Company.

Taylor, T. (1993). *Timothy of the cay*. New York: Harcourt Brace & Company.

Chapter 13
READING ALOUD TO BUILD
SUCCESS IN READING

Teri S. Lesesne

Teachers Reading to Students

I looked around nervously as five sixth-grade classes tromped into the library. Students began to sit on the floor, leaning against book shelves or sprawling on their backs. Teachers were trying to quiet the 150+ students assembled to hear me tell them about new books. How would I get and keep their attention? I began in a hushed tone:

> Because the things that happened to me were so strange, I know that some people will find them hard to believe. It's like when your mind slides from sleeping to waking and something takes place that's so bizarre, you tell yourself, "I have to be dreaming. This couldn't be real." Or when you jolt awake from a nightmare, and there are still unfamiliar shapes that move through your dark room, and you stare at them with wide-open eyes, knowing they can't exist and you must be awake.
>
> There will be more questions, and I'll have to repeat the answers over and over—even to myself—so I've brought a thick, yellow, lined tablet, and I'm going to write down everything that took place, beginning with the day I died.

When I finished, there were audible gasps. This riveting opening from Joan Lowery Nixon's *Whispers from the Dead* (1989) caught their interest. The read-aloud has done its trick: these students wanted to hear more about the books I had brought to share.

Twenty years ago, when I first started teaching middle school students, I read aloud to students as a way to entertain them and to keep them quiet! I also read aloud to them to show them that I liked to read and that I knew good books for them to read. Now I read aloud to middle school students because I have discovered what primary school teachers seem to have always known: being read to is an important part of reading development. Reading aloud to children quickens their minds even as it stills their bodies. It ignites imaginations, lengthens attention spans, introduces thoughts and ideas, and connects us with this thing called story. Reading aloud to children is so important that the Commission on Reading called it "the single most important activity for building the knowledge required for eventual success in reading" (Anderson et al., 1985).

In fact, the commission's findings so highlighted the importance of reading aloud that many predicted that daily reading aloud to students—especially in the elementary school years—would become a typical practice. Couple the commission's findings with any of several other studies that demonstrate the power of reading aloud to preschool and primary school children (Cochran-Smith, 1984; Cullinan, Harwood, & Galda, 1983; McCormick, 1977; Teale, 1984) and you quickly see that reading aloud to children not only affects their attitudes toward reading, but it also helps them learn to read. However, the landmark study by Langer, Applebee, Mullis, and Foertsch (1990) reveals that most teachers do not read aloud daily to their students. The number of teachers reading aloud on a consistent basis to students decreases as the grade level increases, so that by middle school, a small percentage of teachers read aloud daily to their students. This is in spite of the finding that middle school students, especially middle school students who don't like to read or who can't read, report that they not only enjoy being read to, but they learn from it.

An ethnographic study of aliterate seventh graders, students who can read but don't, revealed that being read aloud to by the teacher in an exciting voice was a favorite way for these students to connect with books (Beers, 1996). One student explained that hearing the teacher read a book helped him understand the action in the book. Another student offered that reading a book was boring but hearing a book was fun. But reading aloud to students benefits more than reluctant readers. Livaudais (1985) surveyed students in grades 7 through 12 about what motivates them to read. Of all the activities listed, having the teacher read aloud was the number one choice of these students. Furthermore, a meta-analysis of the research on reading aloud to students in grades kindergarten through 12 (Martinez, 1989) showed that reading aloud contributes to gains in reading comprehension scores, gains in vocabulary scores, and improved scores on sentence structure and usage tests. Anders and Levine (1990) reported that one essential component of middle schools is reading aloud to the students. This practice provides students a model of oral reading, gives them a chance to share an emotional response to a book, allows for interaction between teachers and students, and has a settling effect on the classes.

Being read to not only affects reading ability, but it also impacts reading attitude. My own research with at-risk middle school students has shown that these students wish teachers would read aloud to them, saying it would make them more likely to read on their own. This connection between attitude and being read to isn't new. From the mid-1950s through the mid-1980s, G. Robert Carlsen collected thousands of reading autobiographies from the students he taught in his college adolescent literature classes, all people who were considering a career connected with books. He summarized the findings from those autobiographies in *Voices of Readers: How We Come to Love Books* (Carlsen & Sherrill, 1988). Read what several students had to say about being read to while they were in junior high/middle school:

> In . . . [sixth grade] our teacher read *A Christmas Carol* to us during the few weeks just before our annual Christmas vacation. I thoroughly enjoyed this work and I became most concerned as to whether we would be able to hear the end of the story before classes were dismissed for the holiday. (p. 42)

> In eighth grade the superintendent was the reading teacher. He even read stories from *The Saturday Evening Post* to us. How I wished that I could read aloud like Mr. M. He read with a loud voice and always stopped at the exciting parts. (p. 43)

> Mrs. K. made even *Great Expectations* bearable, her wonderful voice filling out Pip's absurd personality. (p. 43)

The mere act of being read to isn't quite enough to create the positive attitude we are all interested in. It seems that what our parents told us is indeed true: It is not what we say but how we say it that makes the difference. I had a student explain to me that "when my teacher reads aloud with a lot of drama, I can picture what is happening in my head." Another of Carlsen's (1988) students wrote how a seventh-grade teacher "read aloud to the class over a year's time Victor Hugo's complete novel, *Les Miserables* . . . the class—in its entirety—was held spellbound throughout what must have been a sterling oral presentation" (p. 43). Another student shared what happened when the oral presentation was less than sterling: "In seventh grade Miss S. tried hard to make the subject dull. She rarely read aloud and when she did she would sit on a straight-backed chair in front of the room, too low for most of us to see her and in her drab voice, destroy a few paragraphs" (Carlsen & Sherrill, 1988, p. 43).

Reading aloud to students requires the right tone, the correct cadence, the ability to bring the characters to life—if only through our voices and faces. That is because "literature has sound. It has melody and rhythm and tone. And, yes, it has a 'voice'" (Carlsen & Sherrill, 1988, p. 39).

The practice of reading aloud appears, on the surface, easy and perhaps one-dimensional. Get a book, find a listener, begin. In fact, though, there are right ways, wrong ways, and various ways in-between to read aloud to middle school students (see Figure 13.1).

Figure 13.1 Approaches to Reading Aloud to Middle School Students

---

1. Read and Tease

In this approach, you read a sentence or two or perhaps a paragraph in order to whet the students' appetite for the book. The read-aloud should come from a particularly comic or intense passage to be the most effective.

2. Read to Introduce a Genre or Unit of Study

As you begin a new genre or unit of study, select an example or two of that particular genre to share with the class. In this way, you can guide students to deduce the essential characteristics or critical attributes of the new genre or topic.

3. Read an Entire Book

Reading a book a chapter at a time over the course of several days or weeks may make some books heretofore considered too advanced for some students more accessible. Begin with picture storybooks and work toward longer books to increase students' ability to listen.

Differing Approaches to Reading Aloud
Read and Tease

The object behind read and tease is to whet students' appetites for new books. Reading an opening sentence or two or a humorous passage is one way of motivating students to read. The opening sentence of *The Chocolate War* (1974) by Robert Cormier is a prime example of a book made for this approach: "They murdered him." So is the prologue from *Whispers from the Dead* (Nixon, 1989) found at the beginning of this chapter. Alternate between comic and more intense passages so that you will appeal to those students who either love to laugh or those who love to be frightened! Read a few chapters of an exciting book aloud and you will not be able to keep it on your shelves. Keep in mind, though, that some research with aliterate students indicates that reluctant readers prefer to hear an entire book read aloud rather than just a portion of it (Beers, 1996). Reluctant readers aren't likely to read the book on their own and prefer having the teacher read the entire book to them.

The read and tease approach allows teachers the opportunity to note the reading interests of students simply by watching which students take which books. Noting their selections will assist you in recommending more books for these students, books that meet their interests and preferences. My students call read and tease the "groaner" because of the responses of students when I stop reading. Once, after I read the beginning of *Make Lemonade* (Wolff, 1993) to a group of eighth graders, a student demanded that I tell her the rest of the story! When I declined, she turned to the librarian and asked if she could have that book NOW. The librarian was, of course, happy to comply with her request. With all of the booktalks I do with middle schoolers, I always include some read and tease. Classroom teachers and librarians tell me that the books I use for read and tease are always checked out first. Figure 13.2 provides some suggested titles and passages that work well as a read and tease.

Read to Introduce a Genre or Unit of Study

I began each of my 15 years as a middle school teacher with a unit on the short story. It came first in the literature anthologies, did not intimidate my students, and seemed a good place to begin. However, after 5 years or so, I began to tire of the same stories. I started casting about for some new material for the students to read and discovered collections of stories by authors who were writing specifically for and about young adults. The year that I began the study of the short story with Richard Peck's "Priscilla and the Wimps" from Don Gallo's collection *Sixteen* (1984) was a turning point for me and for my teaching. I had found a humorous and very brief story that could be read aloud in a matter of 5 minutes and yet contained all of the elements of the short story that I would teach over the next few weeks: plot, climax, characterization, setting, theme, etc. Here was a story full of wonderful similes and metaphors; plus, it was funny. It never failed to hold the attention of my students, who said they liked reading about something they understood, a school bully. Read Don Gallo's chapter on short stories for middle school students for some more good ideas for sharing short stories.

When it came time for the poetry unit, I tried the same approach. I selected some poems from collections aimed at adolescent readers and commenced reading these poems aloud to the students. I began with the humorous four-line poem "Lasagna" by X.J. Kennedy, found in Paul Janeczko's *Pocket Poems*. Within minutes the class was laughing at the poem and reciting it with me. Our look at poetry continued with poems found in *Where the Sidewalk Ends* (Silverstein, 1974); *Class Dismissed! High School Poems* (Glenn, 1982); *Nightmares: Poems to Trouble Your Sleep* (Prelutsky, 1976); *Tomfoolery: Trickery and Foolery with Words* (Schwartz, 1973); and *Just Give Me a Cool Drink of Water 'fore I Diiie* (Angelou, 1978). Students responded well to hearing poetry read aloud. And they loved hearing poetry that appealed to them. Many mentioned this was the first time that they had not been assigned to read some poems silently and then answer questions about them. I was shocked because poetry, more so than any other genre, begs to be read aloud. For students to hear a poem's meter, which often helps create the meaning, they must *hear* the poem.

Figure 13.2 Suggested Titles for Read and Tease

Note: **Some of the following passages are for younger readers and some are for older ones. The label "one size fits all" is a lie, and the same is true for Read-Alouds. Carefully select only those titles appropriate for your students' needs, interests, preferences, and development.**

- Avi. *True Confessions of Charlotte Doyle* (Prologue) in which the title character tells of how she came to be accused of murder and sentenced to be hanged at the tender age of 17.

- Cormier, Robert. *The Chocolate War* (opening sentence or paragraph) in which Jerry Renault gets his clock cleaned on a football field.

- Faustino, Linda. *Ash: A Novel* (Last Will and Testament of Wesley Libby) in which the narrator deeds his possessions to his friends and family in a humorous and unique voice.

- Holland, Isabelle. *Alan and the Animal Kingdom* (opening sentence) in which readers are left wondering about the fate of the young protagonist and his beloved pets.

- Lowry, Lois. *The Giver* (chapter 15) in which Jonas learns about war.

- Mazer, Anne (ed.). *Going Where I'm Coming From: Memoirs of an American Youth* (final two to three paragraphs of essay by Judith Ortiz Cofer) in which one immigrant child learns about the importance of words and writing.

- Nixon, Joan Lowery. *Whispers from the Dead* (first two paragraphs of the prologue) in which the main character tells about her near-death experience.

- Paulsen, Gary. *Father Water, Mother Woods* (description of the frog pit from chapter on Walleye Fishing) in which Paulsen humorously tells of the dangers of keeping hundreds of frogs captive in a place where anyone might stumble into them.

- Sleator, William. *Oddballs* (opening five paragraphs of chapter entitled "Games") in which Sleator talks about the pleasures of tormenting his siblings.

- Stoehr, Shelley. *Crosses* (opening sentence or two) in which the main character graphically describes her ritual of self-mutilation and destruction.

Soon, my students were joining me as I read poetry aloud to them. Choral reading became a natural part of our poetry time. Then books such as *Joyful Noise!* (Fleischman, 1988) came along. This book, a Newbery winner, is most enjoyed when read aloud and read with two or more readers. Getting middle schoolers into poetry is less difficult when we read aloud poetry that appeals to them. Moving them on into more traditional poetry such as "The Midnight Ride of Paul Revere" (ever present in our literature anthologies) becomes easier—though beware: students will expect you to read it aloud!

Read an Entire Book

While most students enter first grade excited to learn to read, many students enter middle school hating to read. Many conditions contribute to this decline in interest, but only a few factors help curb it. One of the most powerful ways to turn around disinterest is by reading aloud to students. Whether disinterest in reading comes from a fear of reading, of not understanding, of being overwhelmed by too long a book, or simply from being tired of too many questions to answer at the end of too many chapters, hearing an entire book read aloud consistently wins the approval of even the most apathetic, disinterested readers. However, hearing a book read aloud is not only for those with negative attitudes toward reading; many students who love to read express how much they enjoy hearing a story.

Some middle school students won't admit they like being read to. It just seems too "babyish." However, if you don't ask them but just do it, then you quickly discover that they not only like hearing the stories, they love it. Walk into a sixth grade classroom and listen to the sniffles of even the most reluctant readers as the teacher reads aloud *Where the Red Fern Grows* (Rawls, 1974) or *Bridge to Terabithia* (Paterson, 1977). Or visit a seventh grade to hear the laughter that erupts as students listen to *Skinnybones* (Park, 1982) or *Maniac Magee* (Spinelli, 1992). In any middle school classroom where the teacher consistently reads aloud, students look forward to that listening time and become upset if it starts late, is interrupted, or ends early. Hearing an entire book read aloud, though students may not say it aloud, is something middle schoolers enjoy.

When you plan to share a long book with students, you might want to share the reading load with guest readers (respected principals and favorite coaches are ideal candidates) or let students read aloud parts. However, whoever the readers, they must be prepared. This read aloud time is almost a performance time. Students report that they don't like monotone readers, readers who haven't practiced, or readers who stumble over words. Actually, they do not want us to *read* books aloud; they want us to act them aloud. So read ahead, practice, know where to speed up, slow down, change voices, and supply quick sound effects such as knocking on a desk to emphasize a knock on a door. You do not need elaborate staging, props, costumes, and the like, but you do need to be familiar enough with the material to make eye contact with your audience. Most important, know where to end each section of the book so you have them anxiously awaiting the next day's read aloud time.

Remember, many picture storybooks are actually for students in upper elementary, middle, or high school. Don't overlook these powerful books. For example, Patricia Polacco's *Pink and Say* (1994) is a sophisticated picture storybook that middle school students enjoy and appreciate. Books that use irony and satire to develop their humor are also appropriate. *The Dumb Bunnies* (1994) by Sue Denim (pseudonym, get it?) or any of the Jon Scieszka send-ups of the folktales are wonderful to share with middle schoolers. Figure 13.3 lists some of picture storybooks for older readers.

When you read aloud an entire book, whether it is a picture storybook, a short chapter book, or the first book in a trilogy, you provide the students in your class with an in-common text experience (Davidson & Koppenhaver, 1993); everyone will be able to join in the discussion, and will be able to respond in some way to the same text. This type of shared book experience heightens and expands the interaction with a text for everyone. It allows all students, from the gifted reader to the struggling reader, to become a part of the community of readers. In becoming a part of that community, students move one step closer to becoming lifetime readers—all through hearing the book. To help that happen, keep the following additional guidelines in mind:

- Let students respond to the reading every day but do not turn this session into a skill lesson.

- Establish a regular schedule for reading aloud. Reading aloud to students is most effective when it is done on a regular basis.

- Reading daily for 10 minutes or every other day for 15 minutes is optimal. Initially, you may have to begin with a shorter period of reading aloud and work up to the full 10 to 15 minutes as students become accustomed to the routine.

- Preview all material to be read aloud. Not only will this make the presentation more effective, it will avert any uncomfortable situations that might occur because of language or events not appropriate for your students.

- Vary the material to be read. Read nonfiction as well as fiction. Be sensitive to the diverse needs of your students. Sometimes choose books that have males as main characters and others times choose those with females. Include books that show students characters of various ethnic backgrounds.

Figure 13.3 Picture Storybooks for Older Readers

Ahlberg, J., and Ahlberg, A. (1993). *It was a dark and stormy night.* NY: Viking.

Bowen, G. (1994). *Stranded at Plimoth Plantation.* NY: HarperCollins.

Cannon, J. (1993). *Stellaluna.* NY: Harcourt Brace.

Coerr, E. (1993). *Sadako.* NY: Putnam.

Cooper, F. (1994). *Coming home: From the life of Langston Hughes.* NY: Philomel.

Deedy, C. A. (1994). *The library dragon.* Atlanta, GA: Peachtree.

Denim, S. (1994). *The dumb bunnies.* NY: Scholastic.

Denim, S. (1995). *The dumb bunnies' Easter.* NY: Scholastic.

Garland, S. (1993). *The lotus seed.* NY: Harcourt Brace.

Innocenti, R. (1990). *Rose Blanche.* Mankato, MN: Creative Education Inc.

Kroll, S. (1996). *Pony express!* NY: Scholastic.

Lasky, K. (1994). *The librarian who measured the Earth.* NY: Little, Brown.

Legge, D. (1995). *Bamboozled.* NY: Scholastic.

Lowe, S. (selector). (1992). *The log of Christopher Columbus.* NY: Philomel.

McKissack, P. & McKissack, F. (1994). *Christmas in the big house, Christmas in the quarters.* NY: Scholastic.

Pilkey, D. (1994). *Dog breath.* NY: Scholastic.

Pinkney, A. D. (1993). *Alvin Ailey.* NY: Hyperion.

Polacco, P. (1994). *My rotten redheaded older brother.* NY: Simon & Schuster.

Polacco, P. (1994). *Pink and Say.* NY: Philomel Books.

Pomerantz, C. (1980). *The tamarindo puppy and other poems.* NY: Greenwillow.

Price, L. (1990). *Aida.* NY: Harcourt Brace.

Scieszka, J. (1993). *The stinky cheese man and other fairly stupid tales.* NY: Viking.

Stanley, D., & Vennema, P. (1992). *Bard of Avon: The story of William Shakespeare.* NY: Morrow Junior Books.

Stanley, D., & Vennema, P. (1993). *Charles Dickens: The man who had great expectations.* NY: Morrow Junior Books.

Stanley, D., & Vennema, P. (1994). *Cleopatra.* NY: Morrow Junior Books.

Tsuchiya, Y. (1988). *Faithful elephants: A true story of animals, people and war.* (Translated by Tomoko Tsuchiya Dykes.) Boston, MA: Houghton Mifflin.

Yolen, J. (1981). *Sleeping ugly.* NY: Coward-McCann, Inc.

- Have copies of the books you read available for students to check out. This is especially important if you are using a read and tease approach. Students will want to check out the book on the spot.

- Read aloud books that you genuinely enjoy. Our voices give us away. If you do not find a particular book or passage compelling, it will be impossible to read it aloud effectively. Therefore, select materials that you enjoy reading.

While these guidelines will help your read aloud time become more enjoyable, Hoffman, Roser, and Battle (1993) suggest that if we want read aloud sessions to become more than enjoyable, but also educational, then we need to do the following:

- Share literature that is related to other literature. This allows "readers and listeners to explore interrelationships among books, to discover patterns, to think more deeply, and to respond more fully to the text." (p. 501)

- Discuss literature in lively, invitational, thought-provoking ways. For ideas on open-ended questions, look at Chapter 7 by Robert Probst.

- Group children to maximize opportunities to respond. Hoffman, Roser, and Battle (1993) found that "smaller groups and settings in which students are seated in conversational arrangements have been found to increase participation." (p. 501)

- Offer a variety of response and extension opportunities.

- Reread selected pieces.

Students Reading to Students

Paired Reading

Some of us remember the round-robin reading of our early years in school. How many of us read ahead and rehearsed the sentence or paragraph we knew would be ours? How much did we actually gain from this type of reading? I suspect that I missed out on some wonderful adventures because I was more concerned with getting all the words right when it was my turn to read. A new approach to oral reading by students, called paired reading, allows students the opportunity to read aloud in a nonjudgmental situation.

In paired reading, two students read together. Students with like abilities can be paired just as easily as students with unlike abilities. In the latter instance, the less able student might choose to follow along or just listen as the more able student does the reading. This gives the developing reader a model essential for the development of fluency. Good readers are fluent readers; when they read aloud they know where to pause and which words to group together. As developing readers listen to fluent readers, their own reading fluency improves.

Paired reading may also take other forms. Both students may participate in the reading, one following the other, sharing the reading assignment. Allowing students to divide the reading of a chapter in half with a buddy improves attitudes. Paired reading can also mean that the teacher models the reading and then the class echoes in a choral reading of the material. The anonymity of reading in a choral situation may make less able readers take more of a risk and join in the reading.

Paired reading not only helps students practice their own oral reading, but it also acts as a vehicle for some creative assignments. For example, I turned loose an eighth-grade class with a video camera and copies of Paul Fleischman's *Joyful Noise!* (1988), a collection of poems for two readers. The students were instructed to choose a poem, prepare a creative presentation of their reading of the poem, and video the presentation. Later we shared the video with the entire class. I ran into one of the students from that class recently. "Do you remember 'Book Lice?'" he asked. "We had the best time doing that tape. I still have a copy of that book."

Paired reading is reading with a purpose in all of the preceding instances. Just as giving students a real audience for their writing makes for better and more elaborated writing, so giving them a real audience for their reading may make for better reading.

Readers' Theater in the Classroom

The image stays with me several years after it took place. I was sitting with 300+ other enthusiasts of young adult literature at a national conference. At the front of the room were four teens, scripts in hand. For the next 5 minutes, these young people held an audience spellbound as they performed a readers' theater script based on Virginia Euwer Wolff's *Make Lemonade* (1993). I had read this book before this conference and thought I knew it well, but somehow hearing the words of the adolescent characters coming from the mouths of real adolescents made the book more powerful, more real than it had been. Wolff herself was in attendance and was visibly moved by the performance. The power of readers' theater had never been made so real to me as it had in that 5-minute presentation.

What is readers' theater and what elements are essential to its success? Simply, readers' theater is a group project that involves the reading of a prepared script based upon a literary work. Typically, the *actors* sit on stools or chairs in the front of the room and read the scripts; there is little, if any, movement involved as character is developed by dialogue rather than other means such as gesture and costume. In order for readers' theater to be successful, the following elements must be present:

- Students must read the script in such a manner as to capture the interest and imagination of the audience. While hamming it up is to be avoided, some dramatic skills will enhance the presentation.

- Scripts must be kept relatively short (8–10 minutes is long enough) in order to keep the attention of the audience as well as to reinforce the motivational nature of the technique. We want the performance to encourage students who have not yet read the book to do so.

- Vary the genre being used in this strategy. Include nonfiction, poetry, biography, and the like.

- Begin with prepared scripts so that students will have models for their own writing. Latrobe and Laughlin's (1989) *Readers Theater for Young Adults: Scripts and Script Development* offers several scripts that middle school students will enjoy. Once students are ready to begin writing their own scripts, teach them how to select a passage, prepare the script, and conduct the performance. The following five steps should assist you in guiding students toward a successful experience with readers' theater.

  1. Begin with a quality piece of literature.

  2. The scene to be enacted must be one of great dramatic tension. The scene immediately preceding the climax may be a perfect choice.

  3. Any action must be converted to narration for the script. This means that the cast must include a narrator to help set the stage and to keep the action running smoothly.

  4. Once a draft is prepared, students should read it through once to check for extraneous matter. Is there more that can be cut from the script?

  5. After revision, a final rehearsal should be held. The cast needs to decide on the seating arrangements and any costuming notes (i.e., color to help set the mood).

Students learn a lot as they prepare a readers' theater script. First, the act of preparing a script for readers' theater requires synthesis and analysis. Students must be able to take a crucial scene from the book and translate it into a viable script. Dialogue must be written; directions for the staging must be kept simple. Students cannot rely on elaborate props or costumes. The spoken word is the focus of this activity.

The writing of a readers' theater script may serve as an alternative to the traditional book report. Research continues to show that students do not find writing traditional book reports as reading motivation (Livaudais, 1985). In order to adequately prepare and perform the script for a readers' theater production, students must have read and comprehended the story. An eighth-grade reading teacher in Texas uses readers' theater in her classroom as one way for students to demonstrate their understanding of the books they have selected to read. Debbie allows her class to divide into groups based upon the books they have selected. Each group is responsible for writing the script for a crucial scene from the book. All of the class, however, is involved in the production as Debbie videotapes each presentation. She has a person in charge of the camera, of props and costumes, of keeping time, and the like. In this way, every student is a part of every production.

Reading Aloud to Develop a Reader's Ear

When I read a book, a marvelous voice in my head narrates for me. It provides dialects, sets the mood, and directs the pace. I wonder if that is the case for our less able readers? Do they hear the voice? Low-achieving readers report that they don't hear or see anything as they read (Beers, 1996a). This underscores the importance of developing a reader's ear for all of our students. Unless we can hear the words and can form the pictures from a story, the pleasure of reading cannot be fully realized. Read-alouds, paired reading, audiobooks, and readers' theater are a few ways of developing that reader's ear for our students, of ensuring that they have the opportunity afforded to us of becoming lifetime readers.

References

Anders, P. L., & Levine, N. S. (1990). Accomplishing change in reading programs. In G. G. Duffy (Ed.), *Reading in the middle school* (pp. 157–170). Newark, DE: International Reading Association.

Anderson, R. C., Hiebert, E. H., Scott, J. A., & Wilkinson, I. A. G. (1985). *Becoming a nation of readers*. Washington, DC: National Institute of Education.

Beers, K. (1996a). No time, no interest, no way! Part I. *School Library Journal, 42*, (2), 30–33.

Beers, K. (1996b). No time, no interest, no way! Part II. *School Library Journal, 42*, (3), 110–113.

Carlsen, G. R., & Sherrill, A. (1988). *Voices of readers: How we come to love books*. Urbana, IL: National Council of Teachers of English.

Cochran-Smith. M. (1984). *The making of a reader*. Norwood, NJ: Ablex.

Cramer, E. H., & Castle, M. (Eds.). *Fostering the love of reading: The affective domain*. Newark, DE: International Reading Association.

Cullinan, B., Harwood, K., & Galda, L. (1983). The reader and the story: Comprehension and response. *Journal of Research and Development in Education, 16*, 29–37.

Davidson, J., & Koppenhaver, D. (1993). *Adolescent literacy: What works and why* (2nd ed.). New York: Garland Publishing, Inc.

Hoffman, J., Roser, N., & Battle, J. (1993). Reading aloud in classrooms: From the modal toward a "model". *The Reading Teacher, 46,*6, 496–503.

Krashen, S. (1993). *The power of reading: Insights from the research*. Englewood, CO: Libraries Unlimited, Inc.

Langer, J. A., Applebee, A. N., Mullis, I. V. S., & Foertsch, M. A. (1990). *Learning to read in our nation's schools: Instruction and achievement in 1988 at grades 4, 8, and 12*. Washington, DC: The National Assessment of Educational Progress.

Latrobe, K. H., & Laughlin, M. K. (1989). *Readers theater for young adults: Scripts and script development*. Englewood, CO: Teacher Ideas Press.

Lesesne, T. S. (1993). *A survey of read-aloud habits of teachers and librarians*. Unpublished manuscript.

Lesesne, T. S. (1994). *A follow up survey of the read-aloud habits of teachers and librarians*. Unpublished manuscript.

Livaudais, M. (1986). *A survey of secondary students' attitudes toward reading motivational activities*. Unpublished doctoral dissertation, University of Houston, TX.

Martinez, A. (1989). A meta-analysis of reading aloud. Presentation at Phi Delta Kappa seminar, Houston, TX.

McCormick, S. (1977). Should you read aloud to your children? *Language Arts, 54,* 139–143, 163.

Routman, R. (1991). *Invitations: Changing as teachers and learners K-12*. Portsmouth, NH: Heinemann.

Smith, F. (1985). *Reading without nonsense*. New York: Teachers College Press.

Teale, W. H. (1984). Reading to young children: Its significance for literacy development. In J. Goelman, A. A. Oberg, & F. Smith (Eds.), *Awakening to literacy* (pp. 110–121). London, England: Heinemann.

Trade Books Cited

Angelou, M. (1978). *Just give me a cool drink of water 'fore I diiie*. New York: Random House.

Avi. (1991). *Nothing but the truth*. New York: Orchard.

Avi. (1990). *True confessions of Charlotte Doyle*. New York: Orchard.

Brooks, M. (1990). *Paradise cafe and other stories*. New York: Little, Brown.

Brooks, M. (1994). *Traveling on into the light and other stories*. New York: Joy Street.

Cormier, R. (1974). *The chocolate war*. New York: Dell.

Crutcher, C. (1991). *Athletic shorts: Six short stories*. New York: Greenwillow.

Denim, S. (1994). *The Dumb Bunnies*. New York: Scholastic.

Faustino, L. (1995). *Ash: A novel*. New York: Orchard.

Fleischman, P. (1988). *Joyful noise: Poems for two voices*. New York: Harper & Row.

Fox, P. (1984). *One-eyed cat*. New York: Bradbury.

Gallo, D. R. (Ed.). (1984). *Sixteen*. New York: Delacorte.

Gallo, D. R. (Ed.). (1987). *Visions*. New York: Delacorte.

Gallo, D. R. (Ed.). (1989) *Connections*. New York: Delacorte.

Gallo, D. R. (Ed.). (1992). *Short circuits*. New York: Delacorte.

Gallo, D. R. (Ed.). (1993). *Join in*. New York: Delacorte.

Gallo, D. R. (Ed.). (1993). *Within reach*. New York: HarperCollins.

Glenn, M. (1982). *Class dismissed*. New York: Clarion.

Glenn, M. (1986). *Class dismissed* II. New York: Clarion.

Glenn, M. (1988). *Back to class*. New York: Clarion.

Glenn, M. (1991). *My friend's got this problem, Mr. Candler*. New York: Clarion.

Holland, I. (1977). *Alan and the animal kingdom*. New York: Lippincott.

Janeczko, P. (1983). *Poetspeak*. New York: Bradbury.

Janeczko, P. (1985). *Pocket poems*. New York: Bradbury.

Janeczko, P. (1989). *Brickyard summer*. New York: Orchard.

Janeczko, P. (1990). *The place my words are looking for*. New York: Bradbury.

Janeczko, P. (1994). *Stardust hotel*. New York: Orchard.

Lowry, L. (1993). *The Giver*. Boston, MA: Houghton Mifflin.

Mazer, A. (Ed.). (1995). *Going where I'm coming from*. New York: Persea.

Nixon, J. L. (1989). *Whispers from the dead*. New York: Delacorte.

Park, B. (1982). *Skinnybones*. New York: Alfred A. Knopf.

Paterson, K. (1977). *Bridge to Terabithia*. New York: Avon.

Paulsen, G. (1994). *Father water, mother woods*. New York: Delacorte.

Peck, R. (1970). *Sounds and silences*. New York: Delacorte.

Polacco, P. (1994). *Pink and Say*. New York: Philomel Books.

Prelutsky, J. (1976). *Nightmares: Poems to trouble your sleep*. New York: Greenwillow.

Rawls, W. (1974). *Where the red fern grows*. New York: Doubleday.

Rylant, C. (1990). *Soda jerk and other poems*. New York: Orchard.

Rylant, C. (1994). *Something permanent*. New York: Harcourt Brace.

Rylant, C. (1995). *The Van Gogh café*. New York: Harcourt Brace.

Schwartz, A. (1973). *Tomfoolery: Trickery and foolery with words*. New York: Lippincott.

Silverstein, S. (1974). *Where the sidewalk ends*. New York: HarperCollins.

Sleator, W. (1993). *Oddballs*. New York: Dutton.

Soto, G. (1990). *Baseball in April and other stories*. New York: Harcourt Brace.

Spinelli, J. (1992). *Maniac Magee*. New York: HarperCollins.

Stoehr, S. (1991). *Crosses*. New York: Delacorte.

Wilson, B. (1990). *The leaving and other stories*. New York: Philomel.

Wilson, B. (1995). *Dandelion garden and other stories*. New York: Philomel.

Wolff, V. E. (1993). *Make lemonade*. New York: Scholastic.

Wynne-Jones, T. (1995). *Some of the kinder planets*. New York: Orchard.

Yolen, J. (1991). *2041*. New York: Delacorte.

Chapter 14
FOSTERING INDEPENDENT, CRITICAL CONTENT READING IN THE MIDDLE GRADES

Karen M. Feathers

Ms. J.: *What kinds of things do you read?*

Kenneth: *Sports stuff like in the paper, computer stuff, cartoons—.*

Ms. J: *You haven't said anything about reading for school.*

Kenneth: *Oh, you want me to talk about that?*

Ms. J: *Yes, what do you read for school?*

Kenneth: *Last year I read three books for English.*

Ms. J: *What else did you read?*

Kenneth: *Nothing.*

Ms. J: *What about science and social studies? Didn't you read anything for those classes?*

Kenneth: *Well yes, but—I thought you wanted to know about reading.*

Ms. J: *What do you mean?*

Kenneth: *You know, it's not like a story or something. You just find the answers to things.*

While Kenneth's views may not be what we would like to hear, they do represent those of others in his seventh grade class (Saundra, Emilio, Masai, LaShonda, Joyce, for example), and those of many middle grade students. Even those who view reading as a pleasurable activity often separate *that* reading from the informational reading that is part of content classrooms. In this way they are not unlike my own child who in the third grade declared that she "hated" reading. When reminded that she read all the time, she explained, "Oh, I don't hate READING; I hate *READING*! You know, what we do in school," and she took out pages of worksheets to show me. So too, our middle grade students differentiate READING (out-of-school) and *READING* (in-school). Unlike my third grader, they also differentiate between school literature reading and informational reading, classifying literature in with out-of-school "READING" but placing informational reading in a separate category.

How Does This Separation Develop?

Partly separation like this comes about because school reading is unlike reading outside of school in terms of material used and the activities in which readers are engaged. Reading outside of school is done by choice; we choose when to read and what to read. We can begin a book and then decide not to complete it, and we can reread the same book as many times as we want. As we read, we can stop and daydream, and our thoughts relate the text to our personal lives, reminding us of people and places we know and events in our own experience. We often choose to talk with others about our book and share our thoughts and feelings. In school, on the other hand, reading is usually assigned by the teacher who also determines the activities in which readers will engage before, during, and after reading. These activities are focused primarily on the content of the text (the events of the story) and secondarily on readers' responses to the text. School reading is very different from reading outside of school.

In addition, reading informational texts and reading literature in school are very different. Louise Rosenblatt (1980) argues that literary and informational reading are too similar in school—that teachers focus too much on the information in literature instead of focusing on the more appropriate aesthetic response. Although this has been true, there are still differences in how this informational focus has been realized. When teaching narratives at any grade, we ask questions and engage students in activities designed to help them recall major information and to understand the relationships among characters and events in the story. We assume that students have read the entire text and will use all information in that text. When dealing with informational texts, regardless of grade level, questions more typically focus on specific facts with little attention paid to larger relationships or applications. As a result, students like Kenneth can successfully complete worksheets with little reading. As he said, "I read the questions and then I look for the answer in the book. When I find the sentence, I copy it."

Why are These Differing Views Problematic?

Because of these differing views of reading, middle grade students often do not use strategies developed for out-of-school reading with in-school reading or strategies developed for literary reading with informational reading. Thus, Rosa, who naturally predicts what might happen in the story she is reading, has difficulty generating three predictions about what her science chapter on energy might include. If you do not view informational reading as "READING", then you will not use "*READING*" strategies for that activity.

What Other Things Cause Difficulty?

The problems caused by differing views are compounded by a lack of experience reading informational texts. Middle grade students have read narratives in elementary school and written many stories, and they are therefore familiar with this type of reading, but their experience with informational material is usually more limited. Students simply have not had enough experience with informational texts to have developed a variety of successful reading strategies to use with those texts.

Are Informational Texts More Difficult to Read?

Informational and narrative texts are very different; therefore students' lack of experience with informational texts is important. In addition to the charts, graphs, maps, and other graphics that are not typically found in narratives, informational texts are also structurally different. Carolyn Kent (1984) cites three major differences: the point of view, the orientation, and the linkages.

Narratives have a first- or third-person point of view—a narrator can be clearly identified whether it is the author or a character—and the reader determines who is telling the story and develops expectations based on this point of view. If the narrator is speaking in first person, we know that the narrator can only reveal her thoughts on things that she knows about. We will not have the outside view of a third-person narrator who could tell us what everyone is thinking or doing. These factors will help shape our predictions about possible things the author will say in the story. An informational text appears to have no narrator who speaks to the reader. That leaves the reader without the use of narrator information and more dependent on knowledge of text structure for predicting. However, our middle graders who have limited experiences with informational texts have little prior knowledge about text structure to use for predicting.

Narratives also are *agent* oriented in that they focus on characters and deal with personal situations that readers can easily relate to their own lives. Because of experiences with people and interactions with others, readers have a substantial amount of prior knowledge about interpersonal relations that they can use as they read narratives. In contrast, informational texts are *subject* oriented, focusing on topics or subject matter and the transmission of information, something that students have had less exposure to in their own lives. The information usually has little to do with the lives of students today, and the connections are not often suggested in the text. Readers may have some prior knowledge of a topic, but the amount of knowledge will vary greatly across students.

Finally, narrative texts are usually connected by chronological linkages—they are time-based with vocabulary that identifies the passage of time. Specific vocabulary helps readers follow the sequence of events in a narrative, a familiar activity because we constantly tell each other stories about things that happen to us. Informational texts are linked logically through techniques such as making comparisons, supporting main ideas with details, citing examples to illustrate concepts, describing, and listing facts.

These differences do not make informational texts inherently more difficult than narratives. However, limited exposure to informational texts at earlier grades may mean that middle graders have not had the opportunity to develop a variety of strategies for dealing with these differently structured texts independently. We need to help our middle grade students develop such strategies. They not only promote reading ability but also result in better learning of information—the opportunity to "learn about reading" as well as to "learn through reading," as J. Harste says (1989).

The remainder of this chapter will be devoted to strategies that help students learn *how* to read at the same time that they promote learning through reading. While good reading strategies can be used at any time during reading, in this chapter, strategies will be organized to focus on things typically done before, during, and after reading.

Before Reading: Connecting with Prior Knowledge

If any one factor is of importance in the process of reading, it is what we readers bring to the text—our prior knowledge. In order to understand, we must connect new information to what we already know. Middle grade students come to us with substantial knowledge that they can use to understand new concepts. We can promote their comprehension by helping students bring their prior knowledge to a conscious level so that they have readily available links to which they can "attach" or "connect" new information.

Sometimes students do not have specific information related to a particular topic. Amy's sixth grade class ran into some trouble when they reached the section on glaciers in their chapter on erosion. Because they lived in a small southwestern town, few of the students had seen any snow, much less snow piled up to substantial depths. Amy showed videos and films of snow and of Alaskan glaciers, and they read many books with lots of pictures and photographs. The class also did experiments with blocks of wood and sand to see how the wood could gouge out valleys in sand and pile it up into hills. Amy then helped students make connections between their experiments and the things they were reading about glaciers. Like Amy, we can help students understand unfamiliar topics by providing links through lecture, films, supplementary reading, class activities, and demonstrations.

Prior knowledge can also be used to predict what we might encounter in a text. For instance, if we understand something about stories—that they have characters, settings, events, sometimes a difficulty that is eventually solved—and if we have some information about the story such as the title and the picture on the cover, we can make predictions about what the story will involve. Similarly, given prior knowledge about a topic such as glaciers and some understanding of informational text structures, we can also predict what might be included in the chapter.

One way to help students access prior knowledge is brainstorming. Carol's sixth grade class brainstormed what they knew about the Sahara Desert. She asked students to tell everything that they knew or had heard or read about that topic. All information, including things that were inaccurate, was accepted and put on the blackboard (see Figure 14.1):

Figure 14.1 Carol's Class Brainstorming of Sahara Desert

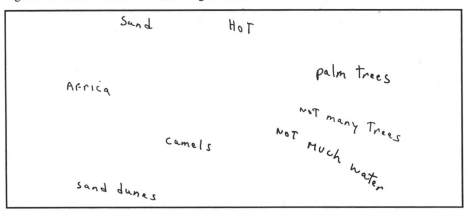

Carol could have stopped at this point and had her students read the chapter. Then they could return to their brainstormed list to reconsider the initial list, confirming accurate information, correcting anything that was inaccurate, and adding new information. Instead Carol asked her students to organize this brainstormed information—What could they group together? This led to the semantic map in Figure 14.2:

Figure 14.2 Carol's Class Organization of Their Brainstorming

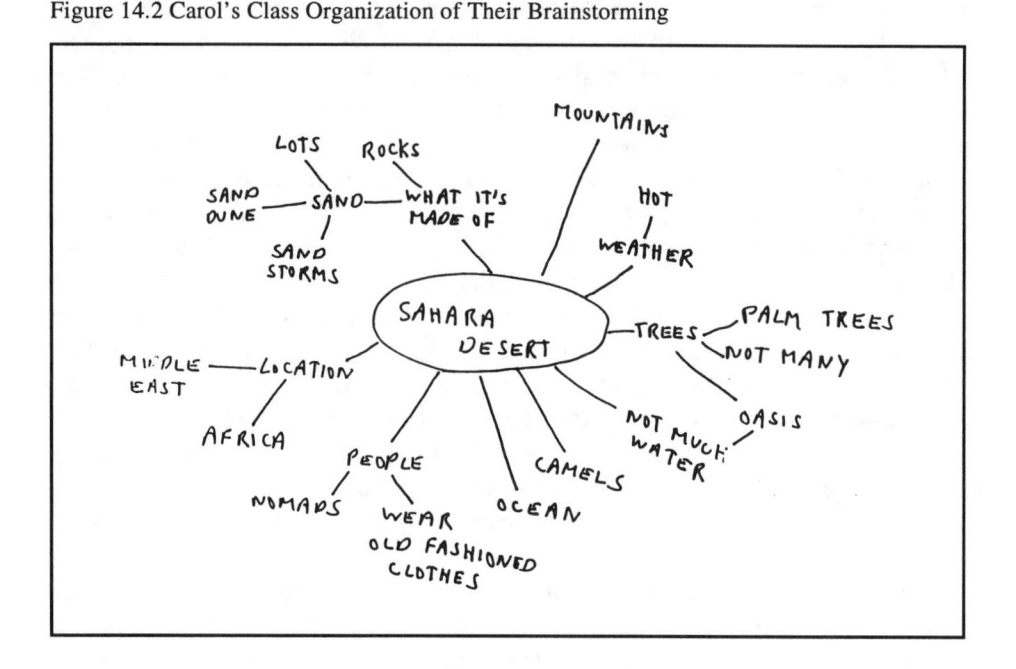

Tammy suggested they connect the information on trees. This then prompted suggestions that "hot" should be under "weather" or "climate" and that "in Africa" should be under "location." Things were also added to the map. When "lots of sand" was placed on the map, Sally said, "Wait! I have something else about sand. Maybe we should just put sand and then have 'lots' off of it and 'sand dunes' off of it." As that was done, Roger raised his hand and added "sandstorms," "They have lots of sandstorms where the sand blows around."

When they could think of nothing more to add, Carol had her students look through their chapter on the Sahara Desert, telling them to look at headings and pictures. She gave them about 3 minutes for this activity, and then she asked them what they thought the chapter might cover that they did not have on their map. They added: "oasis" (which they put connected to "water" and "trees") and "transportation" (because it was used by travelers), "rocks" (which caused them to reorganize sand, as both rocks and sand are found in the desert), "Middle East" (added to "location"), "people" linked to "nomads" and "wear old-fashioned clothes," "mountains," and "ocean."

Carol engaged her students in brainstorming to access prior knowledge and then helped them to use that information in combination with some information from the text (gained from skimming) to predict what the chapter might be about. In addition, she also provided them with the means to organize new information encountered during reading—the semantic map of their brainstorming and their predictions.

Janis, a sixth grade teacher, also used predicting in her math class. To introduce exponents to her class, Janis presented her students with examples of exponents—$2^2=4$, $3^2=9$, $2^3=8$, and then she put them in groups to determine what an exponent is. Using the examples provided, they formulated and then tested hypotheses until they figured it out, and then they shared their attempts. "We thought it meant *times* because 2 times 2 is 4, but 2 times 3 is not 8 so that was wrong." Next Janis put students in groups to generate additional examples for other class members to work out. This final activity led students to discover many new things about exponents. "Hey, guess what! If you do zero to any number, like 024, it still comes out zero," and "It's easy to do the number 10, you just add zeros."

Predictions are actually hypotheses that can be tested, and that is what Janis' students were doing—generating hypotheses (predictions) about exponents, which they then tested by comparing the results of their predictions with the actual examples. As such, Janis was not only engaging her students in good reading, she was also involving them in problem solving, a basic part of math courses. Finally, these students, because they were actively involved in figuring things out for themselves, quickly came to understand exponents—the focus of the chapter.

These strategies help students use what they already know. Other strategies such as K-W-L (Ogle, 1985) in which students identify what they know and what they want to know before reading and what they have learned after reading (see Chapter 12 for an example of how one teacher uses K-W-L) and PReP, which asks students for initial associations to a topic and to reflect on these associations before reading and then asks them to write about new ideas on the topic after reading (Langer, 1981), can also provide ways for students to access prior knowledge (see Figures 14.3a and 14.3b). As they read, they need additional strategies to help them to focus on the construction of meaning and to actively respond to the ideas and information that they encounter.

Figure 14.3a KWL Strategy (Ogle, 1986)

Helps students access prior knowledge and set purposes for reading.

1. Ask students what they know about a topic (K), and put their brainstormed information in that column.

2. Ask students what they want to know about that topic (W), and put their questions in the second column.

3. After students read the text, invite them to put what they have learned (L) in the third column of the chart.

Figure 14.3b PReP, The Pre-Reading Planner (Langer, 1981)

Helps access prior knowledge.

There are three phases.

1. Ask students for their *initial associations* to a topic. This is essentially brainstorming, and the responses are recorded for the group.

2. Ask for students' *reflections on these associations* through questions. For example, "What made you think of electricity?"

3. Ask students to discuss and/or write about new ideas they now have about the topic after reading the material.

During Reading: Encouraging a Focus on Meaning

Middle grade students often think that informational reading is a one-way process—that information flows from the text directly into a reader like pouring water into a glass. This leads them to take a passive role in reading. Even those students who might normally respond actively when reading literature may change their stance into that of a passive reader when approaching informational material.

Ryder (1991) believes that teacher-led discussion and questioning allows teachers to link specific text details to students' prior knowledge and to direct learning and is preferable because "students tend to pay attention when the teacher asks questions" (p. 77). While these things may be true, the long-term results of teacher-led instruction is still a dependence on the teacher.

One way to encourage active reading while also helping students be independent readers is to have students write responses in the margins of their texts. This could begin with a code like those suggested by Smith and Dauer (1984) or Vaughan and Estes (1986) (see Figure 14.4a). Students could develop their own code as Danny did (see Figure 14.4b), or they could simply write their thoughts. Danny used slips of paper because he could not mark in his book, but post-its are also a good alternative. He used a code, but he could also have simply written his thoughts. Placing students in small groups to discuss their thoughts allows students to compare responses and text content that triggered their responses.

Paired think-alouds during which the reader says whatever comes into his/her mind are also helpful. Carol and I demonstrated this for her class with a text that we had not read before. We took turns reading the text orally, interjecting our own thoughts out loud during the reading (see Chapters 5 and 12 for some examples of Think-Alouds). Then we paired students

Figure 14.4a

Insert Code (Vaughan, J., & Estes, T., 1986)

X=I thought differently   +=new information

!=wow   ??=I don't understand

Code (Smith & Dauer, 1984)

A=agree   B=bored   C=confused   D=disagree   M=main idea

C=clear   D=difficult   I=important   S=surprising

---

to read their social studies text and think aloud together. Because Carol's students were used to brainstorming and predicting, we had them begin with that and asked them to continue their predictions as part of their Think-Aloud. This turned Think-Aloud into a Directed Reading/Thinking Activity (Stauffer, 1975).

Once students are used to thinking about what they are reading, they can begin to take notes as they read. Middle grade students need to develop their note-taking ability to help them remember important information from textbooks and lectures. When engaging in inquiry projects where they are gathering information on a topic from multiple sources, the ability to take notes is crucial. More importantly, note-taking helps students focus on meaning and think critically. They have to decide what is important enough to include in their notes, and they have to understand the information well enough to put it in their own words. Depending on the way they are written, notes can also help students begin to organize the information. It is important that these notes are as brief as possible (or they won't use them) and written in the students' own words (or they won't own/learn the information).

One useful format for taking notes is the Cornell System (Pauk, 1984a) sometimes referred to as the *split page* form (Readance, Bean, & Baldwin, 1989). Divide a sheet of paper into two columns with the left column taking up about one-third of the paper and the right one using the remaining two-thirds of the space.

Figure 14.4b Danny's Codes and Markings for a Text

Most of North Africa and the area we call the Middle East is very hot and dry. You can compare the rainfall of these lands with the rainfall in North America by looking at the map on page 72. Which area receives more precipitation on the whole?

mi

Most of North Africa and the Middle East gets less than 10 inches of rain in one year. Land that gets this little rain is usually called a desert. Some of the world's driest and biggest deserts are in North Africa and the Middle East.

Mi

The world's largest desert, the Sahara, covers most of the land in North Africa. *Sahara* means "desert" in Arabic. Almost all of the area we call the Arabian Peninsula is a desert. Riyadh, the capitol of Saudi Arabia, receives only about 3 inches of rain a year. In some parts of the deserts in North Africa and the Middle East there is no rain for years at a time.

Mi

??

People often think of deserts as lands covered with sand, where no plants ever grow. The truth is that only 30 percent of the world's deserts are covered with rocks and stones. Geographers call a sand desert *erg*.

!

?

mi = major idea
?? = don't understand
! I don't know this
? I have questions about this
(why is it called an "erg?" Is that Arabic too?)

Carol helped her students begin note-taking by doing some notes on their social studies book as a class activity similar to a Language Experience Approach activity (Allen, 1976). She read the first section of their chapter, "Where is the Middle East?" aloud and invited her students to tell her what they thought was important information. These were put in the right-hand column (see Figure 14.5):

Figure 14.5 Class Notes of Two Text Sections

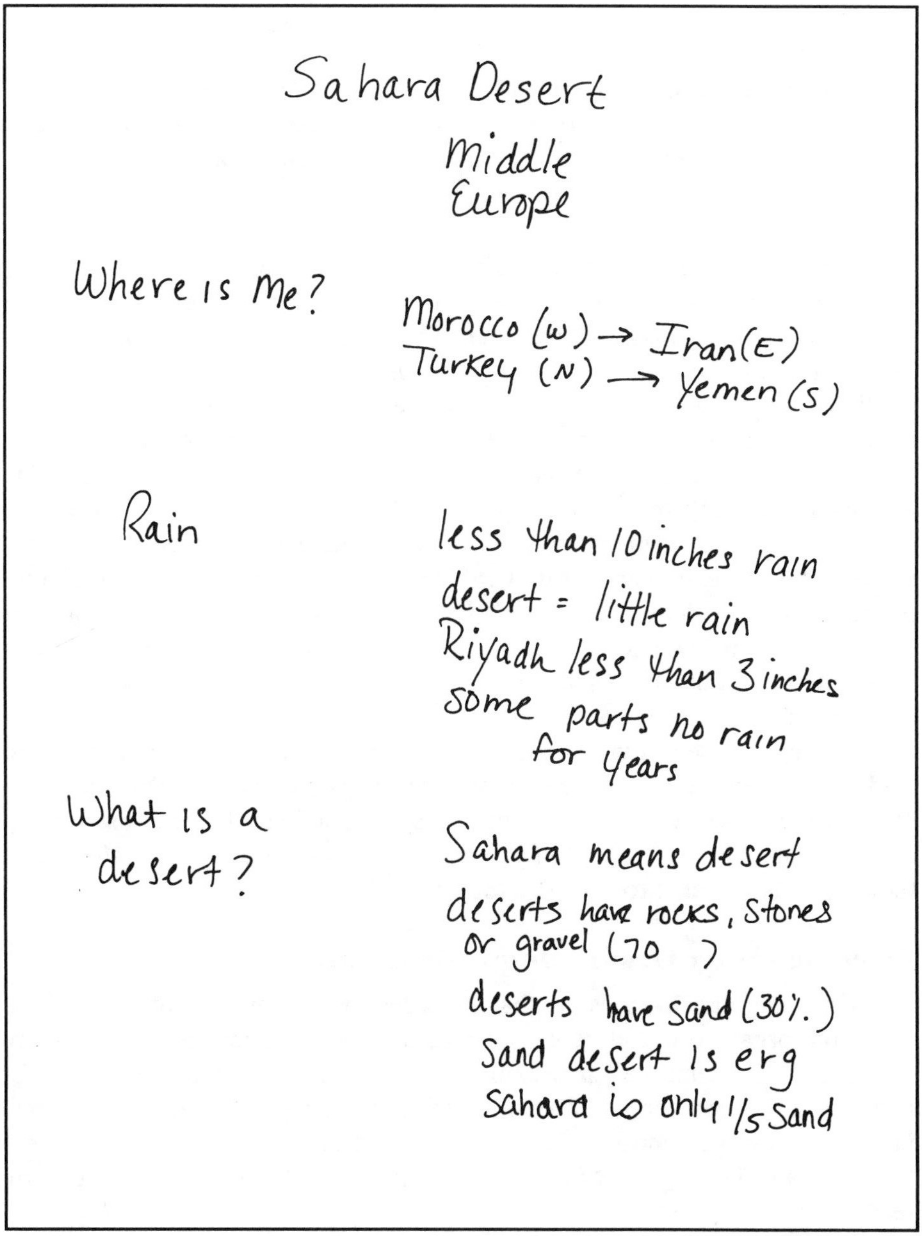

Sahara Desert

Middle Europe

Where is Me?

Morocco (w) → Iran (E)
Turkey (N) → Yemen (s)

Rain

less than 10 inches rain
desert = little rain
Riyadh less than 3 inches
some parts no rain
for years

What is a desert?

Sahara means desert
deserts have rocks, stones or gravel (70)
deserts have sand (30%.)
Sand desert is erg
Sahara is only 1/5 sand

As each item was suggested, she invited students to think of alternative ways to write that fact and, to move them away from copying from the text, had them try to think of the shortest way to write things. For instance:

> Denise: *We could say Middle East from Morocco in west to Iran in east, to Turkey in north to Yemen in south.*

> Emilio: *How about Middle East—Morocco (W), Iran (E), Turkey (N), Yemen (S).*

> Hannah: *I'm going to draw a square and put ME in the middle of the square and Iran on the right side for east, Morocco on the left side for west, Turkey on the top for north, and Yemen on the bottom for south.*

After each item was brainstormed, students selected which one they would put in their own notes. Then Carol had them look over the notes and determine which items went together. Those concepts were put in the left-hand column (Figure see 14.5). This required students to think about the relative importance of information as well as linkages among discrete items, thus focusing them on major concepts and supporting information.

After doing several sections together, Carol paired students to continue reading and writing their notes together. When they met in small groups to discuss their notes, students considered the relative importance of information and made comparisons of how information was summarized by different people. This provided feedback on whether they were identifying the important information, whether they were including more than was necessary in their notes, and how successful they were in putting the information in their own words.

Through these activities and group discussion of responses and notes, students develop and use strategies for meaning construction. They begin to monitor their own reading, focusing on understanding what they have read, and to evaluate and record information. To be effective readers/learners, they must also be able to organize this information.

After Reading: Organizing Information

Frank Smith (1975) says that in order to remember information, we must first organize it and then connect it to items already in our long-term memory. One technique for organizing information that has been used for many years is outlining. An outline categorizes information into separate units based on the subdivisions of the text and the sequential order of these text sections. Thus, an outline represents the organization of the text being read.

However, separating ideas into categories does not help us to generate the linkages we need to store information in memory. Our long-term memory is actually a complex network of interrelated items that includes not just *facts* or *concepts* but also emotions, senses, and narrative memories. My concept of bread is connected not only to facts about bread but also the smell of bread baking, the taste of different kinds of bread, my dislike of certain kinds of bread, the feeling of bread dough in my hands as I knead the bread, images of my grandmother's kitchen, and memories of my attempts to teach a friend how to make bread.

We add new information to our store by attaching it to what is already there. The more connections we can make between new information and what we already know, the easier it will be to retrieve because there will be many alternate retrieval paths. We can help our brain make these connections by organizing new information in ways that show the connections.

Semantic mapping is a means of organizing information in a way that is most likely to facilitate learning and remembering. A semantic map shows relationships among items through placement and connecting lines. Sinatra, Stahl-Gemake, and Morgan (1986) define a semantic map as a means of displaying the relationship of the whole to the parts and the parts to the whole (p. 5). Mapping allows information to be organized based on the connections that the reader sees so that even items separated in the text can be placed near each other and connected on the semantic map. The reader can use the organization of the text to help decide how to organize the information, but the map is not a replica of the text organization. Instead, a semantic map depicts the reader's view of the information, a view that can include prior knowledge and responses as well as the information in the text read. Unlike outlining, which is linear and requires little thought, semantic mapping forces students to think. They have to analyze, evaluate, reason critically, organize, categorize, and show relationships (Miccinati, 1988, p. 543).

Semantic mapping is particularly useful as we involve students in inquiry learning. When students are using multiple sources of information to learn about a topic, they must find ways to pull information together. Semantic mapping is a useful means of integrating information from multiple sources.

Jerry began mapping by providing students with partially incomplete graphic organizers that students filled in. However, because the graphic organizer was produced by the teacher, students had difficulty with this task. They did not view the information in the same way and would not organize it as Jerry did, so they couldn't figure out what he intended them to put in each section. Carol and Pat did not model mapping by showing their students how they would map a chapter because when this is done, students tend to follow the teacher's model instead of figuring out what form works best for them.

Carol began teaching students mapping through the class brainstorming activity (see Figures 14.1 and 14.2). Pat had her students take notes on index cards (you could also use post-its or slips of paper). Then they arranged their notes on a large sheet of paper so that related items were in close proximity to one another. This allowed the students to physically move items and try out different arrangements. Connecting lines were drawn between items, and labels were added as needed. She also had them work in pairs or small groups to promote discussion of the topic of study and to make the process of mapping less threatening. Because her students had been using the Cornell System to take notes, they moved easily into mapping as they had already been organizing information and labeling with concepts. As they continued to map, some students found it easier to continue to take notes first and then map from their notes while others grasped the idea of mapping very quickly and mapped as they read.

Pat and Carol also placed students in small groups to share maps that they had created individually. Erica and Stephanie (see Figures 14.6 and 14.7) discovered that their maps had many similarities but also differences when they shared.

Placing students in groups to discuss their maps allows students to explore the topic in depth and from a variety of perspectives in a nonthreatening atmosphere. Students consider the relative importance of information and the connections among items. They compare the various ways of organizing in their different maps and have a chance to consider other views of the information and alternative organizations.

Other forms of semantic maps include such things as comparison charts, flowcharts, timelines, schedules, graphs, and Venn diagrams, all of which are useful means of organizing information. Students should be encouraged to experiment with these various forms as well as to compare their usefulness for depicting different types of information.

An alternative way to organize information is through summarizing. A summary is a set of statements that condense information and reflect the gist of a text (Hidi & Anderson, 1986). Like semantic mapping, summarizing requires students to make decisions about what information is important (evaluation) and to organize the information in some way. Summary writing is not easy for middle grade students. Hill (1991) suggests that this is because they are not as familiar with the structures of informational texts as with narratives and therefore aren't sure how to organize the material. We need to introduce summarization in ways that provide support for students as they become familiar with the organization of informational material.

Pat had her students use their semantic maps to write summaries. The organization of the map provided a basis for the organization of the summary and the information to be included, although not all of the information on the map needs to be in the summary. Pairing students to write a summary

Figure 14.6 Erica's Semantic Map "Infection Chain"

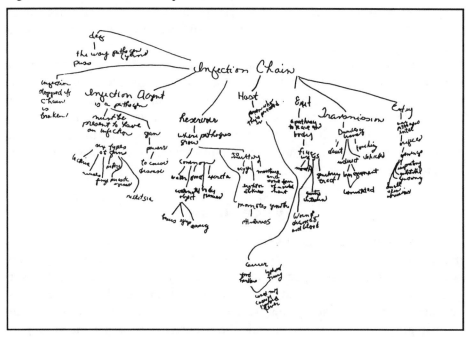

Figure 14.7 Stephanie's Map "Infection Chain"

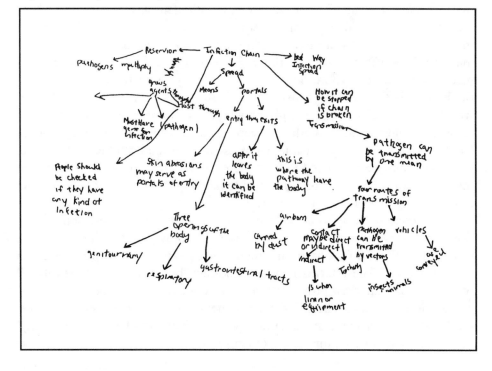

together promotes additional discussion of the topic as well as deeper involvement with the process. Paired writing also reduces the risk associated with trying something new, so it is an effective way to begin summary writing.

Just as individual semantic maps vary, so too will summaries. There is more than one way to organize and present any set of information, and the selection of information, organization, and presentation are dependent upon the prior knowledge of the writer. Small group sharing of summaries allows students to compare their summaries with others and, in the process, to evaluate their own choices in terms of information included, organization, and presentation.

Vocabulary

Vocabulary is a concern when students are reading informational texts particularly if one book, such as a social studies book, serves as the primary source of information. Specific terminology can cause problems for students, but it is not the vocabulary that is difficult for them but the meanings, concepts, and ideas that are represented by the words. All too often we fail to distinguish between the words and the underlying concepts and attempt to teach terms rather than concepts. In other words, we teach the term *pathogen* rather than helping students understand what a pathogen is. The definition in the glossary of the book or a dictionary is not necessarily helpful in developing this understanding. In one textbook, a pathogen was defined as an "infectious agent," which doesn't help much unless you know what an infectious agent is. Definitions within the text itself and other context clues may also be ineffective such as this definition of "oasis": "These were green places in the desert where people grew a few crops in their small garden-fields, which they irrigated from wells." Are oases always irrigated from wells? Do they always have gardens where crops are grown? We do want students to understand specific concepts and to know the terminology related to fields of study—mathematics, science, social studies, art, music, language—but we also need to help them know how to deal with texts that may not always be clear or helpful and to develop strategies for learning and remembering these concepts and terms.

One common way to provide students assistance is to pre-teach the vocabulary that we think is important for them to know and/or which we think might cause them difficulty during their reading—often the words identified in the textbook. These terms may be important, but this will not identify all of the words that may prove difficult for students. Also, some words included on the list may be things that students already know. For example, the list for a sixth grade social studies chapter included the word "journal," something that is very familiar to students today.

To provide her students with a strategy for reading and also help expand their vocabulary, Sally gave them *trouble slips* (Feathers, 1993). These are simply slips of paper like bookmarks. As students read, they wrote anything that they did not understand on a slip and left it marking that page in the text. When they were finished reading, Sally put them in groups to discuss their problems. Mark didn't know the word "peninsula" in his chapter. When Roger explained what a peninsula was, Mark turned to the map of the Middle East and said, "Well, I still don't see why it is called a peninsula. Look at it." Everyone in the group looked at the map and they were puzzled too; so they decided to bring that problem up in the whole-class discussion that followed. Tina wanted help pronouncing "Riyadh," so they all looked at the pronunciation guide in the text and worked it out together. When Kevin asked what "precipitation" was, the group turned to a dictionary to check whether it just meant rain or if it included snow. When Sally brought the groups together to deal with problems that they could not resolve, the entire class benefited from the discussion that resulted from this group's question about "peninsula."

Carol also uses trouble slips, but the brainstorming that she did on the Sahara Desert prior to having students read this section also provided them with help. A specific term for this chapter is "desert," and students had generated many things about deserts (see Figure 14.2). They had also generated things that would help them understand other terms such as "oasis" and "wadi."

An alternative strategy to use prior to reading that still makes use of a predetermined list is to provide students with the list and have them say or write what they think the words mean. Brice wrote her definitions for the vocabulary words before she read the text and then revised her definitions after reading (see Figure 14.8). Charles frequently uses this strategy (developed by J. Harste, 1988) in his science classes because science terms often have common meanings in society but very specific meanings in science. Brice's definitions show this as her initial definitions are related to everyday events while her final definitions are related to her reading.

Semantic mapping also helps students identify important concepts and terminology and to remember them. Erica's and Stephanie's maps from their science text contain the important terms from the chapter (see Figures 14.6 and 14.7). The terms that the teacher had identified and given to his students to define (see Figure 14.8) were found in the maps of these students from another class that did not use the list ("portal of exit," "portal of entry," "host," "reservoir," etc.).

These are strategies that help students focus on specific terms to be learned and that also help them develop strategies for dealing with difficulties, but the most common difficulty is a lack of prior knowledge that could be used to understand. Instead of teaching vocabulary, we need to think about teaching concepts. When Amy engaged her sixth grade class in activi-

Figure 14.8 Brice's Vocabulary Definitions

Words to be defined	1	2
1. Infectious agent	A sore or cut.	Pathogen-germ. There are six.
2. Host	Someone who gives a party.	A person a pathogen gets into.
3. Portal of entry	Door to come in.	Way into the body.
4. Portal of exit	Door to go out.	Way out of the body.
5. Transmission	Part of a car.	Send from one place to another by contact, vehicle, or air.
6. Reservoir	Lake	Place where pathogens multiply.

ties to help them understand glaciers, she was building their conceptual background—the word "glacier" was not difficult; they did not understand the concept *glacier*.

Conclusion

The strategies presented here are not the only ones that could be used, and there are also study plans that combine strategies. For example, ERICA (Downing & Morris, 1984) has four stages: (1) *preparing*—teacher provides structured overview, (2) *thinking through*—teacher provides guides such as Herber's (1970) for guided reading, (3) *extracting and organizing*—use of some form of chart or organizer, and (4) *translating*—writing summaries. PORPE (Simpson, Stahl, & Hayes, 1989) involves five stages—*Predict, Organize, Rehearse, Practice*, and *Evaluate*; and SQ4R (Pauk, 1984b) has six—*Survey, Formulate Question, Read, Record, Recite*, and *Reflect*. Some of these plans are more teacher-directed, such as ERICA, and some are very text-bound, SQ4R for instance, but they do offer some alternative views of how strategies might be used in combination. Strategies, like any tools, should be used when needed, and they should not simply be used as a matter of fact.

The strategies suggested here will provide middle grade students with the tools that will allow them to be independent readers and thinkers. In addition, engagement of students in these strategies deepens their understanding of the topic of study. Karen Wood and K. Denise Muth (1991) argue that middle grade instruction needs to change; there is too much whole-class lecture, little is done to prepare students for assignments, textbooks are still the primary source of content, lectures focus on what is in the text, and activities are still drill and practice and do little to promote higher-level critical thinking. The strategies suggested here will allow both teachers and students to counteract these problems of middle grade instruction and foster independent, critical readers and thinkers.

References

Downing, J., & Morris, B. (1984). An Australian program for improving high school reading in content areas. *Journal of Reading, 28,* 237–243.

Feathers, K. M. (1993). *Infotext: Reading and learning.* Markham, ONT: Pippin Publishing.

Harste, J. (1989). *New policy guidelines for reading: Connecting research and practice.* Urbana, IL: National Council of Teachers of English.

Harste, J., Short, K., & Burke, C. (1988). *Creating classrooms for authors.* Portsmouth, NH: Heinemann.

Herber, H. (1970). *Teaching reading in content areas.* Englewood Cliffs, NJ: Prentice-Hall.

Hidi, S., & Anderson, V. (1986). Producing written summaries: Task demands, cognitive operations, and implications for instruction. *Review of Educational Research, 56,* 473–493.

Hill, M. (1991). Writing summaries promotes thinking and learning across the curriculum—but why are they so difficult to write? *Journal of Reading, 34,* 536–539.

Langer, J. (1981). From theory to practice: A prereading plan. *Journal of Reading 25,* 152–156.

Miccinati, J. (1988). Mapping the terrain: Connecting reading with academic writing. *Journal of Reading, 31,* 542–552.

Pauk, W. (1984). *How to study in college* (3rd ed.). Boston, MA: Houghton Mifflin.

Pauk, W. (1984). The new SQ4R. *Reading World, 39,* 564–569.

Readance, J., Bean, T., & Baldwin, R. (1989). *Content area reading: An integrated approach* (2nd ed.). Dubuque, IA: Kendall/Hunt.

Rosenblatt, L. (1980). What facts does this poem teach you? *Language Arts, 53,* 386–394.

Ryder, R. J. (1991). The directed questioning activity for subject matter text. *Journal of Reading, 34,* 606–612.

Simpson, M., Stahl, N., & Hayes, C. (1989). PORPE: A research validation. *Journal of Reading, 33,* 22–28.

Sinatra, R., Stahl-Gemake, J., & Morgan, N. (1986). Using semantic mapping after reading to organize and write original discourse. *Journal of Reading, 30,* 4–13.

Smith, F. (1975). *Comprehension and learning.* Katonah, NY: Richard C. Owen.

Smith, R., & Dauer, V. (1984). A comprehension-monitoring strategy for content area materials. *Journal of Reading, 28,* 144–147.

Stauffer, R. (1975). *Directing reading maturity as a cognitive process.* New York: Harper & Row.

Stauffer, R. (1980). *The language experience approach to the teaching of reading.* New York: Harper & Row.

Vaughan, J., & Estes, T. (1986). *Reading and reasoning beyond the primary grades.* Boston, MA: Allyn & Bacon.

Wood, K., & Muth, K. (1991). The case for improved instruction in the middle grades. *Journal of Reading, 35,* 84–90.

Chapter 15

AUTHENTIC READING
ASSESSMENT
IN THE MIDDLE SCHOOL

Devon Brenner and *P. David Pearson*

This chapter may be the only chapter in this book explicitly dedicated to assessment techniques, but it is not the only chapter that can help you, as a middle school reading teacher, develop a sound and useful assessment program. In Chapter 8, Mary Santerre provides direction when she tells her story of the negative effect of existing assessments in her classroom and the changes, both in her teaching and her assessments, that she undertook to turn things around. She advocates that you do the same, based upon your views of how students learn and what they should learn. In Chapter 11, Sandra L. Robertson advocates dialectical journals and the projects that they make possible as a means of helping students learn how to respond thoughtfully and deeply, and she talks about how you can use this tool as a window to understanding what students are learning as they read.

Mary and Sandra make strong cases for particular assessment *artifacts*, but even those authors who focus on particular teaching methods or particular sorts of materials, such as Teri Lesesne in her chapter on reading aloud to middle school students, Karen Feathers in her chapter on content area reading, and Judy Wallis in her descriptions of strategy instruction, can help you think about assessment as well as instruction. And that is because the authors write not only about *what* to teach, but about *why* to teach it. They make clear their assumptions about middle school students and the kinds of teaching and learning that this very special group of students responds to. In other words, each of these authors articulates beliefs not only about the what and how of teaching, but also the whys, the reasons for teaching in these particular ways. As you will soon learn, we are committed to the principle that assessment begins with a careful articulation of beliefs and goals.

A thoughtful assessment system will allow you to accomplish many important teaching responsibilities, some of which are detailed in Figure 15.1:

Figure 15.1 Reasons to Assess

A sound system of assessment will help you to:

- ask and answer questions about student performance

- decide what to teach, and when

- find out whether or not your students are accomplishing your established goals

- articulate your own standards more clearly

- think about the opportunities to learn that you have orchestrated for your students

- communicate with audiences outside the immediate classroom

- make decisions about individuals and programs

- describe growth and accomplishment to students and their families

and will help your students to:

- know about the standards by which they are being judged

- judge their own accomplishments

- learn to develop their own learning goals and judge their own progress

Assessment is both the least and the most important piece of any literature-based reading program. It is the *least* important in the sense that teaching and learning are what really count (at best, assessment is simply a support system for allowing teaching and learning to take place). It is the *most* important because if we fail to provide convincing evidence of what our students are learning to those who have a stake in the process (parents, administrators, the public, and, most importantly, the students themselves) it is unlikely that we will be able to sustain good teaching practices, especially when those practices run against the grain of tradition.

In this chapter, we build on all the dazzling ideas about middle schoolers, reading, and teaching that have been shared by our fellow authors in an attempt to describe what a good middle school assessment program looks like and how a single teacher or a school staff or a district faculty might invent such a program. We try to answer one fundamental question:

> What sort of assessment program makes sense for a language arts curriculum in which literature plays a starring role?

We try to answer this question by unpacking the process of literature-based assessment and describing several key phases—phases at once seductively simple and incredibly complex. Finally, we close by describing a few model programs in which teachers have decided not only to teach, but also to assess student accomplishment, according to a set of beliefs and goals.

The Phases

Whenever you assess someone, you are defining how you think of her, and how, to a degree, she should think of herself. If you share your evaluations with other audiences, you are defining how they should think of her. For these reasons assessments must be authentic. In other words, the assessments you choose must be related to the ongoing learning and teaching that takes place in your classroom. Your assessment must be flexible, responsive to both individuals and your teaching goals, and must help students to have access to the educational opportunities you provide.

We see authentic assessment as a process of starting with broad goals for teaching and learning in the classroom and then thinking about those goals more and more concretely, until finally they are transformed into artifacts that can serve as evidence that can be examined by both teachers and students (and their parents) to see how well the original goals for teaching and learning have been met.

Establishing Goals: Broad Brushstrokes

A strong assessment program is built upon clearly stated standards—concrete statements about what students should know and be able to do. But before these are chosen, it is best to begin the process of setting standards by thinking in broad strokes about your own goals for teaching and learning. That means thinking generally about best practices and desirable outcomes. But it is more than that, and it is more personal than our statement suggests. It means knowing what you believe about teaching and deciding what it is you would like your students to learn as they interact with and around literature in the classroom.

This part of the process is the most philosophical. It is where you, as a teacher, ask yourself what is most important, most relevant. This is the part of the process in which *you* decide what you want your students to learn. While these are clearly *your* decisions, you need not, probably should not, make them alone. To the contrary, wise teachers consult broadly before setting instructional goals. First, they consult the other individuals who have a stake in what happens in their classrooms—students, parents, other staff members, even school policymakers. Second, they consult professional resources to help as they think broadly about goals and standards. Publications from the field like this one, district guidelines, or even the state curricular frameworks and standards can all provide guidance and direction. Think of it this way: as you work to find a general idea of where you would like to go as a teacher, and where you would like your students to end up, you ought to engage in a complex negotiation process in which many perspectives, needs, and points of view must be accommodated. State and district standards, the needs of the individuals in your classes, and parents' aspirations and concerns interact with your own professional knowledge and beliefs about teaching and learning. If this negotiation works well, you end up with a cohesive, or at least sensible, set of aspirations and beliefs to guide teaching and learning in your literature-based classroom. These beliefs, these broad brushstrokes of intention, frame all of the other curricular decisions you make.

Most people think of this goal-setting activity as a way to decide what and how to teach, but in our view, it is also the foundational phase of assessment. The ultimate assessment question, "How are we doing?" cannot be answered without asking and answering the more basic question, "Where are we going?" Assessment is a process of collecting evidence in an attempt to answer a particular set of questions. Knowing your own beliefs about teaching and learning is the first step in that process.

Establishing Goals: Filling in the Details

If the goal-setting phase, the place in which you settle on the hopes, dreams, and aspirations you hold for your students, can be thought of as broad brushstrokes, then this second phase of the assessment process may best be thought of as filling in the details of the painting. On the teaching side, this means filling in the curricular details—materials, teaching strategies, student activities, and assignments. On the learning side, it means translating your goals into more specific descriptions of what you would like your students to know and be able to do. One way to accomplish this is to make your goals more and more specific, until they become statements of what your students need to accomplish to demonstrate that they have met your goals.

Consider, for example, Mrs. Bean, a sixth grade teacher at Columbus Middle School. Her guiding belief about using literature in the classroom is that she must do everything possible to foster aesthetic response to literature. Considered more specifically, she would like the students in her classroom to bring their lives, their beliefs, and their feelings to their reading of the literature as they construct relevant models of meaning from the texts they encounter. She would like them to make connections between ideas presented in literature and their own experiences. In this account of Mrs. Bean's thinking in just these few sentences, we already see a transformation. What started as a broad instructional goal for Mrs. Bean (aesthetic response) just became a learning standard (making connections between experience and text), one that is easily translated into an assessment question.

We use the word *question* here very deliberately. Another way to think about assessment is as a process of asking and looking for answers to questions, and then reporting both the questions and the answers to the audiences who care about the learners in your classrooms. Your broad goals for learning, and the more specific standards they become, can both be translated into assessment questions. We illustrate this progression of specificity with Mrs. Bean. In order to promote aesthetic response to literature, Mrs. Bean could ask:

Are my students responding affectively to literature?

This question is too big to assess on its own, but it can drive the rest of the process. Just as her goals became more specific standards for learning, so do the questions. Knowing she'd like to see students making connections between their lives and the texts they read, Mrs. Bean can ask,

Are my students responding affectively to literature *by connecting ideas they read to their own experiences?*

Deciding What Counts As Evidence

If establishing goals is the most important phase of the process of assessment, then the second most important is deciding what counts as evidence. There are two important parts to this question—one physical and one conceptual. Evidence can be thought of as the physical artifacts themselves, the projects and assignments that students complete. Evidence can also be thought of as a more specific description of the goals you have already established, or as a characterization of what the goals might look like in action.

Back to Mrs. Bean. Her standard (connecting ideas they read to their own experiences) would be rendered more specific and concrete in this step. Conceptually, she would have to think about what her standard might look like in action, what she would be hoping to find in their work. And she would also have to decide which physical pieces of student work might be likely to reveal the connections she is hoping to find.

Based upon experience with previous classes, she believes that such connections might best be revealed in dialectical response journals. But her experience has also taught her never to rely on a single source of evidence for any important goal. Indeed, she knows that evidence and artifacts can come from many sources both in and out of the literature classroom. So, she lets students know that they can also include artwork in which they try to depict their feelings about novels, more formal essays in which they analyze and reflect on their aesthetic responses, and even notes they have taken at home or in school as they initially read the novels.

Deciding on the evidence—both the physical matter of what to collect and the conceptual issue of what to look for once you have it—is a phase in which you refine and ground the questions you ask. Mrs. Bean began her assessment process by wondering, "Are my students responding affectively to literature?" She refocused that question until it became, "Are they responding affectively by connecting ideas in literature to their own experiences?" After considering the kinds of evidence that will allow her to answer these questions, Mrs. Bean has a new question:

> Are my students responding affectively by connecting ideas in literature to their own experiences, *as demonstrated by journal entries in which they link their lives to the novels they are reading?*

We have described what might seem to be two very different ways of thinking about evidence—evidence as specific characterizations of the goals, and evidence as physical documentation. These two features of evidence are inseparably intertwined. Knowing what you'd like to see shapes the kinds of documents you collect. At the same time, the documents you collect and what they tell you both enable and constrain what the goals look like in action. The range of appropriate pieces and what you will look for in those pieces are both important questions to consider as you decide what counts as evidence.

This process of selecting artifacts as evidence based upon your goals and standards might remind you of the old skills-management systems that dominated instruction during the seventies and eighties. In these systems, each individual skill that was taught was also measured by a specific question or set of questions, or a particular test item. But ours is not a linear model, nor is it one of discrete units of learning or measurement. This simple, linear mapping is represented in Figure 15.2. We realize that, like instruction, assessment is a recursive, repetitive, overlapping, and ever-changing process.

Any goal can be taught and scaffolded by teachers in many different ways, as you have witnessed while reading the other chapters of this book. Furthermore, any given instructional activity, such as a rich literature discussion, might allow you to teach toward a number of your goals. Assessment is similar. Growth toward or accomplishment of a particular standard might be

Figure 15.2 A Sample Mapping

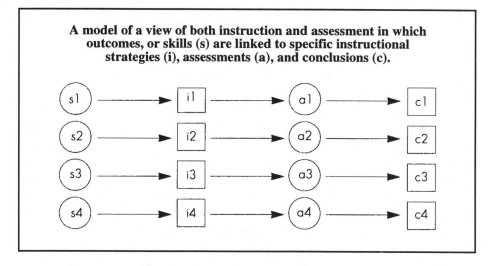

reflected in any of several pieces the teacher assigns or the student chooses to include in a portfolio. At the same time, any given piece you collect and reflect upon might yield information about student accomplishment toward several standards. We have represented this complex mapping between artifacts and standards in Figure 15.3:

Figure 15.3 A Complex Mapping

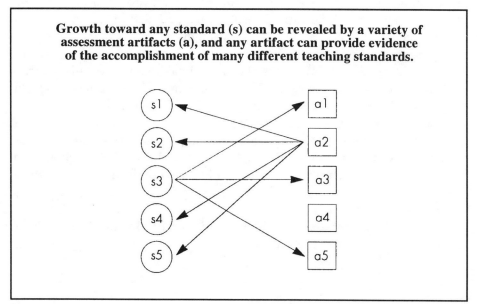

Thus an essay summarizing a student's overall response to *Bridge to Terabithia* (1977) might provide evidence of standards as varied as aesthetic response to literature, understanding and synthesis of key themes in a novel, and the ability to compose a coherent and powerful argument. Finally, just as students learn from many sources, their learning can be reflected by many sources as well. Thus, any given standard or goal can be indexed by any number of types of evidence.

The range of possible documents to provide Mrs. Bean evidence of students' aesthetic response might include papers, book logs, work samples, anecdotal records about classroom discussions, performances, projects, letters, personal or class web sites, and dialectical journals. Each would give students an opportunity to reveal different aspects of their response repertoire. Work done in other subject areas and even pieces from home are potential sources for demonstrating accomplishment of the reading and writing goals you have established in your literature-based classroom. Here's the bottom line: If you are aware of your questions and your students, and you know what you are looking for, there will be no limit to the sources of valuable assessment information.

Teach and Collect

You have established goals, turned them into standards, thought about what they might look like concretely, and determined which artifacts are likely to yield good evidence. Now it is time to teach and collect.

This might mean preserving the work (e.g., placing it in a portfolio) that is naturally generated in class as part of instruction. It might mean paying attention to a single aspect of learning during classroom discussions and keeping an anecdotal record (a teacher journal perhaps) in which you summarize student progress on that aspect. It might mean videotaping a performance at the end of a comprehensive unit or audiotaping a discussion for later student review and reflection. For Mrs. Bean this step entails teaching students how to create dialectical journals, nurturing and supporting students' use of them, and then collecting their contributions.

Teaching to your goals and collecting evidence of student accomplishment should be mutually reinforcing. It is as important to teach students how to do the tasks you are going to collect as it is to collect evidence about what you are trying to teach. In fact, if you fail to provide instruction which includes the rules of the game and the procedure for completing the artifacts, you may inadvertently end up privileging those students who already know how to play, leaving those who did not come equipped with that knowledge to fend for themselves in the dark.

Decide What the Evidence Means

This can be either a simple or a complex task, depending on the questions you ask and the answers you are seeking. In one situation, deciding what the evidence means could turn out to be giving grades or points on an assignment. In a second situation, it could mean telling kids that they either passed or did not pass an assignment. These are the simple versions, in that they are bounded by space and time. You consider only the document at hand and judge it on a set of criteria established for that document in particular, and you, as the teacher, remain the ultimate judge of worth. These first two versions of deciding what the evidence means answer particular questions: Who is up to snuff, and who is not? Who needs to work more? How many can do what I expected?

But in a third situation, deciding what the evidence tells you might mean comparing an artifact produced this week with a similar artifact produced at the beginning of the year; and then you might work with the student to describe how much he or she has grown. And a fourth situation could be an occasion for examining several responses to a particular book, several essays written about a particular theme, or responses to literature across the year, looking for evidence of growing metacognitive awareness of the process of responding to literature. These are more complex in that the evidence might be more ephemeral and the documents themselves less bounded. These latter endeavors take more time and require more thinking. They also answer very different questions: How is Kelly growing, and what can she say about her own learning? Have I provided opportunities for Marcos to demonstrate his growing knowledge? How can I help the students who still need me?

The shape of the final assessment, be it a description, a score, or a ranking, affects both how you look at the artifacts you have collected and the sense you make of them. Judging a piece in order to rank, score, or grade it forces you to hold constant the criteria for performance on that particular document, to hold that artifact up to predetermined criteria. Reflecting in order to describe a piece or to learn from an artifact what a student can do in order to help her describe it to herself, these tasks ask you to look at student work in a very different way, to let the pieces and the students contribute to the meanings constructed as you learn from the evidence. Each version of deciding what the evidence means has its own benefits and costs. A score or ranking might be the most meaningful or traditionally accepted way to communicate with many of your audiences, but it may also be the least flexible and may limit what you learn from the artifacts you collect. A description of the artifacts might be the most authentic way to learn about your students and your own teaching, but it could be quite time-consuming and may not appear *objective*. In any case, the form you choose for your assessments affects not only how you report them, but it affects what you see as you look to them to answer the questions you have about teaching and learning in your classroom.

Up to this point in the process, Mrs. Bean has collected her students' response journals, and she has come to ask herself:

> Are my students responding affectively by connecting ideas in literature to their own experiences, as demonstrated by journal entries in which they link their lives to the novels we are reading?

For Mrs. Bean, deciding what the evidence means changes her question subtly. She is no longer asking herself generally "Are my students responding?" She wants and needs to know about individuals. She studies and reflects upon the artifacts, their journals, to find out not only about her whole class, but about how each student is doing, holding his or her work up to the standards she has set for assessment. Now her question has become:

> *Who is, and in what ways* are my students responding affectively by connecting ideas in literature to their own experiences, as demonstrated by phrases linking their lives to the novels we read in their response journals?

For this phase of the assessment process, she reads the journals with her question in mind, keeping track of and describing the ways her students link their lives to their reading, attending to both her class as a whole and to the individual students. What she finds there may raise a whole new set of questions. Some students will be where she hoped to find them, and she will need to find ways to continue to help them grow as readers. The artifacts will help her to see that others are not responding in the ways she had hoped, prompting her to ask herself about new ways to support their learning.

The goals you have established, your reasons for assessing, and the criteria you have determined to be important: all of these will affect the questions you ask and the answers you learn of the artifacts and what you learn as you attach meaning to the artifacts you use for assessment in your quest for answers.

Deciding what the evidence means is an inherently interpretive process. Making sense of student work requires careful judgment on the part of teachers, and, if a teacher decides to promote self-assessment, on the part of students.

Share the Evaluation

To this point, we have talked about assessment mainly as a process of providing information to you as the teacher. In doing so, we may have misled you. There are many audiences for assessment, each with its own goals

and visions, each with a particular power to shape what happens in the classroom, and each with a particular set of interests and perspectives in the way
it interprets the evaluations you share with them.

Students are perhaps the broadest audience, as they need to know virtually everything that you as a teacher know about them. They also need to
know all the questions you have asked and answered. These questions might
represent your students' perspective:

- What kind of learning is valued in this classroom?

- How can I document my own learning?

- How am I, as an individual, growing according to these criteria? Do I measure up to your expectations?

- What goals should I (or, more likely, you and I together) set
  for myself in the future?

Parents have a slightly different set of needs. While they surely want to
know how their sons and daughters measure up to your standards and how,
as parents, they can help them do better, they also desire normative information. They want to know how their children are doing in comparison to other
students at this grade level—Are they doing better than the average bear?
This complicates matters for teachers who have invested in the logic of portfolio assessment, for to support portfolios is to reject the logic of normative
comparisons (How am I doing in comparison to others?) in favor of allowing
individuals to compare their own accomplishments to clear standards of excellence. Nonetheless, even if you do not accept the logic of normative
evaluation, you must find ways to talk to parents about how their children
are doing in comparison to "what is normal." When you cannot provide a
parent with Johnny's or Amy's grade norm score or percentile rank, you
must find a way to talk about their accomplishments in comparison to some
notion of what is average, normal, or expected for students at this age or
grade level. While difficult, this is not an impossible task.

Administrators, as well as policymakers such as school board members,
use assessments to monitor programs, make recommendations, and allocate
resources. They will not necessarily want or need information about each
and every student; instead they want to know how the class or the school or
the district *as a whole* is doing. As the individuals or bodies held accountable for the teaching and learning, these audiences have good reason to want
information about students and programs. Teachers and school staffs must
come to grips with ways of aggregating data across individuals and classes
in order to provide useful information to these groups.

Each audience for assessment, including the teacher, needs access to
different kinds of information, reported in different formats. Balancing audience needs and preferences is an important phase of any assessment process.

Mrs. Bean, for example, will have to decide who, besides herself, needs to know about student growth in personal response to literature, and how best to describe that growth to individuals and groups who are interested in her students and her teaching.

Do It Again?

The final, as we are listing them here, stage of assessment is that of beginning again. This is intended to capture the reality of new marking periods, new students, new assignments, and new insights. Assessment is ongoing because we are always teaching, and students are always learning.

The title for this phase of the process ends with a question mark very deliberately. This is because each phase of the assessment process provides tools or insights that will help you evaluate not only your students but your assessment process as well. What you learn about your students may cause you to change your teaching practices so that the next time around, they come closer to meeting your instructional goals. Or you may find that the particular artifact you chose didn't help you learn about their progress in the way you had hoped. Or having put together a group of artifacts you love, you may learn that your students have exceeded your original standards, causing you to rethink both your goals and the evidence you wish to collect. For example, in Chapter 10, Jan Wells changed both her teaching and her assessment when she realized her system of keeping track with reading journals didn't meet her standards for teaching or learning. The feedback students received came too late to be helpful to them, and she was not sure they felt ownership of the responses they wrote for her. Her switch to novel studies and literature discussion groups balanced her assessment needs with her goals for teaching and learning.

What Mrs. Bean does the second time around, whether she changes the directions for her response journals, the evidence she seeks from them, or decides to scrap them altogether, will depend upon what she has learned from them and the responses of the audiences with whom she shares the data. Having gone through the process once, she is more than ready to continue to adapt the system to the needs of her classroom.

Authentic assessment is a recursive not a repetitive process. It is not repetitive in the sense that, as a teacher, you find yourself continuously choosing, collecting, and evaluating artifacts in the same way time after time. Instead it is a recursive process: an assessment system can be launched from any of the phases described above, changed at any time, and works only when you continue to ask questions and let those answers uncover new, different, and better questions about your teaching, your students' learning, and the process of assessment itself.

Deciding What Counts as Evidence—Reprise

Next to the goals one uses to guide the entire system, the most important and influential decision you will make is selecting what counts as evidence. In order to address this question more fully, this reprise is devoted to the physical evidence itself—artifacts.

Artifacts are the individual pieces that have been captured in order to allow for reflection and assessment. They may take the shape of written work, of drawings or plays, written notes about a performance, or even a video or audiotape. Artifacts are often the same pieces of work generated out of the teaching and learning that take place in the classroom. Other times, artifacts will have been specially implemented and collected in order to reveal some aspect of accomplishment the teacher or another audience wonders about. There are as many artifacts of literacy assessment as there are ways to teach (a selection of possible artifacts is listed in Figure 15.4), yet none of them are end products in and of themselves. Instead, artifacts are tools teachers use to answer questions.

As you select specific artifacts that will serve as evidence for the assessment system in your classroom, there will be many factors to consider. But since you can't talk or think specifically about tools without thinking about goals, we have listed several possible standards teachers and students might hold for their reading classrooms in Figure 15.5.

Figure 15.4 Possible Artifacts

The following is a list of categories of artifacts that may be useful for assessment in a literature-based reading classroom. This list is only a beginning. There are many more assessment artifacts to choose from. Many of the categories overlap, and many are appropriate for responses to and interactions with both fiction and nonfiction texts.

NOTE: The numbers in parentheses represent chapters of this text that refer to or describe the artifact listed.

Reading Log—list of the books and stories a student has read, often annotated or elaborated with judgements about the quality of each selection (8).

Reading Journal—substantial and ongoing written responses to books, articles, and selections read—which may take the form of informal personal writing, letters to the teacher (8), or a dialectical journal (11).

Literature Discussions—for assessment, these may be audiotaped and transcribed, or notes may be taken about individual participation. Another means of assessing participation in discussion is to tally the number of times each person contributes (9, 10).

Figure 15.4 cont'd.

Written Projects—major piece of work in response to particular selections or units (8, 11, 14), including, but not limited to:

> letters to characters
>
> letters to authors
>
> character diaries
>
> essays and analyses
>
> end-of-book or unit examinations
>
> formal papers

Records of Performances—videos, audiotapes, or notes about performances including book talks, speeches, dramatic presentations, and debates.

Artistic Responses—responses to literature in an artistic form, including sculpture, paintings, drawings, and literature-influenced poetry and prose, often accompanied by a reflective essay explaining the connections between the piece of art and the piece of literature it responds to (5, 8, 11).

Anecdotal Records—teacher's written notes about individuals' participation in class over a period of time (often the writing of anecdotal records is guided by a particular goal or focus).

Surveys—student responses to surveys of interests, habits, attitudes, etc. (2)

Student Reflective Essays—student writing about growth, accomplishment, and performance.

Strategy Use Records—Written records that arise out of student use of particular comprehension strategies, including K-W-L charts, think-aloud tally sheets, GIST statements, strategy logs, and genre reformulations (5, 12, 14).

Portfolio—a purposeful and often annotated collection of many pieces of student work collected over time, with pieces chosen by students and/or teacher to reflect specific goals and accomplishments.

Multimedia Artifacts—including home pages, Web sites, and hypertexts (20).

Intratextual Response Assignments—responses to individual texts including structured response forms such as story frames, charts, character maps, and think-sheets; and less-structured responses such as journal entries, letters, timelines, setting maps, and concept maps. (8, 11)

Intertextual Responses—responses such as those listed for *intra*textual responses, which refer to several texts and understandings across texts.

Figure 15.5 A Selection of Standards

This is a list of possible standards for both teaching and assessing distilled from the other chapters of this book and from our own experiences working with middle school teachers and students. This list of standards is not meant to be either definite or complete, but it is rather to provide examples and descriptions of a wide variety of possibilities. As the classroom teacher, you will need to choose or create for yourself the standards appropriate to your classroom, your students, and your overall goals.

Personal Response—Students make connections between their own lives and the texts they read, responding to them on a personal level.

Aesthetic Response—Students respond to literature as art, attending not only to content but to the affective and emotional experiences evoked by the literature they read.

Critical Stance—When reading, students take a stance of judgment and evaluation based upon literary, cultural, and sociopolitical criteria.

Breadth and Depth—Students read widely (many authors and genres) as well as deeply (digging into an author, topic, or genre.)

Ownership of Reading—When given the opportunity, students choose freely to read and/or discuss literature.

Constructing Meaning—Students make sense of the texts they read based upon the printed pages, their own background and experiences, the context in which they read, possible use of comprehension strategies, and given purposes for reading.

In-depth Analysis—Students not only understand, but they interpret the texts they read, reconsidering and revising the meanings they construct as they talk, write, and reread.

Response in Discussion—Students use discussions as an opportunity to interact around and come to deeper understandings of the texts they read.

Reading/Writing Connections—Students make reference to the texts they read in the writing that they do, using those texts to broaden or deepen or inform their writing.

Authorial Tools—Students develop an understanding of authorial tools such as tone, personification, and voice.

Metacognitive Strategies—Students discuss and explain their own thinking processes, and they possess a repertoire of strategies for use in constructing meaning and overcoming difficulties as they read.

Big Ideas in Literature—Students make connections among the texts they read, identifying major themes and ideas common to many pieces of literature across a variety of genres.

While there are many factors to consider as you select artifacts for assessment, we have chosen to reflect on three of the most important here: The potential that each artifact will reveal student accomplishment on the particular standards in your classroom, consideration of the work on the artifact in light of your curricular goals, and the feasibility of implementing a particular artifact in your classroom.

Potential to Reveal Student Accomplishment Toward the Standards You Have Selected: Perhaps the most important consideration for any artifact is potential to help answer questions about your students. Any individual artifact, such as those in Figure 15.4, has the potential to serve as evidence for one or many aspects of student accomplishment. At the same time, no one artifact will provide a complete picture of any individual learner. For these reasons, it might help you to think about artifacts according to the standards for which they are likely to serve as evidence.

The Artifact by Standard Comparisons Table, Table 15.1, lists several artifacts, and gives some indication of the standards for which those artifacts are likely to yield information. Use this chart only as a launching point for thinking about which artifacts to assign and be prepared to be flexible according to the needs of your students and your curriculum. You can never really predict where important information will come from, and you can never really tell how useful an artifact will be until you try it. Still, it will be useful to consider the possibility that a particular tool will help you answer questions about your chosen curriculum.

Alignment with Curricular Goals: It is also important to think about whether or not an assessment is aligned with your goals. All assessments, all assignments, have a curriculum of their own—that is, they teach about the kinds of knowledge that are important, the processes that are valued, and the range of acceptable responses. It is important to consider whether or not the work that is needed to complete a particular artifact is work that is also likely to support your teaching goals. A multiple-choice test on the characters in *A Wrinkle in Time* (1962) might yield information about your students' sense of character development, but it might at the same time stymie their own individual responses to the characters in that book.

Feasibility of Implementation: Finally, it is important to consider the feasibility of any given piece of work. Student background knowledge and interest levels will determine their ability to reveal accomplishment in (or even complete) a selected artifact. Your ability to make sense of and reflect upon a chosen piece of work will affect whether or not you should choose that piece. Time constraints, required materials, and storage needs can make an assessment piece either workable or unworkable in your particular classroom.

Of course, you must consider the same issues as you select a curriculum to teach, but your decisions take on a special significance in assessment

Figure 15.1   Artifact by Standard Comparisons

A sampling of artifacts is listed across the top of the table. A list of possible standards is listed along the left. This table indicates the likelihood that a given standard will yield valuable information on any given teaching standard.

	Reading Log	Reading Journal	Literature Discussions	Written Projects	Records of Performance	Artistic Responses	Anecdotal Records	Surveys	Intratextual Responses	Intertextual Responses	Student Reflective Essays
Personal Response		Excellent	Excellent	Excellent	Likely	Excellent	Possible		Likely	Excellent	Likely
Aesthetic Response		Excellent	Likely	Excellent	Likely	Excellent	Possible		Likely	Excellent	Possible
Critical Stance		Possible	Excellent	Excellent	Likely	Likely	Possible		Likely	Excellent	Possible
Breadth and Depth	Excellent	Likely					Likely	Possible			Likely
Ownership of Reading		Excellent	Likely	Likely	Likely	Excellent		Excellent			Likely
Constructing Meaning	Possible	Likely	Excellent	Likely	Excellent	Excellent			Excellent	Excellent	Possible
In-depth Analysis		Possible		Likely	Likely	Likely			Likely	Excellent	Possible
Response in Discussion			Excellent				Excellent				Likely
Reading/Writing Connections		Possible		Possible		Excellent			Possible	Possible	Possible
Metacognitive Strategies				Possible			Likely		Possible	Possible	Possible
Big Ideas in Literature	Possible	Possible	Possible	Possible	Excellent	Likely	Possible		Likely	Excellent	Possible

terms. Assessment demands reflection, time to sit with the artifacts and think about what they mean for individual students and for your own accomplishment as a teacher. In order to do this, artifacts must take on a format with which you are comfortable. Audiotapes of student discussion may be the best way to find out whether or not your students really are making connections between texts during small group meetings, but if you will never listen to them, they won't provide the evidence you need. Recordings of performances may be a terrific way for you to assess reading comprehension, but if the students don't yet trust themselves as actors and interpreters, you might not be able to distinguish between a lack of understanding and stage fright.

Finally, a word on portfolios. Since no one artifact reveals all the aspects of student accomplishment, many teachers and school districts are now implementing portfolios as a major portion of their assessment program. A portfolio is a collection of student work over time, selected by the student, the teacher, or both. Several factors move a portfolio beyond a simple collection. A teacher implementing a portfolio system will often consider many pieces at once in order to get a bigger picture of a student or to dig deeper into student learning. Reflection, by both students and teachers as they consider the accomplishment demonstrated in a portfolio, is another important aspect of a portfolio system. Both of the case studies at the end of this chapter are studies of portfolio classrooms, studies in which the assessments were made based on portfolios containing several different types of artifacts.

Students—They're Not Just an Audience Anymore

So far in this chapter, the focus has been on assessment as a process or tool for you, the teacher, to answer your own questions about student accomplishment. This may have been very misleading. Middle school students are highly capable of engaging in every phase of authentic assessment, and they should they be allowed and encouraged to do so.

Establishing Goals: As a first and most basic step in including students in the assessment system, make *them* aware of your overall goals and the specific standards to which they are being held accountable. For even greater involvement, support your students in attempts to set learning goals for themselves. This might mean presenting them with a variety of standards from which to select one or two to focus on, or it may take on a more open-ended format. Either way, allowing students to learn about and set their own goals will help them to recognize their own accomplishment and take responsibility for their own learning.

Deciding What Counts as Evidence: As you will see later in the chapter, one way to help students decide what counts as evidence is to allow *them* to interpret your standards, to elaborate them into specific descriptions of what the goals should look and sound like in action. Or, more traditionally, students can be encouraged to decide on the physical evidence that will demonstrate accomplishment toward your standards as they gather documents for a student-selected portfolio.

If students are allowed to select the artifacts for evaluation themselves in this way, they must be fully aware of the standards they are expected to meet. At the same time, students can be shown how to think about whether or not the artifacts they choose to reflect their growth are likely to allow for demonstration of those standards, are consistent with the standards, and are feasible both to collect and to interpret.

Deciding What the Evidence Means: Students can not only set their own goals and select artifacts to demonstrate their accomplishment, they can also consider their own work for evidence of accomplishment toward your standards or theirs. When they know what to look for, students can evaluate their own work. They can compare artifacts over time, can search their own work for connections between pieces, can look in their writing for evidence of connections between what they read and what they create, and they can think about whether or not they are taking full advantage of the opportunities in the classroom to learn. This process of reflecting on their own work can be very revealing for both students and teachers.

Sharing Their Evaluations: Student participation in the assessment process might end with student self-reflection. Students themselves probably are the most important audience for their own conclusions. But you might find that you learn a lot about how students are understanding the curriculum, about their comprehension of content or their responses to literature, by sharing in and listening to their reflections. Parents may also be an important audience, and you may want to provide times for your middle schoolers to show their parents just what it is they have accomplished.

And Again and Again: Just as you will go back and assess, again and again, changing in light of what you have learned, so will students return to and adapt their goals, choose more reflective artifacts, continue to reflect on their learning, and alter their involvement and interactions around literature in order to answer their own questions and live up to their own standards. In these ways, helping your students to participate in every phase of the assessment process can lead them to become lifelong learners and reflectors.

Charles Ruff: One Case Study

Teachers in the English Department at Charles Ruff Middle School (a pseudonym) in California (see Underwood, 1996) developed and tested a voluntary reading portfolio. In developing, administering, and evaluating their students' portfolios, these teachers engaged in many of the phases of authentic assessment that we have described in this chapter. We will use those phases as an outline for talking about the case.

Establishing Goals: Broad Brushstrokes. The teachers at Ruff were very clear about their overall goal. They wanted their students to become lifelong readers of serious and substantial literature. This strong focus helped them to decide what to teach, what documents to collect, and how to assess the artifacts in the portfolio. Along with their goals, these teachers shared many beliefs and questions. They believed in learning as a social activity, and that school experiences are only one among many social interactions that shape students' learning. They wondered whether or not a shared and systematic assessment plan could authentically reflect their students' learning and at the same time support instructional changes. And they shared questions about performance assessments in general. These standards led them to test a reading and writing portfolio system that would be examined and graded by teachers outside of the portfolio classroom.

Establishing Goals: Filling in the Details: The English Department designed the portfolio process around their ultimate goal of helping students come to think of themselves as and act like readers. This standard was broken into several components. Standards for the students in the portfolio classrooms included frequent voluntary reading, selection of challenging and engaging materials, frequent self-assessment and reflection, greater understanding of the literary elements of texts, and growing strategies for understanding and interpreting their reading.

Deciding What Counts as Evidence: While students selected the items collected in the reading portfolios, they were ultimately assessed by examination teachers—teachers outside the classroom who read, judged, and assigned letter grades to each student's self-selected portfolio based upon the criteria. Because of this, the portfolio teachers very concretely elaborated their goal into specific descriptions of what readers can and should do, which are detailed in Table 15.2. As you can see, each standard was specifically connected to detailed accounts of the evidence that would demonstrate that a standard had been met.

Teach and Collect: Students in the portfolio classrooms also had to decide what counts as evidence, as they chose items from their ongoing work, both in and out of class, for presentation to the examination teachers. In order to help their students meet the portfolio criteria and assume roles as engaged readers of literature, the three portfolio teachers—Jennifer, Martha, and Maria—worked with their students in several different ways. They spent time explicitly teaching the portfolio criteria to their students. They expected their students to read outside of class, and that their reading would include new, challenging, and engaging texts. To bolster this *homework*, they taught the students many literary reading strategies and expected to see students transfer these strategies to their independent reading. And they engaged their students in the process of writing and discussing textlogs.

In fact, *textlogs* (brief, in-class responses to reading done at home) proved to be a central activity in these literature-based classrooms. They

Table 15.2   Criteria for Assigning Letter Grades

GRADE	CONSISTENCY AND CHALLENGE	CONTROL OF PROCESSES	SELF-ASSESSMENT AND REFLECTION	KNOWLEDGE AND WORK PRODUCTS
	**Criteria for Assigning Letter Grades to the Voluntary Reading Portfolio at Charles Ruff Middle School**			

GRADE	CONSISTENCY AND CHALLENGE	CONTROL OF PROCESSES	SELF-ASSESSMENT AND REFLECTION	KNOWLEDGE AND WORK PRODUCTS
A	— reading done habitually almost every day, often for long periods of an hour or so — reads not only to entertain but also to challenge and stretch capabilities — reads widely, experiments with new authors and forms	— Rereads and revises interpretations — supports views with references to the text — uses a variety of strategies end response types — shows persistence	— sets complex goals for reading and achieves them — applies personal/ public criteria and supports judgments — analyzes own processes thoroughly	— reads like a writer—creates organized, complete, and effective work products — learns new vocabulary regularly — pays attention to literary and stylistic features of texts — interprets shared readings personally and deeply
B	— reading done habitually almost every day, often for shorter periods of time — readings entertain, not so much challenge and stretch capabilities — less experimentation with new forms, though perhaps tries new authors	— tends to stick with one interpretation — supports views but may need to explain more thoroughly — uses less variety of strategies and response types — sometimes shows persistence sometimes is satisfied when understanding could be improved	— sets complex goals for reading and works to achieve them — applies criteria to texts but with less clear support — analyzes own processes superficially	— creates organized and complete work products — shows some attention to learning new vocabulary — pays less attention to literary and stylistic features of texts — understands shared readings thoroughly
C	— reading done at least once or twice a week, often for brief periods of 10–30 minutes — reads mainly for entertainment — little evidence of concern for experimenting with new authors or forms	— interprets readings superficially — only occasional support for own views — relies on one or two strategies and response types — may give up easily or quickly when bored or challenged	— sets simple goals for reading and achieves them — applies criteria to texts mechanically — analyzes own processes with clichés, may use reflective type terms with little understanding	— creates only superficially polished work products — occasionally shows interest in learning new vocabulary — rarely pays attention to style/literary features — understands shared readings superficially
D	— reading done quite sporadically — resists even readings that entertains — may not finish books	— sketchy interpretations — little if any support for views — relies on one strategy or response type	— sets simple goals and works to achieve them — seems uninterested in own learning and processes	— work products seem sloppy or "stapled together" little interest in vocabulary development — evidence of exposure to shared readings
E	— little of no evidence of reading	— little evidence that the student interprets reading — little evidence of views	— may set simple or no goals with little work' — doesn't even go through the motions of voicing vague clichés	— few if any work products

played three important roles: (1) the teachers used the textlogs as teaching tools for extending the concepts and strategies taught in their English classes, (2) they made visible for the students the process of explicitly connecting one's ideas and written words to the portfolio criteria, and (3) students used textlogs as artifacts to document accomplishment toward the stated criteria. The process of writing and discussing textlog entries helped students understand the ways in which serious, committed readers would engage with the literature they chose to read; at the same time, they learned how to use the textlogs to demonstrate their developing abilities in making interpretations, setting personal goals, and recognizing literary features of texts.

Decide What the Evidence Means/Sharing the Evaluation: At key points during the year, the examination teachers applied the criteria to assign letter grades to the portfolios, which were reported to parents and used by students as indicators of the quality of their own work in the eyes of the examination committee. In addition, or perhaps more importantly, students wrote summary comments evaluating their own work over each grading period as well as their growth and accomplishment toward becoming engaged readers of literature. One student wrote:

> From what I've talked about, you can see how this portfolio project has helped me understand literature. I've also found out a lot of things about myself as a reader this trimester, and what I'm interested in. I learned that when I'm challenged I'll think of ways to understand things. After the first trimester I thought this portfolio project was a bad idea, because I didn't get the grade I wanted. I cared more about my grade than what I was learning, which I won't be doing anymore. This portfolio to me has been successful in challenging myself to the fullest.

Do It Again? Engaged in both writing and discussion of self-selected and personally meaningful texts, the classrooms of these three teachers became communities of learning in which the teachers' goals, the instruction leading toward those goals, the artifacts collected to demonstrate accomplishment, and the evaluation criteria all supported one another; in other words, the entire instruction-assessment system was aligned with the teachers' beliefs and their desire to help students become lifelong readers. The process was not always easy. Evaluating the portfolios was arduous and time-consuming, and the portfolio teachers did not always agree with the examination teachers. Initially, there was widespread resistance among students. Fortunately, both the students' resistance and the tensions among teachers decreased markedly as they became more familiar with the process and the evaluation criteria. While there were no miracles, in the end, Jennifer, Maria, and Martha recognized that their students had made real growth over the course of the year. After seeing the effect and strengths of the voluntary reading portfolio, the teachers decided to implement the portfolio for all students in all classes during the following school year.

Holt: A Second Case Study

At Holt Junior High School in Michigan, two teachers in the English department have taken a different approach to portfolios (see Sarroub, Dykema, & Lloyd, 1996). In order to ensure that the students were truly engaged in the evaluation process, the teachers, Randy Lloyd and Carmen Dykema, decided to make their class portfolio a part of the grading system for the spring term. Portfolios were not entirely new to the school, the teachers, or the students. In fact, the school had, both because of a state mandate (which ironically has been recently rescinded) and a local initiative, kept portfolios for all students across all subject matter courses. Additionally, in their classes, both Randy and Carmen required the students to keep writing folders. But in neither instance was the portfolio, or its contents, used to make any decisions of consequence to the students or the teachers. Not so with the implementation described here. We tell their story by taking you through the generic set of steps described earlier.

Establishing Goals: Broad Brushstrokes: Because the state of Michigan was in the process of adopting a new set of standards to guide instruction and assessment throughout the state, Carmen and Randy thought that it would be interesting to engage the students in the process of evaluating their work through the filter of the state standards. Besides, when they reviewed the standards, they found the overall goals to be quite consistent with their own conceptualizations of what students should know and be able to do in the language arts. Figure 15.6 lists the broad goals in the Michigan English Language Arts Framework (MELAF).

For purposes of their experiment in using portfolios in grading and because high-stakes portfolios were new to everyone, Carmen and Randy streamlined the process by focusing on one standard, number 5:

> Read and analyze a wide variety of classic and contemporary literature and other texts to seek information, ideas, enjoyment, and understanding of their individuality, or common heritage and common humanity, and the rich diversity in our society.

They also added the elaborations developed by the Michigan Department of Education to their classroom standard:

- Read and respond thoughtfully to both classic and contemporary literature.

- Describe and discuss shared issues in the human experience that appear in literature and other texts from around the world.

- Identify issues and discuss how the tensions, communities, themes, and issues in literature and other texts are related to one's experience.

- Investigate and demonstrate understanding of the cultural foundations for the depiction of themes, issues, and actions in literature and other texts.

Figure 15.6 MELAF Standards

In grades K-12, a locally developed English language arts curriculum, embodying these state content-standards, will ensure that all students are literate and can engage successfully in reading, discovering, creating, and analyzing spoken, written, electronic, and visual texts that reflect multiple perspectives and diverse communities and make connections within English language arts and between English language arts and other fields. All students will:

1. read and comprehend general and technical material;

2. demonstrate the ability to write clear and grammatically correct sentences, paragraphs, and compositions;

3. focus on meaning and communication as they listen, speak, view, read, and write in personal, social, occupational, and civic contexts;

4. use the English language effectively;

5. read and analyze a wide variety of classic and contemporary literature and other texts to seek information, ideas, enjoyment, and understanding of their individuality, or common heritage and common humanity, and the rich diversity in our society;

6. learn to communicate information accurately and effectively and demonstrate their expressive abilities by creating oral, written, and visual texts that enlighten and engage an audience;

7. demonstrate, analyze, and reflect upon the skills and processes used to communicate through listening, speaking, viewing, reading, and writing;

8. explore and use the characteristics of different types of tests, aesthetic elements, and mechanics—including text structure, figurative and descriptive language, spelling, punctuation, and grammar—to construct and convey meaning;

9. demonstrate understanding of the complexity of enduring issues and recurring problems by making connections and generating themes within and across texts;

10. apply knowledge, ideas, and issues drawn from texts to their lives and the lives of others;

11. define and investigate important issues and problems using a variety of resources, including technology, to explore and create texts; and

12. develop and apply personal, shared, and academic criteria for the enjoyment, appreciation, and evaluation of their own and others' oral, written, and visual texts.

- Investigate through literature and other texts various examples of distortion and stereotypes, such as those associated with gender, race, culture, age, class, religion, and handicapping condition.

Given the primacy of literature in their classes, this standard proved a good choice for Carmen and Randy because it allowed them and their students to think about how most, if not all, of their work throughout the year related to that single standard. Interestingly, both the teachers and their students were impressed by how much of their work, even writing assignments and more perfunctory skill activities, was grounded in the literature goal(s) that underlay their program.

Establishing Goals: Filling in the Details: This stage proved to be one of the most interesting at Holt because both Randy and Carmen decided to involve the students in the process of *making the standards real* in their classrooms. Focusing on the Literature Standard number 5, they engaged the whole class in a brainstorming session of what they thought the Standard meant in terms of the kind of work that they were doing in their English classes. After this group discussion, each student completed a *freewrite* on what the Standard meant to him or her. Karla, from fourth hour, wrote this piece:

> The Standard is telling us to read and understand old and new books. We should be able to get information from books, ideas, and enjoyment. Even though all books have these three things, you should also be able to pick out differences between books. They can teach us history, lessons on how the world runs.

Joan, from sixth hour, wrote this interpretation of the Standard:

> To read a lot of books from the 1800s and now and tell what major things happened in the book, to tell the setting, and give descriptions of the characters. They want to have people use books for research, to gain more understanding of different things, and to be able to enjoy a book. They want us to understand about what happened in the past, what's happening now and what is to come in the future.

Both Randy and Carmen found that this process of involving students in the very interpretation of the Standard was a critical step in developing student understanding and buy-in to the process. As one student put it, "The [state] Standard uses too many big words."

Deciding What Counts as Evidence: Again, in order to get the students involved in this process, Randy and Carmen engaged the students in both group and individual consideration of the *what counts as evidence* question. Here are the evidence lists generated by Karla and Joan:

> *Karla*: Every time we read a book or article and analyze it we are meeting the Standard. Our Novel Journals are good examples. We have to understand it to write about it. What we are doing right

now, writing in our own words what we understand from the poster [the Standard was printed on the poster].

Joan: We have done this by setting up journals for sharing ideas about the book to each other while reading novels. We have had tests about what happened in the novel after we have read it to help us remember it. We have also chosen our books to find something we might like.

Karla's insight that the very process of unpacking the Standard could provide evidence for meeting it is a pretty remarkable reflection.

Teach and Collect: Interestingly, Randy and Carmen found that, for the most part, it was pretty easy to adapt their existing curriculum to the portfolio project. Of course, each had a long history of deep engagement with literature as a curriculum cornerstone. Nonetheless, they and their students found that even projects and activities completed earlier in the year, long before the existence of the portfolio and the standard, provided solid evidence for meeting the standard.

Decide What the Evidence Means: While both Randy and Carmen had their own criteria for evaluating the portfolios, they both chose to engage students in the process of interpreting the evidence they collected. Carmen asked students to write a Dear Reader Letter as a way of introducing themselves. Figure 15.7 is Melinda's.

Figure 15.7 Melinda's Dear Reader Letter

Dear Reader,

Let me introduce myself. My name is Melinda, and I am currently in Ms. Dykema's eighth grade English class. I write a lot of personal narratives as well as factual, expository pieces. I also read a lot of novels on a variety of topics. In this portfolio you will read six exhibits that display my abilities and strengths.

The pieces that I chose to put in my portfolio were chosen for many reasons. First of all, they show my aptitude, as well as showing my grades. Some of the pieces you will read are creative and artistic. Some of the pieces are factual and show a lot of information.

They show my maturity and how I've grown as a reader and a writer because they increase in grade as the year goes on. They also show resourcing skills and skills that show following directions.

There are pieces that show my weaknesses in some areas. They also show similar pieces and how I changed them to fit the standards and improve my weaknesses in grammar and my correct word usage. They also show how this class has taught me many things as a student, a reader, and a writer.

Carmen also asked her students to justify their inclusion of each entry by specifying what the entry showed about them as learners. Here are a few such rationales, again from Melinda:

> 1) I followed the standards for this piece by following the outline that was provided for me. I also wrote the paper as an essay, not an opinionated paper. I described issues that humans experienced, I identified the tensions among characters, I demonstrated understanding of the cultural foundations for the depiction of themes, issues, and actions in literature, and I also investigated literature of distortion and stereotypes, such as those associated with race, culture, and class.

> 2) In this paper I followed the directions by correctly writing according to the FCA's. This piece told about contemporary literature and classic literature. I described and discussed in this paper, the issues in the human experience that appear in the book we read. I also found and wrote about examples in the literature that displayed prejudice against race, culture, and class. A lot of the feelings of the people in the book were expressed the same way. They couldn't figure out why people could hate so much.

> 3) The Helen Keller Project (autobiography) was based on her life and the experiences she endured. I looked through her book to find various examples of distortion associated with gender and especially against a handicapping condition. I also discussed the tensions among characters (Anne Sullivan, her mother, father, etc.) and society.

Randy asked each student, as a part of the final exam, to discuss the similarities and differences between tests and portfolios. Their responses were very interesting. As Michaela, from 1st hour, put it:

> In a portfolio, instead of writing definitions for parts of speech, we used them in our portfolio writings. . . . In conclusion, this portfolio was a good test. It demonstrated our skills and our understanding of words and structure. But it was also better than a test because it showed who we are and what we can do.

Or, in the words of Jeffryn, also from 1st hour:

> I would rather do a portfolio than a test anytime. The portfolio shows how great of a learner I am by letting me explore how good of a learner I am and can be.

These examples, we believe, convey clearly the importance and power of involving students at every stage of the process, but especially in the process of reflecting on what the evidence says about them as readers, writers, and learners.

Randy and Carmen each developed their own overall rubric for evaluating the portfolio. Carmen's class used four criteria—purpose, organization, presentation, and details. She elaborated on each criterion with a couple of guiding questions, listed below, and scored them according to a four-point scale (1–4) scale that indexed how consistently the student met each criterion.

> *Purpose*: Does the student identify the purpose for the presentation of his portfolio in his cover letter? Does the student connect choices to the literature Standard?
>
> *Organization*: Are all required pieces there? How many pieces?
>
> *Presentation*: How does it look? Does the student consider the audience? Has the student revised and edited original work?
>
> *Details:* Content, do the portfolio pieces meet the benchmarks of the Standard based on the student's rationale and justification?

Randy used the same *cross rubric* as was used for all major assignments throughout the year:

Form	Content
Voice/Creativity	Mechanics

Randy's rubric was quite extensive, with a different five-point scale (0–4) for each of the four criteria. Here are the standards for earning a 4 for each of the criteria:

> *Form*: Work demonstrates a thorough understanding of vehicles for communicating ideas. Information and evidence are well structured with ideas moving from generalized statements to specific instances and examples.
>
> *Content*: Work demonstrates a thorough understanding of facts and information and uses them to back up the major and generalized points of the piece. It pays attention to the details of the argument and deals well with loose ends.
>
> *Voice/Creativity*: Work has a strong sense of voice and writer's presence. It offers something unique and thoughtful through different uses of language and by bringing a new and unusual perspective to the topic.
>
> *Mechanics*: Work adheres to formal grammatical and spelling practices. Neither of these mechanical elements interfere with the understanding of the work's main purpose and the points the work is trying to make.

Both Randy and Carmen scored the portfolios using their respective rubrics, translated the numbers (for each, the maximum score was 16), and *weighted* the portfolio score as 40% of each student's grade for the quarter. With a few exceptions (students, for example, who did not complete the portfolio at all), the portfolio only served to improve grades for students, indicating that the vast majority of students used the portfolio as a way of demonstrating their learning in the course.

Share the Evaluation: The students and the teachers were the primary audience for the portfolios. In addition to the *grade*, each teacher shared their impressions in the form of comments about what he or she had learned from reading the portfolio. Because this initial experience came at the end of the academic year, communication with parents was not as extensive as it would have been had the portfolio been used throughout the year. In the second year of implementation, for example, parents were informed about the role of the portfolio at the start of the year, and portfolios played a major role in the beginning of the year open house and in the midyear parent-student-teacher conferences.

Do It Again? As we write this chapter, Randy and Carmen are in the midst of revising and fine-tuning their portfolio system. In fact, their effort was so successful that the entire school is examining their approach as a model for expanding the role and consequences of portfolios throughout the curriculum.

Closing Statement

Up to this point, we have described authentic assessment as a set of phases. We want to close by recharacterizing assessment, this time by describing it as a process of asking questions and inventing ways to answer those questions. In a literature-based classroom, questions about individual and group growth and accomplishment arise naturally out of the goals and curriculum. Each phase in the process of assessment we have described above can be seen as an opportunity to ask those questions and to decide for yourself how best to go about answering them. We hope that the descriptions and examples in this chapter have given you ideas, suggestions, and, above all, the license to invent the assessments and to make the decisions that allow you, and your students, to look for answers to your own questions about learning and teaching in your literature-based middle school classrooms.

References

Sarroub, L., Dykema, C., & Lloyd, R. (1996, November). When portfolios become part of the grading process—a case study in a junior high school setting. In P. D. Pearson (Chair), *What happens when new assessments are introduced into school sites—Adaptations to and of alternative assessments*. Symposium conducted at the meeting of the National Reading Conference, Charleston, SC.

Underwood, T. (1996). *The impact of a portfolio assessment system on the instruction, motivation, and achievement of seventh and eighth grade English-language arts students in a northern California middle school.* Unpublished doctoral dissertation, University of California–Davis.

Trade Books Cited

L'Engle, M. (1962). *A wrinkle in time.* New York: Dell.
Paterson, K. (1977). *Bridge to Terabithia.* New York: Avon.

A Focus on Materials—From Books To Computers

Chapter 16
CASTLES TO COLIN POWELL: THE TRUTH ABOUT NONFICTION

Betty Carter and *Richard F. Abrahamson*

We are a country of nonfiction readers. In 1994, Rosie Daley's cookbook, *In the Kitchen with Rosie* (1994), sold a whopping 5.5 million copies, making it "... one of the fastest-selling books in publishing history" (Maryles, 1995, p. 53). John Grisham's book, *The Chamber* (1994), topped the '94 fiction bestseller list with 3.2 million copies—a far cry from the 5.5 million number. And look how diverse our nonfiction reading interests are. *Men Are from Mars, Women Are from Venus* (1992) by John Gray was the second-most popular book of 1994 with total sales of 2.9 million copies, putting him way ahead of top fiction titles by Danielle Steel and Stephen King. Pope John Paul II's book, *Crossing the Threshold of Hope* (1994), sold 1.6 million copies—more than new novels by Ann Rice, Mary Higgins Clark, and Sidney Sheldon (Maryles, 1995).

Just in case you are wondering if 1994 was an atypical year for book sales, consider *The Guinness Book of World Records*, in its various editions, and Dr. Spock's *The Common Sense Book of Baby and Child Care*. Both nonfiction titles appear on the list of "The World's Top 10 Best-selling Books of All Time" (Ash, 1994, p. 124). And as we are writing this, the best-selling book in America, with 1.2 million copies printed so far, is General Colin Powell's autobiography, *My American Journey* (1995). Nonfiction has great reading appeal for millions of us.

What these nonfiction sales show us is the importance this type of writing plays in the reading lives of today's adult readers. These best-selling

313

titles also tell us about the diversity of our nonfiction reading interests, ranging from Oprah Winfrey's chef and her recipes to the writings of Pope John
Paul II. Our adult reading interest in nonfiction didn't just spring up when
we checked our cholesterol at midlife and realized we needed to eat less fat.
It didn't suddenly appear when, at fifty, we searched for spiritual guidance
in our lives. No, for many of us, the love for nonfiction reading sprouted in
elementary school, blossomed in middle school, grew stronger and became
one of our favorite types of reading in high school, and in adulthood is perennially our favorite kind of reading.

Although the fact that middle school readers enjoy nonfiction books
has been documented in studies for years (Carter & Abrahamson, 1995), it is
still one of the best-kept secrets in education. Only in the last ten years or so,
as teachers have tried to implement reading/writing workshops, teach
literature-based courses in social studies and other content areas, and surround middle schoolers with books they like to read, have we come face-to-
face with the importance of nonfiction in the lives of today's teenagers.
What we have also come to realize is that much of the reading we ask adolescents to grapple with on standardized tests is nonfiction material. Many
aren't adequately prepared to deal with it because the literacy curriculum in
middle school has focused far too much on fiction. We often reward teens
for the fiction reading they do, and we ignore or penalize them for their nonfiction reading. For example, here is what an eighth grade teacher in Wis-
consin told us after our speech on the importance of nonfiction books in the
middle school curriculum:

"You should know what you said about some teachers not valuing nonfiction reading—you were talking about me. Yesterday was Friday and in
our middle school we always have free reading on Fridays. An eighth grader
brought a nonfiction book in for free reading. I sent him out of the room and
told him he could come back only when he had a *real* book in his hands! Of
course, I meant a work of fiction."

Middle school readers enjoy nonfiction. You may recall that at the back
of Nancie Atwell's *In the Middle* (1987), she lists the favorite books of her
eighth grade class. That list includes these nonfiction titles: *Eric* (1974),
Never Cry Wolf (1979), *Diary of a Young Girl* (1952), *Lovey: A Very Special Child* (1976), and *A Circle of Children* (1974). Daniel Fader did his research for *Hooked on Books* (1968) about 30 years ago. In the boy's reform
school where he surrounded them with paperbacks and let them read, the
singlemost popular title was *Black Like Me* (1977)—proof that nonfiction is
often the preferred type of reading when teens are free to chose what they
want to read. We believe nonfiction books often hold the key to getting
youngsters on the path, or back onto the path, to a lifetime of reading. But,
nonfiction books can do more than that. They can change lives. As evidence,
we offer this letter from a middle school reader. It is found in a fine new

nonfiction book titled *Dear Author: Students Write About the Books that Changed Their Lives* (1995, pp. 54–55), a collection of students' letters written to authors. This letter is written to the anonymous author of *It Happened to Nancy*, a true story based on the actual diary of a teenage girl who was infected with the AIDS virus as a result of date rape. The book is a highly personal and specific chronicle.

> Dear Anonymous Teenager,
>
> Your story *It Happened to Nancy* about your struggle with AIDS touched my heart and made me realize that the same thing could happen to me if I'm not careful about the kinds of boys I associate with and how I take care of my body.
>
> It was awful to think that you died because of the inhuman behavior of another human—the HIV-positive boy who raped you. I wish I could change that, but I can't. Someday I hope that I can help other people. One of the things that I want to do is work with people with AIDS and other diseases and help scientists find a cure. When I read your book and learned about your friends and family and how they acted before and after they knew you had AIDS, it made me wonder if my family and friends would act the same way. I hope that they'd act in as caring a way as yours did.
>
> I'm really grateful to you for deciding to have Beatrice Sparks help edit your diary so that it could be published after your death. Because your book is a diary, your writing took me inside your head and heart, day to day, even hour to hour. I was there with you, and my feelings were touched. I'm sure that it inspired other people, not just me. I've read your book more than once now, and every time I finish it, I cry, thinking about all that you had to go through. Each time I close the book, I feel closer to you. It's as if I knew you before you died, like you could have been my sister. So as a sister, I hope you are all right in heaven.
>
> Martha Hutchins, 12,
> Center for Teaching and Learning,
> Edgecomb, ME
> Teacher: Nancie Atwell

Martha's letter clearly demonstrates that nonfiction reading evokes powerful responses from young adults.

Of Quality and Popularity

One of the most prevalent misconceptions about the role of nonfiction books in the lives of young teens is that they read nonfiction just to aid them in homework assignments. It's just not true. When you consider that the most circulated nonfiction book in middle school libraries is *The Guinness Book of World Records* and that the most circulated kind of nonfiction book are the how-to-draw books, you realize quickly that these books aren't the ones that would aid a typical middle schooler in his homework assignments (Carter and Abrahamson, 1990). These books are being checked out for pleasure.

In our look at the best-selling adult nonfiction you saw just how diverse our favorites were, from Colin Powell's autobiography to Rosie's low-fat recipes. The same kind of diversity is found in the cornucopia of nonfiction titles written for middle school readers, and this fact is both a blessing and a curse. The blessing is that there is a nonfiction book for every teenager's special interest, from Antarctica to zoology. The curse is that so much nonfiction is unavailable that is difficult for a teacher to decide what titles ought to be available in a reading/writing workshop classroom, or for that matter, in a school library on a limited budget.

Teenagers themselves have given us an answer to this dilemma. The three series we've chosen to highlight in this section are popular ones that were selected by a national sampling of students in either the International Reading Association's annual poll of teens called Young Adults' Choices (International Reading Association, 1992b) or in their survey of readers aged 5–13 called Children's Choices (Children's Choices, 1995; International Reading Association, 1992a; International Reading Association, 1995). In addition, these books received awards, starred reviews, or other indications of quality. These nonfiction books are good bets for reading/writing workshops because they represent the convergence of popularity and quality. We've also chosen to focus on three series of books to show that, just like in fiction, when readers find a book they like, they look for more by the same author, on the same topic, or in the same format.

Incredible Cross-Sections

In terms of beautifully designed, graphically appealing books, few publishers can beat the nonfiction titles put out by Dorling Kindersley publishers. Stephen Biesty's *Cross-Section* books have been consistently chosen by students as favorite nonfiction. So far there are three books in Biesty's series: *Incredible Cross-Sections* (1992), *Cross-Sections Man-of-War* (1993), and *Cross-Sections Castle* (1994). Whether Biesty is slicing up an 18th-century British warship to show youngsters life on board or cutting up a 14th-century castle to examine medieval life, his detailed pictures coupled with Richard Platt's integrated and informative text offer middle school readers nonfiction at its best.

Biesty's *Castle* was chosen by readers as a favorite in the 1995 *Children's Choice* poll (see Figure 16.1). In this work adolescents can examine 14th-century forms of punishment from the finger pillory to pressing to dunking, or worse, to being quartered. You can look inside the various castle rooms to view tapestries and illuminated manuscripts and tables laden with food. You can laugh at table manner tips from the 1400s that include:

- If you wash your mouth out while at the table do not spit the water back into the bowl, but instead spit politely, onto the floor.

- Do not pick your teeth at the table with a knife, straw, or stick.

- Do not belch near anyone's face—if you have bad breath. (1994, p. 20)

Figure 16.1   Stephen Biesty's *Cross-Sections Castle*

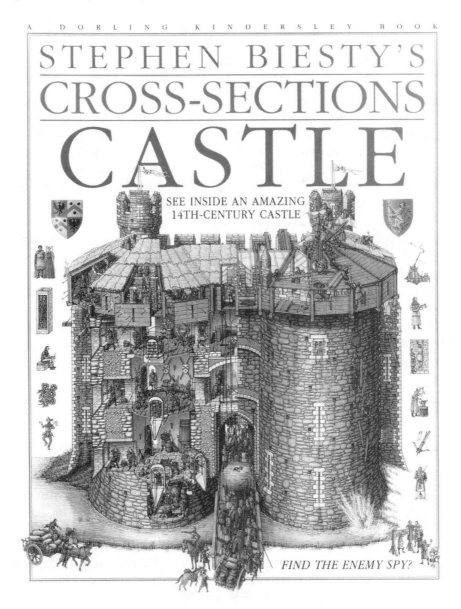

Stephen Biesty's *Cross-Section* books lend themselves to careful browsing, close reading, and integrated units that bring together history and English, and serve as an introduction to other highly-praised nonfiction books by David Macaulay, from *Pyramid* to *The Way Things Work*. Add to all of this Stephen Biesty's CD-ROM *Incredible Cross-Sections Stowaway!* (1995), and you know you've got nonfiction that teens and critics can agree is outstanding and spells reading motivation.

How It Feels

Middle school adolescents show the same diversity in their nonfiction reading that adults do. High on their list of preferred titles are true stories of people who have faced the real struggles of life. Jill Krementz's *How It Feels* books have been popular with young teen readers since the first book appeared—*How It Feels When a Parent Dies* (1988). She followed that with *How It Feels to be Adopted* (1988) and *How It Feels When Parents Divorce* (1988). In each of these books Krementz's skills as interviewer, journalist, and photographer shine through. In what may be her most popular book in the series, *How It Feels to Fight for Your Life* (1989), Krementz uses the same format that proved so successful in the earlier books. She lets 14 brave youngsters, between the ages of 7 and 16, tell their own stories about what it is like to cope with such traumas as heart disease, cancer, diabetes, burns, kidney transplants, and epilepsy. These first-person accounts of grit, determination, and courage are coupled with journalist Krementz's emotion-packed, black-and-white photos of children, family, and friends.

One of the special beauties of the *How It Feels* series is that middle school youngsters can measure themselves and their reactions against those of children younger than themselves, of teens of their own age, and of older adolescents in high school. *How It Feels to Fight for Your Life* gives readers portraits of quiet, uncelebrated heroines and heroes who don't want our sympathy but do want a chance to continue to live and a chance to grab the brass ring of life. The 14 inspiring portraits also make for good read-aloud material in middle school classrooms.

Headliners

A third series that is popular with young teens is entitled *Headliners* and is published by Millbrook Press. *Headliner* books are filled with full-color photos, maps, and charts and take readers behind the newspaper headlines for an in-depth look at major developments in the world, from the Persian Gulf War to the abortion debate to the Los Angeles riots.

Adolescents have always been intrigued with the dual nature of human beings. They read biographies of Hitler and Charles Manson along with Arthur Ashe's *Days of Grace* (1993) and Milton Meltzer's *Rescue: The*

Story of How Gentiles Saved Jews in the Holocaust (1988). Few headline events in recent years have shown more graphically the heights of goodness to which we can soar and the depths of evil to which we can sink as did the Los Angeles riots of 1992 that centered around the Rodney King assault. John Salak's *The Los Angeles Riots: America's Cities in Crisis* (1993) was a 1994 *Children's Choice* book for older readers (see Figure 16.2).

Salak offers middle schoolers the story behind the riots starting with the Rodney King trial and the acquittal of four Los Angeles police officers. The book is replete with gripping color photos of the riots, fires, and looting. Salak takes readers back for a short lesson on the other riots in America's

Figure 16.2   John Salak's *The Los Angeles Riots: America's Cities in Crisis*

history from Haymarket to Watts. The chapter "Anatomy of a Riot" examines the role of the economy, the police, and television on the Los Angeles riots. Salak manages to put the faces and emotions of real people on the riots by focusing in on individuals who owned the looted stores, politicians and a police chief who waited too long to act, and angry young men rioting to vent their frustration. The book ends with a description of the riot's impact and the ways the government and community have tried to heal the wounds. At 64 pages, *The Los Angeles Riots* is brief, visually appealing, and successful in its attempt to explain the real story behind this headline event. In it are portraits of courage and cruelty. Its popularity with young adolescents is proof that they are, indeed, interested in current events.

What these three stories tell us is that middle school readers do find enjoyment in nonfiction books and select them as favorites. The subjects of the highlighted books also tell us just how varied the nonfiction topics are that teens select—from castle battlements to combating cancer to battling rioters. The titles discussed here offer middle school teachers books that come stamped with the approval of a national sampling of adolescent readers and solid assessments of quality from adult literary critics.

Of Structure and Organizational Patterns

Beyond these elements of subject, popularity, and critical acclaim, the series mentioned above show three different faces of nonfiction. Jill Krementz focuses on personal, narrative accounts; Biesty relies heavily on illustrations to illuminate his points; and the *Headliners* series mirrors expository, journalistic prose. These varying series highlight the structural and organizational patterns seen in nonfiction, a difference that must be recognized and nurtured in order to allow middle schoolers to mature in their reading. Youngsters, and their teachers, librarians, and parents, must not limit nonfiction reading to a single structure any more than they should confine fictional reading to narrow genre offerings. Both practices produce the same result: young adults' scholarly development dwindles as they box themselves into formula reading, leaving little room for literary growth.

One of the tensions in encouraging middle schoolers' reading is on the one hand recognizing, and giving value and worth to, that which they choose to read, while on the other hand leading them to move beyond those selections to more sophisticated genres and forms. What students are telling us by selecting books as diverse as those by Krementz, Biesty, and Salak is that they recognize there's more out there than one kind of nonfiction reading. What teachers and librarians must do is listen to these student voices.

Despite this admonition, educators may well favor narrative nonfiction and biography while unconsciously neglecting other formats. The 1993 Best Books for Young Adults (BBYA) committee, for example, choose 24 (out of a total of 97 books) nonfiction titles for its annual list. A close examination of those titles, however, reveals that the majority of the nonfiction books are narrative, telling stories with characters, settings, and plot lines much like their fictional counterparts (Eggers, 1995).

This finding complements an earlier analysis (Carter, 1993) of the starred reviews, or those books of special distinction, recommended for children and young adults that appeared in four major review journals (*Booklist*, *Bulletin for the Center of Children's Books*, *The Horn Book*, and *School Library Journal*) from January, 1991, through June, 1992. During that period, the largest percentage of nonfiction books (excluding those nonfiction works defined by form such as folklore and poetry) that received stars were narratives. Like members of the 1993 BBYA committee, reviewers prefer their information couched in story.

Combined with these data, a telling conversation leads us to believe that teachers and librarians also mirror this prejudice toward narrative nonfiction. At a recent conference, a teacher approached the two of us with an interesting plea. "I understand that my students want to read nonfiction," she said, "and I not only allow it, but I have started including nonfiction in the books we study as a whole class. Still, my kids score low on those items requiring nonfiction reading on the state achievement tests, and their social studies and science teachers tell me they just can't read the materials for their classes. What's wrong here?"

We were bewildered. Here was a teacher doing what, on the surface, appeared to be all she could to introduce her students to a wide variety of literary experiences. The problem had to lie elsewhere, and we were about to agree with her that the state test was a poor performance instrument, or that the textbooks in the content classes were surely so laborious that no one could wade through them. But we asked another question: What nonfiction are you studying in your classes?

Her reply was quick: *Lincoln* (Freedman, 1988); *Freedom's Children* (Levine, 1993); *Woodsong* (Paulsen, 1991); and *Buried in Ice* (Beattie & Geiger, 1993).

"These are wonderful books," we told her, "but they're all stories."

"I know," she replied. "That's why I like them so much."

What we suspect is that many other teachers could recount the same experience. More and more nonfiction is creeping into classrooms, but it appears to be nonfiction that contains the familiar elements of fiction. This practice fails to serve students well.

Just as novelists consider the importance of setting, development of character, progression of plot, revelation of theme, and use of narrative elements such as flashback or foreshadowing, nonfiction writers struggle with identifying precisely the right organizational pattern to best highlight their information. Brent Ashabranner admits that an appropriate ". . . structure may take him almost as long to locate as the usual writing takes" (Ashabranner, 1988, p. 751). Similarly, Jean Fritz reiterates the importance of structure when she writes: "The art of fiction is making up facts; the art of nonfiction is using facts to make up a form" (Fritz, 1988, p. 759).

This art of "using facts to make up a form" represents an author's vision and achievement. Like great architects designing buildings, fine writers lay out a book by blending organization and content as painstakingly as Frank Lloyd Wright melded his designs with the natural world. Specific content determines what a reader will know about a subject: structure directs how that reader will view that content.

Several such structures or organizational patterns emerge in book after book (see Figure 16.3), and these patterns, as respected science author Irving Adler reminds us, provide that foundation upon which readers hang facts and concepts (Adler, 1976, p. 22).

Madeleine Dunphy's *Here Is the Southwestern Desert*, for example, borrows from the familiar nursery rhyme, "The House that Jack Built," for its memorable structure. Here Dunphy lists and illustrates various plants and animals found in the southwestern desert, but she reinforces their interdependency and fragile ecosystems through her cumulative recital:

> Here is the cactus that is covered with spines and can live without rain for a very long time. Here is the southwestern desert.
> Here is the hawk that perches on the cactus that is covered with spines and can live without rain for a very long time. Here is the southwestern desert.
> Here is the lizard who is spied by the hawk that perches on the cactus that is covered with spines and can live without rain for a very long time. Here is the southwestern desert. (Dunphy, pp. 3–6)

Mature readers either consciously or unconsciously look for these organizational patterns and structure their reading, and consequently their thinking, around them. When encountering a chronological history, for example, they key in on those reported events that happened first, then second, and then third. They are thus able to eliminate asides and appositives that have little relationship to the whole, while retaining more crucial information within a familiar cognitive outline. Sophisticated readers need works written in various patterns so that they may polish these skills; less facile readers require the same latitude in order to develop theirs. When students encounter only one pattern such as story narrative, they frequently fail to develop proficiency with different structures, comprehend their textbooks, or perform satisfactorily on the state tests. More important, though, they have limited practice with the language of grownups, a language that extends far beyond story to include listing, compare/contrast, cause and effect, and the like.

Not only should teachers and librarians highlight books with varying structural patterns, but they should also consider these patterns when design-

Figure 16.3   Organizational Patterns in Information Books

Pattern	Definition	Typical Sources	Examples
Alphabetical	Information enumerated in ABC order	Dictionaries Encyclopedias Alphabet Books	*Science Dictionary* *Dinosaur Encyclopedias*
Chronological Order	Subject described by progression of time sequence	Books of directions Historical accounts Scientific texts	*Alligators to Zooplankton* *Acorn Pancakes, Dandelion Salad, and 38 Other Wild Recipes* *Last Stand at the Alamo* *A Flower Grows*
Compare/Contrast	Subject or event discussed by comparing one aspect or viewpoint to another. Typically covers popular issues	Formatted Series Social/Political Questions	*Abortion: Opposing Viewpoints* *Dateline: Troy*
Cumulative	Concepts presented as discrete, chained events which build on one another to create a whole	Science Books	*Here is the Southwestern Desert* *The House That Crack Built*
Enumeration	Subject described by examining relevant parts (specific topics) of the whole.	Reference books Events and topics in all areas	*The Oceans Atlas* *When Plague Strikes: The Black Death, Smallpox, AIDS*
Problem/Solution	Information arranged around a series of situations and followed by possible solutions.	Scientific texts, particularly in books on the environment	*Adventures in Space: The Flight to Fix the Hubble* *Our Endangered Earth*

Figure 16.3 continued

Pattern	Definition	Typical Sources	Examples
Question/Answer	Factual subject broken down to a series of questions posed to the reader, followed by answers.	All subjects containing discrete facts	*100 Questions and Answers About Aids* *If Your Name Was Changed at Ellis Island*
Simple to Complex	Information presented in sequence starting with the most basic element and building to a whole through succeeding elaborate detail.	How-to books	*Draw 50 Endangered Animals* *How to Make Pop-Ups*
Story Narrative	Information presented through story.	Biography and collective biography	*Eleanor Roosevelt* *When I Was Your Age: Original Stories About Growing Up*
		Social Sciences	*Hearing Us Out: Voices From the Gay and Lesbian Community*
		Historical Accounts	*Across America on an Emigrant Train*
		Scientific Events	*Sanctuary: The Story of Three Arch Rocks*

ing specific student responses. Recently we evaluated a district-wide curriculum that had youngsters studying the westward movement through trade books. Their reading emphasized expository accounts such as *Children of the Wild West* (Freedman, 1983) and *The Great American Gold Rush* (Blumburg, 1989). The required responses (write a letter home to a friend, pretend you are on a wagon train and write an exciting adventure that could happen, keep a diary describing your feelings on the journey), however, all depended on narrative structure for completion, despite the fact that the models the youngsters encountered stressed other patterns. Such practices did not reinforce the kinds of learning experiences these middle schoolers were engaged in, so we suggested replacing them with activities ranging from comparing and contrasting a contemporary westward journey with one of 100 years ago to charting the dangers one might encounter on a typical trip from St. Louis to San Francisco in 1849.

Few books aimed at a middle school audience contain a single pattern. Most frequently they utilize a combination of structures such as enumeration for particular chapters and compare/contrast to present information within those chapters. Nonetheless, appropriate responses can address these organizational combinations.

Where to Find Dinosaurs Today (Cohen & Cohen, 1992), for example, is one of the few books capitalizing on place for its dominant organizational structure, although it contains the more common enumeration for a subpattern. Here, the Cohens provide sites, from museums to souvenir shops, that feature the perennially popular prehistoric creatures. Their literary tour begins in the Northeast, moves south and then westward across the continental United States, ventures across the Pacific to Hawaii, goes northeastward to Alaska, and concludes in Canada. Those readers enraptured by raptors should be encouraged to create a wall map of their particular geographical area and designate those sites included in the Cohens' reference. Not only can they determine whether or not they could visit these places, but they can also add additional museums and shops ignored by the Cohens. By allowing youngsters to recreate like patterns in different ways, what such an activity does is to bring nonfiction closer to their lives, encourage individual inquiry, and visually reinforce the written work.

Enumeration and chronological order frequently allow responses that will complement both patterns. *The Great American Baseball Strike* (Layden, 1995) devotes each chapter to a single element of the issue (a history of the game, events leading up to the strike, a discussion of labor relations), while presenting the information within these sections in chronological order. Encourage readers to develop a timeline on the history of the great American pasttime, including information from this book as well as milestones from others, such as Lawrence S. Ritter's *Leagues Apart: The Men and Times of the Negro Baseball Leagues*, Sue Macy's *A Whole New Ball Game: The*

Story of the All-American Girl's Professional Baseball League, or Jack Norwith's *Take Me Out to the Ball Game*. This response not only reinforces the importance of time order, but it also recognizes a community of readers bound by a common subject.

A study of the African-American migration from the south to the north in the first half of the twentieth century triggers a similar activity. Have a small group of students read related accounts of this period in two volumes, Jacob Lawrence's *The Great Migration* and Michael Cooper's *Bound for the Promised Land*. The former chronicles the journey through 60 dramatic paintings, tying each to the other with a skeleton narrative. The latter uses enumeration, covering such topics as the Harlem Renaissance and the Black Metropolis, to present its account. Students will have to use both books to flesh out a timeline. In the process, they should not only meld a pair of patterns but also take the natural opportunity to see how two individuals use different approaches to recreate the same period.

Of Illustrations and Graphics

Jacob Lawrence's vivid palate anchors *The Great Migration*, requiring the reader to pay attention to the art as well as text in order to comprehend his message. This blending of text and graphics, one of the hallmarks of outstanding nonfiction, creates near picture book accounts that require readers to understand both elements in order to fully appreciate the whole. No longer are illustrations inserted as mere filler to break up chunks of text; they are instead an integral part of an aesthetic work. Consequently, teachers should work with students in learning to read pictures in much the same way they help them read text.

Books such as *The Body Atlas* (Parker, 1993) simplify the task of promoting visual literacy. Here, a brief introduction shows youngsters how to "find their way," by providing an overview of the organizational structure. In addition, this front matter also helps them read the illustrations by cracking the graphic code: "In the main illustrations, parts of the body are shown in the same colors throughout the book. Muscles are striped brown, bones creamy-white, nerves and fat yellow, and tendons white. Except for those inside the lungs and umbilical cord, arteries are shown in red, and veins are in blue" (Parker, 1993, p. 5).

Like *The Great Migration* and *The Body Atlas* (above), Agee's *So Many Dynamos!* is also dependent on illustrations to make sense out of text. In this witty collection of palindromes, or phrases spelled the same way when read from left to right and right to left, Agee has created memorable phrases such as "A Santa at NASA," which is only mildly clever until readers see a parade of astronauts queuing up for a chat with the jolly old man. Similarly, the quixotic "Nate Bit A Tibetan" showcases the author's droll humor through the accompanying illustration of a hound, presumably Nate, near the top of a rocky mountain, gazing over a deep gorge where something has apparently fallen (see Figure 16.4). To draw attention to this partnership between text and illustrations, display a series of palindromes on the overhead projector. Have the students guess at the context before showing them Agee's pictorial interpretations.

Figure 16.4   Agee's *So Many Dynamos! And Other Palidromes*

Teachers may also reinforce the importance of illustrations by having youngsters create their own in order to extend text. *The Water Brought Us: The Story of the Gullah-Speaking People* (Branch, 1995) introduces readers to this distinctive population who live on the Sea Islands and adjacent coastal areas of South Carolina. Branch credits the preservation of their unique culture to the isolation of the people, but her argument comes through text and a few photographs of the deserted coastline. The same idea can be reinforced through a student-created map that shows the physical isolation of the Sea Islands, and thus, for youngsters who may have little geographical knowledge of the area, underscores the relationship between topography and culture.

Occasionally, teachers will have to spend some time walking their students through selected illustrations in order to familiarize them with the process of analysis. Martin W. Sandler's *Presidents* affords a few well-chosen examples. The cover, for example, portrays an exuberant Theodore Roosevelt, emphasizing his joy in politics and his zest for life (see Figure 16.5). Compare that illustration with another found inside of the President sporting a rifle and standing over a felled rhinoceros (see Figure 16.6). Certainly questions arise: How could one who enjoyed living so much also enjoy death? How can a president intent on protecting the environment also kill the creatures that inhabit it? Students can be led to consider other questions. Where do rhinos live? for example Did the President have to leave the country in order to participate in this sport? Did presidents routinely travel outside the boundaries of the United States at this time in American history?

Presidents also opens doors for individual inquiry. This photo-essay reveals both the public and the private lives of our chief executives, offering comments on their families, their outside interests, their pets, and the first ladies. Encourage students to visit the White House via the World Wide Web (http://www.whitehouse.gov/WH/Family/html/Life.html) and link to the

Figure 16.5   Martin W. Sandler's *Presidents*

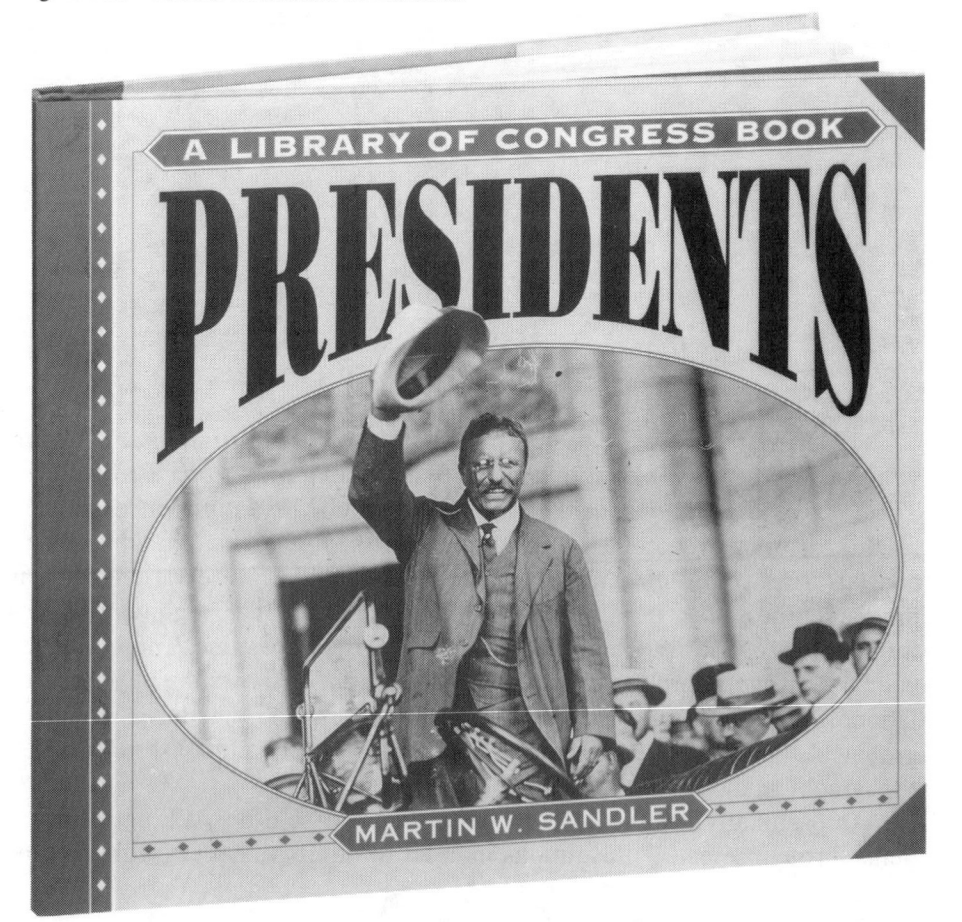

photo-essay of today's family. Ask them to arrange these photographs (as well as Socks's audio caterwauling) under the same general headings Sandler uses. Then encourage these readers to examine the photographs more closely. What can they deduce from the activities of the First Family? What facet of each individual's personality comes through in what they're doing, the clothes they're wearing, and the expressions on their faces. Well-chosen illustrations provide more than mere snapshots of an activity; they allow a unique portrait of distinct individuals. Only through deliberate introduction and reinforcement will students fully appreciate this aspect of the books they read.

Middle school is a time for exploration, for venturing into different worlds, for learning about a myriad of subjects, and for establishing patterns for lifelong inquiry. These beginnings can't be established through fiction alone; they require nonfiction to add substance and texture to that journey. From castles to Colin Powell, we are a country of nonfiction readers. The middle school years are the time when nonfiction reading can flourish if teachers and librarians encourage and value these books. For many middle school youngsters, nonfiction will be the vehicle that will take them down the highway of lifetime reading.

Figure 16.6   Roosevelt Hunting in Africa

References

Adler, I. (1976). The prose imagination. *School Library Journal, 13* (4), 22–23.

Ash, R. (1994). *The top ten of everything.* New York: Dorling Kindersley.

Ashabranner, B. (1988). Did you really write that for children? *The Horn Book, 64* (6), 749–754.

Atwell, N. (1987). *In the middle.* Portsmouth, NH: Boynton/Cook.

Carter, B. (1993). Reviewing nonfiction books for children and young adults: Stance, scholarship, and structure. In B. Hearne & R. Sutton (Eds.), *Evaluating children's books: A critical look* (pp. 59–71). Urbana: University of Illinois Press.

Carter, B., & Abrahamson, R. (1990). *Nonfiction for young adults: From delight to wisdom.* Phoenix, AZ: Oryx Press.

Carter, B., & Abrahamson, R. (1995). Nonfiction—the teenagers' reading of choice, or, ten research studies every reading teacher should know. *SIGNAL, 19* (2), 51–56.

Children's Choices for 1995. (1995). *The Reading Teacher, 49*(2), 133–148.

Dear author: Students write about the books that changed their lives. (1995). Berkeley, CA: Conari Press.

Eggers, C. (1995). *An analysis of nonfiction books on the 1993 best book list for young adults.* MLS professional paper, Texas Woman's University.

Fader, D., & McNeil, E. (1968). *Hooked on books: Program and proof.* New York: Berkeley.

Fritz, J. (1988). Biography: Readability plus responsibility. *The Horn Book, 64*(6), 759–760.

International Reading Association. (1992a). *Kids' favorite books: Children's choices 1989–1991.* Newark, DE: International Reading Association.

International Reading Association. (1992b). *Teens' favorite books: Young adult choices 1987–1992.* Newark, DE: International Reading Association.

International Reading Association. (1995). *More kids' favorite books: Children's choices 1992–1994.* Newark, DE: International Reading Association.

Maryles, D. (1995). Hardcover bestsellers: The big get bigger. *Publishers' Weekly, 242*(12), S3–S8.

Trade Books Cited

Agee, J. (1994). *So many dynamos! And other palindromes.* New York: Farrar, Straus & Giroux.

Ames, L., & Budd, W. (1993). *Draw 50 endangered animals.* New York: Doubleday.

Ashe, A. (1993). *Days of grace: A memoir.* New York: Knopf.

Beattie, O., & Geiger, J. (1993). *Buried in ice: The mystery of a lost Arctic expedition.* New York: Scholastic.

Biesty, S., & Platt, R. (1992). *Stephen Biesty's incredible cross-sections.* New York: Dorling Kindersley.

Biesty, S., & Platt, R. (1993). *Stephen Biesty's cross-sections man-of-war.* New York: Dorling Kindersley.

Biesty, S., & Platt, R. (1994). *Stephen Biesty's cross-sections castle.* New York: Dorling Kindersley.

Biesty, S., & Platt, R. (1995). *Stephen Biesty's incredible cross-sections stowaway!* [CD-ROM]. New York: Dorling Kindersley.

Blumburg, R. (1989). *The great American gold rush.* New York: Bradbury.

Branch, M. (1995). *The water brought us: The story of the Gullah-speaking people.* New York: Cobblehill.

Carter, A. (1990). *Last stand at the Alamo.* New York: Watts.

Cohen, D., & Cohen, S. (1992). *Where to find dinosaurs today.* New York: Cobblehill.

Cooper, M. (1995). *Bound for the promised land.* New York: Lodestar.

Cozic, C., & Tipp, S., (Eds.). (1993). *Abortion: Opposing viewpoints.* San Diego, CA: Greenhaven.

Daley, R. (1994). *In the kitchen with Rosie.* New York: Knopf.

Dunphy, M. (1995). *Here is the Southwestern desert.* New York: Hyperion.

Ehrlich, A. (Ed.). (1996). *When I was your age: Original stories about growing up.* Cambridge, MA: Candlewick.

Fleischman, P. (1996). *Dateline: Troy.* Cambridge, MA: Candlewick.

Ford, M. (1993). *100 questions and answers about AIDS.* New York: Beech Tree.

Frank, A. (1952). *Diary of a young girl.* New York: Doubleday.

Fraser, M. (1994). *Sanctuary: The story of three arch rocks.* New York: Holt.

Freedman, R. (1983). *Children of the wild west.* New York: Clarion.

Freedman, R. (1988). *Lincoln: A photobiography.* New York: Clarion.

Freedman, R. (1993). *Eleanor Roosevelt.* New York: Clarion.

Ganeri, A. (1994). *The oceans atlas.* New York: Dorling Kindersley.

George, J. (1995). *Acorn pancakes, dandelion salad and 38 other wild recipes.* New York: HarperCollins.

Giblin, J. (1995). *When plague strikes: The black death, smallpox, AIDS.* New York: HarperCollins.

Gray, J. (1992). *Men are from Mars, women are from Venus.* New York: HarperCollins.

Griffin, J. (1977). *Black like me.* Boston, MA: Houghton Mifflin.

Grisham, J. (1994). *The chamber.* New York: Doubleday.

Guinness book of world records. (1989). New York: Bantam Books.

Irvine, J. (1987). *How to make pop-ups.* New York: Beech Tree.

Kaufman, L. (1991). *Alligators to zooplankton.* New York: Watts.

Krementz, J. (1988). *How it feels to be adopted.* New York: Knopf.

Krementz, J. (1988). *How it feels when a parent dies.* New York: Knopf.

Krementz, J. (1988). *How it feels when parents divorce.* New York: Knopf.

Krementz, J. (1989). *How it feels to fight for your life.* Boston, MA: Joy Street/Little Brown.

Langone, J. (1992). *Our endangered earth: Our fragile environment and what we can do to save it.* Boston, MA: Little Brown.

Lawrence, J. (1993). *The great migration*. New York: HarperCollins.

Layden, J. (1995). *The great American baseball strike*. Brookfield, CT: Millbrook.

Lessen, D., & Glut, D. (1993). *Dinosaur encyclopedia*. New York: Random House.

Levine, E. (1993). *If your name was changed at Ellis Island*. New York: Scholastic.

Levine, E. (1993). *Freedom's children*. New York: Putnam.

Lund, D. (1974). *Eric*. New York: HarperCollins.

Macaulay, D. (1985). *Pyramid*. Boston, MA: Houghton Mifflin.

Macaulay, D. (1988). *The way things work*. Boston, MA: Houghton Mifflin.

MacCracken, M. (1974). *A circle of children*. Philadelphia, PA: Lippincott.

MacCracken, M. (1976). *Lovey: A very special child*. Philadelphia, PA: Lippincott.

Macy, S. (1993). *A whole new ball game: The story of the all-American girl's professional baseball league*. New York: Holt.

Meltzer, M. (1988). *Rescue: The story of how gentiles saved Jews in the Holocaust*. New York: HarperCollins.

Mowat, F. (1979). *Never cry wolf*. New York: Bantam Books.

Murphy, J. (1993). *Across America on an emigrant train*. New York: Clarion.

Norwith, J. (1993). *Take me out to the ball game*. New York: Four Winds.

Parker, S. (1993). *The body atlas*. New York: Dorling Kindersley.

Paul II, J. (1994). *Crossing the threshold of hope*. New York: Knopf.

Paulsen, G. (1991). *Woodsong*. New York: Bradbury.

Powell, C., & Persico, J. (1995). *My American journey*. New York: Random House.

Ritter, L. (1995). *Leagues apart: The men and times of the Negro baseball leagues*. New York: Morrow.

Robbins, K. (1993). *A flower grows*. New York: Dial.

Salak, J. (1993). *The Los Angeles riots: America's cities in crisis*. Brookfield, CT: Millbrook Press.

Sandler, M. (1995). *Presidents*. New York: HarperCollins/A Library of Congress Book.

Scott, E. (1995). *Adventure in space: The flight to fix the Hubble*. New York: Hyperion.

Simon, S. (1994). *Science dictionary*. New York: HarperCollins.

Sparks, B. (1994). *It happened to Nancy: A true story from the diary of a teenager*. New York: Avon Books.

Spock, B. (1977). *The common sense book of baby and child care*. New York: Pocket Books.

Sutton, R. (1994). *Hearing us out: Voices from the gay and lesbian community*. Boston, MA: Little Brown.

Chapter 17

SHORT STORIES— LONG OVERDUE

Donald R. Gallo

Being short of funds at the end of the month when bills are due is not a pleasant position to be in. A short circuit can be shockingly uncomfortable. Being short of stature in our society is usually not a positive attribute. Nor is it favorable to be shorthanded, shortchanged, or shortsighted. But short stories—aaaaah!—they can offer readers the most enjoyable of literary experiences, while providing teachers with a flexible and varied teaching tool.

For reluctant readers as well as for less able students, short stories can be the most accessible and satisfying literary form—primarily because they are short. In fact, ask any reluctant reader what he (it's usually a he) liked about the story he just read—or heard you read—and he's likely to say: "It was short." Most of them, in fact, are shorter than this chapter. An average short story takes less than one-tenth of the time to read than a typical novel does. Looked at another way, you can read ten or twelve or more short stories in the same time it takes to read a novel.

For people with short attention spans, short stories—at least *good* short stories—don't give you time to get bored or distracted. In addition, if you don't enjoy the first story in a collection you are reading, there is always another one available. And if the collection contains stories written by an assortment of authors instead of by only one individual, the chance for variety is even greater. (The same can be said for poems, of course, but form in short stories seldom presents a problem for students, as it often does with poetry.)

333

Not all people, however, like or appreciate the short story form. The most avid readers in your classrooms are likely to tell you they usually don't like short stories. Why? They're too short! "You just get to know the characters and get involved in their lives and the story ends," a seventh-grade girl complained to me. These are the readers—usually girls—you see carrying around those 400-, 500-, 600-page historical romances or fantasies that I would never pick up because it would take me too long to get to the end. But because those kinds of readers appreciate any kind of good story, they will still read short stories that are offered to them by an enthusiastic friend or persuasive teacher.

Students' enthusiasm, of course, cannot be generated by just any story. Just because it's a short story does not make it readable or interesting to the average middle school (or even high school) student. To see the truth in that statement, all you have to do is think back to the stories you were required to read in school as a young teenager, or honestly assess your own students' responses to the stories that have comprised the traditional anthologies from the past: Guy De Maupassant's "The Piece of String," Nathaniel Hawthorne's "The Minister's Black Veil," Stephen Crane's "The Bride Comes to Yellow Sky," Ernest Hemingway's "The Killers," Edgar Allan Poe's "The Cask of Amontillado," or Jack London's "To Build a Fire." All good stories—some of the world's best, in fact. But were any of them written with kids in mind? Were any of them written from a teenage perspective? Do they contain issues that concern contemporary teenagers? How many of them even contain characters whose age is similar to that of the readers who are assigned to read them? We all know that we are more likely to be interested in and enjoy things that are directly related to our own lives. And for students in the middle grades, this is even more so—for it is natural, developmentally, for them to be more concerned about themselves and finding their place in life than about anything else. "Who am I?" and "Where and how do I fit in?" are the most important questions in the lives of these young people. We need to remind ourselves of the volumes of past research as well as personal observations that show that kids at this age read mostly for vicarious excitement and to see themselves in the stories they read. Older stories such as "The Most Dangerous Game" by Richard Connell, "The Monkey's Paw" by W. W. Jacobs, and several of Edgar Allan Poe's horror stories—"The Tell-Tale Heart," for example—have been liked by teenage readers across generations most likely because of the vicarious thrills they provide, even though they contain no teenage characters with whom readers can identify. But teachers who want stories that are more likely to attract middle school readers in the first place, regardless of the content, will be more successful if the main character or characters in the stories are teenagers at the same age as, or slightly older than, the students in their classes.

David Sohn, while teaching English and reading to junior high school students during the late 1950s and early 1960s, collected numerous short stories from a variety of sources and tried them out with his students. The most successful of those stories became what is still one of the most interesting and longest lasting anthologies available for teenagers: *Top Ten Stories* (1964). It contains a mixture of types of stories such as science fiction and animal stories, while focusing on topics that interest teenagers such as the consequences of cheating on a test or being attracted to a guy from the wrong kind of background.

In 1967, Robert S. Gold attempted to build on Sohn's success by putting together a collection of short stories about teenagers and their concerns. Furthermore, he tried to provide stories that were examples of high-quality writing. He included highly respected writers such as Nadine Gordimer, Elizabeth Enright, William Saroyan, Bernard Malamud, and Howard Nemerov. About half of the stories were selected from collections written by the individual authors; the rest were taken primarily from two literary magazines: *Esquire* and *The New Yorker*. No one needs to be an authority in the field of literature to recognize those published sources as being of the highest literary quality. But that's the problem with them. They are publications that only the rarest of teenagers even knows about, much less reads with any regularity. These stories unquestionably were intended for adult readers— sophisticated, well-educated adults at that—not average teenagers, even though every story in *Point of Departure: 19 Stories of Youth and Discovery* is about a teenager. (In comparison, most of the stories in Sohn's *Top Ten Stories* were selected from magazines such as *Seventeen, Mademoiselle, The Saturday Evening Post*, and *The Magazine of Fantasy and Science Fiction*— publications much more likely to be read by teenagers at that time.) This is not to denigrate the stories in Gold's anthology themselves—they are all excellent pieces of short fiction. And John Updike's "A & P" among them is a story that will and does appeal to contemporary teenagers just about as much as any story can. But teachers who use this or any similar anthology ought to use caution by carefully assessing the ability of their students to handle the sophisticated language and concepts.

There are other, more recent, collections of short stories aimed at teenage audiences that are more readable and more likely to capture the attention of their readers while still providing teachers with works of high quality from which to teach reading strategies and to encourage literary analysis. Some of those collections have been produced for a school market by textbook publishers, incorporating a few contemporary stories among the traditional classics. A recent effort from the National Textbook Company is a good example. Called *Coming of Age: Short Stories About Youth & Adolescence* (1994), edited by Bruce Emra, a New Jersey high school English department supervisor, the collection contains stories by Richard Peck, Gary Soto, Robert Cormier, Toni Cade Bambera, and Sandra Cisneros on the one hand and Margaret Atwood, Katherine Mansfield, Sylvia Plath, Anne Tyler, and Eudora Welty, among others, on the other. While the majority of the selections seem more appropriately directed at senior high school readers because of their sophistication, some of the stories will appeal to some middle school students. However, it does seem unlikely that anthologies like this will ever appeal enough to the average student to make him or her pick up a copy and read through the selections without a teacher's guidance. Part of the lack of appeal is no doubt the typical textbook format, making books like this look as if they are more for work than for enjoyment.

As the literary world for young adults changed in the late 1960s and through the 1970s with more realistic teen-centered books written by the likes of S. E. Hinton, Paul Zindel, M. E. Kerr, and Robert Lipsyte, and later by Richard Peck, Robert Cormier, Rosa Guy, Paula Fox, Bette Greene, Virginia Hamilton, Robert Newton Peck, Walter Dean Myers, and many others, new collections of short fiction began to appear, first from individual authors and then from anthologists who put together collections of stories written by a variety of authors. This trend is stronger now than at any previous time in literary history. All of the stories in these collections feature teenage characters, speak the language of contemporary teens, and appeal to the immediate needs and interests of teenage readers. Among the earliest collections were Nicholasa Mohr's *El Bronx Remembered* (1975), Norma Fox Mazer's *Dear Bill, Remember Me? and Other Stories* (1976), Robert Cormier's *8 Plus 1* (1980), Lois Ruby's *Two Truths in My Pocket* (1982), and Joan Aiken's *A Whisper in the Night* (1984).

In the early 1980s I was fortunate to be in the right place at the right time when short stories were beginning to experience a rebirth of interest among adults as well as among teenagers. With the blessing of George Nicholson, Editor-in-Chief at Dell Publishing Company, I invited several highly successful authors to write a short story for a new kind of collection, a collection featuring teenagers, about teenagers' concerns, and written by authors whose novels were popular with teenagers. That effort became *Sixteen: Short Stories by Outstanding Writers for Young Adults*, published in 1984. In 1994 the Young Adult Services Division of the American Library Association identified this book as one of the one hundred Best of the Best Books for Young Adults published between 1967 and 1992. The table of contents of *Sixteen* reads like a who's who of the top people now in the field. Among those authors are Joan Aiken, Robert Cormier, Bette Greene, Rosa Guy, M. E. Kerr, Robert Lipsyte, Harry Mazer, Norma Fox Mazer, Susan Beth Pfeffer, and Ouida Sebestyen. And among the stories is Richard Peck's "Priscilla and the Wimps," perhaps the most enjoyable and most popular contemporary short story ever written for teenagers, judging from the responses of students and teachers across the country.

Other collections of stories followed *Sixteen*: *Visions* (1987), *Connec-

tions (1989), *Short Circuits* (1992), *Within Reach* (1993), *Join In* (1993), and *Ultimate Sports* (1995), all of which I edited, along with a number of other noteworthy collections produced by knowledgeable people, such as Jane Yolen and David Gale. But before looking more closely at the content of those books, first consider why these kinds of stories appeal to young people.

Kenneth L. Donelson and Alleen Pace Nilsen, in the third edition of their highly regarded textbook *Literature for Today's Young Adults* (1989), list several reasons for the short story's appeal to young readers. In addition to the obvious characteristic of being short, most short stories have "a limited number of characters." In addition: "Their plots are usually straightforward," with the story most often being "direct and to the point" (p. 301). Those characteristics do not necessarily make short stories of lesser literary quality, it should be noted, since the characters can be as well-drawn and memorable as those in longer works of fiction; the quality of the writing can be as distinguished as in any other literary form; and the issues and outcomes of the stories poignant and thought-provoking enough to satisfy even the most jaded readers.

For example, no one who has read Chris Crutcher's "A Brief Moment in the Life of Angus Bethune" (from *Athletic Shorts*, 1991) can forget the indomitable, overweight Angus. The relationship between Mike and his grandmother in Robert Cormier's "The Moustache" (from *8 Plus 1*, 1980) will leave almost any reader with a lump in her or his throat. And Bruce Coville's "Duffy's Jacket" (in *Things That Go Bump in the Night*, edited by Jane Yolen and Martin H. Greenberg, 1989) can easily hold its own against any horror story Edgar Allan Poe ever produced.

From a teaching standpoint, a single short story can be an ideal teaching tool. For one thing, the length of short stories allows the story to be introduced, read, and discussed during one class period. Brevity means teachers can let students spend time focusing on response. Elizabeth Poe in "Student Responses to Don Gallo's *Sixteen*" published in the January, 1988, *English Journal*, explains how her students read and evaluated several short stories in *Sixteen*. With time to attend to students' personal responses, students who had read the same short story met in a small group to discuss their choice and their evaluation and response to it. Then students used their journals to record their thoughts. "Journal entries," Poe notes, "clearly indicated that students learned not only about short stories but also about themselves and others from reading self-selected stories" (p. 69).

Another reason short stories are strong teaching tools is that teachers can use several short stories to illustrate a variety of perspectives on a similar theme, or can use a short story to introduce or reinforce one of the themes in a novel or a play. John H. Bushman and Kay Parks Bushman, in *Using Young Adult Literature in the English Classroom* (1993), note that most of the stories in the contemporary collections fit ideally with the themes often examined in middle and senior high schools today, such as coming of age, peer pressure, boy-girl relationships, death and dying, and conflicts with parents (p. 51).

For example, if your chosen theme has something to do with conflicts between mothers and daughters—as Anne Frank's *The Diary of a Young Girl* (1952) does, for example—students might read Colby Rodowsky's "Amanda and the Wounded Birds*" from *Visions* (1987) and/or Susan Beth Pfeffer's "As It Is with Strangers" from *Connections* (1989) to see how other teenage characters communicate, or don't communicate, with their parents. Or, if you have readers interested in father-son relationships, point them to one of several stories in Graham Salisbury's *Blue Skin of the Sea* (1992) or his "Shark Bait" from *Ultimate Sports* (1995). Then let students read about the father-son conflict in Walter Dean Myers's *Somewhere in the Darkness* (1992).

Donelson and Nilsen offer another reason to teach with short stories. Short stories allow readers to experience many individual works during a specified time, so teachers can present students with a greater variety of perspectives than what could be presented with a single novel or a full-length play (p. 301). This wide reading provides the opportunity to furnish students with multicultural literature that is read thematically. So, instead of doing a unit on "African-American literature," say, where more attention is on the color of the characters' skin than on the universal issues the characters confront, students can now read stories by Gary Soto (Mexican American), Nicholasa Mohr (Puerto Rican American), Walter Dean Myers (African American), and Lensey Namioka (Chinese American), for example, along with stories by Anglo authors who have written stories with the same theme. This allows students to experience multicultural literature in an inclusive setting.

Incorporating short stories into a thematic unit also allows readers to view short stories as a part of the curriculum, not apart from the curriculum. Instead of setting aside a 3- or 4-week block of time to deal exclusively with short stories as an end in themselves, short stories become a means to an end when our curriculum is organized around several key themes. The short stories are used to illustrate and reinforce the theme of the unit, along with poems, nonfiction, newspaper accounts, films/videos, short plays, and a full-length novel or two. This extensive reading also provides students with a greater variety of writing styles than if they read only one novel in the same amount of time.

Teri S. Lesesne provides teachers with even more ways to use short stories in her article "Forming *Connections* and Awakening *Vision*," (1994). In this article, she suggests using them "to introduce readers to different cultures and their customs." As one example, she proposes pairing Lensey Namioka's popular story "The All-American Slurp" with Linda Crew's *Children of the River* (1989) in order to look at the difficulties experienced by teenage characters coming to America from another country whose dress, food, and customs are significantly different from ours (p. 24). She also points out that short stories are "natural lead-ins to historical studies." For instance, two collections written by Paul Fleischman, *Graven Images* (1982) and *Coming-and-Going Men* (1985), provide background for life in New England around 1800 (p. 24). Plus, she advocates using short stories as vehicles for moving readers into new genres. For example, to introduce science fiction or fantasy, use the futuristic stories in *2041* (1991).

Another recommendation from Lesesne is to utilize short stories "as models for student writing" (p. 26). Any story, of course, can be a model for students: by requiring students to write a story following a similar format, or to write a different ending, or to add a scene to the story using the same style as the author. But some stories provide examples of other types of writing in addition to a straight narrative/descriptive one. Robert Lipsyte, in a story entitled "Future Tense," originally published in *Sixteen* (1984), uses a third-person narrative approach punctuated by samples from a story that the main character is writing. Judie Angell's story "Dear Marsha," in *Connections* (1989), is presented entirely in a series of letters exchanged between two individuals, Marsha and Anne Marie. In *Please Do Not Touch* (1993), author Judith Gorog takes "you," the reader, on a journey through a gallery of horror stories by interspersing each story with a page or two written in second person. Folktales provide another kind of style for students to emulate. Look at Lori M. Carlson's and Cynthia L. Ventura's *Where Angels Glide at Dawn—New Stories from Latin America* (1990), the African American folktales in Virginia Hamilton's *The People Could Fly* (1985), and the Jamaican folktales in James Berry's *The Future-Telling Lady and Other Stories* (1991) to see interesting models. Similarly, students can try their hand at writing urban legends like those found in Daniel Cohen's *Southern Fried Rat & Other Gruesome Tales* (1983) or Alvin Schwartz's *Scary Stories to Tell in the Dark* (1981) and their sequels. And Carolyn Meyer provides an unusual format in her *Rio Grande Stories* (1994), where she alternates stories about fictional students in a seventh grade class in the Southwest with essays that each student has written as part of the class's Heritage Project. Included are descriptive essays, biographies, histories, and even a recipe—plenty of lively examples for any middle school student to emulate.

For another teaching tip, I should mention that the short length and lively styles of most of these stories provide ideal material for read-alouds—either in conjunction with the theme of your particular class unit or merely as an entertaining filler for those days when there is an unexpected extra fifteen minutes at the end of class or a day when nobody is interested in any serious learning, like just before a vacation week. A real plus with sharing these aloud with your students is that you'll also have the opportunity to share your personal responses with students. Students can hear you laugh and watch you cry. When you share Cormier's "The Moustache," which will bring tears to your eyes, don't be afraid to shed those tears. As students watch our honest emotions that emerge when reading powerful texts, they see that the main goal of reading isn't just for finishing homework, passing minimum competency tests, or completing worksheet pages; indeed, they see that reading is a way to meet characters and situations that impact feelings and thoughts.

To help you find short stories to share with your students, explore publishers' catalogs, peruse resources such as *Your Reading* from the National Council of Teachers of English, and read reviews of new books in professional journals such as *School Library Journal*, *The New Advocate*, and *The ALAN Review*. There, you will see more and more worthwhile books of short stories in the future, the bulk of which are likely to be fresh, original, never-before published stories, some from a single author, others compiled from works by a variety of authors. But for now, enjoy any of the noteworthy collections listed below, several of which have already been mentioned throughout this chapter.

A word of caution first: don't blindly order a class set of any of these just because they are listed here. A particular collection (such as *Funny You Should Ask*, 1992, or *Don't Open the Door After the Sun Goes Down*, 1994) as a whole might be too easy for the advanced students you have in, say, your eighth grade class; another (*Am I Blue*, 1994, for instance, or *Traveling On into the Light*, 1994) might be too sophisticated for most sixth grade students. In most of the collections that include a variety of authors there are some stories that will seem better suited for younger readers, while others will work better with older students. You need to pick and choose. And because of that, in some cases it might be better for you to purchase five copies of six different books instead of thirty copies of any one book. Or purchase a class set of one collection to use in common, along with one or two copies of several other collections for students to choose for independent reading. Either way, here are several titles for you to consider.

[*Note*: Some titles are included in more than one category. Also, not all of these books are currently in print, but they are included here in case copies are already in your library or school bookroom. Please check *Books in Print* for availability and current editions.]

Books suited more to the younger end of middle school:

> *Baseball in April and Other Stories* by Gary Soto. Harcourt Brace Jovanovich, 1990.
> *Bruce Coville's Book of Nightmares: Tales to Make You Scream* edited by Bruce Coville. Scholastic, 1995.

Don't Open the Door After the Sun Goes Down: Tales of the Real and Unreal by Al Carusone (illustrated by Andrew Glass). Houghton Mifflin, 1994.

Funny You Should Ask: The Delacorte Book of Original Humorous Short Stories edited by David Gale. Delacorte, 1992.

The Future-Telling Lady and Other Stories by James Berry. HarperCollins, 1991.

Raw Head, Bloody Bones: African-American Tales of the Supernatural edited by Mary E. Lyons. Scribner's, 1991.

Scary Stories to Tell in the Dark by Alvin Schwartz. Harper & Row, 1981.

Seven Strange and Ghostly Tales by Brian Jacques. Philomel, 1991.

Short & Shivery: Thirty Chilling Tales retold by Robert D. San Souci (illustrated by Katherine Coville). Doubleday, 1987.

Short Takes: A Short Story Collection for Young Readers edited by Elizabeth Segel. Dell, 1986.

To Break the Silence: Thirteen Short Stories for Young Readers edited by Peter Barrett. Dell, 1986.

Where Angels Glide at Dawn: New Stories from Latin America edited by Lori M. Carlson and Cynthia L. Ventura. Lippincott, 1991.

Within Reach: Ten Stories edited by Donald R. Gallo. HarperCollins, 1993.

Creepy/Scary/Horror/Supernatural stories

Bruce Coville's Book of Nightmares: Tales to Make You Scream edited by Bruce Coville. Scholastic, 1994.

Don't Open the Door After the Sun Goes Down: Tales of the Real and the Unreal by Al Carusone (illustrated by Andrew Glass). Houghton Mifflin, 1994.

Ghostly Tales of Love and Revenge by Daniel Cohen. Putnam, 1992.

Give Yourself a Fright: Thirteen Stories of the Supernatural by Joan Aiken. Delacorte, 1989.

Hair-Raising: Ten Horror Stories edited by Penny Matthews. Scholastic, 1992.

Hidden Turnings: A Collection of Stories Through Time and Space edited by Diana Wynne Jones. Greenwillow, 1990.

Hostilities: Nine Bizarre Stories by Caroline Macdonald. Scholastic, 1991.

Night Terrors: Stories of Shadow and Substance edited by Lois Duncan. Simon & Schuster, 1996.

A Nightmare's Dozen: Stories from the Dark edited by Michael Stearns. Harcourt Brace, 1996.

Oddly Enough by Bruce Coville. Harcourt Brace Jovanovich, 1994.

Please Do Not Touch: A Collection of Stories by Judith Gorog. Scholastic, 1993.

Scary Stories to Tell in the Dark by Alvin Schwartz. Harper & Row, 1981.

Seven Strange and Ghostly Tales by Brian Jacques. Philomel, 1991.

Short Circuits: Thirteen Shocking Stories by Outstanding Writers for Young Adults edited by Donald R. Gallo. Delacorte, 1992.

A Sliver of Glass and Other Uncommon Tales by Anne Mazer. Hyperion, 1996.

Things That Go Bump in the Night: A Collection of Original Stories edited by Jane Yolen and Martin H. Greenberg. Harper & Row, 1989.

Thirteen: 13 Tales of Horror edited by T. Pines. Scholastic, 1991.

A Touch of Chill: Tales for Sleepless Nights by Joan Aiken. Dell, 1980.

Truly Grim Tales by Priscilla Galloway. Delacorte Press, 1995.

Vampires: A Collection of Original Stories edited by Jane Yolen and Martin H. Greenberg. HarperCollins, 1991.

Werewolves: A Collection of Original Stories edited by Jane Yolen and Martin H. Greenberg. Harper & Row, 1988.

A Whisper in the Night: Tales of Terror and Suspense by Joan Aiken. Delacorte, 1984.

Fantasy

Book of Enchantments by Patricia C. Wrede. Harcourt Brace, 1996.

A Knot in the Grain and Other Stories by Robin McKinley. Greenwillow, 1982.

Visions of Fantasy: Tales from the Masters edited by Isaac Asimov and Martin H. Greenberg. Doubleday, 1989.

A Wizard's Dozen: Stories of the Fantastic edited by Michael Stearns. Harcourt Brace, 1993.

Folktales and Legends

The Future-Telling Lady and Other Stories by James Berry. HarperCollins, 1991.

The People Could Fly: American Black Folktales by Virginia Hamilton. Knopf, 1985.

Raw Head, Bloody Bones: African-American Tales of the Supernatural edited by Mary E. Lyons. Scribner's, 1991.

Short & Shivery: Thirty Chilling Tales retold by Robert D. San Souci (illustrated by Katherine Coville). Doubleday, 1987.

Southern Fried Rat & Other Gruesome Tales by Daniel Cohen. Avon, 1983.

Tales from Gold Mountain: Stories of the Chinese in the New World by Paul Yee. Macmillan, 1990.

Where Angels Glide at Dawn: New Stories from Latin America edited by Lori M. Carlson and Cynthia L. Ventura. Lippincott, 1990.

Friendship

Who Do You Think You Are? Stories of Friends and Enemies edited by Hazel Rochman and Darlene Z. McCampbell. Joy Street/Little Brown, 1993.

Historical Fiction

Coming-and-Going Men: Four Tales by Paul Fleischman. Harper & Row, 1985.

Echoes of War by Robert Westall. Farrar, Straus and Giroux, 1989.

Graven Images: Three Stories by Paul Fleischman. Harper & Row, 1982.

Homosexuality

Am I Blue: Coming Out from the Silence edited by Marion Dane Bauer. HarperCollins, 1994.

Humor

Funny You Should Ask: The Delacorte Book of Humorous Short Stories edited by David Gale. Delacorte, 1992.

If This Is Love, I'll Take Spaghetti by Ellen Conford. Scholastic, 1983.

I Love You, I Hate You, Get Lost by Ellen Conford. Scholastic, 1994.

Love and Romance

A Couple of Kooks and Other Stories about Love by Cynthia Rylant. Dell, 1990.

If This Is Love, I'll Take Spaghetti by Ellen Conford. Scholastic, 1983.

I Love You, I Hate You, Get Lost by Ellen Conford. Scholastic, 1994.

Summer Girls, Love Boys and Other Stories by Norma Fox Mazer. Delacorte, 1982.

Multicultural Stories

American Dragons: Twenty-Five Asian American Voices edited by Laurence Yep. HarperCollins, 1993.

America Street: A Multicultural Anthology of Stories edited by Anne Mazer. Persea, 1993.

Baseball in April and Other Stories by Gary Soto. Harcourt Brace Jovanovich, 1990.

Blue Skin of the Sea by Graham Salisbury. Delacorte Press, 1992.

El Bronx Remembered by Nicholasa Mohr. Harper & Row, 1975.

The Future-Telling Lady and Other Stories by James Berry. Harper-Collins, 1991.

A Gathering of Flowers: Stories about Being Young in America edited by Joyce Carol Thomas. HarperCollins, 1990.

In Nueva York by Nicholasa Mohr. Arte Publico, 1988.

An Island Like You: Stories of the Barrio by Judith Ortiz Cofer. Orchard, 1995.

Join In: Multiethnic Short Stories by Outstanding Writers for Young Adults edited by Donald R. Gallo. Delacorte, 1993.

Local News by Gary Soto. Harcourt Brace Jovanovich, 1993.

The People Could Fly: American Black Folktales by Virginia Hamilton. Knopf, 1985.

Raw Head, Bloody Bones: African-American Tales of the Supernatural edited by Mary E. Lyons. Scribner's, 1991.

Rio Grande Stories by Carolyn Meyer. Harcourt Brace, 1994.

Short & Shivery: Thirty Chilling Tales retold by Robert D. San Souci (illustrated by Katherine Coville). Doubleday, 1987.

Tales from Gold Mountain: Stories of the Chinese in the New World by Paul Yee. Macmillan, 1990.

Prejudice

Prejudice: Stories about Hate, Ignorance, Revelation, and Transformation edited by Daphne Muse. Hyperion, 1995.

Science Fiction

Spaceships and Spells edited by Jane Yolen, Martin H. Greenberg, and Charles G. Waugh. Harper & Row, 1987.

2041: Twelve Short Stories about the Future edited by Jane Yolen. Delacorte, 1991.

Sorrow and Pain

Early Sorrow: Ten Stories of Youth edited by Charlotte Zolotow. HarperCollins, 1986.

Sports

Athletic Shorts: Six Short Stories by Chris Crutcher. Greenwillow, 1991.

Ultimate Sports: Short Stories by Outstanding Writers for Young Adults edited by Donald R. Gallo. Delacorte, 1995.

Stories Featuring Girls

Dear Bill, Remember Me? and Other Stories by Norma Fox Mazer. Delacorte, 1976.

If This Is Love, I'll Take Spaghetti by Ellen Conford. Scholastic, 1983.

I Love You, I Hate You, Get Lost, by Ellen Conford. Scholastic, 1994.

Summer Girls, Love Boys and Other Stories by Norma Fox Mazer. Dell, 1982.

A Very Brief Season: Ten Stories by Barbara Girion. Scribner's, 1984.

War

Echoes of War by Robert Westall. Farrar, Straus and Giroux, 1989.

Varied Subjects

Coming of Age: Short Stories about Youth & Adolescence edited by Bruce Emra. National Textbook Company, 1994.

Connections: Short Stories by Outstanding Writers for Young Adults edited by Donald R. Gallo. Delacorte, 1989.

Heartbeats and Other Stories by Peter D. Sieruta. HarperCollins, 1986.

The Leaving and Other Stories by Budge Wilson. Philomel, 1990.

Paradise Cafe and Other Stories by Martha Brooks. Little Brown, 1990.

Point of Departure: 19 Stories of Youth and Discovery edited by Robert S. Gold. Dell, 1967.

Sixteen: Short Stories by Outstanding Writers for Young Adults edited by Donald R. Gallo. Delacorte, 1984.

Ten Top Stories edited by David A. Sohn. Bantam, 1964.

Traveling On into the Light and Other Stories by Martha Brooks. Orchard, 1994.

Visions: Nineteen Stories by Outstanding Writers for Young Adults edited by Donald R. Gallo. Delacorte, 1987.

When I Was Your Age: Original Stories about Growing Up edited by Amy Ehrlich. Candlewick Press, 1996.

One final note. Because of the success of these collections, short stories from many of them are now being included in most new reading and literature textbooks for middle school students. Scott Foresman and Company, for example, has produced *Crossroads: Classic Themes in Young Adult Literature* (1995). The hardcover textbook, using a limited number of black and white illustrations, is divided into six units under themes such as "Who Am I?" "Facing the Enemy," and "Journeys." Each unit consists of between six and eight pieces of literature, about a fourth of which are short stories. Among them are Budge Wilson's "Be-ers and Doers" from *The Leaving and Other Stories* (1990), Todd Strasser's "On the Bridge" from *Visions* (1987), and Robert Cormier's "Protestants Cry, Too" from *8 Plus 1* (1967), as well as Richard Peck's famous "Priscilla and the Wimps."

Numerous contemporary young adult short stories, along with some classical ones, comprise a good portion of D. C. Heath's *Middle Level Literature* anthologies (1995). Eight separately packaged units at each of three levels (corresponding to grades 6–8) are colorfully illustrated and attractively laid out. The selections provide an ideal multicultural variety of short fiction along with nonfiction, poetry, and drama. For example, in the eighth grade unit on myths and folktales, there are short stories by Borden Deal, Lensey Namioka, John Steptoe, Gerald Vizenor, Arthur C. Clarke, and Yoshika Uchida.

Both of the above-mentioned publications are ideal for teachers who prefer pre-selected works (accompanied by ancillary materials) over choosing their own selections and developing their own materials.

Whichever approach you take, there is a wide variety of selections from which to choose. You won't be shortchanged by any of these alternatives. Take a short cut by trying a couple of stories from a variety of these possibilities. In a short time you will have a sense of what will work best for your particular students.

References

Bushman, J. H., & Bushman, K. P. (1993). *Using young adult literature in the English classroom*. New York: Merrill/ Macmillan.

Donelson, K. L., & Nilsen, A. P. (1989). *Literature for today's young adults* (3rd ed.). Glenview, IL: Scott, Foresman and Company.

Lesesne, T. S. (1994). Forming connections and awakening visions: Using short story collections in the classroom. *The ALAN Review, 21* (3), 24–26.

Poe, E. (1988). Student responses to Don Gallo's *Sixteen*. *English Journal, 77* (1), 68–70.

Chapter 18

CREATING LIFETIME READERS:
A NOVEL IDEA

Barbara G. Samuels

> More than just show us order in hypothetical existences, novelists give us demonstration classes in what is the ultimate work of us all, for by days and years we must create the narrative of our own lives. . . . To glance up and see a great novelist offering a story of rare, sweet wit and grace is to feel that our heart has found its home.
>
> So you say that reading a novel is a way to kill time when the real world needs tending to. I tell you that the only world I know is the world as I know it, and I am still learning how to comprehend that. These books are showing me ways of being I could never have managed alone. I am not killing time. I'm trying to make a life.
>
> Kathryn Morton (*New York Times Book Review* Columnist)

I am a novel reader. Like many other reading and English teachers, I became an English teacher and then a reading teacher because I loved to bury myself in the pages of a novel, experience with the characters, live their lives for awhile, think in new ways about myself and the world around me, and view situations in a different way. No other form of literature has had quite the same appeal for me as have novels, and when I ask other readers about their reading history, they often confess the same preference. Like freelance author and columnist Kathryn Morton, novels help me "make a life."

For as long as I can remember, when I read a novel I have been hooked into the world between the pages, lost to the voices around me, deaf to the calls from my mother to come to dinner, disconnected from my husband's voice telling me he was ready to leave, unheeding even of my children's cries for attention. When I read, I vicariously experience the drama created for me by the author. Novels invite an emotional transaction with text.

I was a lucky adolescent. When I was in junior high school, my mother shared her love of reading with me by recommending books she had enjoyed and then discussing my reading with me. I had teachers who encouraged my love of reading. Books helped me to define myself, to expand my understandings beyond the narrow world of a Jewish, suburban New Jersey teenager. They allowed me to step inside the skin of those very different from myself, and by becoming someone else for awhile, to gain understanding, knowledge, and compassion. I learned to live from novels.

Although I was an only child, when I was reading I could grow up in a house full of sisters like Jo March. I became Jane Eyre, dreaming of love with my Mr. Rochester. Novels drew me into their stories. I lost myself for hours, burying my nose in the pages of book after book. For a time I was the character in the story, lived in the settings described, and thought about the ideas suggested by the story. I read animal stories because I dreamed of someday being a veterinarian, a zookeeper, or a farmer. Terhune's books about collies helped me to imagine having a dog of my own when I lived in a sixth-floor apartment building as a child. Maybe someday I could even live in Africa and raise baby lions like Joy Adamson (1960) in *Born Free*. Perhaps my study of animals could help others to better understand their habits and habitats to make the world a safer place for them.

Because reading novels was a total joy to me as a teenager, I wanted to help others experience that excitement. When I decided to become an English teacher, I envisioned myself recommending novels to my students. They would love books as I had. I wanted to play the role for them that my mother and some of my favorite teachers had played for me. But years ago, when I first started teaching English, I discovered that although some students responded very positively to the standard reading lists for secondary English, others hated the traditional classics I was suggesting to them. "It's bo-o-oring!" they would say about *Great Expectations*, or *The Pearl*. "I just can't get into it." Like the poem "Paul Hewitt" in Mel Glenn's *Class Dismissed II* (1986), they would say: "You got any books that deal with real life?" (p. 18) They didn't do the reading assignments. We struggled through class discussions. Although some reading could be done in class, I could not depend upon students to read anything at home. How could I transfer my enthusiasm about reading to kids who couldn't connect with the books I had learned about as an English major? That's when I discovered the appeal of the young adult novel. Teens who refused to finish a book by Dickens and instead read the Cliff Notes eagerly shared the young adult titles they were enjoying.

> I love books that I can actually relate to. In young adult fiction many of the characters encounter or take on problems that we as young adults face everyday. Young adult fiction is exciting when compared to adult fiction. In classical fiction the reader can rarely relate to the problems or conflicts that the character encounters.
>
> (Lonny, eighth grade)

Clearly, other teachers needed to know about the genre.

Studies on Novel Reading

Because I was concerned about the role of the secondary school classroom in creating lifelong readers, and because my own preparation as an English teacher had not included adolescent literature, I conducted a survey of secondary school English teachers to determine their knowledge of and attitude toward the young adult novel (Samuels, 1982). I found that the primary reason teachers didn't use adolescent literature in their classes was that they were not familiar with the titles. Programs that train teachers to teach English do not always include a course in young adult literature as part of the program. As in the teacher preparation program I had experienced, teachers who major in English today often study Chaucer, Shakespeare, Milton, Boswell, Dickens, Hemingway, Dickinson, and Faulkner. Perhaps they have even had a course on multicultural literature to introduce them to Sandra Cisneros, Richard Rodriguez, James Baldwin, and Langston Hughes. Sometimes an English methods course will introduce a few titles published for adolescents, but many English teachers have never had a course in young adult literature. I found that teachers were not familiar with newer titles that might be appealing to their middle school students. When asked if they saw the benefit of a course on young adult literature for new teachers of English, 99% of the junior high school teachers in my survey responded "Yes" (Samuels, 1982).

In addition, according to a recent extensive survey by the Center for the Learning and Teaching of Literature reported by Arthur Applebee (1993), the secondary school literature curriculum in the United States is still relatively narrow. Applebee's study duplicates and confirms an earlier examination of the teaching of high school English completed by Applebee and Squire in 1962–65. The middle school curriculum is slightly more diverse than the high school curriculum. Applebee reports that the selections required in grades 7 and 8 are somewhat more contemporary, more likely to be written by minorities or women, and they are more likely to be by North American authors than those for senior high school. In Applebee's random sample of schools, the most frequent sources of literature materials in all types of schools are anthologies, with 63% of the teachers in public schools reporting that the anthology was their "main source of selections." Junior high/middle school classes placed more emphasis on short stories (43% of class time) and less emphasis on novels or other book-length works (33% of class time). In Applebee's study, for grade 7, the most frequently cited longer works are *Call of the Wild* (London), *The Adventures of Tom Sawyer* (Twain), *The Red Pony* (Steinbeck), and *A Christmas Carol* (Dickens). In Grade 8, the titles most often read are *Diary of a Young Girl* (Frank), *Call of the Wild* (London), and *The Pigman* (Zindel). Of these, the only title written in the past fifty years is Zindel's *The Pigman*. *The Pigman* is also the only title that was published for young adult readers.

While some of the full-length books reported by Applebee as typically taught in junior high school have adolescent protagonists, the primary concerns of the main characters may not be the concerns of adolescents today. Many teens report that they prefer to read novels about teens like themselves. As one seventh grader reported, "Young adult fiction books are about what happens to us as young adults. We can relate with the books." Although many middle school students enjoy reading about a dog and have reported loving *Call of the Wild*, some find it difficult to relate to London's naturalism. They prefer contemporary realistic animal stories like Kevin Henkes' *Protecting Marie* (1995), Patricia Harrison Easton's *Summer's Chance* (1988), or Phyllis Naylor's *Shiloh* (1992). Many middle school students have become fans of animal fantasy novels like British author Brian Jacques' *Redwall* (1987) series, in which a band of heroic mice battle the forces of evil from the Abbey at Redwall.

One measure of middle school students' preferences is the Young Adults' Choices (YA) program of the International Reading Association. Conducted annually since 1987 and published in the November issue of the *Journal of Adolescent and Adult Literacy* (previously the *Journal of Reading*), the YA Choices poll asks students for their preferences among books published during the previous year. An analysis of students' choices done in 1987 and 1988 (Samuels, 1989) found that they liked novels that were "exciting" and "about a character just like me." Problem novels in which protagonists struggle with relationships with friends, parents, abuse, handicaps, illness, and death are particularly evident on the YA Choices list annually. As teachers, we must recognize that many of the classics do not have the power to draw teens away from their activities and into books. They cannot compete with the powerful appeal of contemporary movies and TV, video games, and sports.

Encouraging Reading

"Fight Prime Time. Read a Book!" the bumper sticker on my TV reads. But bumper stickers alone don't challenge the magnet of the television set. Instead, it is the careful monitoring of TV watching, the ready availability of appealing reading material in the classroom and at home, the modeling and encouragement of reading, the reading aloud of high-interest titles, the promotion of choice in students' reading, and a teacher's knowledge of the books that turn couch potatoes into novel readers. Teachers who are enthusiastic readers of books that connect with teens and who share their excitement about the variety of excellent novels available to their students are rewarded with responses like the following from eighth graders:

> Reading young adult fiction has increased my urge to read. I have never really enjoyed reading books until this year. . . . The books are so intriguing and they really relate to everyday life.
>
> (Jennifer)

> I feel like young adult fiction is very important for a youth's mind. It has bridged the gap for me to adult novels. Young adult fiction builds you up for adult fiction by strengthening vocabulary and thinking skills.
>
> (Jonathan)

Whereas the books I read as a teenager were mostly written for an adult audience because I grew up before the explosion of young adult literature, middle school and junior high students today have the wonderful advantage of an entire body of novels that speaks directly to their needs and interests in addition to the classics I read when I was in school. Adolescence is a time when peer relationships, achieving independence, and trying out new experiences assume tremendous importance. Well-written young adult novels with teen protagonists and about these coming-of-age issues are available to middle school and junior high school students today. Teachers who have not read widely in the field of young adult literature are missing the opportunity to draw their students into literature, to help them savor the joys of losing themselves in a book. What middle school teacher doesn't hope for students like the one who wrote in her response letter: "I just couldn't put *Staying Fat for Sarah Byrnes* down. I sat glued to the couch for four hours straight until I finished it."

Some teachers say that they avoid adolescent literature because "it's all formula stuff." Just as many poorly written adult books are published daily, formula novels also exist in the field of YA literature. However, these formula novels and series books fulfill an important role in the reading development of young teens. Almost all of us who are readers went through a stage when we read series books. I read *Nancy Drew, Hardy Boys, Cherry Ames,* and all the horse and dog series books I could find. Like the young teens today who revel in *Baby-sitters' Club* or *Goosebumps* books, I enjoyed the comfort of the predictability and familiarity of the characters I knew and loved. Eventually, like most readers, I had my fill of the formula books and moved on to more sophisticated reading. I do not believe we should deny our students the opportunity to feel secure in the series books they enjoy.

But the field also has a wealth of beautifully written, powerful novels. As one middle school teacher reported in a survey: "I feel strongly that too many teachers are not aware of the excellent young adult literature available. I believe that is why series books are so popular with seventh and eighth graders. They do not know of the alternatives written at their level with far more literary value" (Samuels, 1982). The best novels written for teens explore universal themes and ideas effectively. "Like the best of literature written for adults, good novels written for adolescents possess themes that merit and reward examination and commentary" (Hipple, 1992, p. 4).

Reading about various fictional friendships in novels like Zindel's *The Pigman* (1968), Hinton's *That was Then, This is Now* (1971), Brooks' *The Moves Make the Man* (1984), Crutcher's *Stotan* (1986) or *Staying Fat for Sarah Byrnes* (1993), Spinelli's *Maniac Magee* (1990), Philbrick's *Freak the Mighty* (1993), and Bridgers' *Keeping Christina* (1993), or *All Together Now* (1990) helps teens put in perspective the joys and tensions of different kinds of relationships: across gender and racial lines, between boys and girls, between physically challenged teens, or between a retarded adult and a twelve year old. They are able to test their own friendships against the models in the books they read. Peer relationships are the focus of adolescents' lives. Books like these help them to formulate their own set of values. They learn the importance of trust, loyalty, and empathy. By getting to know characters well in these novels, teens establish their own connections to fictional adolescents and hypothesize how they would act in similar situations.

As physical changes occur during these early adolescent years, teens often become focused on sexual relationships. Junior high teachers know that female readers often chew up one series romance after another. The introduction to *Becoming a Woman through Romance* (Christian-Smith, 1990) reports that "adolescent romances . . . represent 35% of the total non-adult book sales at major national bookstore chains." Diana Mitchell (1996), in an article in the National Council of Teachers of English Standards Consensus Series says, "Besides their being simplistic and of mediocre writing quality, an even greater concern I have about these novels is that girls who read these books will measure themselves against the girls shown in the books. . . . Being told that one is pretty is considered the highest compliment. I also worry that girls take seriously the way females are divided into 'admirable' and 'not-admirable' people." Mitchell proposes constructing a series of questions to guide girls who read these romance series books into a more critical understanding of the gender stereotypes and sexism as illustrated in these books. She admits that the "questioning process may be slow, but, over a period of time, with gentle urging from the teacher, romance series readers can learn to be more objective about what they read" (p. 81).

Having led students who are reading the romances to be more selective, knowledgeable teachers can help girls become more discriminating readers by helping them to evaluate the books they are reading so that they select books that present a more positive image of women, less stereotypical characters, and better writing. Books like *Sex Education* (Davis, 1988); *Heartbeat* (Mazer and Mazer, 1989); *Home Before Dark* (Bridgers, 1976); and *Him She Loves?* (Kerr, 1984) demonstrate that relationships between the sexes need not follow the pattern of many series romances in which a girl's sense of self is totally dependent upon being connected to a boy. After reading Mary Downing Hahn's *The Wind Blows Backwards* (1993), one middle school student wrote,

> This book is incredible! Lauren and Spencer's relationship is wonderfully romantic, and that's one of the main things that kept me hooked. . . . The symbolism with the balloon and letting it go was wonderful. I think that Spencer will be a lot happier in his future life. Letting go of that balloon was like letting go of a horrible burden that has haunted him his whole life.
>
> (Sarah, eighth grade)

while another said about the same book:

> The book makes me wonder if there really are more Spencers (the kind that read poetry and really care about a girl) than I thought. I had to pry the book from my fingers when it was done. I was upset. I wanted to hear more about Spencer and Lauren, and how things turned out between them, even though I can imagine everything turned out great.
>
> (Danielle, eighth grade)

A novel's length and full development of character and situation draws teen readers like Danielle into a transaction with text that sometimes makes it difficult to close the book even when the reader has finished it. Instead of rejecting students' choices of romance novels, effective teachers can help them to become more critical and selective readers of romances.

Another favorite subject for middle school students, achieving independence and surviving independently, takes on a variety of forms in young adult novels from surviving in the wilderness, to overcoming traumatic experiences like the death of a loved one, to making it in sports or with people. Middle school readers enjoy reliving the Robinson Crusoe story in a variety of present and past settings in books like *The Sign of the Beaver* (Speare, 1983); *Deathwatch* (White, 1972); *Beyond the Divide* (Lasky, 1983); and *Julie of the Wolves* (George, 1972). They can experience an urban survival story in *Slake's Limbo* (Holman, 1974); a future scenario in *The Ear, the Eye and the Arm* (Farmer, 1994); or the birth of a legend in *The Lost Years of Merlin* (Barron, 1996). Adventure or mystery novels like *Summer of Fear* (Duncan, 1976); *The Kidnapping of Christina Lattimore* (Nixon, 1979); *Deadly Deception* (Haynes, 1994); *Hatchet* (Paulsen, 1987); *Wolf Rider* (Avi, 1986); or *The Birthday Murderer* (Bennett, 1977) enable teens to vicariously sample the tensions of murder and suspense. But they also become involved in protagonists' survival after an experience with death of a friend, loved one, or stranger in books like *Remembering the Good Times* (Peck, 1985); *A Summer to Die* (Lowry, 1977); and *Driver's Ed* (Cooney, 1994). Testing themselves against the challenges of the characters in these books helps teens to face the daily challenges of their lives.

While some students read novel after novel about real characters like themselves in the contemporary world, some of our most creative students read one fantasy novel after another. They enjoy the adventure and suspense of high fantasy and, as one eighth grade girl said, "They are full of magic, love, and royalty." Robin McKinley's *The Blue Sword* (1982) and *The Hero and the Crown* (1985) and Anne McCaffrey's *Dragonsong* (1976), *Dragonsinger* (1977) and *Dragondrums* (1979) provide excitement and drama with female protagonists who face a variety of adversaries representing the evil forces in imaginary lands. The Terry Brooks fantasy novels, including *Sword of Shannara* (1977) and *Magic Kingdom for Sale: SOLD* (1986) stimulate the imagination with male protagonists who battle the forces of darkness and danger. Others are fascinated with the possibilities of modern science in science fiction novels like *Z for Zachariah* (O'Brien, 1975); *Phoenix Rising* (Hesse, 1994); *Eva* (Dickinson, 1988); or *Keeper of the Isis Light* (Hughes, 1981).

Am I suggesting that teachers avoid study of the classics of literature in the middle school? Of course not. But as Purves, Rogers, and Soter suggest in *How Porcupines Make Love III* (1995), "Teachers tend to want to worship a classic and force students to worship it too. Students tend to see classics as irrelevant because they are not able to see that there is a great deal that is generalizable from the classic to their lives" (p. 73). Instead, I propose that teachers use young adult novels to help develop lifelong readers. Once students discover that reading novels can be meaningful, they can be led to apply what they have learned about the novel form to the reading of the classics.

Teaching About the Novel

Since a main objective of literature in middle school is to teach students about different genres of literature and about the structure of the genre forms, teachers have had success using young adult novels. Yet, both in terms of the specific titles of books typically read in schools and the instructional strategies in classrooms observed, in the late eighties most English classes still consisted of the traditional model of students sitting in seats engaged in teacher-led discussions, often aimed at trying to discover the meaning the teacher decided they should find. According to Applebee (1993), few classes reflected the student-centered philosophies of teaching and learning described elsewhere in this book and in the professional literature today. On the other hand, teachers who have introduced their middle school and junior high school students to young adult titles have found that they can hook reluctant readers on books like *The Outsiders* (Hinton, 1967); *Prank* (Lasky, 1984); *Striking Out* (Weaver, 1993); or *In the Middle of the Night* (Cormier, 1995) and use these titles to teach students about the nature of literary elements and the novel genre. Teens identify with the characters and situations in young adult novels. They feel competent to predict outcomes, make generalizations about motivation, and analyze literature. Rather than wait for the teacher's interpretation of the book, students immediately become involved, participating members of the literature discussion. (See Section II, "A Focus on Reading, Understanding, Connecting" for further discussion of encouraging a response to literature.)

Students in Leigh Van Horn's seventh grade English class, for example, learned about character development by studying *The Outsiders*. As they read, they kept journal notes on a character who interested them. They jotted down descriptive words or phrases, noted how their chosen character responded to situations, and indicated what other characters said about their character. When they completed the book, each student made a wallet belonging to their character from the story. They were asked to pretend that they had found the wallet and were writing a letter to its owner describing at least nine of the objects it contained. Wallets were filled with pictures, ID cards, membership cards, differing amounts of money, etc. As the students explained the reasons for including certain items, they demonstrated a deep understanding of character as well as pride in a job well done.

Students can learn the power of language to create a setting by considering the way Kathryn Lasky uses setting in *Prank* (1984) to emphasize the difference between the dysfunctional world of the Flynn family in East Boston and the glittering skyscrapers of downtown Boston. In *Z for Zachariah* (1975), Robert O'Brien describes a protected valley that has escaped nuclear contamination in the aftermath of an atomic explosion. The setting has a significant effect on the action of the novel. Robert Cormier effectively uses short phrases in his description of setting to build tension in *In the Middle of the Night* (1995).

> Nighttime. Stillness pervaded the room. No hum or beeping of the monitor. The padding of rubber soles in the corridors as the nurses glided to and from the rooms. Venetian blinds shuttered against the outside darkness. Television voices, muted and distant, in the air, his own set suspended high in a corner of the room, like a huge, blind cyclops. (pp. 71, 72)

Students learn how authors use descriptions like this to establish a mood for situations in the novel by exploring authors' styles in young adult books. Then, they can apply this understanding of setting in their own writing.

Building Thematic Units with Novels

Some teachers explore the concept of theme in a middle school classroom with units centered around a variety of young adult novels that address the same theme. A unit on Prejudice: Inhumanity to Human Beings, for example, might include students selecting from books like *Chernowitz* (1981) by Fran Arrick, *Roll of Thunder, Hear My Cry* (1976) by Mildred Taylor, *Number the Stars* (1989) by Lois Lowry, *Beyond the Burning Time* (1994) by Kathryn Lasky, and *The Drowning of Stephan Jones* (1991) by Bette Greene. Each of these novels addresses a different issue of prejudice in a different time and place. In *Chernowitz* the main character is a contemporary teen victim of anti-Semitism. *Roll of Thunder, Hear My Cry* is the story of white prejudice against the Logans, an African American family in Arkansas during the Depression. Anne Marie, the protagonist in *Number the Stars,* helps her best friend and her family escape from the Nazis in Copenhagen during World War II. *Beyond the Burning Time* documents the hysteria and ignorance surrounding the Salem witch trials. And *The Drowning of Stephan Jones* details harassment of homosexuals in society today.

As one teacher said to me, "Adolescent literature is important in developing reading tastes and reading habits. My own ideal situation would be to pair good adolescent books with more classic reading of related themes." An expansion of the thematic unit on prejudice might include classics like *To Kill a Mockingbird* (1960) by Harper Lee and *The Diary of a Young Girl* (1952) by Anne Frank.

Young adult literature paired with classics can help students to explore ideas that otherwise might be very difficult for them. An excellent resource to help teachers make these kinds of connections between readings are the three volumes of *Adolescent Literature as a Complement to the Classics* (1993, 1995, 1997) edited by Joan Kaywell. In the preface, Kaywell writes: "By using young adult novels in conjunction with the classics, teachers can expose students to reading that becomes relevant and meaningful. Additionally, the reading levels of most young adult books are within a range of ease that most students can master" (p. ix). Kaywell draws an analogy to feeding infants. Just as "babies begin with baby foods that are easily digested. . . . So too with reading. Young readers need to start with easy readers, ones that are easily consumed. Eventually, young children desire foods that have a little more substance—vegetables, eggs, and some palatable meats." Young children start reading with picture books, then move into easy chapter books. Kaywell suggests that adolescent literature is the hamburger of reading. Solid, nutritious, tasty, and sometimes prepared in very elaborate ways, it serves as the transition to more sophisticated foods that are appreciated as we approach adulthood.

One chapter of volume 2 of Kaywell's series, for example, centers on the classroom study of *Julius Caesar.* Although this Shakespeare play is frequently read in middle school classes, students struggle with Shakespeare's language and with the ideas presented in play format. Patricia L. Daniel, who wrote this section in the Kaywell book, lists many young adult titles to read in preparation for reading Shakespeare's *Julius Caesar*. Each of the novels suggested introduces characters who manipulate the emotions of others and who struggle for power; comparing those characters and then applying that comparison to Cassius, Mark Anthony, Brutus, and Caesar makes Shakespeare more relevant. Lois Duncan's novel, *Killing Mr. Griffin* (1978), she suggests, works well as a core novel to provide a common understanding of a manipulative character. Mark, like Cassius, who convinces other Romans to join his attack on Caesar, convinces other teens to join his plan to kidnap an English teacher. Daniel's students read and respond in reader response journals first to the young adult novel and then to character connections in Shakespeare's play. Then they extend their understanding with the reading of a variety of other young adult titles with related themes including *Downriver* (1991) by Will Hobbs, *The Contender* (1967) by Robert Lipsyte, and *The Friends* (1973) by Rosa Guy.

In *Tales of Love and Terror* (1993), Hazel Rochman's book about the art of giving booktalks, she notes that in any classroom students are reading at different levels. She proposes that thematic grouping of books can provide readings on a topic to meet the needs of all these reading abilities. Connecting to *Wuthering Heights* (Bronte, 1996), for example, she says she has book-talked "books about love, ghosts, rage, family conflict, mystery, self-betrayal, outsiders, a desolate setting, terror, and survival" (p. 37). In addition to the differing reading levels of students, middle school students "who are themselves bridging the years between childhood and adulthood shift in their reading interests among books for children, books for adolescents, and books for adults" (Samuels, 1992, p. 44). A quick look at a list of readings in a middle school student's reading log often reveals books as varied as *Charlotte's Web*, *Jurassic Park*, and *Jane Eyre*. (See Annie's list in Figure 8.18 in Chapter 8.)

A unit centered around *1984* (Orwell, 1981); *The Giver* (Lowry, 1993); Kurt Vonnegut's short story "Harrison Bergeron"; and Jon Scieszka's *Time Warp Trio* in Leigh Van Horn's middle school class also included readings from *The Time Machine* by H. G. Wells. Students were also introduced to *Z for Zachariah* (1975) by Robert O'Brien, *The Girl Who Owned a City* by O. T. Nelson, and *Invitation to the Game* (1990) by Monica Hughes as well a group of science fiction short stories as supplementary reading. As part of their unit, students engaged in a debate on issues of equality, wrote poems, interviewed older adults about their recollections of events in the past, and researched past events that might have altered the course of history. Students engaged in this unit had opportunities to "write from, of, and about literature," as Robert Probst (1992) suggests, to encourage different kinds of responses. Students' journal writings and research were examples of writing "from" literature, their poems were writings "of" literature, and essays about themes in *The Giver* were "about" literature.

In addition to the tension between classics, adult novels, and young adult novels, teachers contemplating classroom reading of novels in middle school classrooms seem torn between the intensive reading of a single novel for as long as 6 weeks and the extensive reading of large numbers of novels. Arguments can be made for both approaches. Shared reading and various responses to a single novel by students in a classroom offer opportunities for students to learn about the craft of fiction with direct instruction. Students who studied *The Outsiders* together in Leigh Van Horn's class were able to exchange ideas about a number of characters as they planned and wrote about their wallet assignments. They also engaged in whole-class activities like reader's theater, role playing a discussion between Ponyboy and his brothers, and decorating the hall of the school with life-sized figures of characters from the book. These activities deepened their comprehension of the text because they were experiencing it together. An extended study allows for reading aloud large sections of the book in class so that students can discuss particular passages of the book and together explore their predictions and interpretations.

Similarly, a shared reading of *The Giver* in a unit format allows for intensive exploration of a single book in a group-shared experience. If everyone in the class had not read the book in common, debates about the notion of equality would not have been possible. The best of all situations may be a combination of shared intensive reading with self-selected books as independent reading. The unit format described above allowed for an intensive class reading of *The Giver* as well as independent, self-selected supplementary texts to support the ideas from the group novel.

An effective middle school reading program invites students to think about the world of ideas by leading them into thematic units that explore important thoughts. But it goes beyond school reading and discussion. In addition to the reading they do in units like the ones described, students need opportunities to freely self-select the books they read and to read widely. In *Voices of Readers* (1988), their study of thirty years of reading autobiographies by people who eventually sought careers in reading education, Carlsen and Sherill conclude:

> Particularly during the teenage years, young people want to range widely in the world of books. . . . Some readers seemed to revel in the approach whereby a teacher put books out on a table in smorgasbord fashion so that students could discover many types of literature and find out on their own what they enjoyed. A few of the respondents experienced individualized reading classes during the 1960s and 1970s; they felt that they were enthusiastic about reading because they

were encouraged to read what they liked and because blocks of time
were set aside for them to do so. (pp. 149, 150)

Just as we improve our tennis game by practicing our serve and back-
hand frequently and learn to swim by practicing our strokes, students learn
to read by reading regularly. Athletes know that they cannot learn to be basketball players by practicing basketball only at school during physical education class. It takes hours of shooting baskets at hoops in the park or on the
driveway, hundreds of pickup games, and many opportunities to share the
sport with others who play well. Similarly, students become readers by reading every day in DEAR (Drop Everything and Read) or SSR (Sustained Silent Reading) time in school as well as in programs that also encourage and
support regular reading outside of school in books selected by students.
Time and choice are key elements of any school reading program.

The key to helping our students become lifelong readers who choose to
read for pleasure, and who love to bury themselves in books as I did as a
teen is to help them find the right books and then encourage a personal response to them. For many of our middle school students, as for many of us
who are professionals in the field of reading, these books are novels. Knowledgeable teachers can enthusiastically lead students to books they *can* and
will read if we are familiar with a wide range of titles.

Novelist Katherine Paterson (1988) tells the story of meeting a young
nonreader. In preparation for Paterson's visit to his school, the teacher read
her award-winning novel *The Great Gilly Hopkins* (1978) to the class. One
boy was enthralled with the story and stayed after her speech to talk to
Paterson. "How did you know Gilly?" he asked her. After a conversation
about the book with this student, Paterson learned that like her protagonist
Gilly, this boy was a foster child who had experienced serious trauma in his
young years. She sent him a copy of *The Great Gilly Hopkins* and sometime
later received a note from him. He told her that it was the first book he had
ever read himself. She suggested another title. Months afterwards he wrote
to tell her how much he had enjoyed the second book.

Like Paterson, if you can find the right book for the middle school students in your class, they will read the book. In addition, when they like a
book, they will ask for another one like it. As teachers, we must fill our
classrooms with books that will grab our students by speaking to their needs,
their concerns, and their dreams. Novels help us live our lives, face new
situations, understand ourselves and others better. Our own enthusiasm
about the world of literature can help immerse our students in reading. With
our encouragement and knowledge of novels we *can* light the spark for a
lifetime of reading.

References

Applebee, A. N. (1993). *Literature in the secondary school: Studies of curriculum and instruction in the United States*. Urbana, IL: National Council of Teachers of English.

Carlsen, G. R., & Sherrill, A. (1988). *Voices of readers: How we came to love books*. Urbana, IL: National Council of Teachers of English

Christian-Smith, L. (1990). *Becoming a woman through romance*. New York: Routledge.

Hipple, T. (1992). The universality of the young adult novel. In V. Monseau & G. Salvner (Eds.), *Reading their world: The young adult novel in the classroom* (pp. 3–16). Portsmouth, NH: Boynton/Cook.

Kaywell, J. (Ed.). (1993). *Adolescent literature as a compliment to the classics*. Norwood, MA: Christopher-Gordon.

Kaywell, J. (Ed.). (1995). *Adolescent literature as a compliment to the classics, volume 2*. Norwood, MA: Christopher-Gordon.

Kaywell, J. (Ed.). (1997). *Adolescent literature as a compliment to the classics, volume 3*. Norwood, MA: Christopher-Gordon.

Mitchell, D. (1996). If you can't beat 'em, join 'em. In *Teaching literature in middle school: Fiction*. Standards Consensus Series. Urbana, IL: National Council of Teachers of English

Morton, K. The story-telling animal. *New York Times Book Review,* Dec. 23, 1984, pp. 1–2.

Paterson, K. (1988). *Gates of Excellence*. New York: E. P. Dutton.

Probst, R. (1992). Writing from, of, and about literature. In N. Karolides (Ed.), *Reader response in the classroom*. New York: Longman.

Purves, A. C., Rogers, T., & Soter, A. (1995). *How porcupines make love: Readers, texts, cultures in the response-based literature classroom*. White Plains, NY: Longman.

Rochman, H. (1993). *Tales of love and terror*. Chicago, IL: American Library Association.

Samuels, B. (1982). *A national survey to determine the status of the young adult novel in the secondary school English classroom, grades 7-12*. Unpublished dissertation.

Samuels, B. (1989). Why do students "really like" particular books? *Journal of Reading, 32* (8).

Samuels, B. (1992). The young adult novel as transitional literature. In V. Monseau & G. Salvner (Eds.), *Reading their world: The young adult novel in the classroom*. Portsmouth, NH: Boynton/Cook.

Trade Books Cited

Adamson, J. (1960). *Born free: A lion in two worlds*. New York: Pantheon.

Arrick, F. (1981). *Chernowitz*. New York: Bradbury.

Avi. (1986). *Wolf rider*. New York: Collier/Macmillan.

Avi. (1991). *Nothing but the truth: A documentary novel*. New York: Orchard/Richard Jackson.

Barron, T. (1996). *The lost years of Merlin*. New York: Philomel.

Bennett, J. (1977). *The birthday murderer*. New York: Delacorte.

Bridgers, S. (1990). *All together now*. New York: Bantam.

Bridgers, S. (1993). *Keeping Christina*. New York: HarperCollins.

Bridgers, S. (1976). *Home before dark*. New York: Knopf.

Bronte, E. (1996). *Wuthering heights*. New York: Viking Penguin.

Brooks, B. (1984). *The moves make the man*. New York: Harper & Row.

Brooks, T. (1977). *Sword of Shannara*. New York: Ballantine.

Brooks, T. (1986). *Magic kingdom for sale: SOLD*. New York: Ballantine.

Cooney, C. (1994). *Driver's ed*. New York: Delacorte.

Cormier, R. (1995). *In the middle of the night*. New York: Delacorte.

Crutcher, C. (1983). *Running loose*. New York: Delacorte.

Crutcher, C. (1986). *Stotan*. New York: Bantam.

Crutcher, C. (1996). *Staying fat for Sarah Byrnes*. New York: Dell.

Davis, J. (1988). *Sex education*. New York: Orchard.

Dickens, C. (1963). *A Christmas carol*. New York: Airmont.

Dickens, C. (1861). *Great expectations*. New York: Macmillan.

Dickenson, P. (1988). *Eva*. New York: Bantam Doubleday Dell.

Duncan, L. (1976). *Summer of fear*. Boston, MA: Little Brown.

Duncan, L. (1978). *Killing Mr. Griffin*. Boston, MA: Little Brown.

Easton, P. H. (1988). *Summer's chance*. New York: Gulliver/Harcourt Brace.

Farmer, N. (1994). *The ear, the eye, and the arm*. New York: Orchard.

Frank, A. (1952). *Anne Frank: Diary of a young girl*. New York: Doubleday.

George, J. C. (1972). *Julie of the wolves*. New York: Harper & Row.

Glenn, M. (1986). *Class dismissed II*. New York: Clarion.

Greene, B. (1991). *The drowning of Stephan Jones*. New York: Bantam.

Guy, R. (1973). *The friends*. New York: Holt, Rinehart & Winston.

Hahn, M. D. (1993). *The wind blows backward*. New York: Clarion.

Haynes, B. (1994). *Deadly deception*. New York: Delacorte.

Henkes, K. (1995). *Protecting Marie*. New York: Greenwillow.

Hesse, K. (1994). *Phoenix rising*. New York: Puffin.

Hinton, S. E. (1967). *The outsiders*. New York: Dell.

Hinton, S. E. (1971). *That was then, this is now*. New York: Viking.

Hobbs, W. (1991). *Downriver*. New York: Atheneum.

Holman, F. (1974). *Slake's limbo*. New York: Scribner's.

Hughes, M. (1981). *Keeper of the Isis light*. New York: Atheneum.

Hughes, M. (1990). *Invitation to the game*. New York: Simon & Shuster.

Jacques, B. (1987). *Redwall*. New York: Philomel.

Kerr, M. E. (1984). *Him she loves?* New York: Harper.

Lasky, K. (1983). *Beyond the divide*. New York: Macmillan.

Lasky, K. (1984). *Prank*. New York: Macmillan.

Lee, H. (1960). *To kill a mockingbird*. New York: Lippincott.

Lipsyte, R. (1967). *The contender*. New York: Harper & Row.

London, J. (1903). *Call of the wild*. New York: Bantam.

Lowry, L. (1977). *A summer to die*. Boston, MA: Houghton Mifflin.

Lowry, L. (1989). *Number the stars*. Boston, MA: Houghton Mifflin.

Mazer, H., and N. F. Mazer (1989). *Heartbeat*. New York: Bantam.

McCaffrey, A. (1976). *Dragonsong*. New York: Atheneum.

McCaffrey, A. (1977). *Dragonsinger*. New York: Atheneum.

McCaffrey, A. (1979). *Dragondrums*. New York: Atheneum.

McKinley, R. (1982). *The blue sword*. New York: Greenwillow.

McKinley, R. (1985). *The hero and the crown*. New York: Greenwillow.

Naylor, P. R. (1992). *Shiloh*. New York: Dell/Yearling.

Nelson, O. T. (1977). *The girl who owned a city*. New York: Bantam.

Nixon, J. L. (1979). *The kidnapping of Christina Lattimore*. New York: Harcourt Brace Jovanovich.

O'Brien, R. (1975). *Z for Zachariah*. New York: Atheneum.

Orwell, G. (1981). *1984*. New York: New American Library.

Paterson, K. (1978). *The great Gilly Hopkins*. New York: HarperCollins.

Paulsen, G. (1987). *Hatchet*. New York: Bradbury.

Peck, R. (1981). *Close enough to touch*. New York: Delacorte.

Peck, R. (1985). *Remembering the good times*. New York: Delacorte.

Philbrick, R. (1993). *Freak the mighty*. New York: Scholastic.

Scieszka, J. (1991). *The time warp trio*. New York: Puffin.

Speare, E. G. (1983). *The sign of the beaver*. Boston, MA: Houghton Mifflin.

Spinelli, J. (1990). *Maniac Magee*. New York: HarperCollins.

Steinbeck, J. (1947). *The pearl*. New York: Viking.

Steinbeck, J. (1933). *The red pony*. New York: Bantam Books.

Taylor, M. (1976). *Roll of thunder, hear my cry*. New York: Dial.

Twain, M. (1976). *The adventures of Tom Sawyer*. New York: Scholastic/ Apple Classic.

Weaver, W. (1993). *Striking out*. New York: HarperCollins.

Wells, H. G. (1984). *The time machine*. New York: Bantam.

White, R. (1972). *Deathwatch*. New York: Doubleday.

Zindel, P. (1968). *The pigman*. New York: Harper.

Chapter 19
IT AIN'T ONLY IN
BOOKS ANY MORE

Ted Hipple and *Elizabeth Goza*

Think of literature in the middle school English classroom and you think of print: textbooks, novels, short story or poetry anthologies. There's nothing amiss in this perception. After all, print literature has dominated the middle school curriculum for as long—literally—as those middle schools existed. Students read Paulsen and Paterson, *Johnny Tremain* (Forbes, 1945) and *The Pearl* (Steinbeck, 1947), and they read them in print form. But, as the Bob Dylan song suggests, the times are changing.

In this essay we'd like to explore three of these changes and their potential for enriching the middle school literature curriculum: audiobooks (often referred to as "recorded books" or "books on tape"), comic or graphic literature, and CD-ROMs. Each of these, we think, can become a teacher's pedagogical ally, a different and exciting way of presenting literature.

Audiobooks

Rare is the person who does not like to be read to. Suggest, if you want, that this preference recalls the preschool days of our youth, when a parent or grandparent read *Green Eggs and Ham* to us. Or perhaps it's our awareness that much of what is on the car radio or the Sony Walkman that we plug in when we take our daily exercise is banal, pap, beneath, if not our dignity, then our attention. We want something else. For millions, audiobooks provide it.

Yet not many middle school teachers take advantage of this tool. Our experience suggests that not many of them are even aware that such books exist, an ignorance ironically inconsistent with their appreciation of other media. We'd like to change that lack of knowledge, believing that the use of audiobooks can improve literature teaching and learning and act as a bridge to print.

First of all, teachers need to know that the world of audiobooks is rapidly expanding as more and more people are becoming knowledgeable about them and regularly listening to them. Many public libraries have large and growing collections. Private rental operations dot the business landscape. Even national restaurant chains like Cracker Barrel now permit the renting of an audiobook at one location and its return at another, thus making the interstate drive far less boring. And schools are getting into the use of audiobooks, too, recognizing their usefulness with all kinds of students.

Almost always audiobooks are of high quality. Companies that produce them hire professional actors, for the most part, and carefully monitor their reading with what might be called "prooflistening skills" of a high order. Some audiotapes have multiple readers; some add music. But most simply echo grandpa and read to us—and we love it. (Curiously, authors themselves don't always make good readers. Many of them simply do not read well aloud, even when they are reading their own works. Others cannot stop editing and, even if the book is already in print, will pause to make marginal notations or corrections.)

When reading fiction, most readers vary pitch and tone and even pronunciations to distinguish characters. If the text suggests that a character, say, smokes so much that he has developed a smoker's cough, then the reader will probably cough on occasion. Plus, readers will vary the dialect to fit the region so that a character from Boston will sound different than say a character from Houston. In ways like this, the oral text is actually superior to the written one. Some readers get highly dramatic; others are more low key. Sally Darling's rendition of *To Kill a Mockingbird* captures fully the mature Scout remembering incidents from her childhood in rural Alabama and does so with the softest of southern accents imaginable. *Cry, the Beloved Country* is one of those novels possibly better heard than read in print form, if, that is, it is read well. And Maggie Soboil reads it well, making this difficult novel accessible even to middle school readers as she renders Paton's prose about South Africa into an almost poetic form.

Just as these two examples suggest, there are many audiobooks now available that will appeal to middle school students. Just a few of the titles:

The Adventures of Huckleberry Finn by M. Twain.

Athletic Shorts by C. Crutcher.

The Autobiography of Miss Jane Pitman by A. Gaines.

The Barn by Avi.

Beyond the Chocolate War by R. Cormier.

Captains Courageous by R. Kipling.

The Chocolate War by R. Cormier.

The Face in the Frost by J. Bellairs.

The Farthest Shore by U. LeGuin.

Flip-Flop Girl by K. Paterson.

Hatchet by G. Paulsen.

Heidi by J. Spyri.

The Hobbit by J. Tolkien.

Julie of the Wolves by J. George.

Kingdom by the Sea by R. Westall.

Let the Circle Be Unbroken by M. Taylor.

The Man Who Was Poe by Avi.

Nightjohn by G. Paulsen.

Number the Stars by L. Lowry.

The Outsiders by S. E. Hinton.

The Pigman by P. Zindel.

Shiloh by P. Naylor.

Silence of the Lambs by T. Harris.

The Skirt by G. Soto.

The Slave Dancer by P. Fox.

Summer of the Swans by B. Byars.

The Swiss Family Robinson by J. Wyss.

To Kill a Mockingbird by H. Lee.

Where the Red Fern Grows by W. Rawls.

White Fang by J. London.

Wolf Rider by Avi.

Zlata's Diary by Z. Filopovic.

This list, though longish, is by no means complete; in fact, it captures but a few of the titles that are in audiobook form. We include it to show the breadth of books available for classroom use in this format. Note its variety, too: classics like the Twain and London; many standard young adult literature pieces like those by Cormier, Zindel, Hinton, and Paulsen; foreign books like *Zlata's Diary*; and potboilers like *The Silence of the Lambs* that, in print form, may well be beyond the reading competence of young adolescents but are certainly within their listening ken. And more of all of these—the classics, the young adult novels, the foreign best-sellers, the potboilers, collections of short stories—are becoming available every day. Producers of audiobooks are, as we've noted above, tapping into an ever wider and wider reading audience and producing more and more books. Many of these will be valuable additions to the middle school language arts curriculum.

While teachers will naturally vary their uses of audiobooks, it may be useful to become methods-oriented for a bit. Simply letting kids listen to the stories may be the best bet. As Daniel Pennac (1994) argues so persuasively in his excellent book *Better Than Life*, being read to is such a joy that it ill behooves teachers or others to make too many demands on the listeners. We teacher types can, Pennac argues, trust the author and the reader to captivate our students, and we don't need to add our usual instructional demands for book reports or follow-up quizzes. Pennac writes, "A teacher who reads out loud lifts you to the level of books. He gives you the gift of reading!"

Later Pennac quotes Flannery O'Connor: "If teachers are in the habit of approaching a story as if it were a research problem for which any answer is believable so long as it is obscure, then I think students will never learn to enjoy fiction." She is, of course, talking about the classroom study of print literature, but her words are perhaps even more cautionary about audiobooks.

Using audiobooks to introduce students to print literature can be helpful. For many students reading a book, no matter what its size, is a daunting task. Some of these students actually *hear* better than they *read*; that is, they understand what they listen to better than they understand what they read. If they can listen to the opening several chapters and, by so doing, can get hooked on the book, the assignment to read on will be a more agreeable one.

Moreover, students can and should be listening to books that they may not be able to read on their own, books that are, in other words, too difficult in print. As Longfellow put it, narrators can "lend to the music of the poet the rhythm of their voice" and students can, in effect, listen beyond their reading capabilities. Vocabulary and sentence structures that they would not easily understand if they encountered them in print become manageable, and understandable, when met orally.

Audiobooks can and should be studied on their own, *qua* themselves, if you will. We can move beyond a discussion of the content to a discussion of the mode. Questions like the following can get students to recognize that audiobooks are a legitimate form of literature:

- Did you enjoy the reading?

- What made it enjoyable?
- Were the characters well presented?
- Is how the reader presented them how you would have presented them?
- Are there things about the recording you would change?

Audiobooks also facilitate group interactions, something middle school students enjoy, if not demand. Putting six or eight students near the tape player and letting them engage in common listening can generate a collegial enjoyment of the text. Literature takes on a communal appeal, much like the stories told round a campfire or passed from generation to generation in pre-print days. Allowing students to stop the recording at different points and respond to the content and the delivery not only helps comprehension, but also encourages students to "stay tuned."

We must gently demur on one pedagogical strategy, common though it is, and that's the reading-along-while-listening technique. We know that many teachers find this tactic useful in their classrooms, but reading and listening are best regarded, we think, as different skills, more alike than not, to be sure, but separate nonetheless, with neither the handmaiden of the other. Better it is, we believe, to let students listen when they listen, to read when they read.

Thus, we support fully having audiobooks in the classroom. And outside it, too. Young adolescents are seldom too far from their headphones and while we can never completely replace their loyalty to the contemporary top forty or the current rap scene, perhaps now and again a talking book will successfully vie for their attention.

Comic Books and Graphic Novels

Comic books in the classroom? Unconscionable! say many teachers, an abrogation of limited class time. Other teachers find them less objectionable, but still don't want to devote much schoolhouse attention to them, saying that students will read comics on their own and that time in the class should be spent on better—i.e., print—literature. We disagree.

Comics, we think, merit a place in the middle school curriculum. Stan Lee, an illustrator for Marvel Comics, comments that:

> . . . we're bombarded with visual images, television primarily, video games, and yet a kid will still read a comic book of his own volition. They enjoy the comics, and they begin to equate enjoyment with reading. The more they read comic books, the more they develop a facility for reading. The more their world opens up. (quoted in Henderson, p. 33)

We agree. Many language arts teachers experience a daily frustration in trying to get their students to read print literature, a frustration they might overcome if they permitted the use of comics in their classrooms.

Comics combine both pictures and words in ways that often capture readers' attention, the two forms of communication blending symbiotically with text enhancing illustration and illustration enhancing text. Further, comics ARE literature if one thinks of literature in terms of its elements—characters, setting, conflicts, and so on. The major difference pedagogically between "drawn" novels and written novels, for example, is the medium in which the teller tells the story. Comics do have a place in the classroom.

The term *comic books* usually refers to monthly or weekly serial comics, like *Superman*, *X-men*, and *Concrete*. Short in length (about 24 pages), these comic books often end in cliffhanger style, motivating readers to purchase the next issue. Their language is typically easy even for less-able readers and their subject matter usually is geared to a young male audience. Recently, however, comics have appeared that are directed to female and to older readers.

Classroom attention to comics can take on a variety of strategic forms. They can be studied as literature, with analyses of plot, character, and conflict resolutions. They can be studied as art (a legitimate activity, we believe, in an English class), with discussions of their illustrations. They can be studied as literature AND art, with attention to form and content. That they merit such examination may be defended with reference to the scholarship that recently has been done with comics, books like Eisner's *Comics and Sequential Art* (1995) and Harvey's *The Art of the Funnies* (1994). *Understanding Comics* by Scott McCloud (1993) is particularly useful for those who would use comics in the literature class. McCloud's main theme is that reading a comic book is a kind of literacy, one we should attend to. Further, his book is accessible to middle school readers themselves, as it is actually written as a comic book and explains concepts in visual form. Students will enjoy following the pictorial narrator through his adventures in learning about comic books. All three of these works take comics seriously.

The Pulitzer Prize Literature Selection Committee took comics seriously a few years ago when it awarded a "Special Pulitzer" to Art Spiegelman for his *Maus: A Survivor's Tale* (1990). *Maus* is a graphic novel, a distinctive nomenclature for single-issue works that, like novels in print, have beginnings, middles, and ends, a real and identifiable authorial presence, and a seriousness of intent beyond that usually found in comic books. *Maus*, actually a two-volume work, is Spiegelman's story of his father's experiences during the Holocaust and appeals to adults perhaps even more than to young adolescents, though its presentation—in comic form—renders it accessible to them. This is a serious work, meriting serious attention.

Other graphic novels include *The Hiding Place* (1990) by Boatner and Parkhouse, which blends fantasy and reality as a young boy finds himself in the land where extinct mythological characters go when they disappear. This delightful story has many classroom uses, even serving well as an companion piece to studies of mythology and folklore. *Foreign Exchange* (1994) by George Dardess is for older middle schoolers, but is a fine example of the art of the graphic novel.

Comic books and graphic novels can add a dimension to the middle school literature curriculum, but a caveat must be added to our recommendation. We have met teachers who do indeed use comic books and graphic novels, particularly the former, but only with the less able, the *non-readers* in their classroom. Whether these non-readers are those who cannot read or will not read, such literary works as comics and graphic novels are fine. These students will have their enjoyment of reading enhanced, their understanding of literature increased, their skills enlarged, and—who knows?—from such experiences they may well go on to print literature with greater confidence and ability.

But our caveat: Comics and graphic novels deserve to be put in the hands of the ablest students, too. They can benefit from reading these works and sensing their literary worth. They can develop and profit from having this different kind of literacy that McCloud describes. They can, in sum, become better readers of any literature—visual, aural, or print.

Said another way, it's the THAT of reading, not the WHAT of reading, that makes the most classroom sense. And both comic books and graphic novels belong in that THAT.

CD-ROMs

Today even the schoolhouse Luddites admit, albeit perhaps grudgingly, that computers are here to stay in education. Moreover, like the rest of us, they are quite willing to use the many benefits computers can confer upon a classroom—record keeping, word processing, creating graphic handouts, among other uses. And, more recently, teachers of middle school language arts courses are discovering another value of computers: CD-ROMs.

A CD-ROM is a piece of computer software somewhat like the more familiar musical compact disc. The CD-ROM contains a multitudinous amount of information, all of it to be accessed through a computer. CD-ROMs can contain up to a gigabyte of stored information, enough to hold large programs, including several at one time, pictures, books, and entertainment information. Full volume reference works can appear on one disc—a dictionary, a thesaurus, an atlas, an encyclopedia. One present (as we write) disadvantage of the CD-ROM is that it is "read only"; it cannot save work or have other programs fitted into it. But there is technology in the works that will permit CD-ROMs to have storage potential, thus adding even more to the many benefits they can provide teachers and students.

Perhaps the most valuable worth of CD-ROMs in the middle school language arts classroom is their capacity to help improve students' reading ability. Virtually all CD-ROMs require their users to read. Whether it is reading operating instructions, texts with pictures, or cues for further action, the student using a CD-ROM is constantly reading—and usually is doing so conscientiously, eagerly, and with enormous satisfaction. It is this satisfaction that provides motivation for further reading.

CD-ROMs can provide a teacher with a tool that will enable students of vastly differing abilities to have valuable learning experiences. For example, the Broderbund *Living Books* series, though designed primarily for elementary school students, are still sufficiently compelling to attract the attention of middle school readers and enable them to read and explore within a text. A student with greater reading abilities can move to Broderbund's *Alien Tales*, which feature an alien being (and what middle school student can resist an encounter with an alien?) who claims that his planet has authored many classics like *Charlotte's Web* and *Trumpet of the Swan*. It is up to the user—the student—to prove to the alien through quizzes and games that, in fact, humans have written the classics. Most of the titles in this series fall within a traditional middle school literature curriculum. Still more advanced readers can explore *Last Chance to See*, a Voyager CD-ROM, based on the book by Douglas Adams. This disc focuses on many of the last species of certain animals.

These kinds of discs are responsible learning tools. They demand involvement from student users and reward it. While students may regard CD-ROMs as fun and games, and that's all right in our judgment, demands for instructional accountability require that the teacher whose students are using these tools assure and demonstrate that learning is occurring. Teachers can tie CD-ROM use to several assessment techniques. Students can use learning logs 1) to record personal response to content of the CD-ROM, 2) to discuss the satisfaction/dissatisfaction from reading from a CD-ROM, and 3) to outline areas that need clarification. Or, teachers can use conferences, either with individuals or small groups, to determine what students are gleaning from their work with CD-ROMs and, of equal importance, how they view such work as an instructional activity. As we encourage students to think about their computer use as well as what they've learned from that use, we remind them that CD-ROM use in the classroom isn't a euphemism for *Keep Busy But This Doesn't Count*; instead, we show them that computer-assisted instruction is a valuable way to learn.

We know that we write of computers and CD-ROMs a bit at our peril, that our specifics are dated even before we print them out on our own computers. Both the hardware and the software of just a few years ago, so wonderfully imaginative then, is now bordering on the antique. So it is with CD-ROMs we recommend. Think of the writer whose paper is on print literature and who, therefore, can say that Wolff's *Make Lemonade* (1993) and Lowry's *The Giver* (1993) are excellent choices for classroom reading; she can be very secure in her recommendations, knowing that these outstanding books will be read for years to come. But we who treat of the fast-changing world of technology face very different sorts of life-expectancy considerations.

Our suggestions, then, must be understood in this context that by the time these words see the light, the light may have changed. But we do recommend these specific CD-ROMs: *Time Man of the Year* and *Time Almanac*. Both these discs contain articles from the magazine and enrich them with reading and research requirements so that students learn recent history and acquire reading skills at the same time. The BookWorm Student Library produces CD-ROMs somewhat like the audiobooks, though with print features, accompanying fine art, and even music. Students who have difficulty reading passages can click on the mouse and the troublesome passage will be read to them. Titles so far include classics like many of Shakespeare's plays and *The Adventures of Huckleberry Finn* and *Tom Sawyer*, works, especially Shakespeare, that may be too demanding for many middle school students, but stay tuned—the success of this relatively new company promises many more titles.

Subjects a bit tangential to language arts, perhaps, but useful in many literature lessons are commonly found on CD-ROMs. Microsoft Home's *Art Gallery* reproduces paintings from London's National Gallery, with background information on the painters, their techniques, and the periods in which they painted. Imagine asking students to look at a Constable painting while reading about King Arthur. The Voyager Company publishes, among many useful CD-ROMs, *Planetary Taxi*, which explains with compelling graphics and print the solar system. Think of the possibilities of getting writing from students who have encountered this disk.

And we can even tie CD-ROMs with the audiobooks and comics we mentioned earlier in this chapter. Spiegelman's *Maus* is on a CD-ROM. Many of the books in audiobook form are now available—or will be—on CD-ROMs. The field is exciting, it is growing, and it is useful. We recommend it.

Conclusion

And we can go beyond recommendation to an urging that our readers learn for themselves what we are talking about. Listen to a few audiobooks, we suggest. Note their high quality, their ability to capture your attention (indeed: be careful if you're listening while driving), their capacity to help you understand literature in ways different from those you experience in print literature.

Read some comic books and graphic novels. The comic books of our youth in decades recently or long past are themselves long past. New forms are more sophisticated, both their printed content and their illustrations. Just as some children's books captivate middle school readers—those by Jon Scieszka come instantly to mind in this connection—so also do some comic books and graphic novels make excellent choices for these readers, and not simply at home or on Friday afternoon when all the serious work is done, but as regular classroom assignments.

And, finally, pay attention to the business of CD-ROMs. If we had to pick one item of recent technology likely to change the content and the pedagogy of the middle school classroom, it would be CD-ROMs. Their use can open doors yet unimagined, can appeal to minds yet unchallenged. To be sure, for teachers unfamiliar with them or a bit frightened about employing them in their classrooms, the initial attempts may seem daunting. But—just think—not too long ago you feared your computer.

In sum, then, we advocate a somewhat different language arts curriculum. Traditionalists in our field recite, almost as litany, that the language arts in the middle school are reading, writing, listening, and speaking. But the emphasis always seems to be on the first two. We hope we have made a compelling case for attention to listening and to viewing, the former with audiobooks, the latter with comics, graphic novels, and CD-ROMs. Your classrooms will be the richer, we feel, the more exciting. And your students' learning will be the greater.

References

Diegmuller, K. (1995, May 3). Talking books pressed into classroom service. *Education Week, 14*, 6–7.

Eisner, W. (1995). *Comics and sequential art*. Tamarac, FL: Poorhouse Press.

Haremski, M. (1995, December). International video yearbooks. *English Journal, 84*, 82.

Harper, N. (1995, May/June). CD-ROM: Here and now. *Media and Methods, 31*, SE7.

Harvey, R. (1994). *The art of the funnies*. Jackson: University Press of Mississippi.

Henderson, C. (1995, January). Watch out, Little Lulu, here comes Mr. Sinister. *A & E Monthly, 11*, 32–34.

Hipple, T. (1995, Fall). It's not just in print anymore. *The ALAN Review, 20*, 43.

McCloud, S. (1993). *Understanding comics: The invisible art*. Northampton, MA: Kitchen Sink Press.

Novelli, J. (1994, July/August). Make your computer work harder for you. *Instructor, 104*, 108–112.

Roche, D. (1994, November/December). Cutting across the barriers of time with videodiscs and CD-ROMs. *Media and Methods, 31*, 73.

Truett, C. (1993, August/September). CD-ROM storybooks bring children's literature to life. *Computing Teacher, 21*, 20–21.

Wright, G., & Sherman, R. (1994, Spring). What is black and white and read all over? The funnies! *Reading Improvement, 31*, 37–48.

Zientarski, D. P., & Pottorff, D. D. (1994, June). Reading aloud to low achieving secondary students. *Reading Horizon, 35*, 44–51.

Trade Books Cited

Boatner, C., & Parkhouse, S. (1990). *The hiding place*. New York: Prianha Press.

Dardess, G. (1994). *Foreign exchange*. Rochester, NY: Austen Press.

Forbes, E. (1945). *Johnny Tremain*. Boston, MA: Houghton Mifflin.

Gonick, L. (1994). *The cartoon history of the universe*. New York: Doubleday.

Lowry, L. (1993). *The Giver*. New York: Dell.

Pennac, D. (1994). *Better than life*. Toronto, ONT: Coach House Press.

Spiegelman, A. (1990). *Maus: A survivor's tale*. New York: Pantheon Press.

Wolff, V. (1993). *Make lemonade*. New York: Scholastic.

Chapter 20
THE GENIE IN
THE COMPUTER

Elizabeth Stephens

Discovery

Vanessa removed the plastic cover that protected her new computer keyboard. The keys felt strange, not polished like the keys on her well-worn typewriter at home. There wasn't even any lint between the *q* and the *w* or the *o* and the *p*. School starts in three days. Her books were ready, her bulletin boards decorated, and first week's lessons plans finalized. Next week, she promised to herself, she will add the computer to her lesson plans somehow. Maybe. She has six computers in her room and had a 4-day workshop on using the computer during the summer. Now she sat in front of one silent machine wondering how she would work it into her teaching. She placed her hands on the keyboard and typed *h-e-l-p* slowly. Then she typed the letters quickly three times in caps and with no spaces.

As she entered the last *p*, the tiny life-indicating lights on the computer, the monitor, and the keyboard glared a bright chartreuse and a processing hum filled the empty room. Vanessa looked down on the keyboard wondering if she had hit a switch accidentally, yet she was sure that the keyboard switch of her new Macintosh was located on the far, far right corner of the keyboard—nowhere close to where her fingers had been pressing.

"You rang?" someone said in a deep, sonorous voice. Vanessa looked up at the monitor screen and saw a 6-inch cartoonlike figure of a bald, heavy-set man wearing a bright orange tunic and pointed green satin shoes.

"What would you like to know? The electronic age? Information revolution? Global community? Digital man? Virtual reality? Oooh, now there's a groovy one. Edutainment?" he said, twirling on one foot and gracefully waving his arms as he spoke. "I know it all. I see it all. I'm a connoisseur of the billboards of life—the TV, the newspapers, the magazines, the radio—I like the oldies stations, how 'bout you? Wanna dance later? I know what's just immediately ahead and what's coming up down the road—and it's oh-so-cooool. Now, what is your pleasure, hmmmm?"

Vanessa just stared at the screen, trying to make sense of it. She remembered seeing animation like this in the summer workshop, briefly, when she and the other teachers in her school learned about the CD-ROM. She looked down to the place where a CD-ROM is inserted and saw that the tiny light was lit. She tried to peek into it to see if there was a CD-ROM in there but could not tell, so she pressed the button and the carrier slid out. Empty.

"Hey!" the man yelled, startling Vanessa so that she jumped back in her seat. He walked up the screen, closer to it, so that only his face filled it and his big, brown eyes focused on her. "What'll it be?"

"Are you talking to m-m-me?" Vanessa finally said sheepishly.

"Yeah, you, Teach. What'll it be?"

"Who are you? Wha-what are you?"

"I'm the Genie in your computer, Teach, but you can call me Gene. You called me up—said you needed help, so I brought lots of it. Like I said, I know it all, I've seen it all—hey, you're not just teasing ol' genial Gene, are you? You've got a nice setup here. State-of-the-art stuff, as they say in Cyberland."

"A genie? Like a 3-wishes kind of genie?"

"Three wishes? Negative, Teach, you're talking to the Master of Multiplicity, the Prince of Preponderance, the Do-all Duke—you have much more than three wishes, and I have oceans of information to give. Look, do you really need me or did you just wanna dance to some oldies?" Gene snapped his fingers and began strutting away from the front of the screen singing an old '70s tune about a bullfrog.

"Wait." Vanessa rushed to the door of her room and closed it. She sat before the computer again. "I know I'm crazy doing this, but Gene, yes, I need help. I really need help."

Gene twirled twice and strutted back to the screen. "OK, Dorothy, Oz is on-line."

"Um, well, I need help figuring out how to use these things with my seventh graders. I had some training this summer, but I'm still not sure what to do. I mean, I have six computers in here and about 24 students. My principal really wants us to use them, and so do the parents."

"And so do the kiddos, right, Dorothy?"

"Yeah, that's the other thing. They know much more about these computers than I do!"

"Of course, Einstein-ette! They've got that techno-expertise. They're *Nintendo* babies. They're savvy little mouse-armed manipulators who are just as at home with bits, bytes, drives; and discs as they are with pens, pencils, paper, and posterboard. Give 'em a choice. They'll pick the computer every time. Ask them why. They'll say it's 'oh so coooool.' Hey, you've got their attention then, Queen of Sheba. It's what I call the Cool Quotient, or CQ. And you know, there are some things out there for this humming box that have high CQs."

"OK, OK. So what do I do? How do I start?"

Gene started singing a well known song about beginning something from *"The Sound of Music."* "What is your name, Teach?"

"Vanessa Campbell."

"Ah, Vanessa—means the butterfly. Did you know that a few butterflies, including the well-known monarch, may migrate thousands of kilometers to spend the winter in large aggregations at select sites? That's in *Encarta96* (Microsoft), a nifty CD-ROM encyclopedia with a really high CQ. Do you know 'bout multimedia? CD-ROM books? The Net? The Web?"

Vanessa nodded yes, then nodded no, and finally shrugged her shoulders.

"OK, Butterfly, let your wings catch this drift—we're going to migrate through some of the things you can do using this baby (tapping the screen) with your middle school scholars (pointing at Vanessa)."

Multimedia

The screen was filled with phrases—text, graphics, hypertext, hypermedia, animation, digitized video, digitized sound. The phrases were lit like neon signs that alternated between being lit and being dark. Colors were vibrant and there was music. A square that occupied the top right quarter of the screen seemed to open like a window, and Gene's face poked through.

"Boo! Like that music? 1972, voted number 1 oldies song in LA recently. Led Zeppelin's *Stairway to Heaven*. Do you reme—Nah. Let's talk multimedia. You've already made a Christmas list of activities using word processing programs and desktop publishers you tried this summer, right? Think of multimedia as laying a cellophane sheet over it that makes those projects change from one-dimensional to multi-dimensional."

Vanessa's eyebrows wrinkled.

"OK, Chrysalis Queen," said Gene. "Chrysalis—that's the case in which the caterpillar encloses itself before it emerges as a butterfly. I found that in—."

"I know. You found it in *Encarta96*."

"Nope, in the *Grolier Multimedia Encyclopedia*. The same, but different. Now, let me show you what multimedia means." The screen filled with a screen from *Imagination Express* (Edmark). Vanessa saw images of a place deep in a rainforest—fauna depicted in shades of emerald green, flowers in fluorescent reds and oranges, and animals in a rainbow of colors from the muted brown lepirs to the bright yellow and black toucan.

Gene's voice could be heard explaining that the buttons on the left margin of the screen link to a database of animal and people *stickers* that can be used to add to the scene. The stickers can be animated—that is, they'll move on the screen—and the student can record sounds that are linked to the sticker. The story or informational text is added directly on the screen by clicking on the Text tool. The Page Sound tool can be used to select or record sounds and narration for the page. The Fact Book button will take the student to pages of facts about the rain forest that can be woven into a story or added to a report. With the click of a button, the writer can move to the next *page* and continue the story, poem, or report. Once the project is completed, the illustrated book can be published. Of course, to see the vivid colors that were seen on the computer screen, a color printer is necessary.

"And you have one of those gems." Gene's face now replaced the rain forest scene and his hand was pointing to the right side of the screen toward the printer as it started its hum of life.

Gene continued, "There are several create-a-story types of multimedia programs for your inspection, Flutter Wings. There are also some multimedia programs that let you express your imaginative ideas in living color, sound, and motion. And your ideas become interactive. Know what that means? It means that you and anyone who uses what you create can be an *active participant*. That's fancy for saying that you don't have to—as a teacher friend once said to me—'just sit an' git.' You can click buttons and choose what you want to do or go where you want to go in the program." Gene told Vanessa about *hypertext*. He explained that anytime a button on a screen is *hot* or active, it can be clicked and more information appears on the screen or a whole new screen appears. He told her about programs that give students the tools to create their own programs with hot buttons, graphics, sound, and animation.

The printer churned and produced the vivid rain forest scene on paper. "It's just missing the story—your story, Shakespearella," Gene said.

"Or my students' stories. Wow, this is a great addition to the Green Earth Project. What an incentive to do research. After reading and finding the information they need, they can summarize, write a story, publish a book, and have others read and respond to the books in their journals. I see the multimedia in this, now, Gene, and how it encourages both reading and writing. They could create a multidimensional book that has—what did you call it, hypertext? I have a collection of books—novels and nonfiction—that they can choose to read. Books on the environment, like Laurence Pringle's environment books and novels like *Dogsong* (Paulsen, 1985). They might be more motivated to read if they create a multimedia project to showcase what

they learn. Yeah, hypertext, animated characters, recorded narrations, animal sounds—all interactive. And, not only will they be motivated to read, they'll develop communication skills, *and* organization and writing skills. They could even do this in partnership. A *collaborative* interactive book." Vanessa stopped abruptly. " This is getting complicated, Gene."

"Nothing an informed Monarch can't handle."

"Yeah."

CD-ROM Books

"But, Gene, when I thought of computers in my reading workshop, I thought my students would be reading computerized versions of the books we know. Is that what they'll do? Are there multimedia books like this? What are they like? What I really want to know is will it help them enjoy reading and read more?"

Gene stood in his genie pose and rubbed his chin. As he echoed a baritone "hhmmmm," titles of books, short stories, and poems scrolled on the screen beside him from the top down. The scrolling speed increased steadily—faster and faster until Vanessa could not make out the words. There were thousands of them! Then the list ended and Gene said, "Yep, I think there are a few literary works on CD-ROM. Like this one—." Gene held up a CD-ROM. "This is simply a little collection. You choose—would you like to look at Chinese books, Greek books, Indian readings, American readings, European readings, Asian readings, or world history? All in here." He tossed the CD-ROM to the left side and caught another one that flew in from the right side. "Are some multimedia? Sure. Lots. Most. Take the multimedia encyclopedias, for instance—."

"Oh, yes, *Encarta96* and *Grolier Multimedia Encyclopedia* that you've mentioned a few times."

"Bright, she is, she is. Think of it. What would your students say if you asked them to go look something up in an encyclopedia?" Vanessa opened her mouth to speak but before the first word was said, Gene answered, "Yuuuccckkk! You know that's what they're thinking, don't you? When they see the sounds, movies, animation, and automatic links in these encyclopedia productions, well, Wise One, try it and see for yourself."

She expected a visual tour of one such program, but instead Gerne reached behind his back with his other hand and pulled half-a-dozen discs that he held like a fan of playing cards. "There are the databases—on world records, on history, on the old west, on mythology, on ancient lands, on music—they include sound, animation, movies—get the multimedia picture?" He flipped the discs off to the side again and pulled a single one from his sleeve. "And there are the multimedia references. Everything you need—a thesaurus, a dictionary, an almanac, atlas, quotations, right there, in one little disc.

"Multimedia literature? Sure—rivers of it. Check out *The Adventures of Huckleberry Finn* CD (BookWorm). It is Electronic Mark Twain. Hard for those *Ninetendo* babies to figure out that colloquial stuff, huh? Well, I think Huck would have more trouble understanding *their* lingo! Ha! Anyway, that's no reason for your cyber-adventurers to miss out on the river adventures of Huck and Jim. Check this out." On the screen Vanessa saw a page from the book. The mouse arrow moved to different buttons to show how text is *hyperlinked* to graphics, audio recordings, movies, explanations, and references.

"Will they read more? Will they read better?" Gene said as his face rolled up the screen slowly. "I suppose we need to ask the researchers—." Gene told Vanessa about a study that set out to determine if reading scores and attitudes toward reading among middle school students improved when reading software combined with traditional books (Dixon, 1992). The researchers said the remedial reading students in the study did develop positive attitudes toward reading and did increase their reading scores.

He also told her about the research on *Accelerated Reader* (Advanced Learning Systems, Inc.), a reading computer management system. It is not a multimedia learning environment, but it does combine children's and young adult literature with software that tests the reader for comprehension and also manages records and keeps track of reading performance. Based on a point system, he explained, this structured reading program is designed to motivate readers and encourage them to read more challenging literature at an individual pace. The more challenging the book, the higher the points. Tests for more than 7,500 classic and current titles are available.

"Middle school kids showed improvement in reading scores, according to researchers in North Carolina (Peak & Dewalt, 1993)," he said. "You know, Vernal Voyager, there's not a profusion of research out there simply because schools, particularly middle schools, are just testing the waters and the technology is growing and transforming at warp speed. Perhaps you can help us all if you do some research of your own this year."

"Me? What can I do? This is just one little classroom."

"Ah, Worthy Whisperer, a famous scientist Edward Lorenz once asked, 'When a butterfly flaps its wings in Brazil, might it start a series of weather events that result in a tornado in Texas?'"

"Did you read that in *Encarta96* too?"

"Nope, I looked it up on the World Wide Web—oohhh, what you can read through the telephone line. . . ."

Things You Can Do With a Telephone Line

Gene sat down on what seemed to be an invisible plane. Then he lay down on his back and crossed his arms. He stared up as if gazing into the expanse of space, and he spoke in a solemn voice. His speech was different, formal, bordering on monotone. It was as if he had decided he was speaking to the world over a loudspeaker.

"We are close to a time when video, computer technology, and the telephone are merged into one. That is, we will be able to see and hear people and places anywhere in the world—and someday, perhaps, anywhere in our known universe. Tiny camera lenses mounted on computer monitors are allowing us to see as well as to hear each other on the computer as we communicate. Networks link writers in one room or scattered across states or nations—in real time, these writers can work collaboratively on the same document. In other words, all are seeing the same text on the screen and each is reading, commenting, adding, deleting, adjusting." He stopped and was silent for a few moments, still gazing as if in a trance. Vanessa just stared and waited for him to speak again.

"It's all happening very rapidly and although its potential is electrifying, it can become a confusing, out-of-reach reality. How much technology can a teacher use? That really depends on how much is available in the school and how much training and support is provided. Public schools are in many cases not structurally, financially, or emotionally prepared to undertake projects that would make use of this high-end technology. However, all schools have telephones, and that's the basic element needed to use much of the telecommunications technology. . . . Gotta talking machine, Flutter Wings?" Gene flipped his heavy body up to a standing position; his orange tunic shimmied and settled.

"Where did you find that information?" Vanessa asked.

"I told you, Wings, I know all. I see all. That came from little, genius Gene. Well, do you?"

"A talking machine, a phone? Yes."

"Yeah, I know. Just checking. You also have the modem, the software to run it and the kind of phone line that lets us access the World Wide Web—oh, oh, oh, so cooool. High CQ—really high. But let's start with the main vein, the telephone. That's technology, too, you know. And technology you've been able to work since you were tall enough to pull the receiver off the base and drive your young parents crazy!"

"Yeah, mom still tells those stories. . . . How'd you know that?" He shrugged his shoulders and smiled. "OK, so, tell me more, Gene."

"Your wish is my command—thought I'd never say that line, didn't you? Try this idea. . . ." Gene told Vanessa about setting up conferences with authors, experts, or others. Students can interview young adult author Gary Paulsen, for example, in a class session. Teleconferences are real reading motivators, Gene explained, and all the equipment needed is a speaker phone. Of course, there is much planning involved. He suggested that she read an article by R. Chance (1993) that tells about setting up a conference;

taping the experience; teaching etiquette, listening skills, and critical think-ing skills; and becoming motivated to read. Gene quoted Chance: "But best of all, the teleconference has created a community of learners who will be bursting with enthusiasm for an author or a scientist or a historian or a chef. And will it last? Yes. How will you know? You will know by the books the students choose and by the inquiries for more teleconferences."

Vanessa added the information to her notes. "This is terrific—I can't wait to start," she said.

"Wait, wait, wait, *wait*. We've just scratched the surface, Pilgrim. Let's explore more. Like to surf?" He immediately started to sing once again—this time about surfing.

"Beach Boys?" Vanessa suggested. The screen lit up like a TV game show and a flashing "YOU WIN" filled it. She heard applause and Gene in an announcer-like voice said, "Congratulations, contestant number one. Did you look that up in *Encarta96* . . . or on the Net? Heard of the Net?"

The Net

Of course Vanessa had heard of *the Net*. Who hasn't? The Information Highway is probably one of the best known thoroughfares in the country. When Gene asked her if she knew how to surf it, she almost apologetically said she did not.

"Hey, Tenderfoot, don't worry. That's why you called for me. I will tell you the whole Net story—well, maybe not the whole Net story because that could take 5 to 10 of my seconds . . . oh, that's a few hours of your time." Gene explained that the Internet is like the telephone system, except instead of people talking to each other directly by voice, people are using computers that communicate with each other by code. That is, the computer Vanessa is using can link up with a computer in Washington, DC, or a computer in Waikiki, Hawaii, or a computer in Haifa, Israel. Through the Internet, Vanessa could link up her computer with other computers—even huge main-frame computers—for different reasons: to write a message to a friend, to find information stored in a university or government database, to watch video clips, or to hear speeches or music.

"Everyone's heard of the Net," Gene said with a double twirl on one foot, "but it is not something that can be seen or easily understood. Allow yourself to draw a mental picture, my World Traveler. . . . Knowing about the Internet is like knowing about a foreign city like Buenos Aires or Paris. You know where it is and some of its famous landmarks, but you do not re-ally know how to get around *in* it. Until you actually go there, navigate your way around with a map, meet the people, taste the food, inhale the smells, etc., you will not really know it. So what do ya say, neo-Netizen—that's what Net users call themselves—wanna surf?"

"Uh, sure," Vanessa said, feeling quite unsure about this Net-thing de-spite Gene's attempt at simplifying it.

"OK, Brave Heart, imagine that you have entered the travel agency for the Internet. You've picked up brochures for two areas. There are others, but we'll stick with E-mail and the World Wide Web. Let's try out E-mail Land first," Gene said just as he disappeared in a puff of bright orange smoke and the screen went blank.

E-mail Land

"Your pilot today is Captain Gene D. Genie. Please make sure that your seat is in its full upright position as we prepare for takeoff," Vanessa heard Gene say. He suddenly appeared and trotted around the screen with his arms straight out beside him, pretending to be an airplane. He trotted completely off the screen, and Vanessa tried hopelessly to look into the sides of the screen as if the computer screen was a stage. Suddenly, Gene's face filled the entire screen, his big brown eyes sparkling almost as much as his bright white teeth. Startled, Vanessa once again jumped back into her chair.

"You've got to quit doing that, Gene," Vanessa said.

"I'm sorry, Flutter Wings. I just get carried away—get it, carried away?—with the thought of E-mail because E-mail is oh, sooo—."

"—coool, I know, oh, so cool," Vanessa shook her head and smiled. "So tell me about E-mail, Gene."

"Well, it's like this. E-mail means electronic mail," Gene began. He explained that an electronic message is sent from one computer to another. In order for both the sender of the message and the recipient of the message to communicate, each has to have an E-mail or Internet address. An address on the Internet is like an address at a home or post office except it is not a physical place in the same way. It is a location on a central computer that works like a post office. For example, teachers in Texas can get an Internet address on a network called Tenet. Tenet is housed in a big computer in Austin, Gene explained, adding that the computer is where messages arrive and are distributed to tens of thousands of Lone Star State subscribers who have Tenet *accounts*. There are hundreds of networks like this that service Internet users. There are several very large commercial ones for the general public.

"So once I have this account, how can E-mail help me or my students?" she asked.

"E-mailing messages to students is only one of the things you can do. You can contact your teacher buddies, and you can also contact teachers in other schools or states or countries. And your emerging scholars can contact emerging scholars all around the globe," Gene said waving his arms in a large circular motion. "They can start an E-exchange with E-pals and get them interested in books. Yes, books! Let me tell you about just one cool E-pal success story." Gene described a project called STOMP—Student

Teacher On-Line Mentoring Project (Lesesne, in press). At-risk junior high students were matched with student teachers at a university. For 15 weeks they communicated over E-mail and discussed two books selected and read by the junior high students. One of two books was written by Joan Lowery Nixon, who had accepted an invitation to participate in a teleconference with the young readers. An attitude test showed that the young readers had more positive attitudes about reading after this experience and several students went on to read more books by Nixon. The student teachers also gained from the experience; through E-mail, they had motivated these reluctant readers to read and had learned much about teaching and learning from the conversations.

"Sounds terrific, but Gene, tell me, how exactly will I get all of these E-mail addresses?"

"You know just the right questions to ask. OK, Cyber Queen, it's time to talk—," Gene raised his left arm up and a drum roll echoed through the classroom, "—The Web."

Web Talk

A multicolored Persian rug emerged from the front of the screen. Gene hopped on it facing away from Vanessa and sat crossed-legged. "Let's take a magic carpet ride to the Web," he said. The rug carried Gene away as he sang a '70s song about a captain and his mystery ship. His image became smaller and smaller and his voice fainter and fainter as he traveled to some distant point. When he seemed to disappear, Vanessa saw a silver screen with buttons along the top and a small square in the right corner with a white letter "N" sitting on top of a dark sphere.

"This is Netscape Navigator," Gene said from somewhere behind the screen. "It's a software program that will let you *crawl* along the World Wide Web (WWW)." Gene explained the concept of the WWW as well as a genie could. He said it functions on the Internet like E-mail, only it is not strictly text-based. On the Web, the Websters (what Web users are sometimes called) can see graphics and/or video images and hear sound. He explained that there are *Web sites*, places with addresses just like there are people with E-mail addresses.

Anyone can have a *home page* on the Web. There are countless sites right now that belong to individuals, schools, universities, organizations, businesses, and government agencies. And there are *search engines* that help you navigate your way through all of these.

"Watch this," Gene said as he appeared on the silver screen, still seated on his carpet. He reached up toward the top of the screen and pressed the button that said "Net Search" on it. The white letter "N" in the small box was suddenly surrounded by bright white asteroid-like objects that shot from the top right corner to the bottom left corner. Vanessa was fascinated with this logo.

"And as long as the asteroids are flying, Netscape's search engine is traveling the globe searching for information for you." Gene's image was reduced to about a half-inch size, and Vanessa saw a white box with the familiar "I" beam blinking within it.

"Type in 'middle schools' in the white box," Gene suggested. Vanessa did so and the asteroids whizzed by for a longer time than before. They finally stopped and on the screen was a message that her search for "middle schools" resulted in over 100 'hits' or entries. Hong Kong Pui Ching Middle School, Birdville ISD Middle Schools (seven of them), original music pieces from middle school students—a variety of sites were on the list. Anything on the Web that had the words "middle school" in its title was retrieved.

Gene let Vanessa peruse the list and then suggested that she click on one Web site called Cyberspace Middle School. This site's home page said it is "designed for all middle school websters to explore and learn how to crawl around the Web judiciously." Vanessa was fascinated. As she studied the other pages in this site, she found out that Cyberspace Middle School grew out of a 1994 summer program for middle school teachers called Science Feat. The goal of this Web site, she read, "is to provide a concentrated source of information and activities for middle school children and educators within the World Wide Web."

"Try searching for young adult literature," Gene said from somewhere behind the Netscape screen. Vanessa typed in the three words and pressed "Enter." In a few moments she received a listing similar to the one she'd received when she'd typed in "middle schools." This time, the long list of entries had to do with children's books, young adult literature, published writers, illustrators, book awards, works by African American writers, and more.

One in particular caught her attention: the Children's Literature Web Guide. It said this site had information on conferences, book events, book awards, recommended books and best-sellers, on-line children's stories, authors and illustrators, movies/TV based on children's books, and resources (for parents, teachers, storytellers, and writers/illustrators). She found a spot that had information on current and upcoming films based on young adult literature.

Vanessa reached for her spiral notebook to jot down notes about how to use the Web sites she'd seen so far in her teaching, but stopped suddenly. "Gene, how can I get back to this site easily?" No answer. "Gene? GENE!" she yelled.

"Ooops, sorry, Wily Webster," Gene said as he appeared on the screen, rubbing his eyes. "Just thought I'd snooze a bit while you Web-ed. Let's see, how to return? Not a problem for a nimble one like you. See the top bar? See Bookmarks? Just use that command to mark the page you are on. From then on, anytime you use Netscape, you can view the bookmarks and go to that page faster than a Concorde carpet. But, hey, now that you've disturbed my REMs, allow me to suggest some places with astronomical CQs to bookmark. You've seen some that you, Teach, will like. Here's some your kiddos will like." Gene disappeared and Vanessa saw the bright, cheerful home page for KidPub. She could hear Gene singing an old Beatles tune about a paperback writer.

Figure 20.1   Cyberspace Middle School

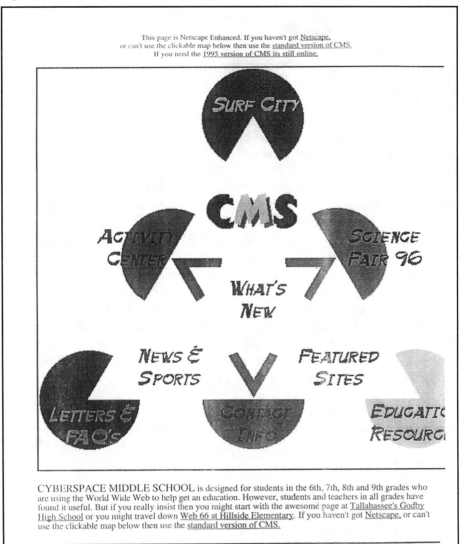

This page is Netscape Enhanced. If you haven't got Netscape, or can't use the clickable map below then use the standard version of CMS. If you need the 1995 version of CMS its still online.

CYBERSPACE MIDDLE SCHOOL is designed for students in the 6th, 7th, 8th and 9th grades who are using the World Wide Web to help get an education. However, students and teachers in all grades have found it useful. But if you really insist then you might start with the awesome page at Tallahassee's Godby High School or you might travel down Web 66 at Hillside Elementary. If you haven't got Netscape, or can't use the clickable map below then use the standard version of CMS.

Special announcements:

KidPub, she found, is a place on the Web where kids can send their writing to be published. There were more than 250 stories and poems available to be read—all written by kids! She chose one story called "The Longest Word" by Erin Chamberlain, age 12, of Canada. She really enjoyed it, so she read "My Worst Experience With a Vegetable" by Sami Sanger, age 14, of Iowa next. Then she read another and another . . . and another.

Figure 20.2   Children's Literature Web Guide

The Children's Literature Web Guide: An Introduction

HOME ~ SEARCH ~ EMAIL ~ STATISTICS

The Children's Literature Web Guide is an attempt to gather together and categorize the growing number of Internet resources related to books for Children and Young Adults. Most of the information that you can find through these pages is provided by others: fans, schools, libraries, and commercial enterprises involved in the book world.

My contribution, besides pulling all these sites together, is to compile book awards lists from a variety of print sources, and from Internet "sources' who generously post news of recent winners to discussion groups, or e-mail me directly (I don't actually decide who wins the book awards. Sorry!).

And, because the film industry seems to have embraced the World-Wide Web in a big way, and because I love movies and movie reviews, I also collect what information I can about movies based on children's books.

I usually find out about the sites I list when their creators tell me about them, or when I see a notice about them on a newsgroup, or one of the major Web Indexes or "What's New" lists. I take quite a thorough look at each site before I list it, so that I can try to describe it in a sentence or two.

Judging from the e-mail I receive, my audience is made up of teachers, librarians, parents, book professionals (writers, editors, booksellers and storytellers), and kids.

My Press Clippings

The Children's Literature Web Guide has received favorable reviews from a number of sources, including The Whole Internet Catalog, Family Planet, and The McKinley Group.

According to The Point Survey, this site is in the top 5% of the Web. I'm not sure what that means, but they gave me a very nice review anyway.

The Children's Literature Web Guide is also proud to be *Clearinghouse* approved. The Clearinghouse for Subject Oriented Internet Resource Guides has included this site in its guide to the guides. If you are looking for something that is "like" the Children's Literature Web Guide, but in another subject, check out the Clearinghouse. You'll be amazed. Of course, none of us are really alike, but we are all trying to do similar things in our respective disciplines.

Who is David K. Brown?

And why is he doing this?

My official title in my Real Job is Director, Doucette Library of Teaching Resources. I am a Librarian with several years of experience in children's materials and educational resources. I work in a Faculty of Education, and an important part of my mandate, as I see it, is to promote both Children's Literature and (in recent years), electronic sources of information such as the Internet. Since children's books and computer technology are both things I love, this is not an onerous task.

I have also recently become Review Coordinator of Canadian Internet Resources for a new Canadian reviewing journal, *Resource Links*. I hope, through that print medium, to make more people aware of the

"Gene, what a great place to have my students' work published! And I know they'll be excited about reading what kids in other schools are writing. This certainly gives the publishing component of the writing process a new definition!"

"Yep," Gene responded. "I thought you'd like this. And don't forget that they'll be reading these cyber-stories. Have you got to the part where you see the counter that lists at the bottom of each story just how many times it has been read since it was posted? Wouldn't you love to know how many times something you've written is read? Did you happen to notice how many times the page you're perusing has been perused by other perusees? Almost 10,000 times as of today! And if you go to the stats page, you'll see

Figure 20.3   KidPub Home Page

You are visitor number 107025!

Welcome to KidPub!

Happy birthday, KidPub! One year old this month!

- Newest Stories
- Older stories (but goodies!):
    - Volume 5: January 96
    - Volume 4: October to December 95
    - Volume 3: September to October 95
    - Volume 2: July to August 95
    - Volume 1: February to July 95
- Search all KidPub stories
- KidPub Schools: Where classes publish their writing
- Gary and Liz at Gateway Mansion: A KidPub collaboration
- Questions and Answers: Common questions about KidPub
- The Story Form: Use this handy form to submit a story...just fill in the blanks!
- How to Publish *Your* Story: A more detailed description of how to send stories to KidPub
- Statistics: How many stories are read each day? Where do our readers live?

To submit a story, just mail it to KidPub@en-garde.com or use the handy form.

Current time at KidPub is: Thu Feb 15 12:33:55 EST 1996

that Perry Donham, the creator of KidPub, has tabulated the number of files and their locations. Take note: Austria, Brazil, Spain, Greece, Hong Kong, Iceland, Kuwait, Singapore, Slovenia, South Africa. A writer on KidPub has an *international* audience. Who read your kids' works last year? You, the kids in the class, Mom and Dad, Grandma, Grandpa—you get the global picture, right?"

"You know, Gene, this is oh, so coooool." Gene was silent momentarily, and Vanessa could only imagine his reaction since she could not see his face. Then she saw his hand zip into the screen overlaid on the Netscape screen. He made a thumbs-up sign and simultaneously said, "Awwwllll-riiiight!"

"Hey," Gene's face was on the screen again. "Had any YAM and 'zine, lately?"

"Huh?"

"Shadow is a 'zine and YAM is the Young Author's Magazine. It's actually a 'zine, too."

"Oh, I get it. Maga-'zine."

"Yep, only on the Web it's an electronic magazine or an 'E-zine.'"

"So let's go, E-gene," Vanessa said, and almost immediately the screen showed the home page of *Shadow—The Fiction 'Zine for Teens.* She read that *Shadow* is an electronic magazine produced on a quarterly basis. It focuses on the young adult population, but the editors invite readers of all ages. Within the "pages" of *Shadow*, she found articles, graphics, and fiction stories.

In his introductory letter, *Shadow's* editor Brian P. Murphy explains that *Shadow* was created "with the sole intent of producing a publication with quality literature that will be appealing to the young adult market." The goal of *Shadow,* it said is "to provide our own slice of literature which we hope may pass as more than just a *fast read.*"

Three fiction pieces were in this issue, and Vanessa saw a brief description of each one in the table of contents at the beginning of the issue. There was also one non-fiction article and short bios on all the authors.

Gene was quiet and Vanessa was glad. She enjoyed having the time to read the piece titled "A Rose" by Margaret Yang in peace. The blurb on it said "Mab Callahan is sick and tired of her first name. Nobody is named Mab. She desperately wants to legally change her name, but the tradition rooted so deeply within her mother seems to be an impassable barrier." Just as soon as Vanessa had read the last line of the story, the screen began to dissolve and then it lit up again showing Gene standing in his cross-armed genie pose. "What'd you think?" he asked.

"Great—this is certainly one I'll recommend to my students this semester."

Gene smiled, waved his arm and said, "Heeeeerrrreeee'sss YAM!" His image was replaced instantly with the graphically sophisticated home page screen of Young Author's Magazine or YAM.

From backstage, Gene explained that YAM is a printed magazine only it's online, too. "I'll let you browse through it on your own," he said and signed off for awhile.

"Have a good nap, Gene!" she answered.

One of the first things Vanessa read was that YAM is "a forum for kids to speak out and express their feelings" and "When they (kids) see their work in print, their self-esteem is strengthened, their anger is refocused, and their problems and personal situations become less threatening."

She read about the three anthologies that feature poems and short stories written by K-12 students for young readers. *YAM*, the classroom anthology is the oldest; the *Showcase Anthology* is the feature anthology, and it is available as a single issue publication through bookstores; and the *Magic Pens* is the electronic anthology that is published bimonthly throughout the year.

YAM also provides The WebLINK Center, a list of locations on the Web that contains information of interest to educators. Here Vanessa found that she could click on a button and link to a Web site called The Discovery Channel Community—educational programs and resources. She could also link to home pages of public and private school programs on the Internet and to educational sites for lesson plans like *The World of Benjamin Franklin* or *Sea World*.

"Wow. Gene, wake up. Thanks for the 'zine and YAM introductions. High CQ ratings, definitely."

The screen changed and it now showed Gene resting peacefully on a hammock suspended on each side by a palm tree. A small radio on the ground was playing Simon and Garfunkel's song about a bridge and troubled water. He was snoring loudly and as he inhaled, the trees would bend down toward him, and then they would straighten back up as he exhaled. She did not want to disturb him. A large dream bubble appeared above him—the kind you would see in a cartoon or comic strip. Inside it she saw these words emerge: "*MidLink Magazine:* The Electronic Magazine for Kids in the Middle Grades—another cool Web site—it won the Global Network Navigator, Inc. Best of the Net Award." The message disappeared and in its place appeared "*Young Adult Reading*: Lists and reviews of young adult literature suitable for teenagers and one kid-written story is featured each month—another cool Web site." Then she saw "*The Dream Machine*, a super-cool Web site featuring the popular Roger Davidson, a 16-year-old Teen Movie Critic; a place to publish original poetry; and *Education Resources,* a plain vanilla listing of various sites of interest to teachers—a very cool Web site." This, too, disappeared and was replaced with "Thought I was sleeping, didn't you?"

"GENE!" Vanessa yelled. She startled him so that he flipped off the hammock and fell belly-first. In a second he was on his feet and the hammock, trees, and radio disappeared.

"I thought you'd never get off that computer, Web-Woman," Gene gently chided. "You've migrated in admirable Monarch style—and I think you can conceptualize the size of this information highway. Your budding scholars can type in *any* topic in that white box and travel the Web, like you did, and read, read, read! There is one more jewel I'd like to show you—." The screen now showed a red, white, and blue highway sign with *Web 66* on it. A large headline read "*Web66*: A K12 World Wide Web Project" and below it was the following: "Route 66. It conjures up all kinds of images. Route 66.

Figure 20.4   Midlink Magazine Home Page

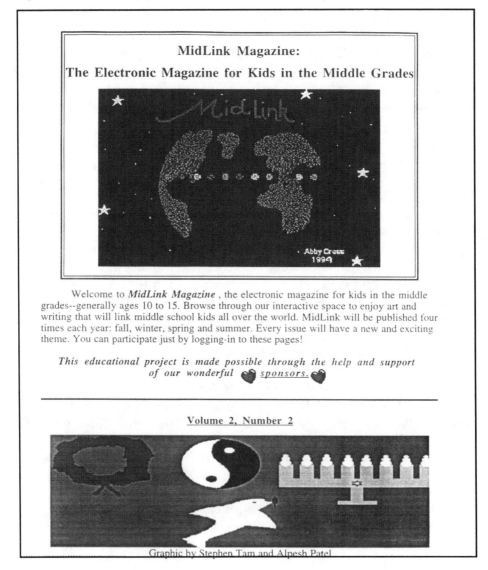

An artery linking much of the nation. Route 66. An inspiration to literature, music, drama, art, and a nation of dreamers. Route 66. A highway fashioned from vision and ingenuity. Route 66. It has forever meant 'going somewhere'.—Michael Wallis, Route 66: The Mother Road."

"How clever," Vanessa said. "This is the Route 66 of the Information Highway." Several links were listed on the home page and they were categorized under Education, Technology, and WWW Information. Vanessa explored the first listing and found an international registry of K-12 schools on the Web.

On the Web66 Technology list, she saw that she could read about how to set up a classroom Internet server in the Internet Server Cookbook. It gives recipes with step-by-step instructions.

"Ooops, I need more experience to do this, Gene."

"There's help and support, Web Hiker," she heard him respond. "See that *Web66 Mailing List*? That's an E-mail discussion group of teachers like you who are using or who plan to use the Web servers in their schools to get kids excited about reading and writing. You can share questions, problems, ideas and successes in there. And you will have successes."

The Questions

Vanessa leaned back on her chair and took a long deep breath. She stared at the computer as if she was sizing it up. "How do I keep up with all the new stuff? How do I know what software is good and what isn't?"

Gene interrupted, "—and does multimedia de-emphasize reading and writing? And will computers replace books? And will we not need schools or teachers anymore? You know, Brilliant Butterfly, my buddy Albert Einstein once said that knowledge is like a circle with questions side by side extending out from the circle's circumference. Each time a question is answered, more questions are created and the circle of knowledge grows bigger and bigger. I know that's true because in all my centuries of helping the literacy-perplexed, I have found that new innovations—the alphabet, the stylus, the printing press, the typewriter, and now the computer—come with huge families of questions. And the circle keeps growing."

"Here's some advice from a lover of the oldies. Know your curriculum. Know your teaching style. Know your students' learning styles and interests. *Then* use the electronic tools to enhance all of those things. Stay informed. And always—ask the questions." Gene took his Genie stance once again, his stately cross-armed figure filling the screen. Vanessa sensed his visit was coming to its closure, and although she was exhausted from her intensive morning *migration*, she was saddened by its conclusion.

"I suppose you're headed on another call, Gene."

"Yep, Magnificent Mentor. I'll know you in Cyberspace—," Gene said, and he twirled on one foot, began singing the same '70s tune he was singing when he arrived. Then he disappeared in an orange puff. Instantly, the printer began delivering sheet after sheet. Vanessa reached for the first one, and at the top it read *1,000 High CQ Sources for the Electronic Middle School Language Arts Classroom.*

References

Chance, R. (1993). Teleconferencing: An overlook technological approach to learning. *Emergency-Librarian, 21,* 20–23.

Dixon, G. O. (1992). The integration of computer software with printed materials to enhance the reading skills of middle school students. Practicum Paper ED350-560.

Encarta96 [CD-ROM]. (1996).

Grolier Multimedia Encyclopedia [CD-ROM]. (1996).

Huckleberry Finn [CD-ROM]. (1994). Knoxville, TN: BookWorm.

Imagination Express [CD-ROM]. (1995). Edmark.

Lesesne, T. (in press). Student teacher on-line mentoring project: Bringing readers on line. *English in Texas.*

Paulsen, G. (1988). *Dogsong.* New York: Bradbury Press.

Peak, J., & Dewalt, M. S. (1993). The effects of the computerized accelerated reader program on reading achievement. Paper presented at the annual meeting of the Eastern Education Research Association.

Netscape Navigator [Computer Software]. (1996).

WWW Sites Cited

Birdland ISD Middle Schools - http://www.birdville.k12.tx.us

Children's Literature Web Guide - http://www.ucalgary.ca

Cyberspace Middle School - http://www.scri.fsu.edu

Hong Kong Pui Ching Middle School - http://www.cs.cuhk.hk

KidPub - http://www.en-garde.com

MidLink Magazine: The Electronic Magazine for Kids in the Middle Grades - http://longwood.cs.ucf.edu

Shadow: The Fiction 'Zine for Teens - http://grimmy.santarosa.edu

The Dream Machine - http://www.dreamagic.com

Webb66: A K12 World Wide Web Project - http://web66.coled.umn.edu

Young Author's Magazine - http://www.yam.regulus.com

Young Adult Reading - http://www.docker.com

For a copy of Vanessa's list, write or E-mail L. Stephens.
Southwest Texas State University
School of Education
San Marcos, TX 78666
E-mail: LCS@tenet.edu

A Focus on Teachers

Chapter 21

HONORING TEACHER VOICES THROUGH PROFESSIONAL CONVERSATIONS

Carol A. Pope and *Karen S. Kutiper*

> In a recent computer usage course, the trainer ignored the fact that he
> had a room full of middle school language arts teachers and gave us a
> generic exercise for a spreadsheet that walked us though calculating
> the bill at "Harry's Hamburger Heaven." It had no application to my
> job, nor did he explain anything about the theory or concepts of what
> we were doing. (*Lea*)

When teachers walk away from a day of staff development like the one
Lea describes above, the most valuable and enjoyable part of the day may be
the time spent eating lunch with colleagues. Conversations during these
gatherings often focus on the content of the presentation or workshop they
just left or on everyday teaching situations. They express concerns, share
ideas, and pose questions in a comfortable collegial setting.

In contrast to these professional conversations, the hours these same
teachers spend in the planned staff development day often lack the ingredients Nancie Atwell (1987) describes as necessary for our middle school
youngsters to develop and hone their literary skills—time, ownership/
choice, and response. One day or half-day presentations can only catch the
attention of the educator if the presenters are dynamic or the new ideas are
appealing. Even on a day when teachers can select from a menu of choices,
the offerings are typically planned by someone distant from the teacher's
classroom and based on broader instructional issues than one teacher's individual needs. Time to grapple with new ideas is left to chance.

> I've been to some awful sessions where I've been lectured to for three
> to five hours with overheads, a dog, and a pony. (*Virginia*)

In the sessions Virginia describes above the time is probably wasted, but whole-group staff development sessions do not have to be all bad. The outside expert or in-district expert may be knowledgeable, entertaining, and focused on real needs of teachers. For example, middle school literacy teachers, eager to learn about new young adult books they can use in reading and writing workshop classrooms, eagerly take notes when the university expert shares new titles. Teacher anticipation builds. Yet with no opportunity to read, to discuss, and to revamp existing curriculum, many teachers forge ahead using the same texts from past years. They are not disappointed with the presentation, but few lasting outcomes occur. According to Jenelle, the best staff development criteria she describes below have not been met.

> Staff development works best if it has some time to evolve. The
> participants need time to incorporate and try out new ideas in their
> classrooms. This (time) serves to increase retention and prevent
> overwhelming the participants with so much new material they will
> just shelve it all.

Traditional vs. Current Views of Staff Development

Recent educational publications, journals, and conferences are not complete without some reference to the constructivist approach to learning. Learners, over time, actively construct and maintain their own knowledge and understandings through ongoing reflection and interaction within the classroom community. As the knowledgeable experts in the classrooms, teachers structure appropriate experiences to support student learning.

As philosophies and views of middle school reading/language arts classroom instruction have changed to a more social constructivist approach, so too have philosophies and views of staff development. No longer do we view teaching or professional development from a deficiency perspective. Students are not empty vessels waiting to be filled by their teachers, and neither are teachers naive, unknowing novices waiting to be enlightened by outside experts. Because we acknowledge that both middle school readers and adult learners have much experience and prior knowledge to bring to their own learning, we view both learning and professional development as a life-long endeavor that builds on learners' existing foundations. The simple syntactical shift from statement ("These students and teachers) don't know . . ." to question ("What do these students (or teachers) know/want to know . . . ?") represents a shift in thinking that successful staff development initiatives reflect.

> The best experiences . . . have been when I was challenged to grow
> beyond my then-current level, to look at things in new ways. I was not

> treated like I was stupid or somehow limited, but was expected to read
> and discuss, achieve and assimilate new concepts on angles at a very
> high level. (*Lea*)

We can speak from some authority, and not a little guilt, in this area. At different times in our careers we have not only been seduced into serving school systems as outside experts invited to enlighten the masses but also have served as system-level coordinators charged with contracting so-called experts to come *do inservice*. While these inservice events may occasionally inspire or affirm a few participants, we are convinced that the long-term impact is minimal. Rather the traditional one-visit inservice may actually alienate rather than support teachers.

We have also learned that, unlike our bank machines where we can immediately get cash or remedy our out-of-money condition, there exists no such parallel with just-in-time inservice. No one speaker or presenter is going to remedy the existing condition in a school or system. Of course, we have all heard inspiring presenters who make us think, who make us want to read further, who entertain, inform, and stimulate us to learn more. However, it is not the speaker alone who has the impact; it is rather the individual or group follow-through that makes a difference. Just as the learners in Nancie Atwell's middle school reading/writing workshop need time, ownership, and response, their teachers also need time, ownership, and response. They need *time* to question, consider, experiment, and reconsider; they need *ownership* of the staff development content and process; and they need *response* both from themselves and others as they change, develop, and grow as professionals.

Our participation in such nationally recognized staff development initiatives as the National Writing Project, Literature Institutes, Accelerated Schools Projects, collegial coaching, and long-standing teacher-researcher groups has confirmed for us that transformative learning and growing experiences occur not by chance but by careful thinking, planning, and building on participants' needs, questions, knowledge, and experiences. These no-longer iconoclastic models of staff development emphasize the importance of invitational processes, teacher-driven inquiry and initiatives, active participation and involvement, questioning and reflection over time, an open, trusting environment, extensive follow-up and follow-through.

In recognition of these needs of learners and of teachers as well as inservice providers, the National Council of Teachers of English (NCTE) Conference on English Education (CEE), through its Commission on Inservice Education, developed and published in 1994 a set of ten principles that serve not only to guide inservice providers but also to offer teachers participating in inservice education programs a way of viewing their own professional growth. These principles affirm that teachers, like any learner, "grow professionally through reflective practice" over time and that "teachers, like other professionals, build new knowledge and revise current beliefs through experiences, reading, discussion, reflection, and interaction with colleagues." (See Figure 21.1.)

Figure 21.1   Inservice Education: Ten Principles

CEE Commission on Inservice Education	
Principle One: Reflective Practice	Principle Six: Sufficient Time
Principle Two: Ownership	Principle Seven: Administrative Collaboration
Principle Three: Theorized Practice	Principle Eight: School-Community Partnerships
Principle Four: Collaboration	Principle Nine: Pluralism and Democracy
Principle Five: Agency	Principle Ten: Explicit and Tangible Support
English Education, **Volume 26, No. 2, May 1994**	

A number of local projects, aware of both the national initiatives and the CEE inservice principles, have evolved around the world. One such project is a group of middle school teacher-researchers in North Carolina who have been meeting monthly for 6 years. The PAL (Power and Literacy Through Speaking and Writing) group began in 1990 as a summer institute that focused on the reading/writing workshop as a viable alternative for middle school students often considered at-risk of academic failure. When recently questioned about the value of this long-term professional development experience, the teachers offered some revealing responses, ones which clearly coalesce with the CEE Principles and successful national staff development projects.

> (PAL) has been a fellowship group . . . one that hasn't been part of me since early in my life. Therefore, the group isn't centered around my family or knowing my children. Rather it's centered around who *I* am, *my* job, *my* interests, *my* concerns. That's important to me. (*Joyce*)

> I think the most important feature of our group is our community and our commitment to do our best for our collective students. Community, however, can't be spread. You need an investment over time. (*Virginia*)

The principles of time and ownership are prevalent in these comments. Virginia speaks of how important it is that the PAL teachers have made this "investment" of time as well as commitment, while Joyce acknowledges that she feels a special ownership of this experience because it focuses on her own professional interests and concerns.

For Joyce and for other PAL teachers it is not only time and ownership that are necessary. They find that the collaboration with other professionals is crucial.

> PAL has provided a sense of community and a forum. Teaching can be a lonely profession. It is good to be among dedicated professionals. (*Shirley*)

This sense of *belonging*, of being part of a community, frees the PAL teachers to explore openly with others, without recrimination, their own challenges in teaching, the areas in which they do not feel they are being successful. Never a meeting passes that several members do not have specific questions about their teaching. Through a process of questioning and talk, they identify and clarify the issues, brainstorm a number of possible responses, and problem-solve the dilemmas together. This part of the meeting is the one most often requested and appreciated, as the words of Joyce and Sue affirm.

> I . . . like to see us meet regularly . . . to help each other. (*Sue*)

> (*We need to meet*) for the support and sharing. The sharing helps me in planning and reevaluating my teaching, and the support strengthens my belief in what we are doing. (*Joyce*)

Besides the awfulizing and problem solving that occur in our monthly meetings, the PAL teachers have also discovered the importance of having meaningful work and goals attached to the group. In Janice's words, they want to make a difference in the larger world and in the world of their students.

> I need to see and talk to my friends, my sisters, about what we are doing to improve the lives and futures of our children. I need to keep in touch with real people dealing each day with real and important problems. I need to know that it is possible to *make a difference* if not daily (though that almost certainly happens whether we recognize it or not), then over the long term. I need to know there are people in the world who care, who try, who *live outside of themselves*, who see a change to be made and do so. I need to be with teachers. (*Janice*)

What a poignant compliment Janice made to the PAL group and to all teachers! Dedicated teachers are those who care about their students, who have not given up, who live outside themselves. It is these kinds of teachers Michael Fullan describes in *Change Forces* (1993) when he says that teachers want staff development that makes a difference in their and their students' daily lives, for that classroom and metaphorical space is the nexus of their school lives.

The combination of time, ownership, collaboration, and doing meaningful work is a powerful one for the PAL teachers. Yet their individual and group identity has been forged by a bond that is even stronger, a bond that has been crucial to the group's success and longevity.

> This group was my lifeline in the early days of (implementing) workshop. Now it has really become for me a coming together of people whom I have known along the way. They know, so there's no need to explain. There's an intimacy that snaps back in place as soon as (I) enter the room no matter how long it's been. So much of my teaching has come from this group it is hard to tell where the group begins and I end. I have a real pride in what I do now. (*Jenelle*)

> I love . . . the encouragement and support I receive from everyone. My belief in what I'm doing in the classroom is supported by teachers I admire. . . . I don't think I would be teaching today if it weren't for PAL. (*Donna*)

> The group gives me energy, excitement, and a fresh vision for tomorrow. (*Amelia*)

The unique quality characterizing the PAL group is that their work, their interactions, and their mutual concerns are supported and nurtured both personally and professionally. As Jenelle says, it is indeed hard sometimes to "tell where the group begins and I end."

These teachers' comments indicate the power of a supportive community in ongoing professional development that is productive for teachers and leads us to believe that ". . . the same principles that increase student learning are relevant to the ongoing professional education of adults" (Hunter, 1990). If students construct their own knowledge and understandings of literacy from their personal experiences, from supportive instruction that encourages developmental growth, and from working within a community of learners, then teachers need similar opportunities to develop and refine their understandings of the teaching/learning process within a professional development program that provides the appropriate instructional scaffolding and a supportive community of fellow learners in which to work.

Dialogue and Staff Development

Just as the type of literacy classroom promoted in this text relies heavily on dialogue, so too must professional development opportunities for teachers. In constructivist classrooms, students have self-selected and shared readings from a variety of rich texts; they participate in literature discussion groups that allow and encourage the development and refinement of student understandings, and their direct instruction component insures acquisition of foundation reading skills. The interactions between student(s) and teacher and student and student form the foundation of these classrooms—conferences, dialogue journals, peer discussion groups. Reflective, ongoing dialogue with self, with peers, and with experts—whether classroom teacher, a guest speaker, or another student—is the key ingredient of the successful work-shop classroom and of any successful professional development initiative for educators.

Dialogue with Experts

Traditional inservice often relies on the services of an expert talking at groups of teachers for a period of time and then leaving to return to another district or university. While this delivery system leaves much to be desired, teachers can benefit from listening to experts who have had success with a particular innovation or with a particular curricular area or who have practical insights into current research, issues and concerns. How then can districts take advantage of outside experts and still maintain the integrity of a staff development program that honors reflective dialogue?

While outside experts play a small role in any ongoing professional development program, they have much to offer when their expertise is used appropriately. They can bring a breadth of experience that goes beyond a single district's often "provincial knowledge, usually limited largely to knowledge of their own school or school system" (Allington and Cunningham, 1995, p. 156). They can become partners in change if the district and experts are willing to commit substantial time to work together. Because of specialization, the outside consultant can have expertise in the theoretical basis for a new innovation, a basis recognized by CEE as a critical attribute of inservice education because it allows teachers to move beyond the *what to do on Monday* syndrome (*English Education*, p. 126).

> The best inservice experiences I had were when the consultants led in clever icebreakers during the sessions. Always teachers were supported and encouraged to be supportive. Inservice tied in with school philosophy and practice. (*Shirley*)

By re-examining the way outside experts are used, districts can maintain the integrity of a change movement or a teacher-centered professional development program. These experts can become involved in ongoing conversations with teachers through a series of visits to the district or through technological innovations such as e-mail, fax, or interactive video. A school district in central Texas recently contracted with an outside expert to help its teachers plan a strong, developmentally appropriate reading program. The contractual arrangement called for not just one but repeated visits. After an initial visit, the consultant returned to the district periodically to dialogue with teachers about their concerns, successes, and questions and to observe and conference with teachers about their efforts to redesign their program.

Experts are not always outsiders. Certainly there are experts in every district and in every building—classroom teachers at various stages in the implementation of an innovation who can share success stories and how-to's with other teachers. When novices have the opportunity to visit the classrooms of expert teachers, important conversations among peers begin. To use these in-house experts effectively, districts must seek ways to maintain the dialogue—visitation days, time on staff development days for conferencing, and recognition of the expertise that exists in the district. E-mail capabilities in the school or classroom also make these conversations with in-district experts more viable. The opportunity to design their own learning experience, to try out the techniques promoted by experts, and to talk through their new classroom innovations makes the time teachers spend with experts, either in-house or out-of-district, a meaningful part of an ongoing professional development program.

Dialogue with Peers

In the team areas, the pods, or the classrooms of a middle school, teachers often work with a group of teachers—a social studies teacher, a science teacher, a mathematics teacher, and a reading/language arts teacher. Certainly collegiality exists among these teachers in the best of situations. This team works together to schedule, to plan, to evaluate, and to support the middle school youngsters with whom they work every day. They often conference with parents together, meeting before the conference to discuss an individual student's social and educational progress. A sense of oneness exists among these team members. Such a framework for interdisciplinary planning can also provide a supportive network for continued professional development. The collegial relationships that emerge offer support for team members' continuing professional growth. Middle school language arts/ reading teachers need these same supportive environments to dialogue with one another about concerns, new learning, and ongoing professional development. Such environments are not often found in the monthly departmental meetings held to dispense information and discuss more generic curricular issues.

> A memorable staff development involved teachers sharing strategies with other teachers. The faculty volunteered to attend and agreed to share one or more times. The sessions were positive, and my opinion of my colleagues was elevated. (*Virginia*)

Many varied opportunities to dialogue with peers exist. Professional organizations, especially at the local and state levels, offer the classroom teacher the opportunity to discuss critical issues informally and formally. While conferences themselves often become just another series of "one shot" presentations, the dialogue that occurs among peers at these meetings provides a needed exchange between educators with like interests and can often be the beginning of ongoing conversations via phone, fax, or electronic mail.

Many school districts now look to well-developed literacy institutes and special projects to provide extensive training for their teachers. Such institutes, initiated by universities, school districts themselves, or independent staff, develop providers and build a camaraderie among participants so that conversations can begin during these days or weeks of the special project and be extended into the regular school year. For example, the staff development division of the Harris County Department of Education in Houston works with the 24 school districts in the county to provide ongoing training through a writing institute patterned on the National Writing Project Model and through a locally developed reading institute for teachers. Such across-grade level institutes provide an environment of shared concerns regardless of grade level and provide rich, theoretical yet practical growth opportunities for teachers that can stimulate ongoing conversations among peers. With follow-up opportunities built into these institutes, beginning conversations can continue throughout the school year.

Dialogue with Self

> The best staff development I have attended was one in which we had reflection time for introspection. (*Janice*)

Classroom teachers naturally spend a substantial amount of time pondering and reflecting on the issues that emerge in their classrooms. They draw upon their accumulated experience and knowledge to solve any problems involving classroom management as well as instruction. All of us at some time or another have asked ourselves questions about our teaching/learning situations: Why did that work so well yesterday and bomb today? What could I do to get those students on task? How can I best help my students make connections between what they are reading and their world? The time spent pondering the questions and issues that evolve from our daily experiences or from our dialogue with experts and peers is a valuable part of ongoing professional development. These inner conversations allow us to grow professionally. Time spent mulling over questions, pondering possibilities, and examining issues and solving problems allow us to monitor our own understandings.

More informal attempts to monitor our professional development often result in written reflection in the form of journals and logs or anecdotal records of our own attempts at innovation and change. When such products emerge from our inner-voice conversations, we can revisit our thinking, see our progress and refine still unanswered questions. In a reflection on her own metamorphosis from traditional teacher to workshop facilitator, Atwell says that writing "fuels my best insights. It makes me understand things I did not know before I wrote" (Patterson et al., p. ix).

(This year in our meetings) I would like to write and publish an article. (*Donna*)

As Donna's request suggests, reflection often leads to more formal inquiry, one fostered by the current focus on the classroom teacher as researcher. In order to help their students learn, teachers seek answers to those inner voice questions related directly to their own classroom practices. They develop a personal plan of action that involves inquiry and written reflection. Whether used for casual reflection or the more formal inquiries of action research, writing provides a record of understanding and growth and often leads to publication.

A Staff Development Conceptual Model

The emphasis on dialogue as a key ingredient to successful staff development cannot be overstated. Making meaning through language is the premise of learning and growth, whether we are middle school students or teachers. This constructivist approach to staff development, parallel with a constructivist approach to teaching reading in middle school, suggests that as learners we construct knowledge and understanding through ongoing reflection and dialogue with self, colleagues, and/or experts. It is this process of considering and interacting singularly as well as with others that not only stimulates but sustains us as learners who are also teachers. (See Figure 21.2.)

Figure 21.2   Successful Staff Development

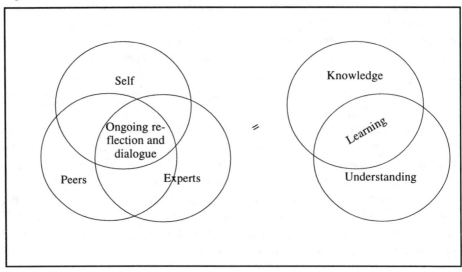

Participating in the New Model of Staff Development

Initiating, establishing, and maintaining a constructivist approach to staff development requires that each of us, in our own roles, views staff development differently. As teachers, we will participate more in deciding what and how to learn and assume more responsibility for our own learning. As arrangers of staff development, we will listen more to the needs of teachers and establish the types of inservice they want and need. As presenters of staff development, we will be colleagues with teachers, not preachers to teachers. This shift will challenge each of us to support and maintain an ongoing approach to staff development, one that respects teachers as knowledgeable professionals who are continually learning.

We offer the following guidelines to teachers, staff development directors, and staff development leaders for surviving and guiding the shift in staff development emphasis from a delivery system to a more constructive one.

Teachers

When we, as teachers, participate in a constructivist approach to staff development, we will assume more responsibility for both the content and outcome of our professional growth. This role may be a new one for those of us who are accustomed to decisions being made for us by someone far removed from the classrooms. We offer the following suggestions to those who find themselves or wish to define themselves as active participants in the staff development process.

Be Issue Detectors: When we serve as teacher-researchers in our classrooms, we constantly question and think about our students, their learning, and our own teaching. We ask ourselves, our colleagues, and our students probing questions about the teaching/learning process; we figure out ways to act on those responses; we implement appropriate strategies; we implement processes for testing the effectiveness of those strategies; and we evaluate the results.

To be an active member of a constructive staff development process, we need to be intimately familiar with our own classroom issues and problems. We need to go beyond complaining to analyze our genuine concerns about students, and we need to use the results of our probes, questions, and classroom research to determine the most crucial issues that are affecting teaching and learning. As Joyce has said about her professional development group:

> I'd like for us to continue to meet for the support and sharing. The sharing helps me in planning and reevaluating my teaching.

We can also best determine our own staff development fate by keeping updated professionally. Reading professional literature, belonging to local, state, and national professional organizations, and attending professional conferences and conventions inform and stimulate at the time and when we return to our classrooms. We learn and think about methods others have tried, we explore current research and theories, and we begin to think differently about our teaching and our students' learning.

Be Pro-active: The stimulation we derive from our own classroom-based research, our professional reading, and our professional experiences serves as a catalyst for determining our own local staff development direction. Armed with information from our classrooms, professional experiences, and the needs of our students, we can request from our principals and other administrators not only the specific content but also the kind and duration of staff development we desire. We can even request the specific person with whom we would like to work, whether that person be an outsider or one or several of our own colleagues. We can ask for a long-term commitment from staff development leaders, we can ask for time during our day to reorganize, plan, and collaborate with parents and our colleagues, and we can ask for follow-up sessions, peer observations, and a demonstration classroom. In short, we can use our knowledge and experience to take the responsibility and ownership for our professional development.

Collaborate with Colleagues: Two resources we sometimes overlook are our own professional colleagues and our students. As teachers participating in a constructive staff development model, we need to share more readily information, questions, struggles, insights, and processes with both our peers and our students. As Amelia explains:

> (This group) will continue to be my professional support. I want us to share in inquiry, using the group for ideas and thoughts. . . . It is what has prompted me to look continually at what I'm doing and what it means for children. (*Amelia*)

The dialogue that accompanies such interchanges is always rich and meaningful. We need to experience the energy and power that comes with all of us is better than one of us.

Staff Development Directors

As a director of staff development, perhaps you have been uncomfortable in your role of deciding for teachers what kind of inservice they should have. You may have felt lonely in this role as you have tried to guess what will be applicable and useful to the greatest majority of teachers. On the other hand, it may have been exciting to shop around for entertaining, informative inservice providers who have valuable messages for teachers. In the new view of staff development, we offer some guidelines that will take you off the hook, that will offer you more collaboration and company in your job. And you will still be able to maintain that exciting part of your role that allows you to find and bring staff development leaders into your school or district.

Consult with Teachers: As people involved in arranging for staff development, the part of our jobs we have found most challenging has been trying to match teachers to the content and inservice providers that best meet their needs. In a more constructivist approach to staff development, we get an opportunity to work more directly with teachers both in determining the inservice needs as well as developing a plan to meet those needs. In our visits to schools and classrooms, we talk with teachers, students, and principals to gain insight about the current problems and issues of teaching and learning. We ask questions, we observe, we listen, we make notes. And we share readings, materials, and experiences we have that might be useful. Through these conversations as well as questionnaires and letters of request to teachers and principals, we also ask for suggestions about inservice foci. This information gives us the starting place for our most important work. Jennifer affirms the importance of this process.

> It seems that most of these (staff development) presenters are out of touch with what is needed. I feel that maybe administrators/planners are not giving us enough credit and that perhaps if faculty members were asked for feedback, they could make these opportunities more effective. (*Jennifer*)

Commit Resources: We have found that no matter how much dialogue, conversation, and open communication we have with teachers and principals, what matters most is what happens AFTER this information-gathering stage. Following through with matching the best inservice provider and process with the teachers' needs is critical.

In our current view of staff development, we think it is important to commit the financial and human resources not only to inform teachers about what they wish to know but also to provide the long-term follow-up. Given what we know now about learning, about knowledge and understanding, we know that we must provide the opportunity for teachers to have an ongoing dialogue with themselves, peers, and experts. Time for such dialogue and professional development requires both budgetary and human commitments. Therefore, we make sure we have an ample budget and sufficient opportunities for teachers to work with consultants over an extended period of time, to have frequent meetings with colleagues as well as consultants, and to have release time for thinking and planning. By offering these substantive blocks of time, we make it more possible for staff development to have an impact on teachers and their students.

Seek a Safe Space: While providing appropriate and long-term support for teacher development is important, probably the variable we have found to be the most valuable to teachers is having a metaphorical *safe space*, a place, a group where they can air their hesitations, their mistakes, their questions and not feel as if they are going to be judged as ineffective, incompetent, or quarrelsome. They need to feel supported, reinforced, and much affirmed in this environment, and the physical space does not seem to matter much. While it is nice to be comfortable, even to have a luxurious space for follow-up meetings, what matters most is the emotional space.

In successful long-term professional development groups with whom we have worked the key ingredients have been: open talking, sharing, and problem solving; time to reflect and create together; pursuing innovation that supports their becoming experts in their classrooms; and doing work that is applicable to their students. In these successful groups the teachers unselfishly celebrate and applaud each other's accomplishments, and they genuinely enjoy each other's professional company.

> (Our group) has meant "belonging" to me. Love. Acceptance. (And we have as our purpose) to help each other. (*Sue*)

Staff Development Leaders

So what do you do if you receive a request to *do inservice* at a school, in a school system, or with a group of teachers? What questions do you need to ask? What general principles should you establish and follow in developing professional development experiences? We have distilled from our experiences and from the Conference on English Education Principles the following premises that are not so different from those we follow when preparing for any teaching experience.

Do Your Homework: Before agreeing to *do inservice,* we try to negotiate for a long-term commitment so as to establish a strong bond with the participants. Then we set about to gather as much information as possible. Our first questions always have to be, "Do the teachers want this staff development? Why?" If we are satisfied with the responses to those seminal questions, we then spend time talking with not only the contact person but also the principal, teachers, and even the students. From these conversations we begin developing a portrait of the entire setting—the school, working conditions, and faculty and students' needs. The last reaction we want is for teachers to feel as Lisa did as she remembered her recent staff development experiences:

> I can barely remember (my staff development experiences) because we didn't engage in anything particularly meaningful. I remember feeling like it was really just a glorified faculty meeting with more food than usual.

Whenever possible, we do this information-gathering in person. By visiting the school or system we can determine faculty interest, student attitudes, and the unique circumstances of place. Through such a process, we gain a clearer view of the educational context than we can just by telephone. We have, on occasion, taken part of a day to interview students in the school to discover their opinions and perspectives on themselves as learners. Such information, when taped and reviewed, can reveal valuable voices to bring to the staff development table.

If visiting the setting is impossible, we recommend communicating with as many teachers as possible by telephone or by sending letters with questionnaires for them to complete and return without names attached. From such data we have received valuable information about the expertise and view of the group. It would take several days to get such data while conducting the inservice.

Honor Existing Knowledge and Experience: Getting the information is all well and good, but using the information is key. We have found that successful staff development experiences build on the existing knowledge and expertise present in the school or system. The idea is not just to develop a presentation that responds to the existing knowledge, but to develop a process plan for hearing and responding to both the professionals and their issues. We accomplish this interaction in a number of ways: by asking questions, by listening attentively to questions and opinions, and by continually referencing these questions and views throughout the staff development process.

Acknowledging and building on the existing professional knowledge and experience of the participants also encourages open dialogue among the participants. This goal sits right at the top of our list throughout the workshop, institute, or study group, for we know that dialogue is the centerpiece of any successful staff development. Building in time for dialogue with self, with peers, as well as with the consultant is well worth the attention. More often than not, we find that, because of compressed schedules, teachers are sadly unaccustomed to talking with each other about their own teaching and expertise, about issues of pedagogy, and about ways of addressing the needs of their students.

Establish a Risk-Free Environment: To assure that open sharing and professional conversation thrives, the staff development consultant needs to model and lead in such a way that power and knowledge are shared equally with the participants. If the consultant and the participants become antagonistic, it is next to impossible to regain any semblance of shared expertise and learning. Imagine a staff development setting like the one Donna describes:

> Our county hired an expert (in business) to "help" us determine outcomes for education. She had never worked in a school and did not care to learn anything about how a school runs. She just knew we were wrong.

We have found that the best environments are established through open dialogue in a safe place where all participants, including the consultant, can share and laugh about pedagogical mistakes, unfortunate choices, and about what some participants will call stupid questions. In such situations we always hasten to say that there are no "stupid questions" and that we need to get all of our concerns openly and honestly on the table. When everyone in the group believes that they will not be chastised or mocked when posing questions, then the group has truly become a community of inquirers who can tackle significant issues together, as Jenelle states here:

> To have a group to go back to and say, "Hey, how do you handle this?" and get some feedback from others in the trenches. It's a support group approach with those who can sympathize and inspire you.

Have Fun: Because our work as educators is challenging and because we face many important daily decisions with our students and colleagues, we sometimes forget how necessary it is that we have fun as we work together. When we refer to "having fun" together, we are not suggesting that all discussions be laden with funny stories or jokes. Rather, our experience has been that staff development participants perceive they are having fun when they can laugh with colleagues about the humorous incidents in their own teaching.

We have also found that teachers report having fun when they are involved in meaningful work together. When they stretch to be innovative, when they become experts, and when they reflect and create together, they do not resent the time they spend in a professional development session. Rather, they see its connections to themselves, their classrooms, and their students. And, if the staff development remains in place over time, the participants have the opportunity to take risks, knowing that support is just a colleague away. They can become teacher-researchers who reinforce their evolving knowledge and experience base through the peer group that provides guidance and encouragement throughout the inquiry process. The staff development leader can, of course, be a part of this alliance as well or can, after a time, leave the group to support itself. To many teachers, and to staff development leaders, this kind of professional development is fun, and they want more of it.

> So when are we going to meet again? I miss seeing everybody.
> (*Barbara*)

Conclusion

In the workshop classroom, we strive to help our young readers and writers discover their voices and to let those voices influence their reading responses and their personal writing. We provide experiences that enable them to see connections between their own lives and their reading and writing, we provide rich models from professionals and peers that illustrate voice, and we encourage this journey of self-discovery in any way possible.

When these students discover their own voice in a particular piece of writing or begin to respond to their reading personally as well as critically, we celebrate. If we want to break the cycle of preacher to teacher staff development, we will do the same in our staff development programs: honor teachers' voices, and encourage and facilitate the ongoing reflective dialogue that leads to self-discovery and growth in our professional lives.

References

Allington, R., & Cunningham, P. (1996). *Schools that work.* New York: HarperCollins.

Atwell, N. (1987). *In the middle: Writing, reading, and learning with adolescents.* Portsmouth, NH: Boynton Cook Publishers.

Fullan, M. (1993). *Change forces: Probing the depths of educational reform.* London: The Falmer Press.

Hunter, M. (1990). Preface: Thoughts on staff development. In *Changing school culture through staff development.* Alexandria, VA: Association for Supervision and Curriculum Development.

Patterson, et al. (1993). *Teachers are researchers: Reflection and action.* Newark, DE: International Reading Association.

Chapter 22

SELECTION AIDS:
PLACES TO GO WHEN THERE'S
MORE YOU NEED TO KNOW

Patricia Potter Wilson

Picture the following scenarios:

- A middle school student needs a complete list of books written by Russell Freedman.
- Another student's best friend is dying of leukemia, and she wants a fictional work in which the main character is going through a similar situation.
- An eighth grade teacher is trying to locate a list of easy-to-read books on topics of interest to middle school students.
- The school library media specialist needs a list of mysteries teens have identified as favorites.

Locating the right book to fulfill personal interests and curricular needs of students can be a time-consuming process, but it doesn't have to be if you use some helpful selection aids that are available in many school and public libraries.

The Value of Selection Aids

Matching children and books is not necessarily an easy task. With thousands of books available for young adults, teachers and librarians naturally find it impossible to read all the books they recommend. This is when it becomes necessary to turn to resources that help teachers, librarians, students, and parents with the selection of print or nonprint materials. These selection aids usually include book reviews or annotated lists of recommended titles. As adult readers we typically select a book for reading enjoyment based on the fact that it appeared on a best-selling list or received excellent reviews. The same can be true in the selection of books for middle school students. Knowledge of *best* lists, award-winning books, and recommended lists can certainly improve our chances of satisfying specific interests and needs.

The recommended titles found in the selection aids are usually selected by the author(s) of the selection aid or by an appointed committee comprised of distinguished teachers, librarians, and university professors. While calling on their specialized backgrounds in various content areas, these experts go about the selection process in an objective manner, usually based on criteria or the use of book reviews. The titles in some selection aids, such as "Young Adults' Choices" list, are selected by students who have read the works and recommend them for the list.

Besides the valuable list of suggested titles to recommend to students, selection aids contain a wealth of information for the classroom teacher. For each recommended title, the entry usually includes bibliographic information useful in ordering or locating the works, a descriptive and/or critical annotation, and an estimate of the book's readability or interest level. These entries are usually arranged according to topics that certainly assist in the development of thematic units. Additionally, the subject, title, and author indexes often included in selection aids provide helpful keys to accessing the various books. Some aids go a step further and provide biographical information on outstanding authors, whereby teachers and students can relate the lives and works of the various authors and examine their creative writing processes.

Classroom teachers and students can call upon selection aids to meet the following needs:

- Books to fulfill personal reading interests.
- Books and nonprint materials to support curricular needs.
- Books and nonprint materials to supplement classroom texts.
- Books that match specific reading levels.
- Books that satisfy bibliotherapy needs.
- Multicultural literature to enrich the classroom.
- Location of book reviews.
- Background information on authors and illustrators.
- Literature and nonprint materials to enrich thematic units.

- Information for ordering the books.

- Books and nonprint materials to support special classroom programs.

Special attention should be given to this final example of a need met through selection aids. Selection aids can assist teachers in locating books and nonprint materials to support classroom programs. On a recent visit to a local middle school, the eighth graders were involved in a special month of activities that focused on cowboys of the wild West. It just so happened that the rodeo was in town that month, and this added a special flavor to the unit. Working with the school librarian, the teachers planned a unit filled with rich learning experiences. The enthusiastic librarian provided the teachers with a bibliography of all the books and nonprint materials on the topic that could be found in the library media center. Next, she introduced the eighth grade teachers to the selection aids available in the library and encouraged them to use the selection aids to become acquainted with other useful works on the topic. To further enrich the unit, the librarian provided the teachers with the phone number of a local rodeo organization that could provide guest speakers. Book displays, student reports, guest speakers, and special projects encouraged much reading and sharing on the topic. As students requested other books on cowboys, the librarian encouraged them to use the selection aids to gain access to new titles.

Choosing Selection Aids

With so many selection aids available, how do we determine which resource is the best to use? Teachers should start by considering their specific needs. What type of books do you need? What is the scope of your needs? Are you looking for books in a specific genre? On a specific topic? For a specific age group? Books published during a specific time period? Books published in a specific country? Once these questions are examined and the needs are identified, teachers can begin to evaluate the various selection aids available that meet their needs. Certain criteria can be used to determine the worthiness of a selection aid: purpose, scope, authority, currency, organization/arrangement, and ease of use.

The majority of the selection aids indicate the purpose and scope in their titles. For example, *Best Books for Children: Preschool Through Middle Grades* (Gilbert, 1985) recommends *best* books for children. The title indicates that the scope is not limited by genre; yet, the scope is limited by grade levels. On the other hand, *Fantasy Literature for Children and Young Adults* (Lynn, 1994) is limited to the genre of fantasy; yet, the book contains works for multilevels. While some idea of the purpose of the tool is given in the title, a special statement concerning purpose is usually included in the preface or introduction of the resource.

The credentials of the author or editor as well as the reputation of the publisher play a critical role in the overall credibility of the selection aid. Equally as important are the credentials of the committee members who select works for the selection aid. Reputable resources usually highlight these credentials in the introduction or preface of the work.

While some teachers in search of outstanding fictional works may not be concerned with currency, many look at the currency of the selection aid as a critical consideration. Middle school teachers who are interested in locating up-to-date nonfiction and recently published fiction will want to use resources such as *Your Reading*, a booklist published every two or three years by the National Council of Teachers of English, which annotates recent books. For the most current information concerning recently published books, book reviews in professional journals can aid selection. The currency feature will be further enhanced as more selection aids move into CD-ROM and on-line formats.

As in all reference works, ease of use is a primary consideration. The resource should be arranged and organized in a way that students and teachers can easily locate specific titles that serve their needs. Most selection aids include a table of contents that lays out the arrangement of the book. The preface provides information about the content of the resource, how the books were selected, and the credentials of the selectors. The indexes are extremely important features in these resources as they allow access by title, author, and subject.

Importance of Preparing Students to Use Selection Aids

On a recent visit to an exemplary middle school library, the librarian was engaged in a two-hour workshop for language arts/reading teachers that focused on "Selection Aids for the Reading Program." While involving the teachers in hands-on activities to acquaint them with the selection aids, the librarian highlighted the various uses for the aids. She went on to emphasize the importance of teaching their students to use selection aids, and at the end of the workshop she provided them with sample activities for acquainting students with selection aids. By becoming comfortable with these selection aids in middle school, students will possess the selection skills that are important for lifelong learning.

Recommended Selection Aids

The selection aids recommended in this chapter will provide middle school teachers and students with useful resources to use in selecting books. To further aid the user in meeting specific needs, the selection tools are listed under specific subheadings. While many selection aids are placed in

Table 22.1 Types of Selection Aids

Type	Purpose	Example
Indexes to reviews	help teachers/librarians find out where to locate the review of a particular book	Book Review Digest
Selection aids that offer titles on a broad range of topics	provide titles/annotations of many books to help students and teachers connect with books	Your Reading
Selection aids that address special needs	provide titles/annotations of many books that address specific emotional and physical problems	More Notes from a Different Drummer
Selection aids that focus on reluctant and at-risk readers	provide titles/annotations of books that meet the needs of middle school students who can't or won't read	High Interest Easy Reading
Selection aids that are genre-specific	provide titles/annotations of books for only one genre such as fantasy or nonfiction	Nonfiction for Children and Young Adults
Selection aids that focus on multicultural literature	provide titles/annotations of books with a multicultural focus	Kaleidoscope
Selection aids that give information on young adult authors	provide information on authors for teacher or student use	Speaking for Ourselves
Selection aids that help with booktalking	provide booktalks for teachers to use with students	Booktalk!
Professional journals	provide current information about newly published books	Booklist
Best lists	provide lists of titles of books that have been designated as outstanding	"Best Books for Young Adults"

the general category, others with a more narrow scope are divided according to genre or specific needs that they address.

The selection aids discussed below (see Table 22.1 for an overview) can be found in a variety of formats—books, journals, CD-ROM, on-line, pamphlets, and reprints of lists. As you examine the various aids, you'll find that the majority of the selection aids fall into four categories: (1) indexes to book reviews; (2) selection guides, both general and specific, which devote the entire work to the selection of books for adolescents; (3) book reviews and recommended lists published in professional journals; and (4) recommended book lists published by professional organizations in pamphlet or reprint form.

Indexes to Book Reviews

Want to know what reviewers say about a particular book you plan to use with students? Access to book reviews is important in the selection process. The following tools will help teachers and librarians locate reviews:

Book Review Digest. New York: H. W. Wilson Company, 1905 to date.

The primary purpose of this tool is to list the location of reviews of books for children and adults. This resource provides citations for reviews from 80 periodicals. Excerpts from the review are also included, thus offering the reader some idea concerning the contents of the review without calling on the primary source.

Book Review Index. New York: H. W. Wilson Company, 1965 to date.

As in the above resource, this tool cites where reviews may be located. Unlike *Book Review Digest*, this aid does not provide excerpts from the reviews. Yet, it does offer the advantage of citing reviews from approximately 375 periodicals. Therefore, if you are unable to find a review citation in *Book Review Digest*, you'll want to try this.

General Selection Aids

The following selection aids recommend books for middle school students. Rather than focusing on a specific genre such as fantasy or nonfiction, these general selection aids recommend titles related to a broad range of genre and topics.

Best Books for Children: Preschool Through Middle Grades (3rd ed.). Edited by J. T. Gillespie & C. B. Gilbert. New York: R. R. Bowker, 1985.

This resource includes titles for beginning middle school readers as well as elementary students that have been recommended by three review sources. Holidays, circuses, mysteries, monsters, curiosities, and crafts are just a few of the broad interest areas under which the more than 6,800 carefully selected titles are listed. Main headings such as *crafts* are further subdivided into specific topics ranging from *American historical crafts* to *woodworking*, making it easier for classroom teachers and students to select recommended books that have a specific focus. With each entry teachers will find an annotation plus information concerning suitable grade levels as well as review citations.

Best Books for Junior High Readers. Edited by J. T. Gillespie. New York: R. R. Bowker, 1991.

This recommended *best* list for junior high readers should encourage teachers to take an active role in reading guidance. The fiction titles are arranged under broad subject headings of interest to junior high readers, and the nonfiction works are arranged by curriculum-oriented subjects. For example, fiction includes subheadings such as *adventure and survival stories*, *mystery and detective stories*, and *sports stories*. The wide range of nonfiction topics include *social concerns*, *guidance and personal development*, and *arts and entertainment*, with each being further subdivided into categories to assure better matches in the selection process. Each entry contains a short, one-sentence annotation along with review sources and grade levels. For ease of use the resource contains an author, title, and subject index.

Best Books for Young Adults: The History, the Selections, the Romance. Written by B. Carter. Chicago: Young Adult Library Services Association of American Library Association, 1994.

This excellent tool offers teachers a compilation of the books that appeared on the "Best Books for Young Adults" lists from 1966 to 1993. This selection aid not only provides annotations of all books chosen for the "Best Books" list, but it also groups them by author and by year. An added feature of the work is the informative historical overview of the Best Books for Young Adults Committee.

Junior High School Library Catalog (6th ed.). Edited by J. Yaakov. New York: Wilson, 1990.

While this tool for grades 7–9 is typically used by librarians for establishing or adding to a basic middle school library collection, it is also valuable to classroom teachers interested in locating highly recommended books. This is the source teachers can go to for verification of bibliographic information such as title, author, publisher, publication date, and price. Short annotations along with readability level are also included. The author, title, and subject indexes as well as the arrangement by the Dewey Decimal Classification System make this tool particularly useful when searching for books about specific topics such as *oceanography*, *archaeology*, and *Europe*.

Teachers' Favorite Books for Kids: Teachers' Choices 1989–1993. Newark, DE: International Reading Association, 1994.

This booklist represents a compilation of five years of "Teachers' Choices" lists that include books that teachers consider outstanding to use with the curriculum. These recommended works for children and adults are grouped by suggested reading level and include short annotations and bibliographic information. An index offers access by title, author, and illustrator.

What Do Young Adults Read Next? A Reader's Guide to Fiction for Young Adults. Written by P. Spencer. Detroit: Gale Research, 1994.

Teens are certain to find a book that will interest them when they or their teacher call on this resource that includes over 1,500 entries for books published for young adults from 1988 to 1992. Each entry provides a summary of the plot and suggests related titles. The ten very specific indexes provide access by author, title, subjects, series, awards, time periods, geographic places, character names, character descriptions, and age levels.

Young People's Books in Series Fiction and Nonfiction, 1975–1991. Written by J. Rosenberg. Englewood, CO: Libraries Unlimited, 1992.

For teachers and students interested in finding which work comes next in a series, this is the selection aid that will help. This handy resource provides an annotation for both fiction and nonfiction series books for students in grades 7 and up. A primary focus of this guide is interest and it includes series that are popular with teens such as *Sweet Valley High*. The nonfiction works are arranged alphabetically by title of series. The fiction series are listed alphabetically by author, and the guide then lists titles in chronological order as they should be read. The combined author and title index further aids users in finding information about series titles.

Your Reading: An Annotated Booklist for Middle School and Junior High, 1995–96 Edition. Edited by B. G. Samuels and G. K. Beers. Urbana, IL: National Council of Teachers of English, 1996.

This book contains over 1,200 annotations of books for middle school students that were published during 1993 and 1994. A committee of teachers and librarians selects the books. The titles of the selected books are then organized by topics of interest to middle school students. The purpose of the book is to help students find books for recreational reading, assist them in finding books needed for assignments, and aid teachers in choosing books for thematic units. Indexes by title, author, and subject help match readers to books.

Books to Meet Special Problems and Needs

Middle school teachers are sometimes approached by a teen who asks for aid in finding a book that will help in dealing with a special problem. That is when teachers and librarians may turn to some of the bibliotherapy resources that can help match a student with an emotional or physical problem to a fictional book in which a main character is tackling a similar problem or an informational work that focuses on the problem. Teachers and librarians should also keep in mind that teens often face problems they do not want to share; therefore, students must be encouraged to use selection aids such as *Bookfinder* (listed below) on their own.

Other selection aids address the difficulties encountered by reluctant and at-risk readers. To encourage these readers to become more involved in reading, these aids offer high-interest tradebooks that are written on a low-readability level.

Both types of selection aids are included in this section for teachers involved in helping students deal with emotional, physical, and learning problems.

Bibliotherapy Aids

Accept Me As I Am. Written by J. Friedberg. New York: Bowker, 1985.

In this nonfiction complement to *More Notes from a Different Drummer* (Baskin & Harris, 1984), Friedberg focuses on children's and young adults' books that deal with physical problems, sensory problems, cognitive and behavior problems, and multiple/severe disabilities. Each annotation includes an analysis of the treatment of the disability as well as a suggested reading level.

The Bookfinder: Volume 2: A Guide to Children's Literature About the Needs and Problems of Youth Aged 2–15. Written by S. S. Dreyer. Circle Pines, MN: American Guidance Service, 1981.

The Bookfinder, Volume 3: When Kids Need Books: Annotations of Books Published 1979–1982. Written by S. S. Dreyer. Circle Pines, MN: American Guidance Service, 1985.

The Bookfinder: Volume 4. Written by S. S. Dreyer. Circle Pines, MN: American Guidance Service, 1989.

If a student is looking for books on topics that focus on various problems and feelings that young people may face, this is the resource that will help. The resource includes both fiction and nonfiction books on a wide range of topics such as *adoption, divorce, suicide, peer pressure, boy-girl relations,* or *cancer.* The specificity of the subject index ensures students of finding books related to their specific problems. Each entry includes a lengthy summary, lists the main themes and sub-themes of the book, and recommends age levels.

Portraying Persons with Disabilities: An Annotated Bibliography of Fiction for Children and Teenagers (3rd ed.). Written by D. Robertson. New Providence, NJ: R. R. Bowker, 1992.

Portraying Persons with Disabilities: An Annotated Bibliography of Nonfiction for Children and Teenagers (3rd ed.). Written by J. B. Friedberg, J. B. Mulliris, & A. W. Sukiennik. New Providence, NJ: R. R. Bowker, 1992.

This companion set, one with a focus on fiction and the other with a focus on nonfiction, provides teachers of preschool through young adults with specific works that deal with various disabilities. The works recommend books that fall into four categories: (1) physical problems such as health problems and orthopedic/neurological disabilities, (2) sensory problems such as hearing and visual impairments, (3) cognitive and behavior problems such as learning disabilities and mental retardation, and (4) multiple/severe and various disabilities.

The annotations are organized according to broad categories. The specific disability addressed is identified, followed by a lengthy, full summary of the book along with a critical analysis that often suggests specific uses of the book as well as strengths and weaknesses. Reading levels are suggested, and the author, title, and subject indexes are available.

More Notes From a Different Drummer: A Guide to Juvenile Fiction Portraying the Disabled. Written by B. Baskin and K. Harris. New York: Bowker, 1984.
Notes From A Different Drummer: A Guide to Juvenile Fiction Portraying the Handicapped. Written by B. Baskin and K. Harris. New York: Bowker, 1977.

This companion set began with *Notes From a Different Drummer*, a comprehensive guide to fiction for children and young adults written between 1940 and 1975 that depicts handicapped characters. Books about characters with a variety of impairments, such as visual, auditory, neurological, and intellectual, are identified and evaluated. Each annotation includes a plot summary and an analysis that evaluates the treatment of the impairment and the literary merit. Suggested reading levels are available for each entry. The subject index points the user with special needs to the various impairments highlighted in the books. The success of this reference tool led to a sequel, *More Notes from a Different Drummer*, which highlights books about the handicapped written between 1976 and 1981.

Reluctant and At-Risk Readers

High Interest Easy Reading: A Booklist for Junior and Senior High School Students (6th ed.). Edited by W. McBride. Urbana, IL: National Council of Teachers of English, 1990.

Over 400 annotated titles of fiction and nonfiction are included in this recommended list of recently published books that will interest reluctant readers in grades 7–12. While none of the books measure above an eighth grade readability level, the selectors searched for works that hold high interest for middle schoolers. Teachers and students will find a mixture of quality books and those considered fast-reads in this list that is used to motivate youngsters. The books are arranged under 24 headings, such as *adventure*, *biographies*, *love and romance*, *social problems*, and *travel*. Subject, title, and author indexes make it easy to match children and books.

High/Low Handbook: Encouraging Literacy in the 1990s (3rd ed.). Compiled and edited by E. V. LiBretto. R. R. Bowker, 1990.

The primary focus of this handbook is the selection, evaluation, and use of high interest/low reading material for at-risk or reluctant teenage readers. The resource includes a "Core Collection" that cites over 400 books with low reading levels that focus on topics of interest to teens. The recommended collection consists of two lists of books, "High/Low Books for the Disabled Reader" and "Books for the Reluctant Reader." A lengthy annotation, other titles in the series, reading levels, and interest levels are given for each entry.

Genre-Specific Aids

Picture Books

Beyond Words: Picture Books for Older Readers and Writers. Edited by S. Benedict & L. Carlisle. Portsmouth, NH: Heinemann, 1992.

The value of picture books extends far beyond the primary grades. The 14 chapters contain essays written by experts who invite teachers to use picture books at all levels. Many of the essays include recommended lists of picture books and ways to use them with older students. The lengthy bibliography of recommended picture books appearing at the end of the book provides middle school teachers with a good selection of picture books they can use in their reading and writing classrooms.

Fantasy

Fantasy Literature for Children and Young Adults: An Annotated Bibliography (4th ed.). Written by R. N. Lynn. New York: R. R. Bowker, 1994.

This annotated bibliography provides recommendations of thousands of fantasy novels and story collections for children and young adults in grades 3–12. Each entry includes a short annotation, grade level appropriateness, review citation, and recommendation symbols. The fantasy works are divided into various categories such as ghost fantasy, animal fantasy, humorous fantasy, and toy fantasy. The resource also supplies valuable information on the genre of fantasy as well as a research guide on the authors who write fantasy for children and young adults. The author and illustrator index, title index, and subject index make the work easy to use.

Nonfiction

Nonfiction for Children and Young Adults: From Delight to Wisdom. Written by B. Carter & R. Abrahamson. Phoenix, AR: Oryx Press.

As the popularity of nonfiction books with teens continues to rise, this resource offers a wealth of information on the genre of nonfiction for young adults. Carter and Abrahamson explore the issues related to information books, examine the reading interests of young adults, discuss the criteria for evaluating works of this genre, and offer ideas for integrating nonfiction into the classroom. Insight into the creative process involved in writing information works is provided through the interviews with popular writers of nonfiction. Conversations with Lee J. Ames, Milton Meltzer, Laurence Pringle, Brent Ashabranner, James Cross Giblin, and Daniel and Susan Cohen provide interesting background information concerning their works. A list of books by each author follows each interview.

Multicultural Literature

When teachers or students are looking for a list of recommended works related to a specific area of multiculturalism, they should consider turning to some of the following selection aids.

Black Authors and Illustrators of Children's Books: A Biographical Dictionary (2nd ed.). Written by B. Rollock. Garland Publishing, 1992.

If you're looking for information about Black authors and illustrators of books for young people, this resource will satisfy your needs. It includes a total of 115 biographical sketches of Black authors and illustrators. Each biographical sketch is arranged alphabetically by author or illustrator, and a selected bibliography of the subject's works follows each sketch. A section of the book is devoted to photographs of the writers and illustrators.

Kaleidoscope: A Multicultural Booklist for Grades K-8. Edited by R. S. Bishop. Urbana, IL: National Council of Teachers of English, 1994.

This resource for K-8 students is a valuable aid for "all teachers interested in diversifying their classroom practice, regardless of their levels of expertise with literature by and about people of color." The National Council of Teachers of English Multicultural Booklist Committee and Editor Rudine Sims Bishop have compiled annotations of nearly 400 books about African Americans, Asian Americans, Hispanic Americans/Latinos, and Native Americans, published between 1990 and 1992. The booklist groups annotations according to genre or theme rather than cultural or racial groups. Chapter headings such as "Ceremonies and Celebrations," "Biography," and "Folktales, Myths, and Legends" make it easy to find just the right book to meet specific multicultural needs. Easy-to-use indexes by author, illustrator, subject, and title help users gain access to a wealth of multicultural books.

Our Family, Our Friends, Our World: An Annotated Guide to Significant Multicultural Books for Children and Teenagers. Written by L. Miller-Lachmann. New Providence, NJ: Bowker, 1992.

The introduction to this useful work contains a discussion of the criteria for selecting multicultural literature. The 18 chapters focus on the four principal minority groups within the United States: African Americans, Asian Americans, Hispanic Americans, and Native Americans. Background information related to each group is given along with a recommended list of books on the countries from which their ancestors came and from which children and their parents come today. The annotated critical bibliography, compiled by an expert in each area, includes approximately 1,000 books published between 1970 and 1990. The lengthy annotations describe strengths and weaknesses of each work. The books are divided according to grade level—grades PreK–Grade 3; 4–6; 7–9; and 10–12. Indexes include author, book title, series title, and subject.

Selection Aids to Support Programming

The selection aids examined throughout the previous sections can certainly be used to support special programs in the classroom and library, as they all can help teachers choose and promote books that enrich and supplement their particular thematic units and programs. The term *selection aid* can also be stretched to include books that supply information about authors as well as those works that focus on booktalking. While books about authors and booktalking certainly provide content information for the programs, they also include lists of titles of books that can be used in programming.

Information About Young Adult Authors

Background information on an author usually adds a new dimension to a book. When students can relate to an author's work and life, they often want to read more by a particular author. The resources about authors and illustrators who create for young people typically include a biographical sketch, list of works, awards, citations to various articles, and reviews about the particular author.

Behind the Covers: Interviews With Authors and Illustrators of Books for Children and Young Adults, Vol. 1. Written by J. Roginkski. Englewood, CO: Libraries Unlimited, 1985.

Behind the Covers: Interviews With Authors and Illustrators of Books for Children and Young Adults, Vol. 2. Written by J. Roginski. Englewood, CO: Libraries Unlimited, 1989.

Interviews, conducted in a question-and-answer format, with authors and illustrators who create books for young people provide insight into the creative writing process as well as interesting tidbits about their works. In addition to the interview, each sketch provides biographical data, a list of works, a list of awards, and a selected list of references about the author or illustrator.

Children's Literature Review. New York: Gale Research, Inc. [Multivolume series.]

This multivolume, ongoing series provides overviews of the lives and careers of authors and illustrators of books for children and young adults. International in scope, the works include outstanding authors and illustrators from around the world. Each entry supplies a biographical sketch and photograph of the author or illustrator, a list of major works, awards, and an author commentary. Of particular importance is the inclusion of excerpts concerning published criticism of the author's or illustrator's works found in books and periodicals. The cumulative indexes to authors, nationalities, and titles make the multivolume set easy to use.

Contemporary Authors. Detroit: Gale Research, 1961 to date. [Multivolume series; also available on CD-ROM.]

This multivolume, ongoing series of references provides information on current writers of fiction and nonfiction for all ages. This biographical guide includes personal and career information, a list of awards and published works, and a listing of critical sources. The more recent volumes of this series provide updated information on writers listed in earlier volumes. The cumulative index is the user's guide to location of the sketches of specific authors.

Major Authors and Illustrators for Children and Young Adults. Edited by L. Collins and J. Nakamura. Detroit, MI: Gale Research, 1993.

This six-volume reference source contains a selection of biographical sketches from *Something About the Author*. The updated and revised sketches focus on over 800 popular authors and illustrators. Each entry provides detailed information concerning the lives and works of significant authors and illustrators who write for young people.

Seventh Book of Junior Authors and Illustrators. New York: H. W. Wilson, 1995.

The first volume of this series, *Junior Book of Authors*, was published in 1935. An advisory committee of children's and young adult literature specialists was chosen to vote on names from the primary list and was invited to suggest additional names for inclusion. Information about the lives and works of the authors is provided along with photographs of the subject.

Something About the Author. Detroit, MI: Gale Research Company. [Multivolume series.]

This multivolume, ongoing reference series focuses on biographical information about authors and illustrators of children's and young adult books. The biographical sketches include photographs of the subjects, detailed information about their lives, a chronological bibliography of their works, a list of awards and honors, and references for further reading. Cumulative author and illustrator indexes cover all volumes.

Speaking for Ourselves: Autobiographical Sketches by Notable Authors of Books for Young Adults. Compiled and edited by D. Gallo. Urbana, IL: National Council of Teachers of English, 1990.

Speaking for Ourselves, Too: More Autobiographical Sketches by Notable Authors of Books for Young Adults. Compiled and edited by D. Gallo. Urbana, IL: National Council of Teachers of English, 1993.

In these companion works authors of books for young adults candidly tell how they became writers and talk about how they create their books. They spend time discussing their youth and the events that prepared them to be writers. Accompanying each biographical sketch is a list of the author's works and a photo of the author. Popular authors such as Bruce Brooks, Sue Ellen Bridgers, S. E. Hinton, Robert Cormier, and Virginia Hamilton are highlighted in these excellent resources.

Speaking of Poets: Interviews with Poets Who Write for Children and Young Adults. Written by J. S. Copeland. Urbana, IL: National Council of Teachers of English, 1993.

Speaking of Poets 2: More Interviews with Poets Who Write for Children and Young Adults. Written and edited by J. S. Copeland & V. L. Copeland. Urbana, IL: National Council of Teachers of English, 1995.

These companion works share interviews with poets who write for children and young adults. Nationally acclaimed poets (including winners of the NCTE Award for Excellence in Poetry) as well as rising stars discuss the role of poetry in the lives of children and share their views about their own works and accomplishments. Highlighting the lives and works of such outstanding poets as Lilian Moore and Aileen Fisher helps bring the genre to life.

Twentieth-Century Children's Writers (3rd ed.). Edited by T. Chevalier. Chicago: St. James Press, 1990.

This reference source provides biographical information about authors of works for young people. Each entry includes brief biographical information about the subject, a complete list of works, a signed critical essay about the author's works, and comments by the author.

Booktalking

Special programs that focus on booktalks provide an excellent means of helping young people select good books to read. Whether the booktalk is developed around books by a single author or books about a specific theme, the purpose is to entice students into picking up a good book.

Booktalk! Booktalking and School Visiting for Young Adult Audiences. Written by J. Bodart. New York: H. W. Wilson, 1980.

Booktalk! 2. Written by J. Bodart. New York: H. W. Wilson, 1985.

Booktalk! 3. Written by J. Bodart. New York: H. W. Wilson, 1988.

Booktalk! 4. Written by J. Bodart. New York: H. W. Wilson, 1992.

Booktalk! 5. Written by J. Bodart. New York: H. W. Wilson, 1993.

Everything you need to know about booktalking can be found in this successful series that encourages teachers to use booktalks to interest young people in reading. The series shares tips and techniques for developing and presenting booktalks. The popular guides provide teachers with hundreds of prepared booktalks that are sure to entice readers of all ages. Bibliographies arranged according to author, age level, and theme/genre will provide teachers with titles of excellent books that adolescents will enjoy.

Juniorplots 3: A Book Talk Guide for Use with Readers Ages 12–16. Written by J. Gillespie & C. Naden. New York: Bowker, 1987.

This rich resource provides teachers with various techniques for introducing books through booktalks, and it shares lengthy plot summaries of 80 fiction and nonfiction titles for readers of ages 12–16. Approximately six to eight additional related book titles are recommended with each selection. The work is divided into various categories popular with adolescent readers such as *teenage life and concerns, adventure and mystery stories, science fiction and fantasy,* and *historical fiction.* The inclusion of information about the authors and the identification of "specific passages and page numbers suitable for retelling or reading aloud" will prove particularly useful to teachers preparing booktalks.

Journals

Professional journals offer teachers the most current information concerning books for adolescents. In addition to the book review section of these journals, featured articles often provide teachers with recommended titles and information about books.

The ALAN Review. Urbana, IL: Assembly on Literature for Adolescents, National Council of Teachers of English.

Articles on topics concerning young adult literature, interviews with authors who write for adolescents, and "clip and file reviews of new hardcover fiction" make this an excellent resource for teachers interested in promoting young adult literature in their classrooms.

Book Links: Connecting Books, Libraries, and Classrooms. Chicago: American Library Association.

Educators of students from preschool level through eighth grade will find this invaluable resource particularly valuable in developing thematic units. Each issue features articles that connect books on similar themes and provide bibliographies.

Book Report. Worthington, OH: Linworth Publishing.

Although targeted at junior and senior high school librarians, teachers will find the book review section handy in discovering new books. This review tool is divided into fiction and nonfiction, with the nonfiction section further subdivided into subject areas. Grade level suggestions are also provided.

Booklist. Chicago: American Library Association.

The section entitled "Books for Older Readers" highlights recommended reviews of books for junior and senior high students. The works are divided into fiction and nonfiction and grade level recommendations are given. The April issue includes American Library Association's *Best* lists such as "Notable Books," "Best Books for Young Adults," and "Recommended Books for Reluctant Readers."

Horn Book Magazine. Boston, MA: Horn Book, Inc.

This review journal offers teachers and librarians quality reviews on the latest books as well as feature articles about authors, illustrators, and literature for young people. Middle school teachers will find reviews of fiction and nonfiction books for "older readers" (age 12 through young adult) particularly helpful. Starred reviews further aid in distinguishing the best.

The New Advocate. Norwood, MA: Christopher-Gordon Publishers, Inc.

Teachers "involved with young people and their literature" will take pleasure in the feature articles about using children's literature in the classroom and across the curriculum. A special section, "Book Review Sampler," rounds out the issue and provides reviews of recently published books for children and young adults. Grade levels for the works are suggested.

Journal of Adolescent & Adult Literacy. Newark, DE: International Reading Association.

Formerly entitled *Journal of Reading*, this journal includes a book review section which reviews books for adolescents on a regular basis.

School Library Journal. New York: Cahners/Bowker.

While this journal is used frequently by school librarians for collection development, middle school teachers will find the book reviews of interest. The book review section, "Junior High Up," focuses on both fiction and nonfiction literature for adolescents, and the starred reviews indicate a stronger recommendation.

SIGNAL Journal. Newark, DE: International Reading Association.

This publication is the journal of the International Reading Association's Special Interest Group on Literature for the Adolescent Reader. It provides feature articles and book reviews related to literature for adolescents.

Voice of Youth Advocates. Scarecrow Press.

Each issue of this journal is packed with reviews of books for adolescents.

Voices from the Middle. Urbana, IL: National Council of Teachers of English.

This new quarterly journal published for middle school teachers highlights a special theme and describes authentic classroom practices related to the theme. A special feature of each issue is the "clip and file" reviews of books for middle level readers. These reviews are written by middle school students.

Book Lists

Various publications highlight notable recommended lists of books for young people. While some of these lists may appear on an annual basis in professional journals, others may be ordered from the professional organizations or publisher. In some cases, the lists that appear in journals may be offered as reprints for a small fee. Teachers should contact the professional organization or publisher for further information concerning how to order any of the lists described in this section. Addresses and phone numbers of the major organizations that publish recommended lists are provided at the end of this chapter.

General *Best* Lists

"Best Books for Young Adults." Young Adult Library Services Division of the American Library Association.

This annual annotated list of books for students ages 12–18 is compiled by a committee of the Young Adult Library Services Division of the American Library Association. Selection is based on the book's appeal to young adults, and the list is divided into fiction and nonfiction and covers a broad range of reading levels and a variety of subjects.

"Best Books of the Year." *School Library Journal*. Cahners/Bowker.

This best list is chosen by the book review editors of the *School Library Journal* as the year's most outstanding books for children and young adults.

"Fanfare." *Horn Book*. Horn Book, Inc.

A special feature in the March/April issue of *Horn Book Magazine*, this annual listing of the best books of the previous year is arranged in various categories.

"Quick Picks for Great Reading." Young Adult Library Services Association of the American Library Association.

Each year the Young Adult Services Association of the American Library Association compiles an annotated list of good books for reluctant teenage readers. The titles are selected by librarians from across the nation who work with teens. The annotated entries, divided according to fiction and nonfiction, are arranged alphabetically by author. The list is published in *Booklist* and reprints of the lists are available from Young Adult Services Division of American Library Association.

"Teachers' Choices." International Reading Association.

This annotated reading list of new books is selected annually by teachers and librarians. These are "books that children might not discover or fully appreciate without the help of a teacher, parent, or other adult." While all the books on the list provide exciting reading, they also relate to various curriculum areas. The "Teachers' Choices" list appears each year in the *Reading Teacher* and *Journal of Adolescent and Adult Literacy*, and reprints of each list may be ordered from the International Reading Association.

"Top One Hundred Countdown: Best of the Best Books for Young Adults." Young Adult Library Services Division of American Library Association.

This annotated list was selected from the past 25 years of "Best Books for Young Adults." It represents the works that are still considered to be the *best* for young adult readers, ages 12–18. Divided according to fiction and nonfiction, the list includes a wide range of subjects and reading interests. The list may be ordered from Young Adult Library Services Division.

"Young Adult Editors' Choice." *Booklist*. Chicago: American Library Association.

Selected for excellence for teenage personal and recreational reading, this list is chosen by the Young Adult book review editors of *Booklist*. The annual list is published in the January 15 issue of *Booklist*.

"Young Adults' Choices." International Reading Association.

Each year adolescents in grades 7–12 are given an opportunity to choose their favorite fiction and nonfiction books. Their selections result in an annotated reading list of approximately 30 new books for adolescents that cover a variety of topics. This "Young Adults' Choices" list also includes ideas for teachers on how to use literature in the classroom. This list appears in the November issue of the *Journal of Adolescent and Adult Literacy* and is available from the International Reading Association as a separate reprint.

Book Lists Related to Specific Genre

"Notable Children's Trade Books in the Field of Social Studies." Compiled as a project of the National Council of Social Studies and Children's Book Council Joint Committee.

In a joint project of the National Council for the Social Studies and the Children's Book Council, a book review committee evaluates and selects outstanding trade books related to social studies for grades K-8. The annotated list is divided according to topics of interest and includes recommended reading levels. The notable trade book list is printed in the April/ May issue of *Social Education*, and single reprints can be ordered from the Children's Book Council.

"Outstanding Science Trade Books for Children." Compiled as a joint project of the National Science Teachers Association and the Children's Book Council.

In an annual joint project of the National Science Teachers Association and the Children's Book Council, a book review committee selects outstanding children's science trade books for grades K-8 that were published during the previous year. This annotated bibliography is divided into various categories and includes recommended grade levels. The list is published in the March issue of *Science Teacher* and is available from the Children's Book Council.

Useful Addresses for Professional Organizations

Professional organizations constantly update selection aids, create new aids, and provide other materials that help us connect students to books and make informed decisions about books. Call an organization (see Table 22.2) to see what selection aids, book lists, journals, membership information, and other materials related to reading it offers. A small fee and a self-addressed stamped envelope is sometimes required when ordering specific lists. Call and ask for their catalogs to help with your selection needs.

Selection aids offer teachers keys to opening the vast world of literature for middle school students. They identify many of the best works available for our young people. At the same time, their indexes and general arrangement provide a means of accessing books according to special topics and interests. To further guarantee the successful match of student and book, it is important that teachers become familiar with each student's personal interests and reading ability. Familiarity with this information about the student and the knowledge of the selection aids presented in this chapter should certainly increase the chance of successfully providing students with books that meet their needs and personal tastes. Thus, we can lay a firm foundation for a love of reading and move the middle schooler on the road to becoming a lifelong reader.

Table 22.2 Professional Organizations' Addresses and Phone Numbers

American Library Association 50 E. Huron Street Chicago, IL 60611 (800) 545-2433	Children's Book Council 568 Broadway, Suite 404 New York, NY 10012 (222) 966-1990
International Reading Association 800 Barksdale Road Newark, DE 19714-8139 (800) 336-READ	National Council of Teachers of English 111 Kenyon Road Urbana, IL 61801 (800) 369-6283

TRADE BOOKS CITED

Adamson, J. (1960). *Born free: A lioness of two worlds*. New York: Pantheon.

Adler, D. A. (1996). *Eaton Stanley and the mind control experiment*. New York: Yearling.

Agee, J. (1994). *So many dynamos! And other palindromes*. New York: Farrar, Straus & Giroux.

Ahlberg, J., & Ahlberg, A. (1993). *It was a dark stormy night*. New York: Viking.

Aiken, J. (Ed.). (1989). *Give yourself a fright: Thirteen stories of the supernatural*. New York: Delacorte.

Aiken, J. (1980). *A touch of chill: Tales for sleepless nights*. New York: Dell.

Aiken, J. (1981). *The wolves of Willoughby Chase*. New York: Dell.

Aiken, J. (1984). *A whisper in the night: Tales of terror and suspense*. New York: Delacorte.

Ames, L., & Budd, W. (1993). *Draw 50 endangered animals*. New York: Doubleday.

Angelou, M. (1978). *Just give me a cool drink of water 'fore I diiie*. New York: Random House.

Angelou, M. (1993). *Soul looks back in wonder*. New York: Dial Books.

Annaya, R. (1991). *Bless me, Ultima*. Berkley, CA: TQS Publications.

Anonymous. (1976). *Go ask Alice*. New York: Avon Books.

Arrick, F. (1981). *Chernowitz*. New York: Bradbury.

Ash, R. (1994). *The top ten of everything*. New York: Dorling Kindersley.

Ashe, A. (1993). *Days of grace: A memoir*. New York: Knopf.

Asimov, I., & Greenberg, M. H. (1989). *Visions of fantasy: Tales of terror and suspense*. New York: Delacorte.

Avi. (1981). *Nothing but the truth: A documentary novel*. New York: Orchard.

Avi. (1986). *Wolf rider*. New York: Collier/Macmillan.

Avi. (1990). *True confessions of Charlotte Doyle*. New York: Orchard.

Babbitt, N. (1975). *Tuck everlasting*. New York: Farrar, Straus & Giroux.

Barrett, P. (1986). *To break the silence: Thirteen short stories for young readers*. New York: Dell.

Barron, T. (1996). *The lost years of Merlin*. New York: Philomel.

Bauer, M. D. (Ed.). (1994). *Am I blue: Coming out from the silence*. New York: HarperCollins.

Bauer, M. D. (1993). *A taste of smoke*. New York: Clarion.

Beals, M. P. (1994). *Warriors don't cry*. New York: Pocket Books.

Beattie, O., & Geiger J. (1993). *Buried in ice: The mystery of a lost arctic expedition*. New York: Scholastic.

Bell, W. (1990). *Forbidden city*. New York: Doubleday.

Bennett, J. (1977). *The birthday murderer*. New York: Delacorte.

Berg, E. (1993). *Durable goods*. New York: Random House.

Berry, J. (1991). *The future-telling lady and other stories*. New York: HarperCollins.

Biesty, S., & Platt, R. (1992). *Stephen Biesty's incredible cross-sections*. New York: Dorling Kindersley.

Biesty, S., & Platt, R. (1993). *Stephen Biesty's incredible cross-sections man-of-war*. New York: Dorling Kindersley.

Biesty, S., & Platt R. (1994). *Stephen Biesty's incredible cross-sections castle*. New York: Dorling Kindersley.

Biesty, S., & Platt, R. (1995). *Stephen Biesty's incredible cross-sections stow away*! (CD-ROM) New York: Dorling Kindersley.

Blumburg, R. (1989). *The great American gold rush*. New York: Bradbury.

Blume, J. (1970). *Are you there God? It's me, Margaret*. New York: Dell/ Yearling.

Blume, J. (1971). *Then again, maybe I won't*. New York: Bradbury.

Bonner, C. (1992). *Lily*. Chapel Hill, NC: Algonquin Books.

Bowen, G. (1994). *Stranded at Plimouth Plantation*. New York: Harper-Collins.

Branch, M. (1995). *The water brought us: The story of the Gullah-speaking people*. New York: Cobblehill.

Bridgers, S. E. (1976). *Home before dark*. New York: Knopf.

Bridgers, S. E. (1990). *All together now*. New York: Bantam.

Bridgers, S. E. (1993). *Keeping Christina*. New York: HarperCollins.

Brightfield, H. (1995). *Island of doom*. Choose your own nightmare. New York: Bantam.

Brin, D. (1980). *The postman*. New York: Bantam.

Bronte, E. (1996). *Wuthering heights*. New York: Viking Penguin.

Brooke, W. J. (1994). *Teller of tales*. New York: HarperCollins.

Brooks, B. (1988). *Midnight hour encores*. New York: Harper & Row.

Brooks, B. (1984). *The moves make the man*. New York: Harper & Row.

Brooks, M. (1990). *Paradise café and other stories*. New York: Little Brown.

Brooks, M. (1990). *Traveling on into the light and other stories*. New York: Joy Street.

Brooks, T. (1977). *Sword of Shannara*. New York: Ballantine.

Brooks, T. (1986). *Magic kingdom for sale: SOLD*. New York: Ballantine.

Brown, J. (1995). *Movie marvels: (Ghostwriter)*. New York: Bantam Doubleday Dell.

Bryant, B. (1995). *Corey's pony is missing*. (Pony Trails.) New York: Skylark.

Bryant, B. (1995). *Jasmine's Christmas ride*. (Pony Trails.) New York: Skylark.

Bryant, B. (1995). *May's riding lesson*. (Pony Trails.) New York: Skylark.

Bryant, B. (1995). *Pony crazy*. (Pony Trails.) New York: Skylark.

Bryant, B. (1996). *May takes the lead*. (Pony Trails.) New York: Skylark.

Burgess, B. H. (1995). *Fred Field*. New York: Delacorte.

Burns, O. A. (1992). *Cold sassy tree*. New York: Ticknor & Fields.

Byars, B. (1968). *The midnight fox*. New York: Viking.

Byars, B. (1984). *Bingo Brown and the language of love*. New York: Viking Kestrel.

Byars, B. (1980). *The pinballs*. New York: Harper & Row.

Cannon, J. (1993). *Stellaluna*. New York: Harcourt Brace.

Card, O. S. (1985). *Ender's game*. New York: T. Doherty Associate.

Carter, A. (1990). *Last stand at the Alamo*. New York: Watts.

Carusone, A. (1994). *Don't open the door after the sun goes down: Tales of the real and unreal*. Boston, MA: Houghton Mifflin.

Clancy, T. (1984). *The hunt for Red October*. Annapolis, MD: Naval Institute Press.

Cleary, B. (1983). *Dear Mr. Henshaw*. New York: Morrow (HB), Dell (PB).

Coerr, E. (1993). *Sadako*. New York: Putnam.

Cofer, J. O. (1995). *An island like you: Stories of the barrio*. New York:: Orchard.

Cohen, D. (1983). *Southern fried rat & other gruesome tales*. New York: Avon Books.

Cohen, D. (1992). *Ghostly tales of love and revenge*. New York: Putnam.

Cohen, D., & S. Cohen. (1992). *Where to find the dinosaurs today*. New York: Cobblehill.

Conford, E. (1983). *If this is love, I'll take spaghetti*. New York: Scholastic.

Conford, E. (1994). *I love you, I hate you, get lost*. New York: Scholastic.

Conrad, P. (1987). *What I did for Roman*. New York: Harper & Row.

Cooney, C. B. (1991). *The cheerleader*. Scholastic/Point Books.

Cooney, C. B. (1994). *Driver's ed*. New York: Delacorte.

Cooper, F. (1994). *Coming home: From the life of Langston Hughes*. New York: Philomel.

Cooper, M. (1995). *Bound for the promised land*. New York: Lodestar.

Cooper, S. (1968). *Over sea under stone*. New York: Puffin.

Cormier, R. (1974). *The chocolate war*. New York: Dell.

Cormier, R. (1977). *I am the cheese*. New York: Pantheon Books.

Cormier, R. (1988). *Fade*. New York: Delacorte.

Cormier, R. (1995). *After the first death*. New York: Dell.

Cormier, R. (1995). *In the middle of the night*. New York: Delacorte.

Coville, B. (Ed.). (1995). *Bruce Coville's book of nightmares: Tales to make you scream*. New York: Scholastic.

Coville, B. (1994). *Oddly enough*. New York: Harcourt Brace Jovanovich.

Cozic, C., & Tipp, S. (Eds.). (1993). *Abortion: Opposing viewpoints*. San Diego, CA: Greenhaven.

Creech, S. (1994). *Walk two moons*. New York: HarperCollins.

Crichton, M. (1991). *Jurassic park*. New York: Knopf.

Crutcher, C. (1983). *Running loose*. New York: Delacorte.

Crutcher, C. (1986). *Stotan*. New York: Bantam.

Crutcher, C. (1987). *Crazy horse electric game*. New York: Greenwillow.

Crutcher, C. (1991). *Athletic shorts: Six short stories*. New York: Greenwillow.

Crutcher, C. (1995). *Ironman*. New York: Greenwillow.

Crutcher, C. (1996). *Staying fat for Sarah Byrnes*. New York: Dell.

Curtis, C. P. (1995). *The Watsons go to Birmingham—1963*. New York: Delacorte.

Cushman, K. (1994). *Catherine, called Birdy*. New York: Clarion Books.

Dahl, R. (1970). *The fantastic Mr. Fox*. New York: Knopf.

Daley, R. (1994). *In the kitchen with Rosie*. New York: Knopf.

Davis, J. (1988). *Sex education*. New York: Orchard.

Dear author: Students write about the books that changed their lives. (1995). Berkeley, CA: Conari Press.

Deedy, C. (1994). *The library dragon*. Atlanta, GA: Peachtree.

Deem, J. M. (1994). *3 NBs of Julian Drew*. Boston, MA: Houghton Mifflin.

Delton, J. (1994). *Pee wee scouts*. New York: Yearling.

Denim, S. (1994). *The dumb bunnies*. New York: Scholastic.

Denim, S. (1995). *The dumb bunnies' Easter*. New York: Scholastic.

Deuker, C. (1993). *Heart of a champion*. Boston, MA: Joy Street.

Dickens, C. (1962). *Great expectations*. New York: Macmillan.

Dickens, C. (1963). *A Christmas carol*. New York: Airmont.

Dickinson, P. (1988). *Eva*. New York: Bantam Doubleday Dell.

Dickinson, P. (1993). *Bone from a dry sea*. New York: Delacorte.

Dickinson, P. (1994). *Shadow of a hero*. New York: Delacorte.

Doyle, B. (1978). *Hey Dad!* New York: Groundwood, Douglas & McIntyre.

Doyle, B. (1986). *Angel Square*. New York: Bradbury.

Dugard, M. (1995). *On the edge: Four true stories of extreme outdoor sports adventures*. New York: Bantam.

Duncan, L. (1976). *Summer of fear*. Boston, MA: Little Brown.

Duncan, L. (1978). *Killing Mr. Griffin*. Boston, MA: Little Brown.

Duncan, L. (1979). *Daughters of Eve*. Boston, MA: Little Brown.

Dunphy, M. (1995). *Here is the southwestern desert*. New York: Hyperion.

Easton, P. H. (1988). *Summer's chance*. New York: Gulliver/Harcourt Brace.

Ehrlich, A. (Ed.). (1996). *When I was your age: Original stories about growing up*. Cambridge, MA: Candlewick.

Ellis, S. (1986). *The baby project*. New York: Bradbury.

Emra, B. (Ed.). (1994). *Coming of Age: Short stories about youth and adolescence*. Lincolnwood, IL: National Textbook Company.

Erickson, W. (1988). *Hank the cowdog*. Houston, TX: Gulf Publishing.

Facklam, H., & Facklam, M. (1991). *Avalanche*. New York: Crestwood House.

Farmer, N. (1994). *The ear, the eye, and the arm*. New York: Orchard.

Flaubert, G. (1989). *Madame Bovary*. New York: Oxford University Press.

Fleischman, P. (1980). *The Half-a-Moon Inn*. New York: Harper Collins.

Fleischman, P. (1982). *Graven images: Three stories*. New York: Harper & Row.

Fleischman, P. (1985). *Coming-and going men: Four tales*. New York: Harper & Row.

Fleischman, P. (1988). *Joyful noise: Poems for two voices*. New York: Harper & Row.

Fleischman, P. (1996). *Dateline: Troy*. Cambridge, MA: Candlewick.

Ford, M. (1993). *100 questions and answers about AIDS*. New York: Beech Tree.

Fox, P. (1973). *The slave dancer*. New York: Bradbury.

Fox, P. (1984). *One-eyed cat*. New York: Bradbury.

Frank, A. (1952). *Anne Frank: the diary of a young girl*. New York: Doubleday.

Fraser, M. (1994). *Sanctuary: The story of the three arch rocks*. New York: Holt.

Fraustino, L. (1995). *Ash: A novel*. New York: Orchard.

Freedman, R. (1983). *Children of the wild west*. New York: Clarion.

Freedman, R. (1983). *Eleanor Roosevelt*. New York: Clarion.

Freedman, R. (1987). *Lincoln: A photobiography*. New York: Clarion.

Freedman, R. (1994). *Kids at work: Lewis Hine and the crusade against child labor*. New York: Clarion.

Gaines, E. J. (1993). *A lesson before dying*. New York: Knopf.

Gale, D. (Ed.). (1992). *Funny you should ask: The Delacorte book of original humorous short stories*. New York: Delacorte.

Gallo, D. (Ed.). (1984). *Sixteen: Stories by outstanding writers for young adults*. New York: Delacorte.

Gallo, D. (Ed.). (1987). *Visions: Stories by outstanding writers for young adults*. New York: Delacorte.

Gallo, D. (ed.), (1989). *Connections: Short stories by outstanding writers for young adults*. New York: Delacorte.

Gallo, D. (Ed.). (1992). *Short circuits: Thirteen shocking stories by outstanding writers for young adults*. New York: Delacorte.

Gallo, D. (Ed.). (1993). *Join in: Multiethnic short stories by outstanding writers for young adults*. New York: Delacorte.

Gallo, D. (Ed.). (1993). *Within reach: Ten stories*. New York: HarperCollins.

Gallo, D. (Ed.). (1995). *Ultimate Sports: Short stories by outstanding writers for young adults*. New York: Delacorte.

Galloway, P. (1995). *Truly grim tales*. New York: Delacorte.

Ganeri, A. (1994). *The oceans atlas*. New York: Dorling Kindersley.

Garland, S. (1993). *The lotus seed*. New York: Harcourt Brace.

Garrigue, S. (1985). *The eternal spring of Mr. Ito*. New York: Bradbury.

George, J. (1972). *Julie of the wolves*. New York: Harper & Row.

George, J. (1995). *Acorn pancakes, dandelion salad and 38 other wild recipes*. New York: HarperCollins.

Ghost Writer. (1995). *Creepy sleepaway*. (Camp at your own risk.) New York: Bantam.

Ghost Writer. (1995). *Daycamp nightmare*. (Camp at your own risk.) New York: Bantam.

Ghost Writer. (1995). *Disaster on wheels*. (Camp at your own risk.) New York: Bantam.

Giblin, J. (1995). *When plague strikes: The black death, smallpox, AIDS*. New York: HarperCollins.

Giff, P. (1988). *Kids of the Polk Street School*. New York: Knopf.

Gipson, F. (1956). *Old Yeller*. New York: Harper.

Girion, B. (1984). *A very brief season: Ten stories*. New York: Scribner's.

Glenn, M. (1982). *Class dismissed*. New York: Clarion.

Glenn, M. (1986). *Class dismissed II*. New York: Clarion.

Glenn, M. (1988). *Back to class*. New York: Clarion.

Glenn, M. (1991). *My friend's got this problem, Mr. Chandler*. New York: Clarion.

Gold, R. S. (Ed.). (1967). *Point of departure: 19 stories of youth and discovery*. New York: Dell.

Gordon, R. (Ed.). (1993). *Peeling the onion*. New York: HarperCollins.

Gordon, R. (1995). *Pierced by a ray of the sun*. New York: HarperCollins.

Gorog, J. (1993). *Please do not touch: A collection of stories*. New York: Scholastic.

Gray, J. (1992). *Men are from Mars, women are from Venus*. New York: HarperCollins.

Greenberg, K. E. (1993). *Nolan Ryan*. Minneapolis, MN: Lerner Publications.

Greene, B. (1991). *The drowning of Stephan Jones*. New York: Bantam.

Griffin, J. (1977). *Black like me*. Boston, MA: Houghton Mifflin.

Grisham, J. (1994). *The chamber*. New York: Doubleday.

Guinness book of world records. (1989). New York: Bantam Books.

Guy, R. (1973). *The friends*. New York: Holt, Rhinehart & Winston.

Hahn, M. (1993). *The wind blows backward*. New York: Clarion.

Hamilton, V. (1982). *Sweet whispers, brother Rush*. New York: Philomel.

Hamilton, V. (1985). *The people could fly: American black folktales*. New York: Knopf.

Haskin, J. (1992). *One more river to cross: The stories of twelve black Americans*. New York: Scholastic.

Hautzig, E. R. (1987). *The endless steppe: Growing up in Siberia*. New York: Harper & Row.

Haynes, B. (1994). *Deadly deception*. New York: Delacorte.

Henkes, K. (1995). *Protecting Marie*. New York: Greenwillow.

Herman, H. (1996). *Crashing the boards*. (Super Hoops.) New York: Bantam.

Herman, H. (1996). *In your face*. (Super Hoops.) New York: Bantam.

Hesse, K. (1994). *Phoenix rising*. New York: Puffin.

Hinton, S. E. (1967). *The outsiders*. New York: Dell.

Hinton, S. E. (1971). *That was then, this is now*. New York: Viking.

Hobbs, W. (1991). *Downriver*. New York: Atheneum.

Holland, I. (1977). *Alan and the animal kingdom*. New York: Lippincott.

Holm, A. (1974). *I am David*. New York: Puffin.

Holman, F. (1974). *Slake's limbo*. New York: Scribner's.

Hughes, M. (1981). *Keeper of the Isis light*. New York: Atheneum.

Hughes, M. (1990). *Invitation to the game*. New York: Simon and Schuster.

Hunt, I. (1964). *Across five Aprils*. New York: Grossett & Dunlap.

Hyppolite, J. (1997). *Seth and Samona*. New York: Delacorte Press.

Innocenti, R. (1990). *Rose Blanche*. Mankato, MN: Creative Education, Inc.

Irvine, J. (1987). *How to make pop-ups*. New York: Beech Tree.

Isaacson, P. (1993). *A short walk around the pyramids and through the world of art*. New York: Knopf.

Jacques, B. (1987). *Redwall*. New York: Philomel.

Jacques, B. (1991). *Seven strange and ghostly tales*. New York: Philomel.

James, M. (1990). *Shoebag*. New York: Scholastic.

James, M. (1996). *Shoebag returns*. New York: Scholastic.

Janeczko, P. (1983). *The place my words are looking for*. New York: Bradbury.

Janeczko, P. (1983). *Poetspeak: In their words, about their work*. New York: Bradbury.

Janeczko, P. (1983). *Stardust Hotel*. New York: Orchard.

Janeczko, P. (1985). *Brickyard summer*. New York: Orchard.

Janeczko, P. (1985). *Pocket poems*. New York: Bradbury.

Jones, D. W. (1985). *Some of the kinder planets*. New York: Greenwillow.

Jones, D. W. (1990). *Hidden turnings: A collection of stories through time and space*. New York: Greenwillow.

Jukes, M. (1996). *Expecting the unexpected*. New York: Delacorte.

Kaufman, L. (1991). *Alligators to zooplankton*. New York: Watts.

Keith, H. (1987). *Rifles for Watie*. New York: Trophy Keypoint.

Kerr, M. (1984). *Him she loves?* New York: Harper.

Kerr, M. E. (1996). *If I love you, am I trapped forever?* New York: Delacorte.

Kerr, M. E. (1981). *Little, little*. New York: Harper & Row.

Klass, D. (1989). *Wrestling with honor*. New York: E. P. Dutton.

Klass, D. (1996). *California blue*. New York: Scholastic.

Klass, D. (1996). *Danger zone*. New York: Scholastic.

Klause, A. C. (1990). *The silver kiss*. New York: Delacorte.

Kline, S. (1993). *Who's Orp's girlfriend?* New York: Putnam.

Kline, S. (1996). *Mary Marony and the snake*. New York: Putnam/Yearling.

Knudson, R. R. (1979). *Zanballer*. New York: Dell.

Kogowa, J. (1988). *Naomi's road*. Oxford, NY: Oxford University Press.

Kormon, G. (1996). *The chicken doesn't skate*. New York: Scholastic.

Krementz, J. (1988). *How it feels to be adopted*. New York: Knopf.

Krementz, J. (1988). *How it feels when a parent dies*. New York: Knopf.

Krementz, J. (1988). *How it feels when parents divorce*. New York: Knopf.

Krementz, J. (1989). *How it feels to fight for your life*. Boston, MA: Joy Street/Little Brown.

Krensky, S. (1995). *The three blind mice mystery*. New York: Bantam.

Krisher, T. (1994). *Spite fences*. New York: Dell.

Kroll, S. (1996). *Pony express*. New York: Scholastic.

Langone, J. (1992). *Our endangered Earth: Our fragile environment and what we can do to save it*. Boston, MA: Little Brown.

Lasky, K. (1983). *Beyond the divide*. New York: Macmillan.

Lasky, K. (1984). *Prank*. New York: Macmillan.

Lasky, K. (1994). *Beyond the burning time*. New York: Scholastic.

Lasky, K. (1994). *The librarian who measured the earth*. New York: Little Brown.

Lawrence, J., & Lee, R. E. (1986). *Inherit the wind*. New York: Dramatist Play Service.

Lawrence, J. (1993). *The great American baseball strike*. Brookfield, CT: Millbrook.

Lawrence, J. (1993). *The great migration*. New York: HarperCollins.

Lawson, J. (1993). *White Jade Tiger Beach*. New York: Holmes.

Lee, H. (1960). *To kill a mockingbird*. New York: Lippincott.

Legge, D. (1995). *Bamboozled*. New York: Scholastic.

L'Engle, M. (1989). *Wrinkle in time*. New York: Dell.

Lessen, D., & Glut, D. (1993). *Dinosaur Encyclopedia*. New York: Random House.

Lester, J. (1995). *Othello*. New York: Scholastic.

Levine, E. (1993). *Freedom's children*. New York: Putnam.

Levine, E. (1993). *If your name was changed at Ellis Island*. New York: Scholastic.

Levy, E. (1993). *Cheater, cheater*. New York: Scholastic.

Lewin, T. (1994). *I was a teenage professional wrestler*. New York: Orchard.

Lewis, C. S. (1950). *The lion, the witch, and the wardrobe*. New York: Macmillan.

Lipsyte, R. (1977). *One fat summer*. New York: Harper & Row.

Lipsyte, R. (1987). *The contender*. New York: Harper & Row.

Little, J. (1986). *Mama's going to buy you a mockingbird*. New York: Viking Puffin.

Little, J. (1989). *Different dragons*. New York: Viking Puffin.

Littlefield, B. (1993). *Champions: Stories of ten remarkable athletes*. New York: Little Brown.

London, J. (1903). *Call of the wild*. New York: Bantam.

Lowe, S. (Selector). (1992). *The log of Christopher Columbus*. New York: Philomel.

Lowry, L. (1977). *A summer to die*. Boston, MA: Houghton Mifflin.

Lowry, L. (1989). *Number the stars*. Boston, MA: Houghton Mifflin.

Lowry, L. (1993). *The Giver*. Boston, MA: Houghton Mifflin.

Lund, D. (1974). *Eric*. New York: Harper Collins.

Lunn, J. (1985). *The root cellar*. New York: Viking Puffin.

Lynch, C. (1993). *Shadow boxer*. New York: HarperCollins.

Lyons, M. E. (1991). *Raw head, bloody bones: African-American tales of the supernatural*. New York: Scribner's.

Macaulay, D. (1985). *Pyramid*. Boston, MA: Houghton Mifflin.

Macaulay, D. (1988). *The way things work*. Boston, MA: Houghton Mifflin.

MacCracken, M. (1974). *A circle of children*. Philadelphia, PA: Lippincott.

MacCracken, M. (1976). *Lovey, a very special child*. Philadelphia, PA: Lippincott.

MacDonald, C. (1991). *Hostilities: Nine bizarre stories*. New York: Scholastic.

MacLachlan, P. (1985). *Sarah, plain and tall*. New York: Harper & Row.

Macy, S. (1993). *A whole new ball game: The story of the All-American girls professional baseball league*. New York: Holt.

Magorian, M. (1981). *Goodnight Mr. Tom*. New York: Harper & Row.

Mahy, M. (1984). *The changeover: A supernatural romance*. New York: Antheneum.

Mahy, M. (1995). *The cousins quartet*. New York: Bantam/Yearling.

Marshall, C. (1976). *Christy*. New York: Avon.

Marshall, J.V. (1984). *Walkabout*. Littleton, MA: Sundance.

Martin, B. (1983). *Brown bear, brown bear, what do you see*. New York: Henry Holt.

Matthews, P. (1992). *Hair-raising: Ten horror stories*. New York: Scholastic.

Mazer, A. (Ed.). (1993). *America Street: A multicultural anthology of stories*. New York: Persea Books.

Mazer, A. (Ed.). (1995). *Going where I'm coming from*. New York: Persea.

Mazer, H., & Mazer, N. F. (1989). *Heartbeat*. New York: Bantam.

Mazer, N. F. (Ed.). (1976). *Dear Bill, remember me? and other stories*. New York: Delacorte.

Mazer, N. F. (1982). *Summer girls, love boys and other stories*. New York: Delacorte.

Mazer, N. F. (1993). *Out of control*. New York: Avon Books.

McCaffrey, A. (1976). *Dragonsong*. New York: Atheneum.

McCaffrey, A. (1977). *Dragonsinger*. New York: Atheneum.

McCaffrey, A. (1979). *Dragondrums*. New York: Atheneum.

McFann, J. (1993). *Nothing more, nothing less*. New York: Avon.

McKinley, R. (1978). *Beauty*. New York: Harper & Row.

McKinley, R. (1982). *The blue sword*. New York: Greenwillow.

McKinley, R. (1985). *The hero and the crown*. New York: Greenwillow.

McKissack, F., & McKissack, P. (1994). *Christmas in the big house, Christmas in the quarters*. New York: Scholastic.

McMurtry, J. (1996). *Beware the snake's venom*. (Choose your own nightmare.) New York: Bantam.

Meltzer, M. (1988). *Rescue: The story of how gentiles saved Jews in the Holocaust*. New York: HarperCollins.

Meyer, C. (1993). *White lilacs*. San Diego, CA, and New York: Harcourt Brace Jovanovich.

Meyer, C. (1994). *Rio Grande stories*. San Diego, CA, and New York: Harcourt Brace Jovanovich.

Mills, C. (1993). *Dinah in love*. New York: Macmillan.

Mitchell, M. (1936). *Gone with the wind*. New York: Macmillan.

Mohr, N. (1975). *El Bronx remembered*. New York: Harper & Row.

Mohr, N. (1988). *In Nueva York*. Houston, TX: Arte Publico.

Montgomery, B. (1995). *Motorcross*. (Choose your own nightmare.) New York: Bantam.

Montgomery, B. (1995). *Possessed!* (Choose your own adventure.) New York: Bantam.

Montgomery, B. (1995). *Tattoo of death*. (Choose your own adventure.) New York: Bantam.

Montgomery, B. (1995). *Typhoon*. (Choose your own adventure.) New York: Bantam.

Morey, J., & Dunn W. (1992). *Famous Asian Americans*. New York: Cobblehill Books.

Mowat, F. (1979). *Never cry wolf*. New York: Bantam.

Murphy, J. (1993). *Across America on an emigrant train*. New York: Clarion.

Muse, D. (1995). *Prejudice: Stories about hate, ignorance, revelation and transformation*. New York: Hyperion.

Myers, W. D. (1981). *Hoops*. New York: Delacorte.

Myers, W. D. (1988). *Fallen angels*. New York: Scholastic.

Myers, W. D. (1988). *Scorpions*. New York: HarperTrophy.

Myers, W. D. (1992). *Somewhere in the darkness*. New York: Scholastic.

Myers, W. D. (1994). *The glory fields*. New York: Scholastic.

Naidoo, B. (1986). *Journey to Jo'Burg: A south African story*. New York: Harper.

Naylor, P. R. (1992). *All but Alice*. New York: Atheneum.

Naylor, P. R. (1992). *Shiloh*. New York: Dell/Yearling.

Nelson, O. T. (1977). *The girl who owned a city*. New York: Bantam.

Nelson, P. (1993). *Sylvia Smith-Smith*. Chicago, IL: Archway.

Nixon, J. L. (1979). *The kidnapping of Christina Lattimore*. New York: Harcourt Brace Jovanovich.

Nixon, J. L. (1987). *The dark and deadly pool*. New York: Delacorte.

Nixon, J. L. (1989). *The orphan train adventures*. New York: Bantam.

Nixon, J. L. (1989). *Whispers from the dead*. New York: Delacorte.

Nixon. J. L. (1994). *Ellis Island trilogy*. New York: Delacorte.

Norworth, J. (1993). *Take me out to the ball game*. New York: Four Winds.

Nye, N. S. (1995). *Words under the words: Selected poems*. Portland, OR: Eighth Mountain Press.

O'Brien, R. (1975). *Z for Zachariah*. New York: Atheneum.

O'Brien, T. (1990). *The things they carried*. Boston, MA: Houghton Mifflin.

O'Dell, S. (1990). *Island of the blue dolphins*. Boston, MA: Houghton Mifflin.

O'Neal, Z. (1982). *A formal feeling*. New York: Viking.

Packard, E. (1982). *The cave of time*. (Choose your own adventure.) New York: Bantam.

Packard, E. (1987). *Journey under the sea*. (Choose your own adventure.) New York: Bantam.

Packard, E. (1991). *Dinosaur island*. (Choose your own adventure.) New York: Bantam.

Packard, E. (1995). *The computer takeover*. (Choose your own adventure.) New York: Bantam.

Palacious, A. (1994). *Standing tall: The stories of ten Hispanic Americans*. New York: Scholastic.

Palmer, D. R. (1984). *Emergence*. New York: Bantam.

Park, B. (1982). *Skinnybones*. New York: Knopf.

Park, R. (1984). *Playing Beattie Bow*. New York: Puffin.

Parker, S. (1993). *The body atlas*. New York: Dorling Kindersley.

Paterson, K. (1977). *Bridge to Terabithia*. New York: Harper & Row.

Paterson, K. (1978). *The great Gilly Hopkins*. New York: HarperCollins.

Paterson, K. (1994). *Flip-flop girl*. New York: Lodestar Books.

Paul II, J. (1994). *Crossing the threshold of hope*. New York: Knopf.

Paulsen, G. (1987). *Hatchet*. New York: Bradbury.

Paulsen, G. (1991). *Woodsong*. New York: Bradbury.

Paulsen, G. (1993). *Dogteam*. New York: Delacorte/Yearling.

Paulsen, G. (1993). *Harris and me*. San Diego, CA: Harcourt Brace & Co.

Paulsen, G. (1994). *Father water, mother woods*. New York: Delacorte.

Paulsen, G. (1995). *Danger on Midnight River*. (World of adventure.) New York: Bantam/Yearling.

Paulsen, G. (1995). *Edge from Fire Mountain*. (World of adventure.) New York: Bantam/Yearling.

Paulsen, G. (1995). *Hook 'em Snottty*. (World of adventure.) New York: Bantam/Yearling.

Paulsen, G. (1995). *Nightjohn*. New York: Dell.

Paulsen, G. (1995). *The rock jockeys*. (World of adventure.) New York: Bantam/Yearling.

Pearce, P. (1991). *Tom's midnight garden*. New York: Dell.

Pearson, K. (1989). *The sky is falling*. New York: Viking Penguin.

Pearson, K. (1991). *A handful of time*. New York: Viking Puffin.

Peck, R. (1977). *Ghosts I have been*. New York: Viking Press.

Peck, R. (1981). *Close enough to touch*. New York: Delacorte.

Peck, R. (1992). *The last safe place on earth*. New York: Delacorte.

Peck, R. (1970). *Sounds and silences*. New York: Delacorte.

Peck, R. (1985). *Remembering the good times*. New York: Delacorte.

Peck, R. N. (1972). *A day no pigs would die*. New York: Knopf.

Philbrick, R. (1993). *Freak the mighty*. New York: Scholastic.

Pilkey, D. (1994). *Dog breath*. New York: Scholastic.

Pines, T. (Ed.). (1991). *Thirteen: 13 tales of horror*. New York: Scholastic.

Pinkney, A. D. (1993). *Alvin Ailey*. New York: Hyperion.

Polacco, P. (1994). *My rotten redhead older brother*. New York: Simon & Schuster.

Polacco, P. (1994). *Pink and say.* New York: Philomel Books.

Pomerantz, C. (1980). *The tamarindo puppy and other poems.* New York: Greenwillow.

Powell, C. with J. Persico. (1995). *My American journey.* New York: Random House.

Prelustsky, J. (1976). *Nightmares: Poems to trouble your sleep.* New York: Greenwillow.

Price, L. (1990). *Aida.* New York: Harcourt Brace.

Pullman, P. (1987). *The ruby in the smoke.* New York: Knopf.

Quattlebaum, M. (1994). *Jackson Jones and the puddle of thorns.* New York: Yearling/Bantam.

Rawls, W. (1974). *Where the red fern grows.* New York: Doubleday.

Ray, K. (1995). *To cross a line.* New York: Puffin.

Rinaldi, A. (1992). *A break with charity: A story about the Salem witch trials.* New York: Harcourt Brace Jovanovich.

Rinaldi, A. (1993). *In my father's house.* New York: Scholastic.

Ritter, L. (1995). *Leagues apart: The men and times of the Negro baseball league.* New York: Morrow.

Rivers, G., & Brooks, B. (1994). *Those who love the game.* New York: Holt.

Robbins, K. (1993). *A flower grows.* New York: Dial.

Robinson, B. (1994). *The best school year ever.* New York: HarperCollins.

Rochman, H., & McCampbell, D. Z. (1993). *Who do you think you are? Stories of friends and enemies.* New York: Joy Street/Little Brown.

Rodowsky, C. F. (1992). *Lucy Peale.* New York: Farrar, Straus & Giroux.

Rubin, S. G. (1993). *Emily good as gold.* New York: Harcourt Brace.

Rylant, C. (1990). *A couple of kooks and other stories about love.* New York: Dell.

Rylant, C. (1990). *Soda jerk and other poems.* New York: Orchard.

Rylant, C. (1990). *The Van Gogh café.* New York: Harcourt Brace.

Rylant, C. (1994). *Something permanent.* New York: Harcourt Brace.

Salak, J. (1993). *The Los Angeles riots: America's cities in crisis.* Brookfield, CT: Millbrook Press.

Salisbury, G. (1992). *Blue skin of the sea.* New York: Delacorte.

Salisbury, G. (1994). *Under the blood-red sun.* New York: Delacorte.

San Souci, R. D. (1989). *Short & shivery: Thirty chilling tales.* New York: Doubleday.

Sandler, M. (1995). *Presidents.* New York: HarperCollins/A Library of Congress Book.

Schecter, E. (1995). *Real live monsters.* Milwaukee, WI: Gareth Publications/Bank Street.

Schwartz, A. (1973). *Tomfoolery: Trickery and foolery with words.* New York: Lippincott.

Schwartz, A. (1981). *Scary stories to tell in the dark.* New York: Harper & Row.

Scieszka, J. (1989). *Math curse.* New York: Viking.

Scieszka, J. (1989). *The true story of the three little pigs.* New York: Viking.

Scieszka, J. (1991). *The time warp trio.* New York: Puffin.

Scieszka, J. (1993). *The stinky cheese man and other fairly stupid tales*. New York: Viking.

Scott, E. (1995). *Adventure in space: The flight to fix the Hubble*. New York: Hyperion.

Sebestyen, O. (1994). *Out of nowhere*. New York: Orchard.

Segel, E. (1986). *Short takes: A short story collection for young readers*. New York: Dell.

Sharmat, M. (1977). *Nate the great*. New York: Yearling.

Sieruta, P. D. (1986). *Heartbeats and the other stories*. New York: HarperCollins.

Silverstein, S. (1974). *Where the sidewalk ends*. New York: HarperCollins.

Silverstein, S. (1981). *Light in the attic*. New York: HarperCollins.

Simon, S. (1994). *Science dictionary*. New York: HarperCollins.

Sleator, W. (1974). *House of stairs*. New York: Dutton.

Sleator, W. (1993). *Oddballs*. New York: Dutton.

Sohn, D. A. (Ed.). (1964). *Ten top stories*. New York: Bantam.

Soto, G. (1990). *Baseball in April and other stories*. New York: Harcourt Brace.

Soto, G. (1993). *Local news*. New York: Harcourt Brace Jovanovich.

Sparks, B. (1994). *It happened to Nancy: A true story from the diary of a teenager*. New York: Avon.

Speare, E. G. (1958). *Witch of blackbird pond*. Boston, MA: Houghton Mifflin.

Speare, E.G. (1983). *The sign of the beaver*. Boston, MA: Houghton Mifflin.

Spielgelman, A. (1986). *Maus: A survivor's tale*. New York: Pantheon Books.

Spinelli, J. (1986). *Jason and Marceline*. Boston, MA: Little Brown.

Spinelli, J. (1992). *Maniac Magee*. New York: HarperCollins.

Spock, B. (1977). *The common sense book of baby and child care*. New York: Pocket Books.

Sports Illustrated for Kids. (1994). *You call the play: Baseball*. New York: Bantam.

Sports Illustrated for Kids. (1995). *You call the play: Football*. New York: Bantam.

Stanek, L. W. (1991). *Katy did*. New York: Avon.

Stanley, D., & Vennema, P. (1992). *Bard of Avon: The story of William Shakespeare*. New York: Morrow Junior Books.

Stanley, D., & Vennema, P. (1993). *Charles Dickens: The man who had great expectations*. New York: Morrow Junior Books.

Stanley, D., & Vennema, P. (1993). *Cleopatra*. New York: Morrow Junior Books.

Staples, S. F. (1993). *Haveli*. New York: Knopf.

Steinbeck, J. (1947). *The pearl*. New York: Viking.

Steinbeck, J. (1965). *The red pony*. New York: Bantam Books.

Stoehr, S. (1991). *Crosses*. New York: Delacorte.

Stone, T. B. (1994). *Don't eat the mystery meat!* (Graveyard schools.) New York: Skylark Press.

Stone, T. B. (1994). *The headless bicycle rider.* (Graveyard schools.) New York: Skylark Press.

Stone, T. B. (1994). *The skeleton on the skateboard.* (Graveyard schools.) New York: Skylark Press.

Stone, T. B. (1995). *Little pet werewolf.* (Graveyard schools.) New York: Skylark Press.

Stone, T. B. (1995). *Revenge of the dinosaurs.* (Graveyard schools.) New York: Skylark Press.

Sutton, R. (1994). *Hearing us out: Voices from the gay and lesbian community.* Boston, MA: Little Brown.

Taylor, M. (1976). *Roll of thunder, hear my cry.* New York: Dial.

Taylor, T. (1963). *The cay.* New York: Doubleday.

Taylor, T. (1993). *Timothy of the cay.* New York: Harcourt Brace.

Temple, F. (1992). *Taste of salt: A story of modern Haiti.* New York: Orchard.

Temple, F. (1993). *Grab hands and run.* New York: Orchard.

Thesman, J. (1991). *The rain catchers.* Boston, MA: Houghton Mifflin.

Thomas, J. C. (1990). *A gathering of flowers: Stories about being young in America.* New York: HarperCollins.

Tolan, S. S. (1996). *Welcome to the ark.* New York: Morrow Junior Books.

Tolkien, J. R. R. (1990). *The hobbit.* Oxford, NY: Windrush.

Townsend, S. (1982). *The secret diary of Adrian Mole, aged 13 ½.* New York: Avon.

Tsuchiya, Y. (1988). *Faithful elephants: A true story of animals, people and war.* Boston, MA: Houghton Mifflin.

Twain, M. (1976). *The adventures of Tom Sawyer.* New York: Scholastic/Apple Classic.

Ulrich, G. (1995). *My tooth ith loothe: Funny poems to read instead of doing your homework.* New York: Yearling.

Ventura, C., & Ventura, C. L. (1991). *Where angels glide at dawn: New stories from Latin America.* Philadelphia, PA: Lippincott.

Voigt, C. (1990). *On fortune's wheel.* New York: Atheneum.

Weaver, W. (1993). *Striking out.* New York: HarperCollins.

Wells, H. G. (1994). *The time machine.* New York: Bantam.

Westall, R. (1989). *Echoes of war.* New York: Farrar, Straus & Giroux.

Westall, R. (1996). *Gulf.* New York: Scholastic.

White, E. (1952). *Charlotte's web.* New York: Harper & Row.

White, R. (1972). *Deathwatch.* New York: Doubleday.

White, R. (1992). *Weeping willow.* New York: Farrar, Straus & Giroux.

Wiesel, E. (1982). *Night.* Toronto, ONT: Bantam.

Wilson, B. (1990). *The leaving and other stories.* New York: Philomel.

Wilson, B. (1995). *Dandelion garden and other stories.* New York: Philomel.

Wolff, V. E. (1993). *Make lemonade.* New York: Scholastic.

Woodruff, E. (1995). *Ghosts don't get goosebumps.* New York: Yearling.

Wrede, P. (1990). *Dealing with dragons.* San Diego, CA, and New York: Harcourt Brace Jovanovich.

Yee, P. (1990). *Tales from Gold Mountain: Stories of the Chinese in the new world.* New York: Macmillan.

Yep, L. (Ed.), (1993). *American dragons: Twenty-five Asian American voices*. New York: HarperCollins.

Yep, L. (1992). *The star fisher*. New York: Puffin.

Yolen, J. (Ed.). (1991). *2041: Twelve short stories about the future*. New York: Delacorte.

Yolen, J. (1981). *Sleeping ugly*. New York: Coward-McCann.

Yolen, J. (1990). *The devil's arithmetic*. New York: Puffin.

Yolen, J., & Greenberg, M. H. (Eds.). (1991). *Vampires: A collection of original stories*. New York: Delacorte.

Yolen, J., & Greenberg, M. H. (1988). *Werewolves: A collection of original stories*. New York: Harper & Row.

Yolen, J., & Greenberg, M. H. (1989). *Things that go bump in the night: A collection of original stories*. New York: Harper & Row.

Yolen, J., Greenberg, M. H., & Waugh, C. G. (1987). *Spaceship and spells*. New York: Harper & Row.

Zindel, P. (1968). *The pigman*. New York: Harper.

Zolotow, C. (1986). *Early sorrow: Ten stories of youth*. New York: HarperCollins.

AUTHOR BIOGRAPHIES

Kylene Beers is an adjunct assistant professor of children's and young adult literature at Sam Houston State University in Huntsville, Texas. A former middle school teacher, her interest continues to be finding ways to connect middle schoolers to reading. Kylene presents frequently at both NCTE and IRA, is the co-editor of the journal *English in Texas*, is a co-author of the "Books for Adolescents" column in the *Journal of Adolescent and Adult Literacy* (formerly *Journal of Reading*), serves as a board member on the Assembly on Literature for Adolescents (ALAN) of NCTE, and was co-editor, with Barbara  Samuels, of *Your Reading: An Annotated Booklist for Middle School and Junior High, 1995–96 Edition.* Kylene lives in Houston, Texas, with her husband, their six-year-old son, twelve-year-old daughter, and a too old to mention dachshund.

Barbara G. Samuels is an associate professor of language arts and reading at the University of Houston-Clear Lake where she teaches courses in adolescent literature and secondary school reading. She is also director of the Greater Houston Area Writing Project. She is past president of the Assembly on Literature for Adolescents (ALAN) of NCTE and currently serves on the Board of the Special Interest Group on Adolescent Literature (SIGNAL) of IRA. She is a frequent contributor of articles about young adult literature to books and journals and recently co-edited *Your Reading: An Annotated Booklist for*  *Middle School and Junior High, 1995–96 Edition* with Kylene Beers. Barbara and her husband Vic have three grown sons and live in Houston, Texas, with their dog Sam.

Richard F. Abrahamson teaches children's and young adult literature at the University of Houston. Dr. Abrahamson has been named the Outstanding English Language Arts Educator in Texas by the Texas Council of Teachers of English. He is the recipient of the University of Houston's Teaching Excellence Award, and is a past president of The National Council of Teachers of English Assembly on Literature for Adolescents (ALAN). In addition, Dr. Abrahamson currently serves on the Manuscript Review Board for *English Journal* and the Proposal and Manuscript Review Board for the IRA. He and co-author Betty Carter edited the 1988 edition of *Books for You* for NCTE, and together the two wrote *Nonfiction for Young Adults: From Delight to Wisdom* which was published by Oryx Press in 1990.

Barbara Baskin is the Chair of the Child and Family Program at the State University of New York-Stony Brook as well as Chair of the Board of Directors of the Verbal Interaction Project/Mother Child Home Program, an international preschool literacy program. She is the co-author of several professional books, as well as *How's Business*, a child's book on punning. Barbara has written and contributed many articles as well as being much in demand as a lecturer and presenter.

Devon Brenner is a former teacher and current graduate student at Michigan State University in the Department of Teacher Education, focusing on instruction in both social studies and language arts. Ms. Brenner's research interests include the content and use of children's literature and the role of assessment in professional development.

Betty Carter teaches children's and young adult literature at Texas Woman's University. Dr. Carter is a past president of NCTE's Assembly on Literature for Adolescents (ALAN), a former board member of the Young Adult Library Services Association, and a past chair of the Best Books for Young Adults Committee (BBYA). In 1994, she wrote a history of BBYA for the American Library Association entitled *Best Books for Young Adults: The History, The Selection, The Romance*. In addition, she and co-author Richard F. Abrahamson edited the 1988 edition of *Books for You* for NCTE, and together the two wrote *Nonfiction for Young Adults: From Delight to Wisdom* which was published by Oryx Press in 1990.

Karen Feathers received her Ed.D. from Indiana University. Her current research is on using retellings to understand comprehending process, the impact of inquiry curriculum on learning, and the impact of portfolio evaluation on students. She is a past chair of the IRA's Committee on Reading/Language in the Secondary Schools and Citation of Merit Committee.

Donald R. Gallo received his Ph.D. from Syracuse University. For many years he was a Professor of English at Central Connecticut State University where he supervised student teachers in English and taught courses in literature for young adults, expository writing, and American ethnic literature. Don has been the past president of NCTE's Assembly on Literature for Adolescents (ALAN), Vice-Chair of the Conference on English Education, a Trustee of the NCTE Research Foundation, a member of the NCTE Editorial Board and an Editor of the *Connecticut English Journal*. He is the editor of six highly acclaimed collections of short stories written by outstanding writers for young adults. His first collection, *Sixteen: Short Stories by Outstanding Writers for Young Adults*, was named by the American Library Association as one of the 100 Best of the Best Books for Young Adults published between 1967 and 1992.

Elizabeth Goza graduated from the University of Tennessee with a BA in English and an MS in Curriculum and Instruction. After graduating, she moved to Seattle, WA, and is currently teaching at Jackson High School, a member of Ted Sizer's Coalition of Essential Schools. In her spare time, she likes to hike in the nearby Cascade Mountains, explore the Seattle arts scene, and develop other independent projects.

Margaret H. Hill received her doctorate in Education from the University of Houston, and she is currently an Assistant Professor in Reading and Language Arts at the University of Houston–Clear Lake. She has been the past President of the Greater Houston Area Reading Council. She is the president-elect of the Texas State Reading Association and is Co-Director of the Greater Houston Area Writing Project. She is also the Director of the University of Houston–Clear Lake Student Literacy Corps.

Ted Hipple is a professor of English education and adolescent literature at the University of Tennessee-Knoxville. He is also one of the founders of ALAN, a past president, and currently its Executive Secretary. Ted is a contributor to Christopher-Gordon's *Adolescent Literature as a Complement to the Classics* Series and is editor of Scribner's *Writers for Young Adults*.

Karen Kutiper received her Ed.D. from the University of Houston-University Park and is now an English Language Arts Consultant. She is a recipient of the Texas State Reading Association Distinguished Service Award. Karen has written and published extensively on the subject of young adult literature and is a member of IRA and NCTE.

Teri S. Lesesne is an Assistant Professor of Library Science at Sam Houston State University where she teaches courses in children's and young adult literature. Teri edits the "Books for Adolescents" column for the *Journal of Adolescent and Adult Literacy* (formerly the *Journal of Reading*), is Past-President of the Texas Council of Teachers of English, and co-edits *English in Texas*. Teri's articles on motivating middle school readers have appeared in numerous journals.

Hollis Lowery-Moore is an Associate Dean of the College of Education and Applied Science at Sam Houston State University. She is a longstanding member of NCTE, IRA, and many other professional organizations. Her research interests include young adult literature, English education, and middle and secondary school instruction, where she has published many articles.

Yolanda N. Padrón is an Associate Professor of Education at the University of Houston-Clear Lake where she teaches courses in the areas of bilingual and multicultural education. She is a former Assistant Editor of the National Association for Bilingual Education's *Bilingual Research Journal* and is on the Editorial Advisory Board of *The Reading Teacher*. She is also president of the American Educational Research Association's Special Interest Group on Classroom Observations. Also, she has served as the 1994 AERA Division K (Teaching and Teacher Education) Section Chair on Teaching in Multicultural and Multilingual Settings, and the 1997 AERA Division G (Sociocultural Contexts) Section Chair on Sociocultural Contexts of Multiple Language and Literacies. Dr. Padron received her Ed.D from the University of Houston.

P. David Pearson holds the John A. Hannah Distinguished Professorship of Education in the College of Education at Michigan State University, where he is a member of the Department of Teacher Education and the Department of Counseling, Educational Psychology, and Special Education. He continues to pursue a line of research related to reading instruction and reading assessment policies and practices at all levels—local, state, and national. His recent work focuses on attempting to validate standards-based approaches to portfolio and performance assessment.

Elizabeth A. Poe is an associate professor of English Education at Radford University in Virginia where she teaches young adult and children's literature. She previously taught junior high and high school English for thirteen years in Colorado and English education courses for four years at the University of Wisconsin-Eau Claire. A past president of ALAN, NCTE's Assembly on Literature for Adolescents, and the current editor of IRA's *SIGNAL Journal*, a publication dedicated to young adult literature, Elizabeth is the author of Twayne's *Presenting Barbara Wersba*, as well as two books for ABC-CLIO's Teenage Perspectives Series, *Focus on Sexuality* and *Focus on Relationships*. She has written numerous book chapters, teaching guides, journal articles, and book reviews.

Carol A. Pope, Associate Professor of English Language Arts Education at North Carolina State University, works in middle school teacher education. She has a longstanding commitment to middle school teachers and to those who are preparing to become middle school teachers. The PAL (Power and Literacy) teachers quoted in the article have become partners with her in classroom research, teacher research, and teacher preparation. With that group she edited and published an NCTE issue of *Voices from the Middle/ From At-Risk to Promise: Pathways to Literacy.* Her current interests include middle school teacher education reform, the power of grassroots groups in reform, and the value of teachers' voices in reform efforts. She has received several Outstanding Teacher Awards at North Carolina State. She earned her doctorate in English Education from the University of Virginia.

Robert Probst is Professor of English Education at Georgia State University in Atlanta. He was before that an English teacher—in both junior and senior high school—in Maryland, and Supervisor of English for the Norfolk, Virginia, Public Schools. He is a member of the National Council of Teachers of English where he has worked on the Committee on Research, the Commission on Reading, the Commission on Curriculum, and the Board of Directors of the Adolescent Literature Assembly. He is also a Colleague and faculty member of the Creative Education Foundation and a member of the National Conference on Research in Language and Literacy.

Sandra L. Robertson has been a classroom teacher at the high school and middle school levels for twenty-four years. She is a Fellow of the South Coast Writing Project of the University of California-Santa Barbara, a site of the National Writing Project, and a Fellow of the NEH-sponsored Literature Institute for Teachers, also at UCSB. Ms. Robertson is a teacher in the Masters of Education Program at UCSB, is a frequent inservice and conference presenter, and is a member of the Early Adolescent/English Language Arts Standards Committee of the National Board for Professional Teaching Standards. Previous publications include articles in *English Journal* and *Voices From the Middle.* Both Ms. Robertson and her students are contributing authors to *The Writer's Craft.* She is currently English Department Chair at Santa Barbara Junior High School in Santa Barbara, California.

Linda Robinson taught high school and junior high school before she moved to the elementary level as a reading specialist. For the past twelve years she has been the principal of Alvin Junior High, where she has led the school from a traditional junior high to a school that is built on the middle school concepts that were recommended by the 1989 Carnegie Foundation report. As a result of this reform, Alvin Junior High was selected as one of 19 middle schools in Texas to become a Carnegie mentor school and professional development school. Linda recently served as President of the Texas Middle School Association and is currently serving as South Region Trustee on the National Middle School Association Board.

Mary Santerre is an eighth grade English teacher in Texas. She is a member of the Texas Council of Teachers of English, where she is frequently asked to present. In 1996, she was named Teacher of the Year by the Texas Council of Teachers of English Middle School.

Judith A. Scott is an Assistant Professor at Simon Fraser University where she works in undergraduate, graduate and teacher education programs. She has authored and co-authored several articles on reading, vocabulary development, cognition and instruction, word learning, and teacher development. Her most recent research examines how intermediate level students learn new word meanings.

Liz Campbell Stephens, Ed.D., teaches preservice English/language arts and reading teachers at Southwest Texas State University, San Marcos, Texas. She has given numerous presentations and workshops on technology and literacy and has co-authored a book on the topic.

Judy Wallis received her doctorate from the University of Houston. Judy is the Language Arts Coordinator for the Alief Independent School District. Her research interest centers on children's and young adult literature. She is a member of NCTE and IRA, as well as many other state and national affiliations.

Jan Wells has taught in elementary schools in England and in Canada. She was a reading consultant in Ontario and a Faculty Associate at Simon Fraser University in British Columbia. Jan has co-authored four books on the teaching of reading for Pembroke Publishers and is much in demand as a workshop leader. She currently teaches fifth grade in Vancouver. Jan has one son, William, who has always inspired her research into children's learning and reading.

Patricia Potter Wilson is an Associate Professor in the School of Education at the University of Houston-Clear Lake where she teaches courses related to school libraries and reading education. She received an Ed.D. in Curriculum and Instruction from the University of Houston in 1986. She co-authored *Happenings: Developing Successful Programs for School Libraries.* Her articles have appeared in professional reading and library journals, and many of these articles focus on her research interests related to children's preferences for literature.

Author Index

457

Title Index

Subject Index

Abstract
  devices, 75
  matters, 68
  thinking, 11
Academic
  divergence, 69
  exposition, 213
Active listening, 172
Aesthetic,
  experience, 15, 61
  reading, 16, 52, 128
  response, 53, 173, 262, 285, 288, 295
  stance, 44, 46, 48, 50, 52, 53, 127-129
  transaction, 48
Aliteracy, 44, 59
  types of, 44-50
  understanding, 37-54
Aliterates, xiv, 44, 46, 55
Analytic
  activity, 73
  skills, 75
Anecdotal record, 294
Anticipation guide, 226, 231-232
Appreciation, 200, 206-209
Art
  activities, 57, 58
  connecting readers to, 58
Artifacts, 288-290, 293-294
  by Standard Comparison, 277
Assessment
  authentic, 281-310
  case studies, 299
  establishing goals for, 283-285
  evidence for, 285-290, 293, 296, 298-299
  phases of, 283
  process, 147
  program, 283
  reading, 177, 281-310
  reasons for, 282
  sharing, 290
  system, 282
  techniques, 281, 370

Audience awareness, 205
Audiobooks, xi, xix, 82, 83, 257, 363-367, 371-372
Authentic appraisal, 173
Author and You, 238
Autobiographies, 25, 29, 71
Background knowledge, 86-88, 115, 116, 117
Basals, 34, 53, 66, 69
Behavior, 54
Bibliotherapy aids, 423-424
Bilingual
  education, 107
  programs, 111
  reading teachers, 106
Biography, 71, 74
Book
  aids, 57
  fairs, 55
  reports, 13, 55, 58
  selection, 67
Booklists, 117, 432-434
Books,
  audio, xi, xix, 82, 83, 257, 363-367, 371-372
  children's, 30
  classic, 13, 354
  clubs, 169, 179
  comic, xix, 363, 367-369, 372
  comparison of film to, 57
  fantasy, 70, 142, 334, 353, 425
  fiction, xi, 34, 70, 75
  graphic, 363, 367-369, 372
  historical, 30, 31, 70, 142, 334
  horror, 83, 334
  how-to, 34
  humor, 29, 30, 71
  multimedia, 377-379
  mystery, 15, 83, 353
  nonfiction, xi, xv, 30, 34, 425-426
  picture, 13, 425
  reference, xi, 72
  reviews, 156
  romance, 15, 30, 31, 353
  science fiction, 70, 142
  share, 55
  sports, 29, 30